STUDIES
IN PERCEPTION

Edited by

Gerald M. Murch

The Bobbs-Merrill Company, Inc.
Indianapolis

The Bobbs-Merrill Company, Inc.
4300 West 62nd Street
Indianapolis, Indiana 46268

First Edition
First Printing 1976
Design by Anita Duncan

Library of Congress Cataloging in Publication Data

Murch, Gerald M   1940–   comp.
    Studies in perception.

    Bibliography: p.
    1.   Perception—Addresses, essays, lectures.
I.   Title.   [DNLM: 1.   Auditory perception.   2.   Visual
perception.   WW103 M973s 1974]
BF311.M69   153.7   74–8398
ISBN 0–672–61189–9

Preface

This collection of research papers in the study of perception has been assembled on the basis of two considerations. First, I have attempted to select presentations of major *historical* importance, each of which has provided either a basis for further research or a fundamental piece of knowledge upon which many of the concepts of current approaches to perception are founded. Second, I have chosen papers from the *contemporary* literature that represent current trends in perceptual research and appear to be providing the impetus for future work. In retrospect, I note that my bias towards research on short-term perceptual processes is reflected in the choice of articles for this second category.

In order to reduce the volume of possible candidates for inclusion in the book, only papers dealing with visual and auditory perceptual processes were considered. The visual category carries by far the lion's share.

The topics of each chapter reflect the breakdowns found in most current texts on perception. The papers included in each chapter make no attempt to cover in full the material relevant to that area; rather, they provide concrete examples of some of the experimental approaches to the topics. I have included a section on color vision, although most current texts on perception do not discuss this topic. The two selections are basic and provide a starting point for any approach to color perception. While a reader unfamiliar with psychological research may find the work of Wald and particularly the study by Hurvich and Jameson very difficult, both papers reflect the painstaking care devoted to detail which is characteristic of research on color mechanisms.

I should like to thank all of the authors who have allowed me to reproduce their work in this volume. In particular I should like to express my gratitude to George Wald, Lewis Harvey, Jr., H. W. Leibowitz, and Harry Helson for their aid in editing their respective presentations, so that these might fulfill the objectives of this book. I am also indebted to the American Psychological Association, the American Association for the Advancement of Science, The Canadian Psychological Association, The Optical Society of America, The American Philosophical Society, Scientific American Inc. (W. J. Freeman and Co.), Van Nostrand Publishing Co., The University of Illinois Press (*The American Journal of Psychology*), and *The Psychological Record* for granting permission to reproduce the articles contained in this book.

G.M.M.

Portland, Oregon

Contents

**STUDIES
IN PERCEPTION**

CHAPTER 1
The Perceptual System

Psychology emerged as an independent scientific discipline in the last half of the nineteenth century. Prior to that time several other kinds of scholars had pondered various aspects of the perceptual process. Philosophers had long queried the nature of the relationship between the external physical world and the internal state of mind produced by that external stimulus. Physicists studied these relationships in a more scientific manner, analyzing the physical properties of stimuli that evoked perceptual responses. At the same time, physiologists and anatomists were examining the sensory mechanisms and studying their functions.

The new experimental psychology of the 1880s drew its proponents from among such physicists, physiologists, and philosophers, many of whom had dealt previously with certain aspects of perception. Hence it is not surprising that the study of perception was one of the first areas of study for psychology. To an interest in physical stimulation via sensory mechanisms, the new discipline added a concern for the behavioral response of the individual. Even with this early start, and even with a number of significant contributions made during the last ninety years, there is much left to be done in the areas of perception and perceptual research.

Sensation versus Perception

A major concern of perceptual psychology is the study of conditions causing the transmission of impulses along afferent pathways of the nervous system. If an external stimulus evokes any kind of a nervous response in the organism, we speak of *sensation.* The individual is said to be sensitive to this or that particular stimulus. *Perception,* in contrast, is something more than the introduction of stimuli into a sensory system. In perception, the individual is aware of the incoming stimuli; he is able to rely on past experience to draw inferences about the nature of the incoming stimuli, to develop response patterns to particular stimuli, and to establish relationships between stimuli.

The line separating sensation from perception is very narrow. Consider, for example, a study attempting to establish the threshold for "perceiving" a moving stimulus. Such a study would, at first glance, belong in the realm of sensation. However, previous experience of the individual could play an important part. Knowledge about objects that tend to remain stable or that are characteristically in motion would narrow the number of possible moving stimuli; as a result, the threshold would be lowered. If one were slowly to move a ticking watch closer to another person's ear, an auditory threshold could be established. The farthest point from the ear at which the subject reported hearing a sound would represent a sensory threshold. If he reported, however, not just sound, but the ticking of a watch, one would be dealing not simply with sensation but also with perception. To hear a sound is a sensory response; but to hear a particular sound, identifiable on the basis of past experience, is a perceptual response. Another borderline area is found in the study of color sensation. A light stimulus with certain physical properties evokes the psychological sensation of a particular color. Colors themselves are capable of evoking more complicated, perceptual responses. For example, some colors seem to belong together; others seem to be warm or cold, bright or pale.

The problem of sensation versus perception can also be approached from a practical aspect. In studying perception, we are attempting to describe adequately the interaction of a perceiving organism with the external world. Hence, all aspects of physical stimuli and all individual response characteristics affecting this interaction are valid areas of study for perception.

Traditionally, we refer to five different sensory systems. These are the visual, auditory, gustatory, olfactory, and tactile-kinesthetic systems. By means of each of these the organism interacts with his environment, although past experience may modify his response behavior. For the more highly developed organisms, such as the vertebrates, two of these systems appear to dominate. These are the visual and auditory systems, which are involved in most interactions with the environment, and which often tend to override the information relayed by other systems. In our discussion of perception we will confine ourselves to these two systems.

Visual Stimuli

Light is the primary instigator of visual sensation. Of course it is not the only stimulus capable of producing a visual sensation, as anyone who has ever been punched in the eye can attest. Visual sensation also occurs in the absence of external stimulation, as in dreams or hallucinations. The latter need not concern us here, however.

Light is an electromagnetic radiation traveling at 186,000 miles per second and exhibiting several definite characteristics. One is the length of the oscillating wave motion, or *wavelength*. The range of wavelengths extends from short cosmic rays, which may be only four ten-trillionths of an inch long, up to transoceanic waves utilized in broadcasting, which reach lengths of over eighteen miles. Only a very small portion of these wavelengths evoke responses from the vertebrate eye. These are the wavelengths falling between sixteen and thirty-two millionths of an inch. Since the inch is a rather cumbersome unit of measurement, most scientific studies utilize the metric system. The range of adequate visual stimuli in meters lies between 380 and 760 millimicrons (abbreviated as mμ, or millionths of a meter). This range can be extended, as Judd (1951) has demonstrated, down to about 320 mμ and up to about 1,000 mμ by increasing the intensity of the light stimulus. The intensities necessary to evoke sensations at these outlying wavelengths are damaging to the eye and probably play only a minor part in our perceptual response patterns.

A second important characteristic of light is the intensity of the light stimulus. In physical terms, intensity is the amplitude or height of the wave. Any given light stimulus has the properties of intensity and wavelength. Usually light is complex, containing a number of different wavelengths and intensities.

Auditory Stimuli

To turn now to the second source of perceptual information, we want first to consider the physical aspects of the auditory stimulus. The primary source of auditory stimulation is the sound wave, which can be described as a longitudinal vibratory disturbance in a medium. Such a wave exhibits positive and negative pressure around a base line of neutral pressure. The usual medium through which a sound wave reaches the ear is air, although the ear also responds to pressure waves transmitted through various other mediums such as water, metal, or wood. The speed of sound at sea level is about 760 miles per hour. A sound wave, then, reaches its target at a rate over 14,000 times more slowly than a light radiation reaches its target.

Sound waves have two primary physical attributes. The first is *frequency*, defined as the number of completed cycles of positive and negative deflection per second. The human ear is sensitive to sounds with frequencies within the range of 20 to 20,000 cycles per second (cps or Hz). Whether or not a sound of a given frequency will be heard depends to a great extent upon the intensity of the sound. The threshold, measured in sound pressure level, is lowest in the range 1,000 and 4,000 Hz.

The second primary attribute of a sound wave is its *intensity*, which is determined by the size or height of the swing of the wave away from the base line. The greater the oscillation, the more intense the sound. The psychological unit of measurement of sound intensity is the *decibel* (db). The decibel scale is used to describe the ratio of energy levels of two given auditory stimuli. It is logarithmic, so that if the ratio of energy levels of two stimuli is 10 to 1, we have a value of 10 decibels. A ratio of 100 to 1 equals 20 decibels, and so on. In psychological research, one takes the mean threshold value for an auditory stimulus with a frequency of 1,000 Hz and relates the energy ratio of the second stimulus to this value. The log unit of this ratio provides the sound intensity in *bels*. Multiplying this value by 10 produces the decibel unit. Thus, for a sound 17 times more intense than threshold, the bel unit would be log 17, or 2.3 bels. The decibel unit would be 2.3 times 10, or 23 decibels. The ear is able to cope with sounds of very high intensity; however, sounds above 130 decibels evoke responses of pain and are damaging to the ear.

Outside the laboratory, one seldom encounters pure sounds of a single frequency and single intensity. Rather, everyday sounds are complex, containing many frequencies of varying intensity. A sound containing all audible frequencies is called *white noise;* a sound containing a conglomerate of frequencies, but with no repetitive pattern, is called *noise* or *impulsive sound*.

The Detection of a Stimulus

We have indicated that sensation occurs when a nerve impulse conducted along the afferent pathway evokes a response. Will the same response always occur? Will a stimulus of the same intensity, duration, and other physical attributes always be perceived or never be perceived? Such questions help to define the problem of stimulus detection. If a light of very low intensity begins to increase, at some point an observer will report the presence of the light at a certain energy value of the stimulus. At the original energy level the light was *subliminal* (below threshold) and evoked no observable response in the subject. As the intensity of the stimulus was increased, the light became *supraliminal* (above threshold), so that it could be reported by the subject. Actually the idea that, at a particular level of energy, a threshold is crossed, after which the observer will report the presence of the light, has proved to be a difficult problem for psychophysics. That under the same physical conditions the energy level necessary for the subject to report the presence of the light varies from trial to trial is an assumption that speaks against the concept of a specific sensory threshold. Furthermore, the response of the subject observed by the experimenter may not be the first sensation evoked by the stimulus. Perhaps a more sensitive measure would reveal a sensation at a lower level of stimulus energy.

The complexity of the problem increases when we consider the proposed distinction between sensation and perception. Sensation probably occurs at a number of different levels. If the observer is attending to some other aspect of the environment, sensation may occur even though the subject is unable to report the presence of the stimulus. If, for example, I am looking at a tree, I may fail to notice a small bird in the upper branches. Some receptors of my optical system may have responded to that particular stimulus, however. I failed to direct my attention to the object and therefore failed to *perceive* the bird. On the other hand, if I had focused my attention on the bird, sensation or perception might have occurred at the same energy level as that of the tree. In other words, there is a continuum of relative sensitivity for sensory input ranging from the inability to identify a stimulus up to the exact description of all of the attributes of the stimulus. The actual points at which sensation and perception occur will depend on a number of factors and not solely on the physical intensity of the stimulus.

For many years psychologists have attempted to deal with the problems of stimulus sensitivity. The early concept of threshold—even though its application has practical value in the laboratory—has probably confused thinking on the subject more than it has added to an understanding of the process. One individual leading modern work in the field of stimulus detection is John A. Swets. In a report first published in *Science*—the organ of the American Association for the Advancement of Science—in 1961, Swets discusses the historical concept of threshold and the empirical observations concerning the ability of observers to detect stimuli. After testing several models of stimulus detection, he offers some practical applications in the area of psychophysics known as *signal detection theory*.

Is There a Sensory Threshold?

John A. Swets

One hundred years ago, at the inception of an experimental psychology of the senses, G. T. Fechner focused attention on the concept of a sensory threshold, a limit on sensitivity. His *Elemente der Psychophysik* described three methods

—the methods of adjustment, of limits, and of constants—for estimating the threshold value of a stimulus (Fechner, 1860). The concept and the methods have been in active service since. Students of sensory processes have continued to measure the energy required for a stimulus to be just detectable, or the difference between two stimuli necessary for the two to be just noticeably different. Very recently there has arisen reasonable doubt that sensory thresholds exist.

The threshold thought to be characteristic of sensory systems has been regarded in the root sense of that word as a barrier that must be overcome. It is analogous to the threshold discovered by physiologists in single neurons. Just as a nervous impulse either occurs or does not occur, so it has been thought that when a weak stimulus is presented we either detect it or we do not, with no shades in between. The analogy with the neuron's all-or-none action, of course, was never meant to be complete; it was plain that at some point above the threshold sensations come in various sizes.

From the start the triggering mechanism of the sensory systems was regarded as inherently unstable. The first experiments disclosed that a given stimulus did not produce a consistent "yes" ("I detect it") response or a consistent "no" ("I do not detect it") response. Plots of the "psychometric function"—the proportion of "yes" responses as a function of the stimulus energy—were in the form of ogives, which suggested an underlying bellshaped distribution of threshold levels. Abundant evidence for continuous physiological change in large numbers of receptive and nervous elements in the various sensory systems made this picture eminently reasonable. Thus, the threshold value of a stimulus had to be specified in statistical terms. Fechner's experimental methods were designed to obtain good estimates of the mean and the variance of the threshold distribution.

It was also assumed from the beginning that the observer's attitude affects the threshold estimate. The use of ascending and descending series of stimulus energies in the method of limits, to take one example, is intended to counterbalance the errors of "habituation" and "anticipation"—errors to which the observer is subject for extrasensory reasons. Typically, investigators have not been satisfied with experimental observers who were merely well motivated; they have felt the need for elite observers. They have attempted, by selection or training, to obtain observers who could maintain a reasonably constant criterion for a "yes" response.

The classical methods for measuring the threshold, however, do not provide a measure of the observer's response criterion that is independent of the threshold measure. As an example, we may note that a difference between two threshold estimates obtained with the method of limits can be attributed to a criterion change only if it is assumed that sensitivity has remained constant, or to a sensitivity change only if it is assumed that the criterion has remained constant. So, although the observer's response criterion affects the estimate of the threshold, the classical procedures do not permit calibration of the observer with respect to his response criterion.

Within the past ten years methods have become available that provide a reliable, quantitative specification of the response criterion. These methods permit isolation of the effects of the criterion, so that a relatively pure measure of sensitivity remains. Interestingly, the data collected with these methods give us good reason to question the existence of sensory thresholds, to wonder whether anything more than a response criterion is involved in the dichotomy of "yes" and "no" responses. There is now reason to believe that sensory excitation varies continuously and that an apparent threshold cut in the continuum results simply from restricting the observer to two categories of response.

The methods that permit separating the criterion and sensitivity measures, and a psychophysical theory that incorporates the results obtained with these methods, stem directly from the modern approach taken by engineers to the general problem of signal detection. The psychophysical "detection theory," like the more general theory, has two parts. One part is a literal translation of the theory of testing statistical hypotheses, or statistical decision theory. It is this part of the theory that provides a solution to the criterion estimation problem and deals with sensitivity as a continuous variable. The second part is a theory of ideal observers. It specifies the mathematically ideal detection performance—the upper limit on detection performance that is imposed by the environment—in terms of measurable parameters of the signal and of the masking noise (Tanner and Swets, 1954).

We shall turn in a moment to a description of the theory and to samples of the supporting data. Before proceeding any further, however, we must note that, although Fechner started the study of sensory functions along lines we are now questioning, he also anticipated the present line of attack in both of its major aspects. For one thing, he regarded Bernoulli's ideas on statistical decision as highly relevant to psychophysical theory. More important, while advancing the concept of a threshold, he spoke also of what he called "negative sensations"—that is, of a grading of sensory excitation below the threshold. That subsequent workers in the field of psychophysics have shown little interest in negative sensations is apparent from the fact that, seventy-five years after Fechner's work, Boring could write:

> So also a sensation either occurs from stimulation or it does not. If it does not, it has no demonstrable intensity. Fechner talked about, negative (subliminal) degrees of intensity, but that is not good psychology today. Above the limen we can sense degrees of intensity, but introspection cannot directly measure these degrees. We are forced to comparison, and there again we meet an all-or-none principle. Either we can observe a difference or we cannot. Introspection as to the amount of difference is not quantitatively reliable.
>
> (Boring, 1933)

Decision Aspects of Signal Detection

How detection theory succeeds in estimating the response criterion may be described in terms of "the fundamental detection problem." The experimenter defines an interval of time for the observer, and the observer must decide whether or not a signal is present during the interval. It is assumed that every interval contains some random interference, or noise—noise that is inherent in the environment, or is produced inadvertently by the experimenter's equipment for generating signals, or is deliberately introduced by the experimenter, or is simply a property of the sensory system. Some intervals contain a specified signal in addition to the background of noise. The observer's report is limited to these two classes of stimulus events—he says either "yes" (a signal was present) or "no" (only noise was present). Note that he does not say whether or not he saw (or heard) the signal; he says whether, under the particular circumstances, he prefers the decision that it was present or the decision that it was absent.

There is presumably, coinciding with the observation interval, some neural activity in the relevant sensory system. This activity forms the sensory basis—a part of the total basis—for the observer's report. This "sensory excitation," as we shall call it, may be in fact either simple or complex; it may have many dimensions or few; it may be qualitative or quantitative; it may be anything. The exact, or even the general, nature of the actual sensory excitation is of no concern to the application of the theory.

Only two assumptions are made about the sensory excitation. One is that it is continually varying; because of the ever-present noise, it varies over time in the absence of any signal, as well as from one presentation to the next of what is nominally the same signal. The other is that the sensory excitation, insofar as it affects the observer's report, may be represented as a unidimensional variable. In theory, the observer is aware of the probability that each possible excitatory state will occur during an observation interval containing noise alone and also during an observation interval containing a signal in addition to the noise, and he bases his report on the ratio of these two quantities, the likelihood ratio. The likelihood ratio derived from any observation interval is a real, nonzero number and hence may be represented along a single dimension.

The Likelihood-Ratio Criterion.   The observer's report after an observation interval is supposed to depend upon whether or not the likelihood ratio measured in that interval exceeds some critical value of the likelihood ratio, a response criterion. The criterion is presumed to be established by the observer in accordance with his detection goal and the relevant situational parameters. If he wishes to maximize the number of correct responses, his criterion will depend upon the a priori probability that a signal will occur in a given interval. If he chooses to maximize the total payoff, his criterion will depend on this probability and also on the values and costs associated with the four possible outcomes of a decision. Several other detection goals can be defined; the way in which each of them determines the criterion has been described elsewhere (Swets, Tanner, and Birdsall, 1961). In any case, the criterion employed by the observer can be expressed as a value of the likelihood ratio. Thus, the observer's decision about an interval is based not only on the sensory information he obtains in that interval but also upon advance information of various kinds and upon his motivation.

Next, consider a probability defined on the variable likelihood ratio—in particular, the probability that each value of likelihood ratio will occur with each of the classes of possible stimulus events: noise alone and signal plus noise. There are, then, two probability distributions. The one associated with signal plus noise will have a greater mean (indeed, its mean is assumed to increase monotonically with increases in the signal strength, but for the moment we are considering a particular signal). Now, if the observer follows the procedure we have described—that is, if he reports that the signal is present whenever the likelihood ratio exceeds a certain criterion and that noise alone is present whenever the likelihood ratio is less than this criterion—then, from the fourfold stimulus-response matrix that results, one can extract two independent measures: a measure of the observer's response criterion and a measure of his sensitivity.

The Operating Characteristic.   The extraction of these two measures depends upon an analysis in terms of the operating characteristic. If we induce the observer to change his criterion from one set of trials to another, and if, for each criterion, we plot the proportion of "yes" reports made when the signal is present (the proportion of hits, or p_1) against the proportion of "yes" reports made when noise alone is present (the proportion of false alarms, or p_0), then, as the criterion varies, a single curve is traced (running from 0 to 1.0 on both coordinates) that shows the proportion of hits to be a nondecreasing function of the proportion of false alarms. This operating-characteristic curve describes completely the successive stimulus-response matrices that are obtained, since the complements of these two proportions are the proportions that belong in the other two cells of the matrix. The particular curve generated in this way depends upon the signal and noise parameters and upon the observer's sensitivity; the point on this curve that corresponds to any given stimulus-response matrix represents the criterion employed by the observer in producing that matrix.

It has been found that, to a good approximation, the operating-characteristic curves produced by human observers correspond to theoretical curves based on normal probability distributions. These curves can be characterized by a single parameter: the difference between the means of the signal-plus-noise and noise-alone distributions divided by the standard deviation of the noise distribution. This parameter has been called d'. Moreover, the slope of the curve at any point is equal to the value of the likelihood-ratio criterion that produces that point.

The Yes-No Experiment.   The procedure employed in the fundamental detection problem is often referred to as the "yes-no procedure," and we shall adopt this terminology. Two operating-characteristic curves resulting from this procedure are shown in Figure 1.1. The data points were obtained in an auditory experiment in which the observers attempted to detect a tone burst in a background of white noise. The curves are the theoretical curves that fit the data best. The inserts at lower right in the two graphs show the normal probability distributions underlying the curves, and the five criteria corresponding to the data points. In this particular experiment the observers changed their

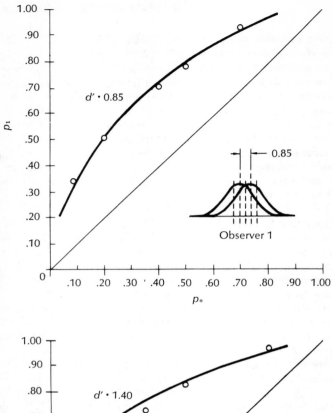

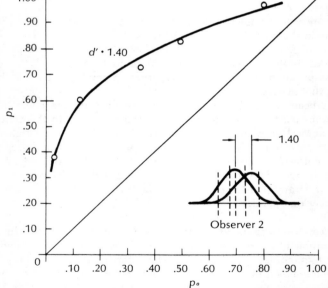

Figure 1.1: Two theoretical operating-characteristic curves, with data from a yes-no experiment.

criteria from one set of trials to another as the experimenter changed the a priori probability of the occurrence of the signal. The distance between the means of the two distributions is shown as 0.85 for observer number 1 and as 1.40 for observer number 2; this distance is equal to d' under the convention that the standard deviation of the noise distribution is unity.

We may note that the curve fitted to the data of the first observer is symmetrical about the negative diagonal, and that the curve fitted to the data of the second observer is not. Both types of curves are seen frequently; the second curve is especially characteristic of data collected in visual experiments. Theoretically, the curve shown in the graph at left will result if the observer knows the signal exactly—that is, if he knows its frequency, amplitude, starting time, duration, and phase. A theoretical curve like the one shown in the graph at right results if the observer has inadequate information about frequency and phase, or, as is the case when the signal is a white light, if there is no frequency and phase information. The probability distributions that are shown in the inserts reflect this difference between the operating-characteristic curves.

Both of the curves shown are based on the assumption that sensory excitation is continuous, that the observer can order values of sensory excitation throughout its range. Two other experiments have been employed to test the validity of this assumption: one involves a variant of the forced-choice procedure; the other involves a rating procedure. We shall consider these experiments in turn.

The Second-Choice Experiment. In the forced-choice procedure, four temporal intervals were defined on each trial, exactly one of which contained the signal. The signal was a small spot of light projected briefly on a large, uniformly illuminated background. Ordinarily, the observer simply chooses the interval he believes most likely to have contained the signal. In this experiment the observer made a second choice as well as a first.

The results are shown in Figure 1.2. The top curve is the theoretical function relating the proportion of correct first choices to d'; the lower curve is the theoretical relation of the proportion of correct second choices to d'. The points on the graph represent the proportions of correct second choices obtained by experiment. They are plotted at the value of d' corresponding to the observed proportion of correct first choices.

It may be seen that the data points are fitted well by the theoretical curve. The rather considerable variability can be attributed to the fact that each point is based on less than 100 observations. In spite of the variability, it is clear that the points deviate significantly from the horizontal dashed line. The dashed line may be taken as a baseline; it assumes a sensory threshold such that it is exceeded on only a negligible proportion of the trials when noise alone is presented. Should such a threshold exist, the second choice would be correct only by chance. The data indicate that the observer is capable of ordering values of sensory excitation well below this point. Two sensory thresholds are shown in the insert at lower right in Figure 1.2. The threshold on the right, at three standard deviations from the mean of the noise distribution, corresponds to the horizontal dashed line in the upper part of the figure. The data

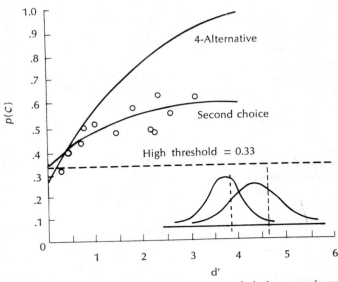

Figure 1.2: The results obtained in a second-choice experiment shown with the prediction from detection theory. (*Data from Swets, Tanner, and Birdsall, 1956.*)

indicate that, were a threshold to exist, it would have to be at least as low as the left-hand threshold, at approximately the mean of the noise distribution.

The Rating Experiment. In the rating procedure, as in the yes-no procedure, a signal is either presented or not presented in a single observation interval. The observer's task is to reflect gradations in the sensory excitation by assigning each observation to one of several categories of likelihood of occurrence of a signal in the interval.

The results of a visual experiment are displayed in Figure 1.3. The abscissa represents a six-point scale of certainty concerning the occurrence of a signal. The six categories were also defined in terms of the a posteriori probability of occurrence, but, for our purpose, only the property of order need be assumed. The ordinate shows the proportion, of the observations placed in each category, that resulted from the presentation of the signal.

Five curves are shown in Figure 1.3. Four of them correspond to the four observers; the fifth, marked by X's, represents the average. It may be seen that the curves for three of the four observers increase monotonically, while that for the fourth has a single reversal. The implication is that the human observer can distinguish at least six categories of sensory excitation.

It is possible to compute operating-characteristic curves from these data, by regarding the category boundaries successively as criteria. The curves (not shown here) are very similar in appearance to those obtained with the yes-no

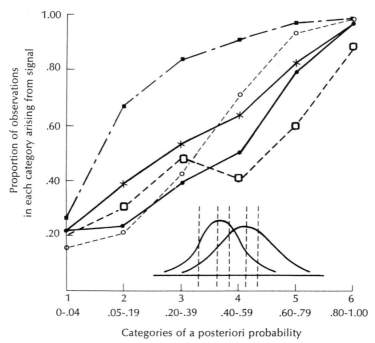

Figure 1.3: The results of a rating experiment. (*Data from Swets, Tanner, and Birdsall, 1956.*)

procedure. By way of illustration, the five criteria used by one of the observers (the one represented by solid circles) are shown in the insert at lower right in Figure 1.3.

The Experimental Invariance of d'. It has been found experimentally, in vision (Swets, Tanner, and Birdsall, 1961) and in audition (Tanner, Swets, and Green, 1956), that the sensitivity measure d' remains relatively constant with changes in the response criterion. Thus, detection theory provides a measure of sensitivity that is practically uncontaminated by the factors that might be expected to affect the observer's attitude.

It has also been found that the measure d' remains relatively invariant with different experimental procedures. For vision and audition the estimates of d' from the yes-no procedure and from the four-interval, forced-choice procedure are very nearly the same. Again, consistent estimates are obtained from forced-choice procedures with 2, 3, 4, 6, and 8 intervals (Swets, 1959). Finally, the rating procedure yields estimates of d' indistinguishable from those obtained with the yes-no procedure (Egan, Schulman, and Greenberg, 1959).

Thus, the psychophysical detection theory has passed some rather severe tests—the quantity that is supposed to remain invariant does remain invariant. This finding may be contrasted with the well-known fact that estimates of the threshold depend heavily on the particular procedure used.

Theory of Ideal Observers

Detection theory states, for several types of signal and noise, the maximum possible detectability as a function of the parameters of the signal and the noise. Given certain assumptions, this relationship can be stated very precisely. The case of the "signal specified exactly" (in which everything about the signal is known, including its frequency, phase, starting time, duration, and amplitude) appears to be a useful standard in audition experiments. In this case, the maximum d' is equal to the quantity $(2E/N_0)^{1/2}$, in which E is the signal energy and N_0 is the noise power in a one-cycle band.

It can be argued that a theory of ideal performance is a good starting point in working toward a descriptive theory. Ideal theories involve few variables, and these are simply described. Experiments can be used to uncover whatever additional variables may be needed to describe the performance of real observers. Alternatively, experiments can be used to indicate how the ideal theory may be degraded—that is, to identify those functions of which the ideal detection device must be deprived—in order to accurately describe real behavior.

Given a normative theory, it is possible to describe the real observer's efficiency. In the present instance, the efficiency measure η has been defined as the ratio of the observed to the ideal $(d')^2$. It seems likely that substantive problems will be illuminated by the computation of η for different types of signals and for different parameters of a given type of signal. The observed variation of this measure should be helpful in determining the range over which the human observer can adjust the parameters of his sensory system to match different signal parameters (he is, after all, quite proficient in detecting a surprisingly large number of different signals), and in determining which parameters of a signal the observer is not using, or not using precisely, in his detection process (Tanner and Birdsall, 1958).

The human observer, of course, performs less well than does the ideal observer in the great majority of detection tasks, if not in all. The interesting question concerns not the amount but the nature of the discrepancy that is observed.

The human observer performs less well than the ideal observer defined for the case of the "signal specified exactly." That is to say, the human observer's psychometric function is shifted to the right. More important, the slope of the human observer's function is greater than that of the ideal function for this particular case—a result sometimes referred to as "low-signal suppression." Let us consider three possible reasons for these discrepancies.

First, the human observer may well have a noisy decision process, whereas the ideal decision process is noiseless. For example, the human observer's response criterion may be unstable. If he vacillates between two criteria, the resulting point on his operating-characteristic curve will be on a straight line connecting the points corresponding to the two criteria; this average point falls below the curve (a curve with smoothly decreasing slope) on which the two criteria are located. Again, the observer's decision axis may not be continuous. It may be, as far as we know, divided into a relatively small number of categories—say, into seven.

A second likely cause of deviation from the ideal is the noise inherent in the human sensory systems. Consistent results are obtained from estimating the amount of "internal noise" (that is, noise in the decision process and noise in the sensory system) in two ways: by examining the decisions of an observer over several presentations of the same signal and noise (on tape) and by examining the correlation among the responses of several observers to a single presentation.

A third, and favored, possibility is faulty memory. This explanation is favored because it accounts not only for the shift of the human observer's psychometric function but also for the greater slope of his function. The reasoning proceeds as follows: if the detection process involves some sort of tuning of the receptive apparatus, and if the observer's memory of the characteristics of the incoming signal is faulty, then the observer is essentially confronted with a signal not specified exactly but specified only statistically. He has some uncertainty about the incoming signal.

If uncertainty is introduced into the calculations of the psychometric function of the ideal detector, it is found that performance falls off as uncertainty increases, and that this decline in performance is greater for weak signals than for strong ones. That is, a family of theoretical uncertainty curves shows progressively steeper slopes coinciding with progressive shifts to the right. This is what one would expect; the accuracy of knowledge about signal characteristics is less critical for strong signals, since strong signals carry with them more information about these characteristics.

It has been observed that visual data and auditory data are fitted well, with respect to slope, by the theoretical curve that corresponds to uncertainty among approximately 100 orthogonal signal alternatives. It is not difficult to imagine that the product of the uncertainties about the time, location, and frequency of the signals used in these experiments could be as high as 100.

It is possible to obtain empirical corroboration of this theoretical analysis of uncertainty in terms of faulty memory. This is achieved by providing various aids to memory within the experimental procedure. In such experiments, memory for frequency is made unnecessary by introducing a continuous tone or light (a "carrier") of the same frequency as the signal, so that the signal to be detected is an increment in the carrier. This procedure also eliminates the need for phase memory in audition and location memory in vision. In further experiments a pulsed carrier is used in order to make unnecessary memory for starting time and for duration. In all of these experiments a forced-choice procedure is used, so that memory for amplitude beyond a single trial can also be considered irrelevant. In this way, all of the information thought to be relevant may be contained in the immediate situation. Experimentally, we find that the human observer's psychometric functions show progressively flatter slopes as more and more memory aids are introduced. In fact, when all of the aids mentioned above are used, the observer's slope parallels that for the ideal observer without uncertainty, and it deviates as little as 3 decibels from the ideal curve in absolute value (Green, 1960).

Relationship of the Data to Various Threshold Theories

Although there is a limit on detection performance, even ideally, and although the human observer falls short of the limit, these facts do not imply a sensory threshold. We have just seen that the human observer's performance can be analyzed in terms of memory, and, conceivably, additional memory aids could bring his performance closer to the ideal. Moreover, consideration of ideal observers concerns an upper rather than a lower limit. The human observer, while falling short of the ideal, can still detect signals at a high rate. Ideally, any displacement of the signal-plus-noise distribution from the noise-alone distribution will lead to a detection rate greater than chance. Although it is difficult to obtain data near the chance point, the theoretical curves that fit the plots of d' against signal energy for human observers go through zero on the energy scale.

This last-mentioned result, of course, based as it is on extrapolation, cannot stand by itself as conclusive argument against the existence of a threshold. The result also depends on a measure of performance that is specific to detection theory. So we shall not be concerned with it further. It is possible, however, to relate the various threshold theories that have been proposed to the experimental results discussed earlier—results obtained with the yes-no, second-choice, and rating procedures, as shown in Figures 1.1, 1.2, and 1.3. We shall examine these results in relation to threshold theories proposed by Blackwell (1953), Luce (1960), Green (1960), Swets, Tanner, and Birdsall (1961), and Stevens (1961).

Blackwell's High-Threshold Theory. Blackwell's theory assumes that, whereas the observer may be led to say "yes" when noise alone is presented, only very infrequently is his threshold exceeded by the sensory excitation arising from noise—so infrequently, in fact, that these instances can be ignored. There is a "true" value of p_0—call it p_0'—that for all practical purposes is equal to zero. Corresponding to p_0', there is some true p_1', the value of which depends on the signal strength. Since the observer is unable to order values of sensory excitation below $p_0' \approx 0$, if he says "yes" in response to such a value he is merely guessing and will be correct on a chance basis. The operating-characteristic curve (for a given signal strength) that results from this theory is that of Figure 1.4. It is a straight line from (p_0'', p_1'') through $(p_0 = 1.00, p_1 = 1.00)$. The insert at lower right shows the location of the threshold. The data of observer 1 shown in Figure 1.1 are reproduced for comparison.

This theoretical curve is described by the equation

$$p_1 = p_1' + p_0(1 - p_1')$$

The observed proportion of "yes" responses to a signal (p_1) equals the proportion of true "yes" responses (p_1') plus a guessing factor (p_0) modified by the opportunity for guessing $(1 - p_1')$. The beauty of this high-threshold theory is that, if it is correct, the influence of spurious "yes" responses can be eliminated, the proportion of true "yes" responses being left. The familiar correction for chance success

$$p_1' = \frac{p_1 - p_0}{1 - p_0}$$

is a rearrangement of the first equation. The correction serves to normalize the psychometric function so that, whatever the observer's tendency to guess, the stimulus threshold can be taken as the signal energy corresponding to $p_1' = 0.50$.

However, the theory does not agree with the data. The empirical curve shown in Figure 1.4, like the great majority of operating-characteristic curves that have been obtained, is not adequately fitted by a straight line. The horizontal line in Figure 1.2, which follows from this theory, does not fit the second-choice data shown here. The rating data of Figure 1.3 also indicate ordering of values of sensory excitation below a p_0 of approximately zero. Further, yes-no and forced-choice thresholds calculated from this theory are not consistent with each other.

Luce's Low-Threshold Theory. Luce has suggested that a sensory threshold may exist at a somewhat lower level relative to the distribution of noise— that is, that p_0' may be substantial. Apart from this, the low-threshold theory

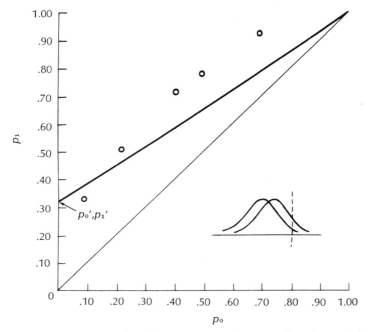

Figure 1.4: The results of a yes-no experiment and a theoretical function from Blackwell's high-threshold theory.

is like the high-threshold theory, only twice so. Whereas Blackwell's theory permits the observer to say "yes" without discrimination when the sensory excitation fails to exceed the threshold, Luce's theory also permits the observer to say "no" without discrimination when the sensory excitation does exceed the threshold. Thus the operating-characteristic curve of this theory contains two linear segments, as shown in Figure 1.5. Again, the data for observer 1 in Figure 1.1 are shown for comparison. The location of the threshold indicated by these data is shown in the insert at lower right.

It may be seen that the two-line curve fits the yes-no data reasonably well, perhaps as well as the nonlinear curve of detection theory. Although the calculations have not been performed, it seems probable that this theory will also be in fairly good agreement with the second-choice data of Figure 1.2. It provides for two categories of sensory excitation, and two categories would seem sufficient to produce a proportion of correct second choices significantly above the chance proportion. However, on the face of it, a two-category theory is inconsistent with the six categories of sensory excitation indicated by the rating data of Figure 1.3. (We may note in passing that the theory raises the interesting question of how another threshold, the one above which a more complete ordering exists, might be measured.)

Green's Two-Threshold Theory.   Green has observed that operating-characteristic data, perhaps adequately fitted by Luce's curve of two segments,

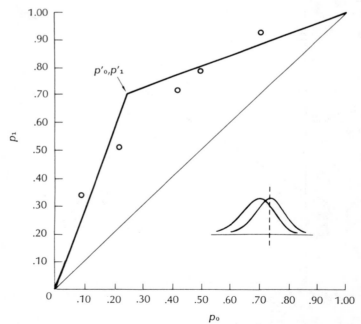

Figure 1.5:   The results of a yes-no experiment and a theoretical function from Luce's low-threshold theory.

are certainly better fitted by a curve with three linear segments. This curve, shown in Figure 1.6, corresponds to a theory that includes a range of uncertainty between a lower threshold, below which lies true rejection, and an upper threshold, above which lies true detection. The insert at lower right shows the location of the two thresholds.

As is evident from Figure 1.6, the curve of three line segments fits the yes-no data at least as well as the nonlinear curve of detection theory. Again, the calculations have not been performed, but it seems very likely that a three-category theory can account for the second-choice data. Even a three-category theory, however, is inconsistent with the six categories of sensory excitation indicated by the rating data.

There is, of course, no need to stop at two thresholds and three categories. A five-threshold theory, with a curve of six line segments, would fit any operating-characteristic data very well indeed and would also be entirely consistent with the second-choice and rating results. However, such a theory is irrelevant to the question under consideration. It is hardly a threshold theory in any important sense. It may be recalled that we considered it earlier as a variant of detection theory.

Swets's, Tanner's, and Birdsall's Low-Threshold Theory.   Tanner, Birdsall, and I proposed a threshold theory that may be described as combining some of the features of Blackwell's and Luce's theories. This theory permits ordering of

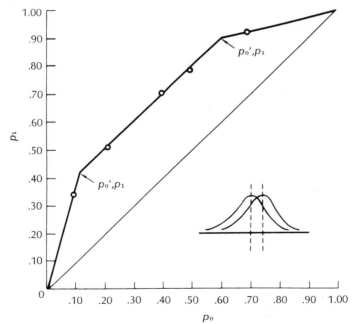

Figure 1.6: The results of a yes-no experiment and a theoretical function from Green's two-threshold theory.

values of sensory excitation above the threshold but locates the threshold well within the noise distribution. The corresponding operating-characteristic curve is composed of a linear segment above some substantial value of p_0 (say, 0.30 to 0.50) and a curvilinear segment below this value. Inspection of Figure 1.1 shows that such a curve fits yes-no data rather well. It is evident that the second-choice data, and rating data exhibiting six categories, could also be obtained without ordering below this threshold.

Stevens's Quantal-Threshold Theory.   The quantal-threshold theory advocated by Stevens cannot be treated on the same terms as the other threshold theories. The data of Figures 1.1, 1.2, and 1.3 are not directly relevant to it. The reason is that, whereas the other threshold theories give a prominent place to noise, collection of data in accordance with the quantal theory requires a serious attempt to eliminate all noise, or at least enough of it to allow the discontinuities of neural action to manifest themselves.

We may doubt, a priori, that noise can in fact be reduced sufficiently to reveal the "grain" of the action of a sensory system. Although the other theories we have examined apply to experiments in which the noise is considerable and, as a matter of fact, are typically applied to experiments in which noise (a background of some kind) is added deliberately, they are not generally viewed as restricted to such experiments. In adding noise we acknowledge its universality. The assumption is that the irreducible minimum of ambient noise, equipment noise, and noise inside the observer is enough to obscure the all-or-none quality of individual nervous elements in a psychological experiment. Noise is added in order to bring the total, or at least that part of it external to the observer, to a relatively constant level, and to a level at which it can be measured.

A recent article reviewing the experiments that have sought to demonstrate a quantal threshold has questioned whether any of the experiments suffices as a demonstration (Corso, 1956). Even if we ignore some technical questions concerning curve-fitting procedures and grant that some experiments have produced data in agreement with the quantal-threshold theory, we must observe that obtaining such data evidently depends upon the circumstance of having elite experimenters as well as elite observers. A relatively large amount of negative evidence exists; several other experimenters have attempted to reproduce the conditions of the successful experiments without success (Corso, 1956).

A striking feature of the quantal-theory experiments, in the present context, is the stimulus-presentation procedure employed. Although not contingent upon anything in the theory, the recommended procedure is to present signals of the same magnitude on all the trials of a series and to make known to the observer that this is the case. This procedure provides an unfortunate protection for the theory; if the observer is likely to make noise-determined "yes" responses, the fact will not be disclosed by the experiment. Licklider has expressed aptly the growing discomfiture over this procedure: "More and more, workers in the field are growing dissatisfied with the classical psychophysical techniques, particularly with the [methods that ask the observer] to report 'present' or 'absent' when he already knows 'present.' It is widely felt that the 'thresholds' yielded by these procedures are on such an insecure semantic basis that they cannot serve as good building blocks for a quantitative science" (Lick-lider, 1959). Although the original intent behind the use of this procedure in the quantal-theory experiments was to make the task as easy as possible for the observer, from the point of view of detection theory the procedure presents a very difficult task—it requires that the observer try to establish the response criterion that he would establish if he did not know that the signal was present on every trial.

Thus the advocates of the quantal theory specify a procedure that makes detection theory inapplicable. The result is that, as things stand, the conflict between the two theories cannot be resolved to the satisfaction of all concerned, as it conceivably could be if both theories could be confronted with the same set of data. However, there is reason to hope—since the quantal-theory procedure is not intrinsic to the theory but rests rather on a sense of experimental propriety, which is a relatively labile matter—that such a confrontation will some day be possible.

Is There a Sensory Threshold?

We have considered the data of three experiments—the yes-no, second-choice, and rating experiments—in relation to five competing theories concerning the processes underlying these data. The three sets of data are in agreement with detection theory, a theory that denies the existence of a sensory threshold, and also with the version of a low-threshold theory proposed by Tanner, Birdsall, and me. Blackwell's high-threshold theory is inconsistent with all three sets of results. Luce's low-threshold theory is consistent with the first, perhaps consistent with the second, and inconsistent with the third. Green's two-threshold theory hits the first two sets of results but not the last. We also considered the only other explicit threshold theory available—the quantal theory, to which the three experiments are not directly relevant.

The outcome is that, as far as we know, there may be a sensory threshold. The possibility of a quantal threshold cannot be discounted, and certainly not on the basis of data at hand. On another level of analysis, there may be what we have termed a low threshold, somewhere in the vicinity of the mean of the noise distribution. The low-threshold theory proposed by Tanner, Birdsall, and me fits all of the data we examined. If the rating experiment can be dismissed (there is now no apparent reason for giving it less than full status), then Luce's and Green's theories, which involve a low threshold, fit the remaining data.

On the other hand, the existence of a sensory threshold has not been demonstrated. Data consistent with the quantal theory are, at best, here today and gone tomorrow, and the theory has yet to be tested through an objective procedure. With respect to a low threshold, we may ask whether demonstration of such a threshold is even conceivable.

It is apparent that it will be difficult to measure a low threshold. Consider the low-threshold theory that permits complete ordering above the threshold in connection with the forced-choice experiment. The observer conveys less information about his ordering than he is capable of conveying if only a first choice is required. We saw in the preceding discussion that the second choice conveys a significant amount of information. Another experiment, in which the observer tried to be incorrect, indicated that he can order four choices (Tanner, Swets, and Green, 1956). Thus it is difficult to determine when enough information has been extracted to yield a valid estimate of a low threshold.

Again, it is difficult to imagine how one might determine the signal energy corresponding to the thresholds of Luce's and Green's theories. The determination is made especially difficult by the fact that, in general, empirical operating-characteristic curves for various signal energies are fitted well by the theoretical curves of detection theory. Consequently, the line-segment curves that best fit the data have lines intersecting at a value of p_0 that depends upon the signal energy. The implication is that the location of the threshold depends on the signal energy that is being presented.

Implications for Practice

We have, then, the possibility of a threshold, but it is no more than a possibility, and we must observe that since it is practically unmeasurable it will not be a very useful concept in experimental practice. Moreover, even if the low threshold proposed by Tanner, Birdsall, and me did exist, and were measurable, it would not restrict the application of detection theory. We may note that yes-no data resulting from a suprathreshold criterion depend upon the criterion but are completely independent of the threshold value. The same limitation applies to the quantal threshold. It appears that a compelling demonstration of this concept will be difficult to achieve, so that in practice a theory and a method that deal with noise will be required.

Accordingly, with any attempt to measure sensitivity by means of "yes" and "no" responses, a measure of the observer's response criterion should be obtained. The only way known to obtain this measure is to use catch trials—randomly chosen trials that do not contain a signal. The methods of adjustment, limits, and constants in their usual forms, in which the observer knows that the signal is present on every trial, are inappropriate.

A large number of catch trials should be presented. It is not sufficient to employ a few catch trials, enough to monitor the observer, and then to remind him to avoid "false-positive" responses each time he makes one. This procedure merely forces the criterion up to a point where it cannot be measured, and it can be shown that the calculated threshold varies by as much as 6 decibels as the criterion varies in this unmeasurable range. Precision is also sacrificed when, because highly trained observers are employed, the untestable assumption is made that they do maintain a constant high criterion. Even if all laboratories should be fortunate enough to have such observers, we would have to expect a range of variation of 6 decibels among "constant criterion" observers in different laboratories. To be sure, for some problems, this amount of variability is not bothersome; for others it is.

The presentation of a large number of catch trials—enough to provide a good estimate of the probability of a "yes" response on such a trial—is still inadequate if this estimate is then used to correct the proportion of "yes" responses to the signal for chance success. The validity of the correction for chance depends upon the existence of a high threshold that is inconsistent with all of the data that we examined. It should be noted that the common procedure of taking the proportion of correct responses that is halfway between chance and perfect performance as corresponding to the threshold value of the signal is entirely equivalent to using the chance correction.

In summary, in measuring sensitivity it is desirable to manipulate the response criterion so that it lies in a range where it can be measured, to include enough catch trials to obtain a good estimate of this response criterion, and to use a method of analysis that yields independent measures of sensitivity and the response criterion. One qualification should be added: we can forego estimating the response criterion in a forced-choice experiment. Under the forced-choice procedure, few observers show a bias in their responses large enough to affect the sensitivity index d' appreciably. Those who do show such a bias initially can overcome it with little difficulty. As a result, the observer can be viewed as choosing the interval most likely to contain a signal, without regard to any criterion. For this reason, the forced-choice procedure may be used to advantage in studies having an emphasis on sensory, rather than on motivational or response, processes.

Editor's Note: Growth of a Percept

If a seven-letter English word is flashed briefly in a viewing apparatus, the observer may have a sensation (e.g., of a shadow or line) but not a perception (the identification of the word). With an increase in duration or intensity the observer may accurately report several letters but still fail to perceive the entire word. A further increase of either variable provides the subject with a clear perception of the word. Obviously increases in duration and intensity in such a perceptual task are associated with improvement in the task of word identification. According to Swets in the preceding paper, another important variable is the frequency of presentation of the word without changes in duration or intensity.

Let us assume that the chance or probability of correctly identifying the word is about 33 percent. If the subject fails to report the word correctly on the first trial, we might conclude that the word was below the perceptual threshold. However, if the same word is presented a second time, under the same conditions as on trial one, we find the probability of correctly identifying the word to be much greater than 33 percent. Although the subject failed to identify the word, some kind of information about the word had been gained on the first trial. Often the subject is unable to report any aspect of the first presentation, yet his performance upon the occasion of the second presentation of the word is markedly improved. Such observations support the contention of the detection theorists that one cannot speak of thresholds in the classic sense.

In a recent publication, the present author reported on research into changes in the probability of correctly identifying a word presented successively under standard conditions (*Journal of Experimental Psychology*, 1969). This line of study is an outgrowth of the results of the signal detection theorists. Investigation into the probability of correctly identifying a word as a function of presentation frequency has been led by Ralph Norman Haber of the University of Rochester. He has referred to the process of identification as the "growth of a percept." In addition to tracing the growth of the processes of perception, the following essay also considers the effect of the interval between each successive presentation of the word. Parts of the following publication have been omitted for the sake of brevity.

Growth of a Percept as a Function of Interstimulus Interval

Gerald M. Murch

Recently, Haber and Hershenson (1965) addressed the problem of the effects of the repeated exposure of a meaningful word on the probability that the word would be correctly identified. They noted that studies of word recognition thresholds, using the method of limits, apply a number of independent variables, e.g., set, word frequency in print, word length, etc., while confounding the variables of exposure duration and exposure frequency. Using several durations, Haber and Hershenson varied the frequency of the exposure of common seven-letter words and showed the relationship between identification probability and frequency of exposure to be a negatively accelerating function approaching an asymptote after approximately ten presentations of the word.

Recognition accuracy in the Haber and Hershenson (1965) study could be predicted with several empirical functions. Of these functions, the best fit of the data points for the varying durations of exposure (threshold, threshold plus 5 msec, threshold plus 10 msec) was $p_n = A - B/n$, where A is the maximum probability that the word would be perceived, B is the probability of incorrect identification on the occasion of the first exposure, and n is the number of exposures.

While the work of Haber and Hershenson (1965) provides a useful description of the relationship between recognition probability and presentation frequency, it fails to incorporate the variable of the interval between successive stimulus presentations (interstimulus interval or ISI). The importance of this variable in studies observing an interaction between temporally separate perceptual inputs is emphasized by recent work on *critical durations* in visual acuity tasks. Kahneman (1964, 1966) has traced the length of time over which the time–intensity reciprocity (Block's law) is shown to hold. The research on visual masking (Eriksen and Collins, 1965) and on short-term perceptual memory (Sperling, 1963) has indicated that critical temporal periods exist in the visual mechanism within which input and energy appear to summate or interact.

Experiment I

The purpose of Experiment I was to observe the relationship between recognition accuracy and frequency of exposure as a function of the interval between successive presentations of the stimulus words. In the study by Haber and Hershenson (1965), the ISI was held constant at approximately 10 seconds.[1]

A further difference between Experiment I and the earlier work of Haber and Hershenson (1965) relates to the visual angle of the stimulus array. Their stimuli (English words) subtended small visual angles (4°). In the present study, a *scanning* task was introduced in that the words subtended visual angles of 13°. Whereas in the study by Haber and Hershenson all elements of the words could be perceived simultaneously, in Experiment I a scanning or re-fixation would be required in order to sample all the elements.

Method.   The 220 most frequent seven-letter words from the Thorndike-Lorge (1944) list were selected. The list excluded proper names. All words were printed on white 4 × 6 inch file cards with a ½-inch LeRoy stencil.

The words were presented in a two-field mirror tachistoscope (Gerbrands Model T-2B-1). Field 1 was always illuminated except for the duration of the presentation of the word in Field 2. Field 1 contained two penciled horizontal lines (1 inch apart). The luminance of the fields was held constant at 4.6 ftc.

Four exposure frequencies (1, 3, 5, and 10) and four interstimulus intervals (50, 100, 250, and 1,000 msec) were used. Each subject was shown 10 words at each of the 16 Frequency × ISI conditions, the order of conditions being randomized across subjects (Ss).

The subjects (N = 16) were unpaid volunteers from the author's introductory psychology class. At the start of each experimental session, the deck of 220 words was mixed and ten words were selected for the establishment of the presentation duration for the subject. The subject was informed that seven-letter English words would be shown several times. Each time the signal light, mounted below the viewer of the tachistoscope, came on, [the] subject was to try to identify the word presented. Each word was presented ten times, with an ISI of 1,000 msec. The duration was set at 1 msec on Trial 1 and increased by 1 msec after each ten presentations until the subject correctly identified the word. A duration for each subject was desired that would allow the probability of word identification after ten presentations with an ISI of 1,000 msec to approach 1.0. Therefore, the lowest duration at which at least six of the ten words were correctly identified was taken as the presentation duration for Experiment I for the particular subject.

[1] R. N. Haber, personal communication, October 15, 1965.

For Experiment I, the subject was given an answer sheet containing the numbers 1–160. After each number were seven blank spaces in which the subject was to record his answers. He was told to record what he saw, even if it was not a complete word. After each word, the experimenter gave the subject a code number to be entered in a special column to the left of the number of the trial. The presentation of each word for the specific Frequency × ISI condition occurred when the subject depressed a Morse key located below the tachistoscope. That is, the stimulus appeared either 1, 3, 5, or 10 times at one of the four ISIs. Naturally, the condition of one word presentation at each ISI represented a control condition. The signal lamp below the viewer came on at the end of the presentation, at which time the subject was to record his answer. While the subject recorded his perception of the word presented, the experimenter changed the word, selecting the new word from the mixed deck of words. After ten words, a new Frequency × ISI condition was set.

Results.   An analysis of variance of the number of words correctly identified for the three frequency conditions (3, 5, and 10 presentations of each word) and the four ISIs revealed a significant effect for frequency, $F (2, 45) = 11.26, p < 0.01$, and for ISI, $F (3, 129) = 12.04, p < 0.01$.

The four control conditions of one presentation of the word at each of the ISIs were compared with a Friedman test. The resulting value of $\chi^2_r = 3.51$ was not significant at the 0.10 level.

Figure 1.7 presents the relationship between presentation frequency and the probability of correct word identification over all ISI conditions. As the analysis of variance indicated no ISI × Frequency interaction, the data for the ISIs of 100, 250, and 1,000 msec have been summed for this curve. Also included in Figure 1.7 is the curve predicted by the function offered by Haber and Hershenson (1965). That function overestimates the slope of the observed function obtained in Experiment I for the summed intervals.

The data for the 50-msec ISI were not included in the summed curve as it showed a marked deviation from the other three ISIs. The mean number of words correctly identified for each frequency was compared for each ISI condition by Duncan's multiple-range test. The means for the 50-msec ISI deviated significantly ($p = 0.01$) from all other ISI means for frequencies of five and ten presentations.

The effects of ISI are shown in Figure 1.8. As can be observed, reductions in ISI appear to result in a monotonic decrease in recognition accuracy over the intervals used.

Discussion.   Under the conditions of Experiment I, the relationship between identification probability and frequency of exposure is found to be a negatively accelerated function. This result is comparable to the data obtained by Haber and Hershenson (1965). The slight overestimation by their function can probably be attributed to the large visual angle subtended by the stimuli in Experiment I. The observation of a reduction in recognition accuracy with decreasing ISI would be expected in a task such as that imposed on the subject in Experiment I. A 5-inch, seven-letter word presented at a distance of

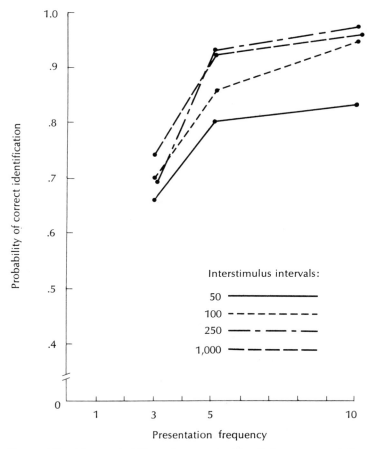

Figure 1.7: The probability of correctly identifying a seven-letter English word with increasing frequency as a function of interstimulus interval.

21 inches subtends a horizontal visual angle of 13.6°. In order to accurately perceive the word, the subject must fixate the first part of the word and then refixate the last part of the word. Assuming that such refixations can occur as rapidly as once each 300 msec, additional information about the word could only be obtained with total presentation times (Frequency × ISI) greater than 300 msec. As the interval decreases, the subject has less time to scan the array and recognition accuracy decreases.

The data from Experiment I can be adequately explained with the assumption of information loss due to a reduction in scanning time at shorter ISIs. The purpose of Experiment II was to observe the effects of shorter ISIs on recognition accuracy as a function of the frequency of presentation.

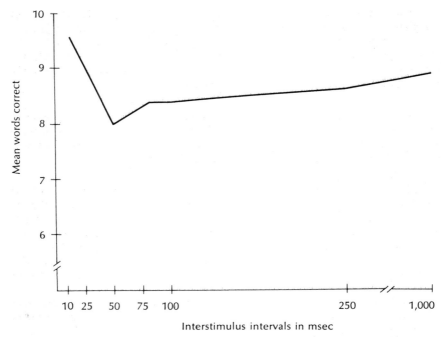

Figure 1.8: The average number of words correctly identified for each of the inter-stimulus intervals used in experiments I and II.

Experiment II

A number of experiments have demonstrated the existence of a perceptual time unit somewhere in the region of 50–100 msec (White, 1963). Although a variety of interpretations have been advanced, the empirical evidence speaks for a process of visual summation in which successive visual stimuli falling within the critical time period interact. Such critical durations relate on one hand to the time–intensity reciprocity, in which visual responses are found to be dependent on the total energy of the stimulus ($E = I \times t$, where I equals illumination and t the duration of the stimulus). Kahneman (1964) demonstrated a nonmonotonic relationship between stimulating energy and acuity with regard to the critical duration within which the reciprocity law is shown to hold. As luminance increased, the critical duration decreased from 200 msec to somewhere between 50 and 100 msec. Further increases in energy resulted in an increase in the critical duration to about 300 msec. In a recent study by Eriksen and Collins (1967), two patterns of dots, which when presented simultaneously produced a legible nonsense syllable, were presented at varying interstimulus intervals ranging from 0 to 500 msec. The probability of the correct identification of the syllable was observed as a function of the ISI. At very short ISIs (below 25 msec), performance approached 100 percent correct identification. As the ISI increased, performance decreased, reaching an asymptote somewhere in the region of 100–300 msec.

Thus on one hand, some tasks (Kahneman and Norman, 1964) result in complete reciprocity for illumination and duration and no reduction in recognition performance over critical durations up to 300 msec (Kahneman, 1964). Other tasks, such as those employed by Eriksen and Collins (1967), yield a monotonic decrease in recognition accuracy in which performance is inversely related to ISI and reaches an asymptote between 100 and 300 msec.

Method.   The method was the same as Experiment I with the exception of the ISIs used (10, 25, 50, and 75 msec). All other aspects of the study, including the measurement of threshold, paralleled Experiment I. The subjects ($N = 16$) were again unpaid volunteers from an introductory class.

Results.   An analysis of variance for the number of words correct for the three frequencies of presentation (3, 5, and 10) revealed a nonsignificant value, $F_{(2, 45)} = 1.10$, $p > 0.10$. The ISI variable was significant, $F_{(3, 129)} = 6.46$, $p < 0.01$, and the Frequency $\times$ ISI interaction was not significant, $F_{(12, 129)} = 1.51$, $p < 0.10$. The insignificant value for the frequency condition was found to be due to the deletion of the control condition of one presentation at each ISI. In a subsequent 4×4 analysis, the value for frequency was found highly significant, $F_{(3, 45)} = 17.28$, $p < 0.01$.

Again the control conditions of one word presentation at each ISI were compared with a Friedman test. The resulting value of $\chi^2_r = 4.03$ again failed to reach a 0.10 level of significance.

Figure 1.8 presents the relationship between recognition probability and ISI for Experiment II. Also included in Figure 1.8 are the data from Experiment I.

Discussion.   The probability of correct identification of the words was shown to decrease from 1,000 to 50 msec (see Experiment I). For the very short ISIs in Experiment II (10 and 25 msec), an increase in the number of correct identifications resulted. This observation confirms the observations of Eriksen and Collins (1965) in the masking situation and Eriksen and Collins (1967) in the successive presentation of dot patterns forming a nonsense syllable. The summation effect decreases monotonically from zero-delay periods to an asymptote around 100 msec. It does not fit with the expectations of the critical durations for the time–intensity reciprocity function, which would predict no reduction in response accuracy within the confines of the critical duration (Kahneman and Norman, 1964). Such a discrepancy between functions for form perception and for brightness summation with regard to a critical duration has been observed by Schurman, Eriksen, and Rohrbaugh (1968). They concluded that perceived brightness within a critical duration is solely a function of the amount of energy present within the critical duration. For form perception, critical durations were found only when the light energy was continuously distributed over the interval of stimulation.

The data of Experiment II, then, appear compatible with a visual summation hypothesis in which the probability of correct word identification decreases linearly as the interval between successive stimulus presentation is lengthened.

The large discrepancy between recognition probabilities in Experiments I and II for the 50-msec ISI seem worthy of note. If one considers the subject's task in Experiment I as compared to Experiment II, it would appear reasonable to assume that the subject would adopt a different strategy in each study to maximize the probability of identifying each word. In Experiment I, all but one of the ISIs were longer than 100 msec. An efficient strategy for the long ISIs would involve fixating both the front and back parts of the word. On those trials using the 50-msec ISIs, this strategy would be most inefficient as the subject would have time to fixate only one portion of the word. In Experiment II, however, all ISIs were below 100 msec. In this case, the subject would never have time to fixate on various sections of the word and would use a single fixation point in the center of the word as the most efficient strategy.

CHAPTER 2

Some Aspects
of Color Vision

The perception of color has interested and puzzled scientists for a number of years. Several physical characteristics have been identified which appear to stand in a constant relationship to the sensation of a given color. The primary physical aspect is the wavelength of the stimulating light radiation. If a light with a wavelength of 580 mμ is projected on a white screen, most subjects will report seeing yellow. Different wavelengths evoke the sensations of different colors.

The relationship between wavelength and the sensation of color might lead us to the conclusion that wavelength *is* color. A second possibility is that wavelength *induces* color. If the latter were the case, it might be possible to find other stimuli capable of evoking the sensation of color. Such a stimulus was discovered in 1826 by a French monk, Benedict Prevost, and later described in detail by the noted psychophysicist G. T. Fechner. The latter observed that when a disc diagonally divided into a black-and-white section was rotated at about five revolutions per second, the disc changed color. Various colors not usually produced by mixing black and white (which should produce an achromatic gray) appeared at slow revolutions of the disc. If the speed of the disc was increased above a critical level, fusion occurred, and the expected achromatic gray appeared. Obviously, wavelength was not the stimulus evoking the sensation of color. Rather, the retinal cells were being activated in rapid succession by the black-and-white stimulus.

More recently, the physicist Edwin Land (1959) has developed several experiments demonstrating the sensation of color independent of wavelength. In Land's basic experimental design, first devised by Sir Isaac Newton in 1660, white light is broken down by means of a prism into the visible spectrum. The wavelengths separated by this process produce the sensations of red, orange, yellow, green, blue, indigo, and violet. By placing filters in front of the spectral light, it is possible to allow only narrow bands of these wavelengths to pass through to a target screen. Mixing these bands of light on the screen produces new colors located somewhere between the two mixed bands on the visible spectrum. Land set up this experiment using two narrow beams from the yellow portion of the spectrum. When combined, they produced a yellow falling between the two beams of the spectrum. In front of the combined beams he placed two black-and-white transparencies, each showing a collection of colored objects. There was, of course, no color in the transparencies, but only lighter and darker areas which allowed more or less of the light to pass through to the screen. The image of the collection of objects projected to the screen was not yellow, varying in brightness; rather, the image showed distinct colors. As with Fechner's experiment, the color is produced by evoking a response in the eye that does not utilize wavelength as the critical stimulus element.

The important point to remember is that the sensation of color is produced by the discharge of certain retinal receptors, and is not a specific property of the stimulating object. Many theories have been advanced to describe these receptors and their functions. Observations of the structures of eyes of certain animals that are not color sensitive have led scientists to nominate the cone-shaped receptor as the likeliest part of the retina responsible for color sensation. Of the various theories of color perception developed around this idea, two have received the most support and acclaim. These are the trichromatic theory, first advanced by Thomas Young in England and Hermann von Helmholtz in Germany; and the opponent-processes theory, developed by Ewald Hering in Germany.

Recent research, while confirming the basic assumptions of the trichromatic theory at the level of the retina, has led to the supercession of other aspects of the theory. In particular, the explanation of the transmission of sensory information to higher visual centers appears to conform more with the hypothetical formulations of Hering.

The physiological, biological, and biochemical function of the receptors of color vision at the level of the retina is best described by George Wald, a biologist at Harvard University, who recently was awarded a Nobel Prize for his work in the photochemistry of vision. His report of the present-day knowledge of receptors of color vision first appeared in *Science* in 1964.

Wald, a noted proponent of the trichromatic theory, presents data to support this explanation. The second paper in this chapter is by Leo Hurvich and Dorothea Jameson, both advocates of the opponent-processes theory. They examine the problem of luminosity and the sensitivity of the fovea to different colors, and offer data supporting the opponent-processes theory.

The nature of the research into color vision requires highly sophisticated equipment and a rather technical language is employed. Since the latter may prove difficult for the reader unfamiliar with such research, the following list describes several terms utilized in the two papers. For definitions of other unfamiliar terms the reader should consult the book by Graham (1965) and the *Dictionary of Psychology* by Chaplin (1968).

CIE standard observer: Standard curves of spectral luminosity as established by the Commission *Internationale* de l'*Eclairage* (International Commission on Illumination).

chromatic adaptation: An increase in the lower threshold of sensitivity to light of a certain wavelength or hue. In research into color vision the term often refers to a decrease in the perceived strength of a hue after prolonged exposure.

deflection galvanometer: A device for measuring variations in the strength of an electric current.

footlamberts: The usual unit for the measurement of luminance.

luminosity: The relative brightness of a light depending upon the conditions of illumination and the reflectance characteristics of the object viewed.

luminosity function: Luminosity or brightness values of all visual wavelengths.

monochromater: A device used for isolating certain portions of the visual spectrum (i.e., narrow bands of wavelengths).

radiant flux: The rate of emission of radiant energy as a function of time.

thermophile: A device for measuring the energy of radiations falling on a blackened surface through temperature increases in the absorbing surface.

Trolands: A unit of visual stimulation. Defined as the retinal illuminance equal to the illuminance produced by viewing a surface with a luminance of one standard candle per square meter. (Also called a photon.)

Wratten wedges: A particular kind of filter for reducing the intensity of a light beam allowing equal reduction in intensity over the entire spectrum or for specific portions thereof.

The Receptors of
Human Color Vision
George Wald[1]

> From three simple sensations, with their combinations, we obtain several
> primitive distinctions of colours; but the different proportions, in which they
> may be combined, afford a variety of tints beyond all calculation. The three
> simple sensations being red, green, and violet, the three binary combinations
> are yellow, consisting of red and green; crimson, of red and violet; and blue,
> of green and violet; and the seventh in order is white light, composed by all
> the three united.
>
> —Thomas Young, *Lectures on Natural Philosophy*, 1807

That normal color vision involves the operation of three independent variables was first stated plainly by Thomas Young (1802); yet it was not until this
notion was embodied in the color mixture experiments and equations of Helmholtz (1852) and Maxwell (1871, 1890) that it gained general currency. Young
had expressed his idea in terms of three primary color sensations—red, green,
and violet—excited by three types of retinal receptors differing in spectral sensitivity. With Max Schultze's (1866) recognition that color vision is exclusively
the business of cones, this came to mean three types of cone with different
spectral sensitivities. That posed, a century ago, the problem of determining
what those spectral sensitivities are. It is a task that must be approached directly, since it has been clear for some time that there is no unique theoretical
solution: that an infinite array of hypothetical trios of spectral sensitivity functions, all interconvertible by linear transformations, can satisfy the formal demands of most color vision measurements. Rather than go on with such formal
constructions, we need to determine the properties of the receptor mechanisms
that in fact govern human color vision.

In the past Stiles (1949, 1959) has come closest to solving this problem by
sensory methods. Recently also we have had direct microspectrophotometric
measurements of the difference spectra of the light-sensitive pigments in the
human fovea (Brown and Wald, 1963) and in single parafoveal cones (Marks,
Dobelle, and MacNichol, 1964).

The present paper describes a further analysis of such mechanisms. I
came to these experiments indirectly. Having extracted two visual pigments
from a crayfish eye, I tried to learn what they were doing. It turned out that the
crayfish possesses an apparatus suitable for color vision, having at least two
visual pigments segregated in different receptors and poised at about the same
level of sensitivity. A simple procedure was devised for analyzing these ar-

rangements. The sensitivity throughout the spectrum was measured in the dark-adapted eye. Then, one type of receptor being selectively adapted to a colored light, a redetermination of visual thresholds throughout the spectrum revealed the spectral sensitivity of the other type of receptor. So, for example, with the eye continuously adapted to red light, the spectral sensitivity measured was that of the blue-receptor. Conversely, on adaptation to blue light one could measure the spectral sensitivity of the red-receptor. The response of each type of receptor is not at all distorted by such background adaptations. This could be shown in organisms possessing a single visual system—for example, lobsters or horseshoe crabs—in which the spectral sensitivity is identical whether measured in the dark-adapted eye or under red or blue light.

Such invariance with the conditions of adaptation is an essentially photochemical criterion, characterizing the operation of a single visual pigment. The spectral sensitivities measured in this way have the force of action spectra of visual pigments. This is not necessarily the criterion for isolating a single receptor type, for instance, a single type of cone; for a cone containing a mixture of visual pigments, or any more central photoreceptor mechanism responsive to several visual pigments, would change in spectral sensitivity with the color of the adapting light.

The experiments reported here extend this type of procedure to the human eye. In retrospect it was clear that this method is a limiting case of Stiles's two-color threshold technique. As ordinarily employed this involves determining the way in which the increment threshold at one wavelength rises with the brightness of background at another wavelength. The present measurements correspond to increment thresholds measured on steady backgrounds of very high brightness. On inquiry it turned out that Stiles had made similar measurements, a short account of which he generously agreed to append to this article. Related procedures have also been used to partially isolate the spectral sensitivities of the blue-receptor and of the green- and red-receptors.

Procedure

The experimental arrangement is shown in Figure 2.1. It involves two light paths, one for monochromatic test flashes, the other for a steady, colored background radiation upon which the test flashes are superimposed. Both are seen in Maxwellian view, a field lens in each pathway focusing the light upon a fixed exit pupil. Both lenses are therefore seen as evenly illuminated, the background appearing as a circular field subtending an angle of 3.5° with the eye, the test field as a 1° circle entered upon it. Central fixation is maintained either with a luminous white fixation point for dark or dim backgrounds (made by passing light down a tapered quartz rod to appear as a bright point at its tip), or with a black fixation point when the background is too bright for a luminous point to be easily visible.

For the test field the light of a 100-watt zirconium arc was projected through a Bausch and Lomb grating monochromator with slits set to transmit a wave band 3.3 mμ wide throughout the spectrum. A photographic shutter set

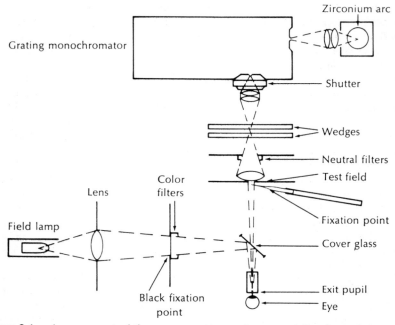

Figure 2.1: Arrangement of the apparatus. It consists essentially of two light paths, one for presenting monochromatic test flashes of graded intensity, superimposed on steady colored backgrounds provided through the other light path. Both the test and background fields are seen in the Maxwellian view.

the exposure at 45 msec. The intensity was regulated by a pair of neutral wedges rotating in opposite directions so as to compensate each other, and by neutral filters.

Observations

The subject, with head held in a chin-and-forehead rest, looked through the 3.5-mm exit pupil, either at a luminous white fixation point in an otherwise dark field, or at a black point at the center of a colored background field, 3.5° in diameter. The test field was exposed for flashes of 45 msec, beginning at a subthreshold intensity, and brightened step by step until the subject reported just seeing it. Since the test field was 1° in diameter and fixated centrally, its image fell entirely within the area of the fovea, effectively 1.5° to 1.7° in diameter, which contains only cones. The data are expressed in terms of the logarithm of the relative sensitivity, the sensitivity being the reciprocal of the relative number of photons per flash needed to just see the test field. Some idea of absolute sensitivities can be gained from the fact that under the conditions of these experiments the first subject (R.H.), when dark-adapted, required about 10^4 photons per flash at 560 mμ to see the field, and the second subject (D.G.) required about 1.6 times this quantity.

Spectral Sensitivities at the Corneal Level. Figure 2.2 shows measurements on the right eye of R.H., in terms of relative numbers of photons incident upon the cornea. The log sensitivity of the dark-adapted fovea is greatest at about 562 mμ, falling symmetrically to both sides except for an abrupt shoulder in the blue. This curve represents the overall sensitivity of the fovea, a composite of the spectral sensitivities of all the types of cone it contains.

To isolate the individual functions that make up this composite, background radiations of various colors and brightnesses were chosen on the basis of a priori considerations and empirical trial. It has already been noted that this procedure tends to isolate the spectral sensitivities (action spectra) of visual pigments rather than specific types of cone. To the degree that the pigments are segregated, one to a cone, it does both; but in the event that some cones contain mixtures of pigments, it would isolate only the pigments. I use such terms as blue- or red-receptor below to refer more particularly to a pigment than to the cone that contains it, and attempt to clarify these distinctions further in the discussion that follows.

When the fovea is continuously adapted to bright yellow light containing all wavelengths longer than 550 mμ (Corning filter 3482; log footlamberts, 6.00; log effective trolands, 7.01), the spectral sensitivity curve is that of the blue-receptor. It consists of a high, narrow band, maximal at about 440 mμ. The low, broad shoulder at long wavelengths apparently is not an intrinsic part of this function but represents the residual sensitivities of other receptors.

Simultaneous adaptation to wave bands in the blue and red, and hence to purple light, isolates the green-receptor. In Figure 2.2 this involves adaptation to a background radiation that includes all wavelengths shorter than 462 mμ and longer than 645 mμ (Wratten filter 35; log footlamberts, 4.34; log effective trolands, 5.42). The spectral sensitivity is greatest at about 548 mμ and displays a broad shoulder in the blue, which is, as will appear, an extraneous effect of the ocular pigmentation.

Adaptation to blue light isolates the red-receptor. Figure 2.2 shows two such experiments, involving different color filters and brightnesses. The upper curve was obtained with a blue background radiation rising from 500 mμ to a peak at 430 mμ (Wratten filter 47B; log footlamberts, 4.27; log effective trolands, 5.35). The lower curve was measured on a background radiation rising from 530 mμ to a peak at 440 mμ (Wratten filter 47; log footlamberts, 5.12; log effective trolands, 6.15). Both curves show peaks at about 580 mμ and are nearly identical in shape, showing the invariance of such action spectra with the conditions of adaptation once a reasonable isolation has been achieved.

Figure 2.3 shows a similar analysis of the foveal sensitivities of subject D.G. The results differ only in detail from those for R.H. The spectral sensitivity of the dark-adapted fovea is maximal at about 568 mμ; and the sensitivity curves for the blue-, green-, and red-receptors show peaks at about 435, 550, and 585 mμ. The two latter curves, like that for the dark-adapted fovea, lie at slightly longer wavelengths than those for R.H.; and the curves for the dark-adapted and purple-adapted eye display only gentle inflections in the blue, whereas those for R.H. have large and abrupt shoulders. The reason for these differences will appear shortly.

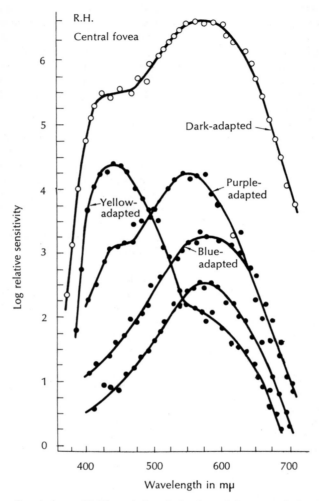

Figure 2.2: Spectral sensitivities of the dark-adapted fovea and the single color vision pigments measured at the corneal level in R.H. The sensitivity of the total fovea is greatest at about 562 mμ (average of 2 experiments). Adaptation to yellow light isolates the action spectrum of the blue-sensitive pigment (λ_{MAX} 438 mμ); to a mixture of violet and red, hence purple light, that of the green-sensitive pigment (λ_{MAX} 548 mμ); and to blue light, that of the red-sensitive pigment (λ_{MAX} 580 mμ). The results of two different blue-adaptations demonstrate the invariance of such action spectra with the condition of adaptation. Ordinates are log relative sensitivity (log 1/threshold), expressed in terms of relative numbers of photons per flash incident upon the cornea of the eye. Absolute sensitivities can be judged from the fact that the maximal sensitivity of the dark-adapted fovea corresponds to a threshold of about 10^1 photons.

The isolation of individual spectral sensitivity curves by these methods involves trying numbers of filters and brightnesses. The blue-receptor is isolated rather easily, since it lies so far from the others. Separating the curves of the green- and red-receptors is more difficult, since they overlap so widely, and it may be too much to expect absolute isolations. The conditions finally chosen were those that yielded the narrowest and simplest shapes of spectral sensitivity function, on the assumption that these criteria should mark the most complete isolations.

We can derive some assurance that the individual receptor curves of Figures 2.2 and 2.3 succeed in this to a degree from experiments in which they

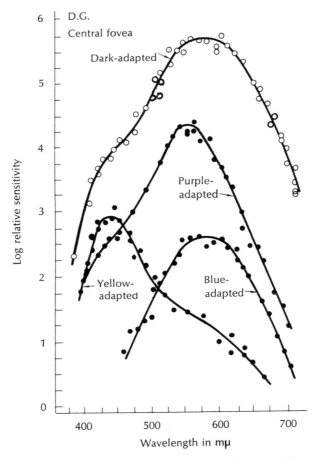

Figure 2.3:   Spectral sensitivities of the dark-adapted fovea and the single foveal pigments, measured at the corneal level in D.G. The foveal sensitivity is greatest at about 568 mμ where the visual threshold is about 1.6 X 10^1 photons per flash. The blue-, green-, and red-sensitive pigments display maximum sensitivities at about 435, 550, and 585 mμ. Otherwise as in Figure 2.2.

are isolated two at a time. In Figure 2.4 the curves marked "red-adapted" were obtained with two brightnesses of a red background radiation containing only wavelengths longer than 630 mμ (Corning filter 2403. Upper curve: log footlamberts, 2.60; log effective trolands, 3.77. Lower curve: log footlamberts, 5.42; log effective trolands, 6.44). The red light having selectively adapted the red-receptor, these spectral sensitivity curves display the peaks of the blue- and green-receptors. At the lower brightness of background, the green-receptor has λ_{MAX} about 550 mμ, as in Figure 2.2; the minor maximum of the blue-receptor is pulled toward longer wavelengths by some degree of fusion with the major band, so that it lies at about 450 mμ. Conversely, at the higher brightness, the principal peak, that of the blue-receptor, lies at its proper position, 440 mμ (compare Figure 2.2), whereas the minor green-sensitivity maximum is pulled toward it, so as to lie at about 535 mμ.

Similarly (Figure 2.4), a bright green background (Ilford filter 604; transmission 500–40 mμ, peaking at 520 mμ; log footlamberts, 4.85; log effective trolands, 5.90) selectively adapts the green-receptor, so that the residual spectral-sensitivity curve displays the maxima of the blue- and red-receptors, at about 440 mμ and 585 mμ (compare Figure 2.2).

The fact that the sensitivity peaks take about the same positions when in pairs as when isolated singly indicates that we are dealing with genuine properties of the receptor pigments.

Ocular and Macular Absorptions.   Such spectral sensitivity curves, measured in terms of light incident on the surface of the cornea, govern how we see; yet relative to the intrinsic properties of the cones or visual pigments, their shapes are distorted by the filtering action of colored structures in the eye. These are principally the yellow lens and the yellow pigmentation of the macula lutea.

Figure 2.5 shows an estimate of the average absorbance (extinction, optical density) of the refractive structures of the human eye, prepared from the measurements of Ludvigh and McCarthy (four eyes, 1938), Boettner and Wolter (nine eyes, 1962), and my own comparison of the average spectral sensitivity of rod vision with the absorption spectrum of dark adapted human rods (absorbance $= \log I_0/I$, in which I_0 is the incident and I the transmitted intensity) [Wald and Brown, 1958]. Figure 2.5 shows also the absorption spectrum of the human macula (average of eight eyes). Adding these together yields an estimate of the total absorbance of the ocular structures, from the corneal surface to the cones, in the human fovea. This added to the log spectral sensitivity measured at the cornea yields the spectral sensitivity at the level of the cones. Such an average correction is suitable for dealing with the averaged data from numbers of subjects. Ocular and macular pigmentations vary widely, however, and the data for individual observers require individual correction.

Individual Differences in Spectral Sensitivity.   Several years ago I prepared a curve for the average cone sensitivity ("photopic luminosity"), combining the results of a number of investigations. It includes measurements on several hundred subjects, and is highly reliable. (See the normal cone sensitivity curves in Figures 2.11 and 2.12.)

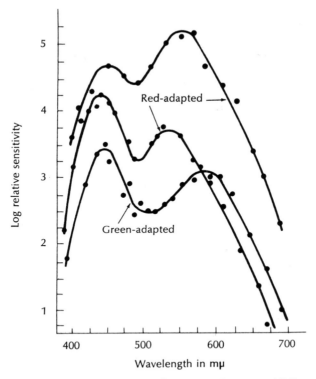

Figure 2.4: Spectral sensitivities of the color vision pigments of R.H., measured in pairs at the corneal level. Adaptation to two brightnesses of red light (wavelengths greater than 630 mμ) selectively adapts the red-receptor, the resultant sensitivity curves displaying in different proportions the peaks of the blue- and green-sensitive pigments, at about 440 and 550 mμ. (In each instance the minor peak is displaced toward the major peak by some degree of fusion with it.) Adaptation to green light, selectively adapting the green-sensitive pigment, exposes the peaks of the blue- and red-sensitive pigments at about 440 and 585 mμ.

The spectral sensitivity of R.H.'s dark-adapted fovea (Figure 2.2) agrees well with this function from about 700 to 480 mμ. At shorter wavelengths, however, the curve for R.H. displays a bulge of higher sensitivity, greatest at about 440 mμ, and resembling the sensitivity curve of the blue-receptor. I would conclude that R.H. possesses nearly the average ocular and macular transmissions but departs from the average subject in having a considerably higher blue-sensitivity (0.3 log unit higher, hence about twice as high at 440 mμ).

In an earlier investigation in which I was able to make measurements at only a few wavelengths, I thought that R.H.'s relatively high foveal sensitivity in the blue, like that of her brother, was caused by a lack of macular pigmentation (Wald, 1945, 1949). This sensitivity now appears in both cases to be caused by a greater than average amount of blue-receptor. We do not yet know

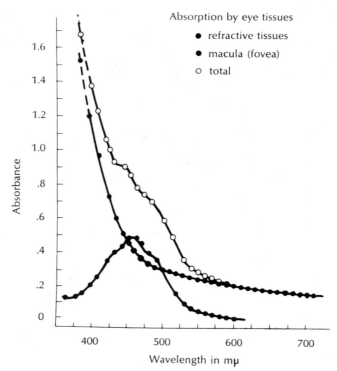

Figure 2.5: An estimate of the average absorption by the dioptric tissues of the human eye (cornea to retina) and of the macular pigmentation (average of eight eyes). (*Data from Brown and Wald, 1963.*)

whether this departure from the average is sufficient to categorize these subjects as color-anomalous. In any case this condition, just the opposite of blueblindness (hence blue-richness, "hypercyanopia") appears, like color blindness, to be genetically determined.

The spectral sensitivity of D.G.'s dark-adapted fovea (Figure 2.3) departs from the average luminosity curve in an entirely different way. Compared with the average, D.G.'s sensitivity decreases more and more from the red to the violet. On subtracting her curve from the average function, one obtains a curve looking much like the one for total ocular and macular absorbance shown in Figure 2.5. I conclude that D.G. has nearly the average distribution of color receptors, but a considerably denser ocular and macular pigmentation. Adding her departure from the photopic luminosity curve to the total ocular absorbance of Figure 2.5 yields her individual correction.

These two subjects exemplify the two kinds of individual differences that underlie changes in the shape of "corneal" spectral sensitivity curves even within the normal range: differences in ocular and macular transmission, and differences in the relative sensitivities of the color mechanisms. Such differences also are found within a single retina. The macular pigmentation is concentrated in the central retina, thinning out peripherally, and very dilute or absent beyond 5° from the fovea. The proportions of the color receptors may change also from the center to the periphery. In some subjects the far periphery behaves as though red-blind (Maxwell, 1871; Auerbach and Wald, 1954, 1955); and Weale (1953) has reported finding this region of his own eye markedly blue-sensitive relative to the fovea and parafovea.

Spectral Sensitivity at the level of the Cones.   The data for R.H. can therefore be brought to the cone level by adding to her spectral sensitivities the average ocular and macular absorbances shown in Figure 2.5; and the data for D.G. can be similarly corrected by adding her own denser ocular and macular absorbances to her spectral sensitivity curves. In this way the curves shown in Figure 2.6 are obtained. Below 400 mμ, where these corrections are unreliable, the curves are drawn with broken lines.

The sensitivity curve of the dark-adapted fovea at the cone level consists of a major band showing a peak at about 550 mμ in both observers, with a minor maximum or inflection in the blue. In the "corneal" curves of Figures 2.2 and 2.3 the inflection in the blue was caused mainly by the depression of sensitivity in this region by the macular pigmentation. Now this factor has been removed, and the remaining bulge of sensitivity in the blue is caused by the blue-receptor. R.H., who is particularly rich in blue-sensitive cones or pigment, displays a maximum at about 430 mμ; but even the curve for D.G., which represents the average condition more closely, has a broad inflection in in this region.

The curves for the individual receptors in Figure 2.6, to the degree that the corrections are adequate, should represent the intrinsic action spectra of the blue-, green-, and red-sensitive pigments, and by the same token their absorption spectra—in terms of log relative absorbance—as measured in situ. They have many interesting features: (1) the maxima now lie at about 430, 540, and 575 mμ. (2) Though the "corneal" sensitivity curves of these two subjects differ in shape and position, the corrected curves for blue (B), green (G), and red (R) are invariant, as they should be if they represent the action spectra of single pigments. A small difference appears only at long wavelengths in the B curve, one indication that the broad inflection in this region is due to the residual sensitivity of the other receptors rather than to the blue-receptor itself. (3) These curves, unlike those for the "corneal" sensitivities, remain high at short wavelengths. The absorption spectra of all known visual pigments remain at least one-fifth as high in the violet and near ultraviolet as at their peaks (Wald, 1958). In Figure 2.6 the G and R curves fall at 400 mμ to 22 and 14 percent of their maxima, not a bad approximation to the behavior of absorption spectra in view of the uncertainties of correction for ocular transmission at short wavelengths. The B curve at 400 mμ is about 0.6 percent of its maximum.

Figure 2.7 shows the same data plotted on the more familiar arithmetic ordinates. The features just described appear more clearly here. The same figure shows with broken lines the difference spectra of the green- and red-sensitive pigments of the human fovea, measured in situ by Brown and Wald (1963).

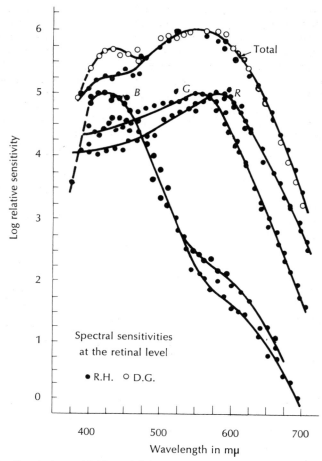

Figure 2.6: Spectral sensitivities of R.H. and D.G., as in Figures 2.2 and 2.3 corrected for ocular and macular absorptions. The resulting curves are as though measured at the level of the cones, and have the force of action spectra or absorption spectra of the foveal pigments. The sensitivity of the dark-adapted fovea (total) displays a main peak at about 500 mμ, and a minor peak or inflection at about 430 mμ due to the blue-receptor, in which R.H. is particularly rich. The action spectra of the blue-, green-, and red-sensitive pigments, following individual correction for ocular and macular absorptions, are invariant in shape and position, with λ_{MAX} at about 430, 540, and 575 mμ.

The difference spectrum of the green-sensitive pigment agrees well with the present measurements, except for the expected falling off of the difference spectrum below about 510 mμ owing to the formation of colored products of bleaching (retinaldehyde). The difference spectrum of the red-sensitive pigment, however, lies at slightly shorter wavelengths (λ_{MAX} 565 to 570 mμ) and is somewhat broader than the action spectrum. Both types of departure suggest that in measuring this difference spectrum, some green-sensitive pigment had been bleached along with the red-sensitive pigment. The present measurements not only represent absorption rather than difference spectra, but seem to involve a more complete isolation of the red-sensitive pigment than we had achieved previously.

Discussion

Composition of Total Foveal Sensitivity.   Figure 2.8 assesses the contributions of the three receptor pigments to R.H.'s total foveal sensitivity, as measured at the corneal level (main graph) and that of the cones (inset). R.H. was

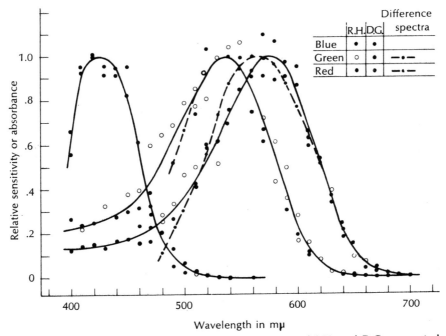

Figure 2.7:   Action spectra of the color vision pigments of R.H. and D.G., corrected for distortions caused by ocular and macular absorptions. λ_{MAX} of the blue-, green-, and red-sensitive pigments appear at about 430, 540, and 575 mμ. Difference spectra of the green- and red-sensitive pigments measured directly in the human fovea are shown with broken lines. All curves have been given the same arbitrary height for comparison.

chosen for this computation because of her blue-richness, ensuring that her blue-receptor would appear significantly, as it might not in an average observer.

The computation starts with the recognition that beyond about 650 mμ the red-receptor accounts entirely for the total sensitivity. One can infer this not only from the curves of Figure 2.7, but also from the fact that beyond this wavelength hues are no longer discriminated—every wavelength matches every other in hue, an expression of the fact that only one type of receptor still functions.

I begin therefore by fitting the red-receptor curve to the total sensitivity curve at long wavelengths, using such a logarithmic plot as that of Figure 2.2, which offers a long stretch of these curves for matching between 650 and 700 mμ. This sets the height of the red-receptor curve in the composite function. Then, subtracting the red-sensitivity data from the total, in such an arithmetic plot as Figure 2.8, yields the vertically barred circles (plotted only to 500 mμ, below which the blue-sensitivity function would intrude). R.H.'s directly measured green-sensitivity data, brought to the same height, are shown in Figure 2.8 with horizontally barred circles. The good agreement of both sets of points speaks well for the accuracy of the analysis. Subtracting the sum of the red- and green-sensitivity curves from the total indicates the height of the blue-sensitive component; and R.H.'s blue-sensitivity data, brought to this height, are shown in Figure 2.8 as small open circles. The ratios of sensitivity maxima in this subject come out to be $R : G : B = 0.542 : 0.575 : 0.053$.

The ocular and macular absorptions particularly depress the sensitivity of the blue-receptor. A comparable analysis of spectral sensitivity at the level of the cones is shown in the inset of Figure 2.8. The ratios of maxima are now $R : G : B = 0.52 : 0.59 : 0.28$; that is, about $1 : 1.13 : 0.54$.

It has already been stressed that R.H. is particularly blue-sensitive. The same analysis carried out with her red- and green-sensitivity curves and the average photopic luminosity function leaves no room at all for a blue-receptor; the sum of the red- and green-sensitivities accounts for the total within the errors of measurement. Other data, however, indicate that in the average observer the blue-sensitive component is about one-third as high as in R.H. In the average normal observer, therefore, when the total luminosity curve is set at a maximum of 1.0, the component curves should have maxima $R : G : B$ of about $0.54 : 0.58 : 0.018$ at the corneal level; and $0.52 : 0.59 : 0.09$ at the level of the cones.

Segregation of Visual Pigments in Cones.   Though the method of selective adaptation tends to isolate visual pigments rather than types of cone, for cones that contain only one pigment it does both.

The yellow lights used to isolate the spectral sensitivity of the blue-receptor cause so little light adaptation in the violet region that it seems unlikely that the blue-sensitive cones contain appreciable amounts of other visual pigments. It is known that bleaching very little visual pigment causes a large rise of threshold (Rushton and Cohen, 1954; Wald, 1954); and if the blue-sensitive cones contained considerable green- or red-sensitive pigment, the bleaching of the latter should raise their thresholds much higher than we observe in isolating the blue-sensitive pigment.

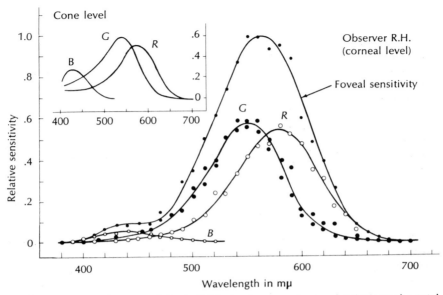

Figure 2.8: Contributions of the individual color receptor mechanisms to the total foveal sensitivity of R.H. The main graph shows measurements at the corneal level, the inset, corresponding curves at the level of the cones. In this particularly blue-sensitive observer, when the total foveal sensitivity is given a maximal height of 1.0, the heights of the B, G, and R curves are as 0.053 : 0.575 : 0.542 at the corneal level, and 0.28 : 0.59 : 0.52 at the level of the cones. In the average observer the blue-component is only about one-third as high.

A like inference can be drawn from the fact that hue discrimination ceases beyond about 650 mμ, owing apparently to the fact that only red-sensitive cones continue to function. If the blue- and green- sensitive cones contained red-sensitive pigment, they should still function at such long wavelengths, and it should still be possible to discriminate between hues. It is probable, therefore, that neither the blue- nor the green-sensitive cones contain red-sensitive pigment.

These arguments leave open the possibility that the red-sensitive cones contain mixtures of visual pigments.

Blue or Violet as a Primary Sensation. This distinction, though irrelevant to the main burden of this paper, has plagued color vision theory since its beginnings. After careful consideration, Young, Helmholtz, and König all settled upon violet rather than blue as the primary color sensation. It is not common practice at present, however, and I depart from it here only to avoid raising an extraneous issue.

Comparisons with Other Measurements. The comparison of Stiles's measurements (1964) in which he used much the same techniques of selective adaptation as in the present work, with mine shows that his curve I (λ_{MAX} 443 mμ) is almost identical with the peak of my curve for the blue-receptor.

His curve M comes closest to my green-receptor curve, though skewed toward shorter wavelengths, with about 533 mμ. Stiles's curve H, the closest to mine for the red-receptor, displays a peak near 590 mμ superimposed on a general rise of sensitivity toward shorter wavelengths. The divergences from my measurements in curves M and H seem to go with different choices of adapting lights and much lower intensities of adaptation. Other of Stiles's curves display two, in some instances (G for example) even three maxima from the individual receptors (compare Figure 2.4).

It is more informative to make such comparisons with Stiles's color "mechanisms," based upon his extensive measurements (1959) of increment thresholds on backgrounds of graded brightness. Such a comparison with my measurements on R.H.—chosen because they involve close to average ocular and macular absorptions—is shown in Figure 2.9.

In evaluating his experiments, Stiles invoked two criteria: homogeneity of the relation connecting increment threshold with brightness of background, and conformity with what he calls "displacement rules"—that is, invariance of shape of the sensitivity function with the conditions of adaptation. These seem to me to imply two different approaches to the underlying mechanisms, the first physiological, the second photochemical. Homogeneity of the increment threshold function probably distinguishes a single neural unit, involving one or more cones and their central connections; whereas conformity with the "displacement rules" indicates the isolation of the action spectrum of one visual pigment. Among Stiles's "mechanisms," only those associated with the blue-receptor (π_1, π_3) obey the displacement rules. The green-mechanism (π_4) and the red-mechanism (π_5) do not, and must therefore involve mixtures of visual pigments.

The comparison shown in Figure 2.9 reveals a number of interesting features. In π_1 and even more in π_3, Stiles has achieved more complete isolations of the blue-sensitive pigment than mine. π_3 indeed displays a single-banded action spectrum, with no indication of a shoulder at long wavelengths. This series of curves, added to what has gone before, makes it relatively certain that the long wavelength shoulder is not an intrinsic part of the action spectrum of the blue-sensitive pigment.

My measurements of the green-receptor display a narrower band than Stiles's π_4, implying a more complete isolation of the action spectrum of the pigment. This is implied also in the failure of π_4 to follow the displacement rules. (My measurements also display a slightly higher shoulder in the blue, owing probably to individual differences in macular pigmentation.)

The most illuminating comparison, however, involves Stiles's π_5, for as Figure 2.9 shows, this traces almost perfectly the envelope of my curves for the green- and red-sensitive pigments. I think there can be little doubt that the π_5 mechanism depends upon roughly equal contributions from both pigments. The interesting question is whether such a mixture of pigments is present in the red-sensitive cones or in some other way converges its effects upon a single neural channel—that is, whether π_5, though composite in terms of pigments, may represent a single physiological mechanism. It may be recalled that my discussion of the segregation of visual pigments among the cones left this possibility open in the case of the red-receptor.

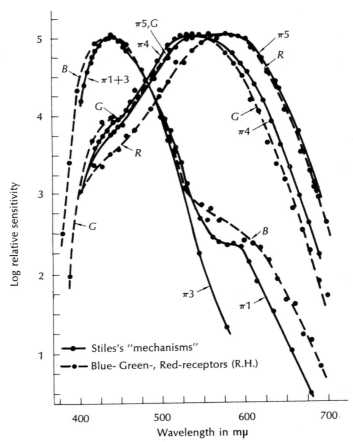

Figure 2.9: Spectral sensitivities of R.H.'s foveal pigments (*B, G, R*) compared with Stiles's color-vision "mechanisms." These curves are uncorrected for ocular and macular absorptions, and have all been brought to the same arbitrary height for comparison.

It is consistent with this interpretation that the red- and green-receptors seem to follow a different principle in combining to form the π_5 mechanism than in composing the luminosity curve. In the latter instance they simply add together, as in Figure 2.8, a straightforward photochemical type of behavior. In making up π_5, however, the increment threshold at each wavelength seems to depend primarily on whichever receptor is the more sensitive, so yielding a peculiarly broad function—considerably broader than the total luminosity curve—that represents the *envelope* of the red- and green-sensitivity curves rather than their sum.

Rushton (1959) and Weale (1959) have attempted the superbly difficult feat of measuring the difference spectra of foveal pigments directly, by the spectrophotometry of light reflected from the fundus of the living eye after passing twice through the retina. Rushton originally reported finding green- and red-sensitive pigments at about 540 mμ and 590 mμ, Weale at about 540 mμ and 600 mμ. For understandable reasons this procedure offered no approach to the blue-sensitive pigment; it has tended also to yield inconsistent results with the red-sensitive pigment. Rushton (1964) has recently "disclaimed" all his measurements of this kind prior to 1963. We are left with (1) his new measurements of the green-sensitive pigment which, though they rise from the red to a maximum near 550 mμ, do not descend again significantly, that is, do not describe a peak; (2) a computation "correcting" the absorbance of this pigment from a measured value of 0.07 to 0.35, which I judge to be at least five and perhaps as much as ten times too high; and (3) a remeasurement of the red-sensitive pigment in deuteranopic and normal eyes, which, though accompanied by elaborate tests to show that a single pigment was measured, is said to match Stiles's π_5 mechanism, which we have just seen to involve both the green- and red-sensitive pigments.

This procedure has yielded valuable information on the rise and fall of visual pigments in the living eye, and seems to measure reasonably well the difference spectrum of such a relatively dense pigment as rhodopsin; but it may not be capable of measuring reliably the difference spectra of the foveal pigments.

Color Blindness

> The mathematical expression of the difference between Colour-Blind and ordinary vision is that colour to the former is a function of two independent variables, but to an ordinary eye, of three; and that the relation of the two kinds of vision is not arbitrary, but indicates the absence of a determinate sensation, depending perhaps upon some undiscovered structure or organic arrangement, which forms one-third of the apparatus by which we receive sensations of colour.
>
> —*James Clerk Maxwell*, letter to G. Wilson, 1855

Whereas normal human color vision is trivariant, the usual types of color-blind vision are divariant (Maxwell, 1855). Young suggested that the red-blindness of his contemporary, the chemist Dalton, might be caused by the lack of one of the three color mechanisms. This idea, taken up by Helmholtz and Maxwell as a general explanation of color-blindness, later ran into the difficulty that many color-blind persons possess a nearly normal spectral sensitivity. Fick (1879) suggested that in such dichromats, two of the color channels—red and green—may be fused to yield a single sensation. Yet there has been no common agreement on this or other mechanisms of color blindness, and some years ago it became customary to bypass questions of mechanism by using arbitrarily—though he himself attached mechanisms to these terms—von Kries's classification (1905) of dichromats into protanopes, deuteranopes, and tritanopes.

Most color-blind persons—about 2 percent of all human males—are protanopes and deuteranopes. Both groups see only two hues in the spectrum, apparently blue and yellow, with a neutral point between that can be matched with white. The neutral points lie near 493 mμ in protanopes and near 497 mμ in deuteranopes, depending in part on the white chosen for matching (Judd, 1943). Protanopes and deuteranopes are therefore much alike except in one respect: the protanopes are abnormally insensitive to red light, whereas the deuteranopes are said to have a nearly normal spectral sensitivity. Tritanopes are rare (about 0.002 percent of men); they have an almost normal spectral sensitivity, and a neutral point at about 572 mμ.

One of the main difficulties in understanding color blindness is resolved with the recognition that it includes, not three, but four main types.

Figure 2.10 shows the foveal luminosity data of fourteen protanopes measured by various observers, compared with the "corneal" action spectrum of R.H.'s green-sensitive pigment. The agreement of these data shows that, as usually supposed, protanopes lack the red-sensitive pigment. They possess also, like normal trichromats, so little blue-sensitivity that the total luminosity function is dominated by the green-sensitive pigment alone. [The data for R.H. are chosen for these comparisons because she possesses close to the average ocular and macular transmissions. The measurements of Pitt (1935) involved comparisons between the halves of a 2° unfixated field, those of Hsia and Graham (1957) a centrally fixated 42' field, and those of Willmer (1955) a 10' field such as he believed to be blue-blind even in trichromatic subjects.]

A word should be said here about neutral points. Though for a variety of reasons they may depart considerably from the wavelengths at which the sensitivity curves of dichromats cross in such a diagram as Figure 2.8, they do bear a relationship to such crossing-points. The fact that in protanopes a neutral point occurs near 493 mμ suggests a crossing of the B and G curves near that wavelength. Obviously in Figure 2.8 this crossing comes too low, near 450 mμ, even though drawn for R.H., for whom the B curve is about three times as high as the average. Evidently the blue-receptor has a far larger white-making valence than its contribution to the foveal sensitivity function indicates; but that is another problem. Much the same comments will apply to the "deuteranopes" of Figure 2.12.

Figure 2.11 shows the average foveal luminosity function of seven tritanopes measured by Wright (1952), compared with that of normal observers. The tritanope curve displays a small loss of sensitivity in the blue and violet. The difference between the normal and tritanope sensitivities has the same shape and position as the action spectrum of the blue-sensitive pigment. The loss of sensitivity is greatest at about 450 mμ (0.23 log unit or about 40 percent). This is about what is expected from the contribution of the blue-receptor to the spectral sensitivity of the normal observer. The presence of a neutral point in tritanopes at about 572 mμ is consistent with the crossing of the G and R curves near that wavelength (Figure 2.8).

Figure 2.12 shows measurements on seven "deuteranopes" whose spectral sensitivity curves correspond with the action spectrum of R.H.'s red-sensitive pigment. By the same token they depart widely from the average photopic luminosity function, shown here with a broken line. Such subjects apparently lack the green-sensitive pigment.

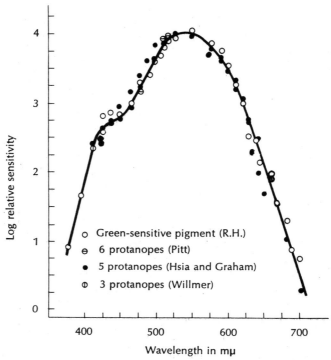

Figure 2.10: Action spectrum of R.H.'s green-sensitive pigment, measured at the corneal level, compared with the foveal luminosity function of fourteen protanopes. These dichromats apparently possess only the green- and blue-sensitive pigments, the latter contributing so little to the luminosity function as hardly to appear in the measurements. It can be concluded that protanopes lack the red-sensitive pigment, and in this sense are literally red-blind.

There are therefore three types of dichromat, each of which lacks one of the color-vision pigments. They might in that sense be called red-, blue- and green-blinds or, if Greek roots are preferred, anerythropes, acyanopes and achloropes. The general phenomenon might be called *achromia*.

What central arrangements one postulates to accompany the presence of only two visual pigments in such dichromats depends upon how seriously one takes the reports that protanopes and deuteranopes see the long-wave-length end of the spectrum as *yellow*. I am inclined to think them significant, particularly in view of the observations on unilateral dichromats, who match all wavelengths longer than the neutral point in the dichromatic eye with yellow in the normal eye. On this basis the simplest assumption is that such dichromats retain all three sensory channels and the capacity to experience all three primary sensations, but that in each case two sensations are excited by a single visual pigment. So one might assume that in protanopes the green-sensitive pigment, and in the deuteranopes of Figure 2.12 the red-sensitive pigment, ex-

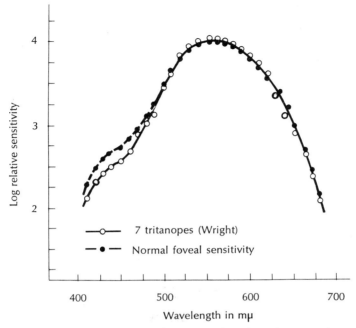

Figure 2.11: The average photopic luminosity function of seven tritanopes measured by Wright (1952), compared with that of normal observers. The small loss of
sensitivity of tritanopes in the blue and violet has the shape and position of the
action spectrum of the blue-sensitive pigment, with λ_{MAX} about 450 mμ, and a difference at that wavelength of about 0.23 log unit, representing a loss of relative sensitivity of about 40 percent. Such observers appear to lack the blue sensitive pigment,
and in that sense are blue-blind.

cites indiscriminately the red- and green-sensations, thus yielding a sensation
of yellow.

Editor's Note

In the foregoing paper as it first appeared in 1964, Wald discussed the possibility of two kinds of deuteranopic color blindness. One involved the lack
of a green sensitive pigment, while the second depended on a "fusion" of
the red-green mechanisms into a single sensory system. Previous research
had indicated the feasibility of such a fusion mechanism. Subsequent research by Wald has indicated, however, that such a mechanism does not
exist. Accordingly, this section was deleted from the original article. A discussion of this research can be found in the papers by Wald (1965, 1966a).
For a summary of current thinking concerning mechanisms of color blindness
the interested reader should consult the paper presented by Wald to the
National Academy of Sciences in 1966.

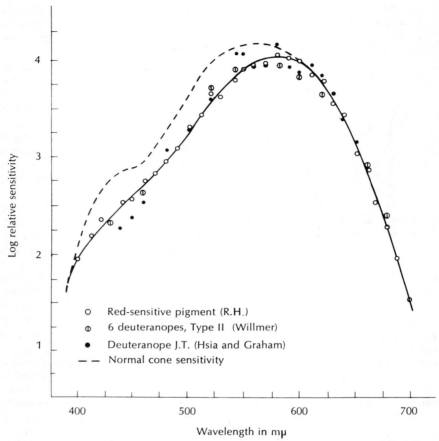

Figure 2.12: The foveal luminosity function of "deuteranopes" who display a relative loss of sensitivity at short wavelengths, compared with the action spectrum of R.H.'s red-sensitive pigment, measured at the corneal level. The good agreement of these data shows that this class of deuteranope lacks the green-sensitive pigment, and in this sense is literally green blind. For comparison the normal photopic luminosity function is shown with a broken line.

Foveal Sensitivity

Another area of color vision research involves the effect of various wavelengths upon the color sensitive fovea of the eye. The intensity of the light radiation is increased until the subject responds to the presence of a light stimulus (threshold). In this manner it is possible to map the sensitivity of the fovea to different wavelengths.

On the basis of biochemical evidence, one would expect that the human fovea would be more sensitive to light radiations of certain wavelengths than to others. In order to evoke a response, longer or shorter wavelengths located toward the edges of the visible spectrum would require higher intensities than wavelengths located closer to the center of the visible spectrum.

In a now-classic study, the husband-and-wife team of Leo M. Hurvich and Dorothea Jameson attempted to establish the exact relationship between wavelength and foveal sensitivity. This relationship proved to be somewhat analogous to the relationship between frequency and stimulus intensity reported by studies of the auditory threshold. In the latter experiments a significant increase in the intensity of the stimulus was found to be necessary in order to evoke a response at the lower and higher audible human frequencies. A similar relationship, including the greater dependence upon intensity at shorter wavelengths, is observable in the visual process.

The present experiment also considers spectral sensitivity for the dark-adapted and light-adapted eye in relation to the so-called Purkinje shift. Named after the Czech physiologist Purkinje, the shift accounts for the apparent brightness of objects containing longer wavelengths in their light radiations under conditions of low illumination. This phenomenon is assumed to be the result of differing peaks of spectral sensitivity for the rods and the cones. Although the rods evidently do not convey color information, they display differing sensitivities to various wavelengths. Hurvich and Jameson observed a slight shift in spectral sensitivity under conditions of dark and light adaptation despite the lack of rods in the 1° area of fovea which they stimulated.

This experiment was first reported in the *Journal of the Optical Society of America* in 1953. It is suggested that the reader skip over the sections on apparatus and calibration, and after the introduction proceed to the discussion of the methods and results. After studying the basic design the reader should reread the paper, paying close attention to the exact method of stimulus control discussed in the sections on apparatus and calibration.

Spectral Sensitivity of the Fovea: Neutral Adaptation

Leo M. Hurvich and Dorothea Jameson

It is well known that there are two fundamental luminosity functions which represent the spectral sensitivity of the human eye. One function has a peak at about 555 mμ, while the other is displaced toward the short wavelengths and has a peak at about 510 mμ. These functions are taken to represent the spectral sensitivity of the eye in fully bright-adapted day vision and fully dark-adapted night vision, respectively. Between these two extremes, a family of transition curves characterized the intermediate states of adaptation. The curve with a peak at about 510 mμ is commonly identified as the rod, scotopic luminosity function, and that with the peak at about 555 mμ is commonly identified as the cone, photopic curve. As this distinction implies, it is generally assumed that there is but one photopic function for any given individual and, since it is normally measured for foveal areas where the cones are maximally concentrated, that there is only one *foveal* luminosity function. In practical photometric and colorimetric applications, moreover, this assumption is, as a rule, either implicitly or explicitly accepted as fact.

The notion of a single fixed foveal luminosity function is not based on a conclusive body of experimental data, nor do the various current theoretical formulations of the nature and mode of operation of the visual mechanism all postulate such a fixed response function. They do, in fact, offer quite different predictions concerning the possible changes in the form of the foveal luminosity function with changes in the state of the visual system, particularly with changes in the chromatic state.

The theoretical formulations most frequently proposed to explain how the brightness attribute of visual experience is mediated are of three general types: (1) a fixed number of chromatic mechanisms is postulated—usually three—and brightness is determined by the total response generated by the combined activities of the individual elements; (2) brightness is mediated by the activity of a single receptor or neural process (the process responsible for this quality may be any one of the individual chromatic mechanisms, or a completely separate and independent brightness component may be introduced); and finally, (3) brightness is mediated primarily by the activity of a single, separate, nonchromatic process but the activities of the various chromatic processes also contribute in specific ways to the total brightness effect.

Each of these views ordinarily leads to a different general prediction concerning the relation of the foveal luminosity function to selective chromatic adaptation: (1) a strong dependence of the luminosity function on chromatic adaptation; (2) no dependence whatsoever of the luminosity function on chromatic adaptation; and (3) some dependence on chromatic adaptation but of lesser degree than ordinarily predicted by (1).

The absence in the practical situation of adaptive effects of the magnitude required by traditional three-component theory has been at least partly responsible for the assumption of a single, fixed luminosity function as a first-order working hypothesis. This apparent contradiction between practical experience and traditional expectation concerning the dependence of luminosity on chromatic adaptation strongly suggests the need for intensive experimental analysis.

As is unfortunately so frequently the case, the experimental evidence on this question is conflicting and inconclusive. There is evidence which claims to show that chromatic adaptation has no effect on luminosity, while other experimental evidence demonstrates the contrary.

Among the latter experiments the extent of the dependence shown varies considerably. Abney (1913) measured effects, for example, that were relatively large in magnitude and in the direction required by his theoretical analysis. On the other hand, when Troland (1922) was finally able to detect changes in brightness resulting from specifically chromatic effects, they were so small that he questioned their significance.

In the context of the general problem of the dependence of the luminosity function on chromatic adaptation, much of the previous experimentation is found to be fragmentary, unsystematic, or at best only preliminary. In other instances, the experiments are designed in such a way as to leave room for ambiguity in the meaning of the rather clear-cut results obtained. Furthermore, in experiments dealing with heterochromatic comparisons, further ambiguities arise because of the difficulties met in distinguishing between the visual attributes of saturation and brightness.

One source of difficulty has been the lack of a rigorous control condition against which to evaluate the effects of specific chromatic adaptations. This control can be achieved only by comparing the effects of chromatic adaptations with results obtained for the eye in a chromatically neutral state. The latter may be either one of dark adaptation or bright adaptation. In the bright-adapted condition the perceptually unique white-adapting stimulus must also be "physiologically neutral."

Each of these control states offers certain advantages, the dark-adapted state the advantage that it represents a condition of maximal sensitivity and the bright-adapted neutral condition the advantage that its luminance can be equated to that of the chromatic adapting fields. Both control conditions were therefore investigated. The present paper deals only with the results of the experiments for the two neutral states.

Apparatus

The apparatus used in the present experiments provides a number of stimulus controls for the study of various aspects of the luminosity function. It makes possible variations in, and accurate control of: (1) the wavelength, radiance, angular size, and exposure duration of a test stimulus; (2) the wavelength, radiance, angular size, and exposure duration of a comparison stimulus; (3) the wavelength, radiance, and angular size of an adapting field and surround; and (4) the wavelength and radiance of a stimulus added to both the test and comparison stimuli.

In the study reported here measurements were obtained of the absolute light threshold in a $1°$ foveal area for different adapted states and hence only controls (1) and (3) were used.

A schematic plan of the optical system of the complete apparatus is shown in Figure 2.13. M_2 is a Farrand monochromator (Model 300 Vis.) which, in conjunction with the optical elements shown, provides the primary test field. The second monochromator M_1 (Farrand, Model 300 Vis.) provides an independently variable comparison stimulus and with the optical cube C in the position indicated, the observer views the stimuli from M_1 and M_2 in a circular bipartite field. The light sources S_1 and S_2 are identical 6-volt, 18-ampere flat-ribbon filament lamps run at constant voltage to maintain the source at constant emittance and wavelength distribution. Monochromator M_1 was not employed in the present study (except for calibration cross checks), and with the optical cube C removed the homogeneous stimulus provided by monochromator M_2 is seen in a circular test field. Calibrated photographic shutters, at position C, control the exposure duration of the test stimulus from M_2. The alternative S'_2 system provides a heterogeneous, rather than monochromatic, comparison field when the cube C is in position and M_1 is used to supply the test field beam. It has not been used in the present experiments. Filters to eliminate stray light and to attenuate the beams from M_1 and M_2 in fixed density steps are placed next to W_1 and W_2, which are continuously variable neutral Wratten wedges. The latter permit continuous variation of the radiant flux of the monochromatic light beams. The achromatic lens L_1 is located at a distance of twice its focal length from the M_1 and M_2 exit slits, in the plane of the lens of the observer's eye. With this optical arrangement the aperture stop at L_1, which is conjugate with the principal focus of the ocular, may be used to control the test image size. The aperture at L_2, conjugate with the slit plane, may be used to reduce the flux of the two beams nonselectively.

A reflector-aperture (RA) is located at the principal focus of the ocular lens, and forms the central field stop. This front-silvered metal plate contains a centered circular aperture which determines the total angular size of the test and comparison field. The plate is oriented at an angle of approximately 35° to the primary optic axis and reflects the beam which provides the surround illumination into the eye-lens of the ocular. The horizontal angular dimension of the test field is correspondingly reduced in size.

The surround and adapting stimuli are provided by a diffraction-grating double monochromator M_3 of zero dispersion. The light source S_3 is a 6-volt, 18-ampere, flat-ribbon filament lamp maintained at constant voltage. This monochromator permits the presentation of a single monochromatic beam, a mixture of two or three homogeneous wavelength bands, or a heterogeneous beam of variable spectral distribution. The wavelength bands are isolated by means of a single, double, or triple slit placed in the plane of the primary spectrum formed by the first half of the double monochromator. The slit, or slits, are mounted on a metal frame with both vertical and horizontal rack and pinion adjustments and carry a horizontal vernier scale calibrated in wavelength units. Three neutral-density Wratten wedges, each of which can be moved independently in a vertical plane through the primary spectrum, provide a means for (1) varying the flux of the monochromatic wavelength band transmitted by a single slit or (2) varying the ratio of fluxes of the several bands which pass through the multiple slits. To obtain a pure white (physiologically neutral) adapting field, the slit frame is moved completely out of the spectrum locus, and the three vertical wedges are then used to vary the spectral distribution of the heterogeneous light which is recombined at the exit slit of the double monochromator. The flux of this heterogeneous beam is varied nonselectively by means of a variable diaphragm inserted at the anterior surface of the achromatic lens L_2'.

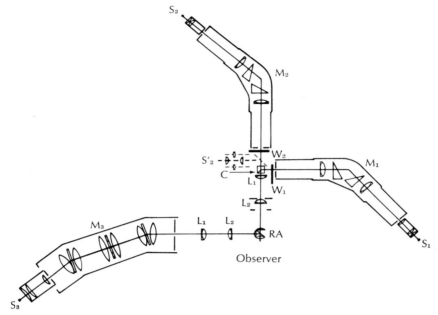

Figure 2.13:   Schematic diagram of optical system.

The lens system $L_1'L_2'$ duplicates the primary system $L_1'L_2$ and thus the image planes of test and surround beams are conjugate, and lie in the plane of the exit pupil of the apparatus and the entrance pupil of the observer's eye. The slit heights were adjusted so that the former served as an effective artificial pupil.

By centering a stop with very small central aperture at the posterior surface of L_1', and placing a thin wafer of cover glass over the aperture of the central field stop RA, the surround field can be replaced by a tiny reflected fixation dot located optically in the center of the test area. Such a red fixation dot, which is actually seen as double because of the secondary reflection from the rear surface of the wafer, is used in obtaining measurements of foveal sensitivity in the dark-adapted eye. The intensity was just adequate to enable the observer to obtain steady foveal fixation in the dark-adapted state.

The observer was seated in an enclosed cubicle shielded from all extraneous light and a Bausch and Lomb combination rest-and-head support was used to reduce extraneous head movement.

Calibration

Energy.   We have attempted to guarantee the validity and reliability of our energy calibration by employing a number of different instruments and procedures and by both repeating and cross-checking the measurements at every stage of the calibration. Measurements of the radiant flux were made with each of three different measuring devices: (1) a thermopile (Eppley Bi-Ag surface, linear type) and deflection galvanometer (Leeds and Northrup); (2) a Welch Densichron model 2150 employing a Cetron CE 34R phototube with an S-4 surface; and (3) a Photovolt Multiplier Photometer model 520-M. The multiplier tube used was an RCA 1P21 with S-4 surface.

The spectral sensitivities of the Densichron and Photovolt instruments were themselves first determined. Two separate calibrations were made for the Densichron instrument. Its spectral response properties were measured in our own laboratory for a constant light source with the available mono-chromators and thermopile-galvanometer combination, and a completely inde-pendent calibration was made in the Kodak Research laboratories. The results were reproduced to within ±2 percent. The Photovolt instrument was cali-brated in our laboratory and, to validate the instruments one against the other, measurements of the same spectral distribution of radiant flux were then cross-checked with the two different photoelectronic instruments.

The spectral energy calibration was carried out in triplicate form and the replications served as an additional check on the reliability of the results. In one series of measurements, the spectral distribution of radiant flux was deter-mined at the exit slit of the monochromator with the thermopile-galvanometer combination; and, with the transmittance losses through each of the inter-vening optical elements taken into account, the relative flux distribution at the observer's eye was calculated. The spectral transmittances of each of the optical elements had been separately measured with the General Electric re-cording spectrophotometer. A similar calculation was made for a second series of results obtained by using the calibrated Densichron at the exit slit of the monochromator.

As a final check, direct readings of the relative spectral distribution of radiant flux at the exit pupil of the instrument were obtained with the Photo-volt photometer. The directly measured response at the exit pupil confirmed the values computed from the measured flux distribution at the exit slit of the monochromator and the separately determined transmittances of the optical elements.

Filter and Wedge Transmittances.   The spectral transmittance of each of the neutral-density Wratten filters used to vary the energy in fixed steps and the Corning filters used to eliminate stray light were measured independently on the General Electric and Cary Model 11 recording spectrophotometers. Spot checks were also made with various filters in place by means of the Densichron instrument.

The spectral transmittance of the neutral-density Wratten wedge was measured in place with the Densichron instrument for wedge positions sepa-rated by 10 mm. At each wedge position the densities were measured for each of 31 wavelength settings from 400–700 mμ. A separate density calibration curve was thus available for each wavelength at which threshold measure-ments were obtained.

Wavelength. The wavelength scale of each monochromator was initially calibrated with a General Electric FH-4 mercury-cadmium lamp. Periodic wavelength checks using the same source were made during the course of the experimentation by optically substituting it for the incandescent light source normally used. For this purpose a small mirror oriented at 45° to the optical axis was placed between the fixed source and the entrance slit of the monochromator, and the arc was then positioned on a line which made an angle of 90° with the axis of the monochromator. The wavelength band width with the entrance and exit slits fixed at 0.2 mm ranged from 1.5 mμ at 413 mμ to 7.6 mμ at 680 mμ.

Photometric Values. The luminance level of the white adaptation and surround field was determined directly with a Macbeth illuminometer using a binocular matching technique.

Method and Procedure

The spectral sensitivity of the fovea of the right eye of each of two practiced observers was measured at 10 mμ intervals from 400 to 700 mμ for the dark-adapted neutral state, and from 405 to 700 mμ for the bright-adapted neutral state (white, 10 mL). Ten complete luminosity functions were obtained for each observer for each of the two states of adaptation.

The foveally fixated test field was elliptical in form and subtended 1° × 0.8° at the observer's eye, and the circular surround for the bright-adapted condition subtended a visual angle at 37° at the observer's eye. In the dark-adapted neutral condition central fixation was achieved by the use of a small reflected red fixation dot, and in the bright-adapted state, by fixating the dark elliptical 1° field centrally located in the illuminated surround. The test stimulus appeared within the fixated area and was exposed for 0.045 second.

The selection of an absolute white-adapting stimulus which satisfies the conditions of both perceptual and physiological neutrality was achieved separately for each observer in a similar series of steps. At a given luminance level, the wavelength distribution of the light from the double monochromator (using the whole spectrum) was first adjusted to evoke an achromatic sensation in the partially dark-adapted neutrally tuned eye. The luminance of the "white" stimulus was then reduced to enable the observer to detect any residual chromaticity and the wavelength distribution was continuously readjusted as required until no trace of hue was reported throughout the luminance range.

Finally, the loci of the pure hues in the spectrum were determined following adaptation to the white stimulus thus selected, and these loci were checked against the positions as measured in the control condition, that is, the partially dark-adapted neutral state. Only a physiologically neutral bright adaptation has no effect on the loci of the spectral stimuli which are unique in hue. When the adapting light satisfied the above conditions for perceptual and physiological neutrality, it was accepted as an adequate standard for the given observer.

In a single experimental session, spectral sensitivity was measured for one state of adaptation. All experimental sessions, whatever the state of adaptation investigated, began with a fixed period of preliminary dark-adaptation. For the dark-adapted state the initial period of light exclusion was 30 minutes. For the bright-adapted state a 10-minute period of light exclusion preceded a 5-minute period of bright adaptation. Ten minutes of light exclusion is normally adequate for the eye to reach a chromatically neutral state. For the bright-adapted state the surround field was continuously fixated between test exposures. When the test stimulus was to be exposed, the observer, upon a signal from the experimenter, fixated the center of the 1° dark area appearing in the center of the 37° illuminated white surround. Following the test exposure, the observer again fixated somewhere on the surround field preparatory to the next stimulus presentation.

A modified method of limits was used to determine the threshold. To avoid interserial physiological effects of suprathreshold test flashes, an ascending series of stimulus presentation was used throughout. An arbitrary criterion of two "yes" responses out of three repeated flashes at the same radiance was ordinarily adopted for a threshold response. In isolated instances, however, when the observer reported, say, an unusually bright and/or colored light experience, the experimenter recorded a threshold value without repeating the test exposure. "Uncertain" responses were occasionally obtained, and in these circumstances the test flash was simply repeated. The observer sometimes reported colors, as well as the presence of a simple light flash. No attempt was made to measure the chromatic threshold as such, but all reports of colored flashes were recorded in the protocols. Blue and red hues were reported with greatest frequency at the threshold level and yellow least frequently.

The specific technique used for threshold measurements of this sort will depend to a large extent upon the nature of the questions posed for experimental answer. Measures of threshold and sigma-values based on frequency-of-seeing functions at each wavelength probably yield more total information than do the threshold techniques now more commonly used. The frequency-of-seeing method is currently being employed by Crozier (1950), for example, to study the photosensitization of the retina, and is demonstrated by his work to be a useful analytical tool. In the present study, however, the form of the threshold function per se, and changes in its form with changes in adaptation, are of principal concern. For this purpose, a method which permits measurements at a large number of wavelengths in a single experimental session provides a body of data with greater homogeneity for wavelength than the frequency-of-seeing technique permits. For a comparable number of observations, the technique used in the present experiment provides a greater amount of first-order information concerning the form of the luminosity function and its modification with adaptation.

A single experimental session lasted one to one-and-a-half hours, and the sequence of wavelength presentation was varied from one session to the next. The radiance required for a threshold light response was measured in arbitrary units at every 10 mμ from 400 to 480 mμ, and from 460 to 700 mμ in separate experimental sessions for the dark-adapted condition. Since angular subtense of field and duration of flash were held constant, the relative values of radiance may be taken as relative energies. For the bright-adapted state measurements were obtained throughout the entire spectral range in each single session. Ten repeated sessions for each of the two observers comprise an experimental series for any one state of adaptation.

Results

Measurements of the stimulus energies necessary to evoke a threshold response as a function of wavelength are shown for the dark-adapted fovea in Figure 2.14 for observer J. Log relative energy is plotted as ordinate; wavelength, in millimicrons, is abscissa. Each plotted point represents a single threshold determination for that wavelength. Where two threshold energy measurements were identical, the plotted points are shown as half-solid, and solid circles indicate three or more identical threshold values for that wavelength. The figure contains the results of 320 threshold measurements, 10 determinations at each of 32 wavelengths. The function exhibits, on the whole, the characteristic form associated with such threshold determinations. The average spread of the individual threshold measurements is approximately 0.2 log unit of radiant energy, with four regions of minimal spread at 470, 500, 550, and 580 mμ. The results for observer H are similar and for both observers the average spread of the individual measurements is well within the range to be

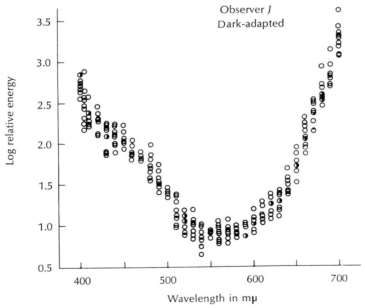

Figure 2.14: Threshold data: dark adaptation for Observer J.

expected on the basis of Crozier's intensive study of the variability of foveal threshold measurements.

The form of the threshold function is fairly well defined by the overlapping points plotted in Figure 2.14. It is of interest to note, however, that appreciable fluctuation occurs among the results of individual experimental sessions for a given observer for any one condition. Results of ten single runs are shown in Figure 2.15 for observer H for the bright-adapted state. The ordinate scale is correct for the lowest function. The other functions are displaced successively by 0.5 log unit on the ordinate scale.

The average log sensitivity functions for the dark-adapted state are shown for the two observers in Figure 2.16. A comparison of these average functions reveals that observer H is somewhat more sensitive than observer J throughout most of the visible spectrum except in the region from 400 to 430 mμ, where the difference is reversed. The differences in sensitivity are very small in the long-wave region from 630 to 700 mμ, and the functions are more widely separated throughout the mid-spectral range. Except for the short-wave inversion the differences between the two observers are comparable to some of the individual differences reported by Abney and Watson (1916) in their classical study of visual thresholds. The sensitivity inversion which occurs at the short-wave end and is probably due to selective differences in the transmittance of the various ocular media and/or differences in macular pigmentation in the two observers. This assumption is consistent with the differential coloring of the eye media known to exist for the age difference between the two observers, and it is also consistent with the differences assumed to exist among the absorption curves of macular pigmentation of different individuals.

Paired average log sensitivity results for the dark-adapted and bright-adapted states are presented in Figures 2.17 and 2.18 for the two observers. For both observers, the sensitivity functions show a marked shoulder in the short-wave region starting at about 450 mμ. The presence of this shoulder is by no means a new discovery. It was known to Gibson and Tyndall (1923), although they appear to have been reluctant to accept it as a valid experimental result. It was reported by Stiles and Crawford (1933) almost twenty years ago, and the existence of this shoulder has been repeatedly confirmed in more recent studies. The failure of the average luminosity curve for the CIE standard observer to represent the relatively high sensitivity to short-wave radiant flux (see Figure 2.19) indicated by this shoulder has given rise to important technical difficulties, and is partly responsible for the international redeterminations of the standard curve that are now in progress.

In addition to the prominent shoulder at the short-wave end of the curve, the bright-adapted foveal sensitivity functions for our observers show inflections at 409 mμ and the curves for both states have inflections in the long-wave spectral region at about 600–20 mμ. The presence of the latter shoulder has also been reported elsewhere, and it has most recently been emphasized in a report on the sensitivity of the dark-adapted fovea by Hsia and Graham (1952). It is of interest to note that Granit (1947) has also reported an inflection of this sort in his electrophysiological studies of the luminosity response of the cat's eye.

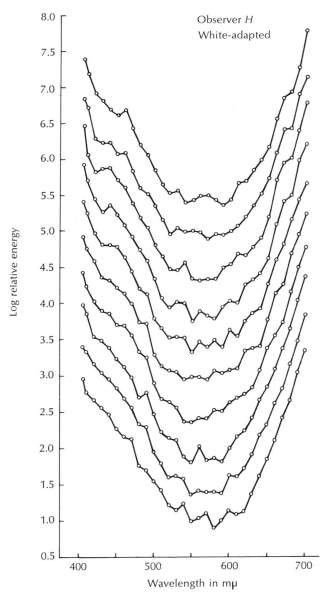

Figure 2.15: Threshold data: bright adaptation with single runs for Observer H.

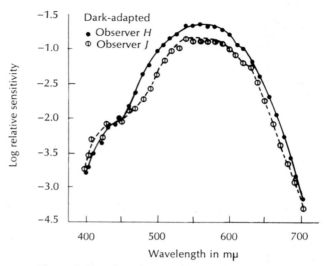

Figure 2.16: Foveal sensitivity: Dark adaptation.

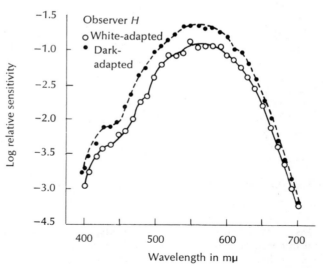

Figure 2.17: Foveal sensitivity and adaptation level for Observer *H*.

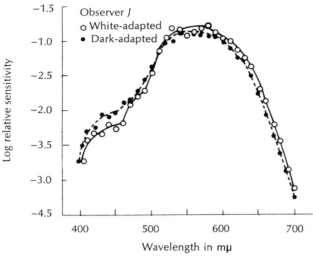

Figure 2.18: Foveal sensitivity and adaptation level for Observer *J*.

For both the bright- and dark-adapted states, the data, in particular those for observer *J*, show a tendency toward a depression in the region of maximal sensitivity, suggesting the presence of a double maximum in the mid-spectral region. Small deviations of the average points from the smooth function take on a magnified appearance in this region, however, and since the actual significance of such deviations has not been thoroughly explored, the average sensitivity curves have not been drawn to emphasize them. Still the tendency warrants some attention, particularly since our results are not unique in suggesting such a mid-spectral depression in light sensitivity. Walters and Wright (1943), for example, made note of the fact that at very low luminances approaching the foveal threshold, both of their observers on occasion obtained curves for the fovea showing two peaks, with maxima at about 540 and 600 mμ. Such curves could not be repeated with consistency, however, and they were not included in the published results since the authors thought it unwise to give them a prominence which they might not merit. The individual runs for observer *H* shown in Figure 2.9 are in accord with Walters's and Wright's observation.

More recently, a number of other investigators have reported a similar result. Weale's (1951) spectral sensitivity data for both the fovea and parafovea "exhibit a double prong in the green" at each of two brightness levels, 2.4 and 75 E.F.C. (equivalent footcandles). Spectral sensitivity measurements made by Thomson (1951) also show this "double prong" in the mid-spectral region, and Bouman (1950) and his co-workers call attention to the fact that two peaks occur between 500 and 600 mμ in the foveal sensitivity curves for the dark-adapted eye of normal, deuter-anomalous, and tritanopic observers. Finally, data presented by Stiles (1949) and by Hsia and Graham (1952) show

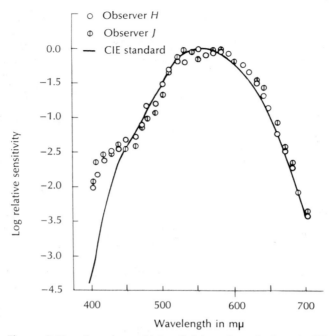

Figure 2.19: Foveal sensitivity (bright adaptation) and CIE standard luminosity function.

a similar tendency toward double maxima, although in both the latter cases the curves drawn through the plotted points again fail to emphasize this property, possibly for the same reasons that these irregularities are not emphasized in the present report.

The data that show the most striking inflections in the luminosity function at each of the wavelength regions discussed above are those obtained by Crozier (1950) for 1.6' and 1.5° test fields in his frequency-of-seeing experiments. Crozier, has, moreover, discussed the reality of these inflections and their relation to the absorption characteristics of specific enzyme systems.

It is amply clear that a considerable body of experimental evidence is now available which contradicts the more traditional notion that the luminosity function exhibits "a notable symmetry." We are in agreement with Thomson (1951) who, on the basis of a detailed statistical analysis, concludes that "one can say with confidence that the spectral sensitivity of the centre of the central fovea cannot be a smooth single-humped function."

The paired sensitivity curves plotted in Figures 2.17 and 2.18 show clearly the differences brought about by a change in the level of adaptation. In comparison with the dark-adapted condition, the spectral locus of the maximal sensitivity values for the bright-adapted state is shifted toward longer wavelengths for both observers and sensitivity is reduced throughout the shortwave spectral region. The shift is small, approximately 10 mμ for both observers, from about 560 to 570 mμ for observer H, and from 550 to 560 mμ for observer J. There is one major difference between the two observers: for one (J) the maximal sensitivity values are not widely different for the two states, while for the other (H) sensitivity for the bright-adapted state is considerably lower throughout the entire spectral range. Thus, the bright-adapted function changes its form and undergoes a lateral displacement for both observers, and for one of them a vertical displacement as well. In the two instances, however, the meaning is the same: a slight Purkinje shift occurs in the fovea as we pass from the bright- to the dark-adapted state.

Discussion

The question of whether or not a Purkinje shift occurs in the fovea has long been a matter of controversy. The present experiments were not undertaken to reopen this controversy. Rather, our primary interest and purpose was simply standardization for a series of experiments concerned with chromatic adaptation.

Although authoritative opinion usually holds that no Purkinje shift can occur in a 1° foveal area, the dispute has never been completely resolved, despite, or possibly because of, its important theoretical implications.

In contrast to those who report no evidence for a Purkinje shift in the fovea with a change from bright to dark adaptation, Sloan (1928), for example, was able to demonstrate such a shift in her thorough analytical study of the luminosity function. Using the equality-of-brightness method, and controlling adaptation and stimulus luminance independently, she found a typical, even though small, Purkinje effect for a 57′ field with a change in adaptation. When adaptation was fixed and luminance alone was varied a direct Purkinje shift did not necessarily occur even for a large extrafoveal field.

Hering (1895) first argued and demonstrated that adaptation rather than stimulus luminance is the critical determinant of the Purkinje shift and Sloan's experimental results provide quantitative evidence that confirms Hering's demonstration. Experiments which fail to isolate the experimental variables of luminance and adaptation are likely to produce ambiguous results which are difficult to interpret. Moreover, as Sloan has pointed out, no general conclusions should be drawn from experiments in which determinations are made at only a small number (usually two) points in the spectrum.

The spectral-sensitivity results presented in this report provide clear evidence that a slight Purkinje shift occurs in the 1° fovea as the level of adaptation is changed from bright (10 mL) to dark. A change in form and displacement of the log sensitivity function with a shift from the bright- to the dark-adapted state is, of course, usually attributed to a change in the relative contributions made by the rod and cone elements to the luminosity response. If we were to interpret the foveal shift in the same way that we explain its more pronounced occurrence in larger, or noncentral, retinal areas, the two foveal sensitivity curves would simply represent different ratios of rod and cone function, each kind of receptor having its own characteristic luminosity response. Such an interpretation, however, faces a number of difficulties. Although it has sometimes been assumed that a small number of rods are present in the foveas of some individuals, the most recent anatomical evidence is that there is "a central island, measuring only 500 μ across, absolutely free from the rods, corresponding to 1°40' of arc in the field of vision" (S. Polyak, *The Retina* [Chicago: U. of Chicago Press, 1941], p. 203). Thus, a rod-cone interpretation of the foveal shift conflicts with the histological evidence. It also conflicts with one of the commonly accepted functional properties of the rods. The achromatic scotopic rod system not only has its characteristically spectral response curve, but also has, characteristically, a sensitivity level which is considerably higher than that of the cone system. Although the foveal function shifts in the expected direction for both of our observers, the data for one observer fail to show the increased sensitivity required by increased "rod participation."

An alternative hypothesis to explain the Purkinje shift and one which does not require different degrees of rod-cone participation was proposed by Hering (1895) and Hillebrand (1889). In this hypothesis the luminosity response is attributed mainly to the activity of a separate white-black system, with some auxiliary contributions to brightness from the paired red-green and yellow-blue chromatic mechanisms. The red and yellow processes possess an inherent relative brightening power while the blue and green processes possess an inherent relative darkening power. The total brightness effect is represented by the algebraic sum of the contributions of both the chromatic and achromatic systems, and since the former are further assumed to play a greater functional role when the eye is bright adapted, their increased participation in the spectral response would lead to a relative darkening of the blue and green spectral regions and a relative brightening of the yellow and red regions. In terms of spectral sensitivities, there results a relative loss in sensitivity to short-wave energy, and a relative loss in sensitivity to longer-wave energy. These relative changes yield the differences in form and lateral displacement of the spectral-sensitivity function identified as the Purkinje shift. Displacements in the overall sensitivity level of the spectral response function are, in this theory, the result of changes in the sensitivity of the white-black mechanism per se, the principal determinant of brightness.

This theoretical possibility has been examined quantitatively, with the result shown in Figure 2.20. The solid line represents the experimentally measured relative luminosity of the dark-adapted fovea for observer *J*. To predict the form and locus of the bright-adapted luminosity function we assume that for this observer there is only an increased participation of the chromatic processes with bright adaptation. The measured dark-adapted curve is then modified to reflect the increased chromatic function by adding to the experimentally determined sensitivities at each wavelength the relative sensitivity values for the chromatic processes. The values used are those given by the Judd (1951) equations which relate the chromatic functions of the Hering primaries to the CIE tristimulus values. (See Figure 2.21.) The predicted spectral-sensitivity curve derived in this manner for the bright-adapted state is plotted as a dashed line in Figure 2.20 and the crosses represent the ex-

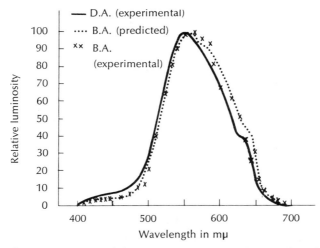

Figure 2.20: Foveal luminosity curves: Experimental and derived for dark and bright adaptation for Observer *J*.

perimentally determined average sensitivity values for observer *J* for the bright-adapted fovea. The predicted curve is seen to be reasonably good fit to the experimentally determined spectral-sensitivity values.

The prediction is illustrated here for observer *J* since the values for the chromatic primaries used by Judd are nearly identical to the experimentally determined wavelengths of the unique hues in the spectrum for this observer. (Hurvich and Jameson, 1951, and Jameson and Hurvich, 1951.) A test of observer *H*'s data would require an additional ad hoc assumption concerning the decreased sensitivity of the white process with bright adaptation as well as the calculation of a different set of chromatic-sensitivity values for this observer's primaries.

The inherent brightness hypothesis is examined here as an alternative to the rod-cone explanation of a Purkinje shift in the fovea, not because this theoretical possibility has received any wide acceptance or confirmation in its specific details, but simply because it provides a coherent explanation of our experimental facts, and is not in conflict with the best available anatomical evidence that there are no rods in the central 1° fovea.

Dartnell's (1948) recently advanced hypothesis concerning the photochemical pigments related to luminosity can also be reconciled with the anatomical evidence. This hypothesis assumes that visual purple underlies both scotopic and photopic luminosity, and the shift in the luminosity function from scotopic to photopic vision is attributed, not to a shift from rod to cone function, but to the visual purple bleaching products which come into play when the eye is bright adapted. Dartnell demonstrates quantitatively that the accumulation of indicator yellow from the breakdown of visual purple would gradually displace the maximum of the luminosity curve until it reaches a limiting position which agrees with the standard CIE photopic curve. Since Dart-

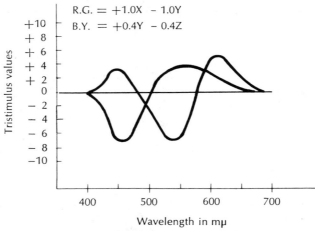

Figure 2.21: Chromatic functions for primaries of Hering's theory. The white function is not shown. (*Judd, 1951*.)

nell's hypothesis calls for a reduction in sensitivity where a shift occurs for the bright-adapted state, it does not account for the results of both of our observers. A more basic objection to Dartnell's view is that it leaves no room for contributions to luminosity by the visual processes underlying chromatic sensations. This objection will be discussed in a later paper concerned with the dependence of the foveal luminosity function on the state of chromatic adaptation.

Summary

The spectral sensitivity of the 1° fovea of the right eye of two practiced observers was measured at 10 mμ intervals from 400 to 700 mμ for the dark-adapted state and for the bright-adapted (10mL), chromatically neutral state. Ten complete luminosity functions were obtained for each observer for each of the specified adaptations. The data of these experiments are intended to provide controls against which to evaluate luminosity data for different chromatic states. A number of inflections and shoulders are found in the functions for both states of adaptation. Moreover, the functions for both observers are shown to undergo a change in form and a displacement from the bright- to the dark-adapted state. These changes in the foveal functions, although small in magnitude, are in the same sense as the familiar "Purkinje shift." Alternative theoretical explanations of the data are discussed and analyzed.

CHAPTER 3
The Basic Organization of Perception

The discussion of sensation and perception emphasized the *organization* of incoming sensory stimuli as an important aspect of perception. Some stimuli are perceived to be central, capable of commanding the attention of the perceiver, while other stimuli are relegated to less important roles. The central stimuli—those elements upon which the responding organism focuses attention—are said to compose the *figure*. Other entering stimuli not composing the figure are perceived as a background, or simply, *ground*. The figural elements are usually seen as specific forms standing in some relationship to one another; the ground is formless, or less structured and organized.

The perception of figure-ground relationships naturally requires an inhomogeneous field of stimuli. The figure must possess some characteristic which differentiates it from the ground. In other words, there must be some element of form or structure to stand out. The existence of figures can be considered prerequisite to visual perception since without figures, no organization could take place.

Questions arise concerning what is perceived or sensed in the absence of figures. What does an individual experience when viewing a ground that displays no field inhomogeneity? What sensations arise when the incoming visual stimuli are completely homogeneous?

At one time or another the reader has probably experienced homogeneous visual stimulation. While walking in a dense fog, for example, one can suddenly lose all spatial orientation. Skiers often experience a homogeneous field when skiing in a snowstorm.

The achievement of an exact experimental situation in which no inhomogeneity of the visual field exists has proved to be difficult, although interest in the problem was expressed rather early by experimental psychologists. Most of their early attempts failed to devise a situation in which the field was completely homogeneous. Walter Cohen, working with Carl Brown at the State University of New York in Buffalo, tackled the problem of the homogeneous field, or Ganzfeld, and developed an experimental situation in which a completely homogeneous visual stimulus could be presented to the subject. This paper, first published in 1957, appeared in the *American Journal of Psychology*.

Spatial and Textural Characteristics of the Ganzfeld

Walter Cohen

There have been several partially successful attempts to study the effects of uniform stimulation over the entire visual field. Metzger (1930) has reported that under low illumination the entire visual field (Ganzfeld) appears as "a mist of light which becomes more condensed at an indefinite distance." When intensity is increased, the fog becomes a filmy surface separated from the observer by empty space. The distance of the surface is judged to be about the same as its objective distance. With further increase in level of illumination, the distance is judged to be greater, and the filmy curved surface is transformed into a flat plane surface with microstructure. It is difficult to interpret these results since uniformity of stimulation was not achieved by Metzger. Under high illumination, the physical texture of the surface was perceived.

Gibson and Waddell (1952), using a translucent globe, found that under high illumination their observers described a "sea of light" with something vaguely surface-like in front of the face. Their naive observers did not consistently report the impression of space-filling fog. Gibson and Waddell attribute the occasional reports of other qualities to central processes rather than to peripheral stimulation.

There have been two basic sources of inhomogeneity in all previous studies dealing with the Ganzfeld. First, physical microstructure was present. In addition, parts of the observer's face prevented uniform stimulation of the entire retina—for example, the nose must have produced a shadow on the peripheral nasal area of the visual field. The apparatus developed for the present investigation provided an adequate uniform Ganzfeld by eliminating both these sources of inhomogeneity. Although additional information was collected, this paper will be limited to the 'mode of appearance' and spatial characteristics of the Ganzfeld. The following three questions guided the design of the experiment: (1) In what manner is the appearance of the homogeneous Ganzfeld dependent upon intensity and wavelength? (2) How does the appearance of the inhomogeneous Ganzfeld differ from that of the homogeneous Ganzfeld? (3) How are these differences in appearance related to stimulus-distributions?

Method

Apparatus.   A new method was devised which would produce a uniform Ganzfeld as well as permit the introduction of a spot into the field. The principle utilized was similar to that of the photometric sphere—as a result of direct illumination of a small part of the inner surface, there is indirect uniform illumination of the entire surface of the sphere.

Two spheres, each having a diameter of 1 m, were joined together (Figure 3.1). The smooth inner walls were sprayed with high albedo and no visible texture at viewing distance. The observer looked into Sphere A, and the light entered by way of two openings in Sphere B. At the junction of the two spheres was a circular aperture 8 cm in diameter. A special mask was made to fit the contours of the observer's face. The mask formed a removable section of the wall of Sphere A and was used as a headrest. Each mask had an opening which permitted unobstructed monocular vision. When the observer looked to the right, no part of his mask or face was visible. The left eye was kept in complete darkness. Since the opening of the mask was directly opposite the center of the 8 cm aperture, the observer's line of sight was perpendicular to the plane of the aperture.

A beam of light was projected onto the inner surface of Sphere A, 20 cm above the observer's eye. Sphere B was uniformly illuminated by a beam of light that could be independently varied. By use of appropriate filters, the luminosity of both spheres was so controlled as to produce either equality or some desired difference. When the luminous flux-density in the two spheres was made equal, the aperture ceased to exist optically, and a uniform Ganzfeld was produced. When the luminous flux in the two spheres differed as to dominant wavelength, purity, or intensity, inhomogeneity was produced. Light coming from the aperture area was different from that coming from the rest of

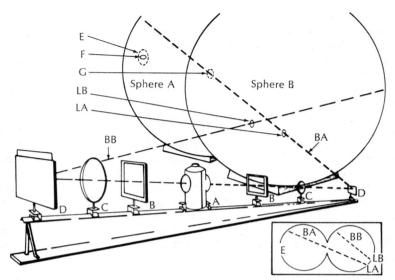

Figure 3.1: Diagram of apparatus (*A*, light-source; *B*, filter; *C*, lens; *D*, mirror; *E*, mask; *F*, eye-piece; *G*, 8-cm aperture; *BA*, beam for sphere *A*; *BB*, beam for sphere *B*; *LA*, opening for *BA*; *LB*, opening for *BB*.

the field, and the observer was confronted with a simple homogeneity in an otherwise uniform field.

The two beams of light originated from the same source. With appropriate lenses and mirrors, the beams were directed through two 5 cm openings in Sphere *B*. These openings were not visible to the observers looking into Sphere *A*. Neutral and colored filters altered the intensity and composition of the light. Chromatic illumination was obtained by the use of the following Wratten filters; (1) red (608 mμ) CC-50R, excitation-purity 21 percent; (2) green (554 mμ) CC-40G, excitation-purity 21 percent; (3) green (554 mμ) CC-30G, excitation-purity 16 percent; (4) blue (461 mμ) CC-30B, excitation-purity 20 percent. The following notation will be used to designate the manner of illumination: The chromatic filters will be designated by the letters *R*, *G*, *GX*, and *B* respectively. The letter *A* will signify the absence of a chromatic filter. The luminance will be expressed in millilamberts. Thus, (*R*2.1-*A*4.9) signifies a field having a dominant wavelength of 608 mμ and a brightness of 2.1 mL, with an achromatic spot having a brightness of 4.9 mL.

Observers. Thirteen men and three women served as observers. The median age of the group, which was made up of three undergraduates, ten graduate students, and three faculty members of the University of Buffalo, was twenty-five years. Although all specialized in psychology, they were naive as to the purpose of the present study. All had normal color vision, but only six had normal visual acuity.

Procedure.   Each observer was studied in an average of five one-hour sessions. A complete record of the observer's responses was made with a tape recorder. Tasks of two kinds were performed: (1) the observer was required to compare two situations with respect to fog density, distance, distinctiveness of figure, hue, and saturation. Each of the situations was presented for twenty seconds, with an interval of five seconds between the two members of each pair and an interval of 15 seconds between pairs. (2) The observer remained in the experimental situation for three minutes to report on the effects of adaptation. Each situation was followed by a two-minute rest period.

The order of presentation was counterbalanced to control for time-error, practice, and adaptation. Each observer was presented with approximately half of the experimental situations, thus providing an N of eight for each. There were five basic kinds of visual field with which the observers were presented: (1) homogeneity; (2) inhomogeneity due to a difference in chromaticity between field and spot; (3) inhomogeneity due to a difference in intensity; (4) inhomogeneity due to a difference both in intensity and chromaticity; (5) inhomogeneity due to a difference in purity.

Results and Discussion

Homogeneity.   The most characteristic description of the field for all observers was "fog-like." Reports as to density and degree of immersion varied. The following phrases are representative: "A diffuse fog." "A hazy insipid yellow." "A gaseous effect." "A milky substance." "Misty, like being in a lemon pie." "Smoky."

The observers of Gibson and Waddell reported other impressions with considerable frequency, a disparity which may be traced to procedure as well as to apparatus. Gibson and Waddell used a questionary and a training procedure which may have influenced their observers to seek something other than fog. Failure to control for facial shadows may account for the reports of a boundary. During the present investigation, there were a few descriptions of a "cracked ice effect" or a "web-like structure" which could be eliminated by slight adjustments in the illumination of Sphere B. It may be that gradients of intensity which are insufficient for the formation of a spot result in other forms of phenomenal inhomogeneity.

The homogeneous Ganzfeld was reported to be "close at hand" by all observers. Only one consistently described the field as being more than six inches away, and the modal judgment of distance was two inches. The fog itself was, however, seen to extend for an indefinite distance. Several observers described an experience of complete immersion in the fog, and, in a few instances, space was internalized, described as being "inside the head." Werner (1929) has described a similar internalization of sound. There was a high degree of uncertainty as to distance and most observers were extremely hesitant about making distance judgments.

A nonparametric technique gave no indication, within the range of 1.8–4.9 mL, that either fog density or fog distance was significantly related to intensity of illumination ($P > 0.10$), a result which does not correspond to Metzger's findings. This discrepancy may be accounted for by the absence of surface-texture in the present experiment. The "blue" field ($B2.4$-$B2.4$) was consistently judged ($P < 0.05$) as less dense than either the "red" field ($R2.1$-$R2.1$) or the achromatic field ($A2.4$-$A2.4$). In addition, the observers reported feeling less immersed in the "blue" field, which suggests that receptors sensitive to long wavelength are more densely concentrated than those sensitive to short.

During the course of adaptation, five of the sixteen observers reported a complete cessation of visual experience. Two reported "black-out" almost every time they were confronted with prolonged, homogeneous stimulation. This was a unique experience which involved a complete disappearance of the sense of vision for short periods of time, and not simply the presence of a dark, undifferentiated visual field. The following description is representative: "Foggy whiteness, everything blacks out, returns, goes. I feel blind. I'm not even seeing blackness. This differs from the black when lights are out." It may be conjectured that the perceptual mechanism has evolved to cope with a differentiated field, and, in the absence of differentiation, there is a temporary breakdown of the mechanism (which might be detected electro-physiologically). Anxiety and fear of blindness under somewhat similar conditions also were reported by Hochberg, Triebel, and Seaman (1951).

Although uniform proximal stimulation does not provide a basis for articulation, the separation of the field into a fog in front of a ground occurs. This effect may be related to the process of figure-ground segregation. It should be noted that when hue is experienced in the chromatic Ganzfeld, it is seen as a phenomenal characteristic of the fog, whereas the ground behind the fog may appear as neutral.

Inhomogeneity.   Introduction of inhomogeneity reduced fog density and increased fog distance ($P < 0.05$) in most instances. When figure-ground segregation was poor because of the absence of steep gradients of intensity, the field, as fog, continued to be seen as close, while the figure was seen as far away. Thus, the "normal" relationship between figure and ground was reversed. Distance judgments for the figure under these conditions ranged from five inches to six feet, with a mode of two feet. Increasing the difference in intensity between field and spot resulted in a closer figure and a more distant ground. When the difference in intensity was maximal, judgments of figural distance ranged from "next to the eye" to three feet away, with a median of six inches. The ground usually was judged to be a few inches behind the spot, although a few observers judged it to be several feet behind the spot. Each observer was consistent in his judgments of distance. There were, however, marked differences among observers in the range of values used to describe the distance of the figure. The terms "close" and "far" varied considerably in meaning for different observers. For one, an apparent distance of five inches was considered far, while for another an apparent distance of 3 feet was considered close.

Inhomogeneity due either to intensive or to chromatic differences between field and spot reduced fog-density and increased fog-distance in most cases. There were, however, no consistent differences ($P > 0.10$) between homogeneous and inhomogeneous fields when (1) differences in intensity between field and spot were at about 1 *jnd* (just noticeable difference), or (2) inhomogeneity was due to a difference in purity between field and spot. In both cases, the spot was unstable and often disappeared for brief intervals.

The results of comparisons between inhomogeneous fields are shown in Table 3.1. Increasing the difference in intensity between field and spot tended to decrease the apparent density and to increase the apparent distance of the fog (*a, b, c, d*). The direction of the difference was not relevant (*e*). There was no consistent difference between those situations involving both chromatic and intensive inhomogeneity and those involving only intensive inhomogeneity (*f, g, h, i*). The appearance of the fog of an achromatic field was dependent upon the dominant wavelength of the spot (*j, k, l*). The fog was reported as denser and closer when the dominant wavelength of the spot was short than when it was long.

An amorphous field, as well as an amorphous figure, appears to characterize those situations in which gradients of intensity are absent. The assertion that gradients of intensity are more effective than chromatic gradients in reducing the amorphous characteristics of the field would not, however, be completely warranted. Such a conclusion would require the comparison of fields in which the two types of gradient were equated as to magnitude. Since such an equation would be arbitrary, and articulation of the field is dependent upon the magnitude of the stimulus-gradients, no direct test of this hypothesis is possible (Koffka, 1931).

The mode of appearance of the field seems to be related to the definiteness of figure-ground segregation. With increased sharpness of boundary, there is greater definiteness of surface. Gibson and Dibble (1952), in their study of visual surface, found that the steepness of gradients of luminous intensity was a determinant of surface hardness. The same was found to be true in the present study to a limited extent. Even when steep gradients of intensity were present, fog was reported more than 50 percent of the time. In only a few cases did the observers actually report the ground as appearing hard, but the figure was frequently described as hard when differences in intensity between field and spot were large.

An expansion of the field was experienced when steep gradients were introduced. Koffka (1935) suggested that contraction and expansion of space may be a function of "forces" related to articulation of the field. In accordance with his formulation, well-articulated fields are perceived as being at a greater distance than those which are poorly articulated.

In most cases, the figure was judged to be about one-and-one-half times as large as its "real" size. It has been suggested that there is an invariant relationship between phenomenal size and phenomenal distance (Boring, 1952). If there were such a relationship, the underestimation of the apparent distance of the figure should have been accompanied by an underestimation, rather than an overestimation, of its apparent size. When steepness of the intensive gradients was increased, the figure appeared closer, but there was no

Table 3.1

Relative fog density and fog distance of the ground areas of inhomogeneous fields

	Situations Compared		Density-Judgment				Distance-Judgment			
	1	2	1-Greater	Equal	2-Greater	P*	1-Nearer	Equal	2-Nearer	P*
a	(A2.1-A2.0)	(A2.1-A1.8)	6	2	0	<0.03	5	3	0	<0.05
b	(A2.1-A1.8)	(A2.1-A0.0)	8	0	0	<0.01	6	2	0	<0.03
c	(A2.1-A2.2)	(A2.1-A2.4)	7	1	0	<0.03	5	3	0	<0.05
d	(A2.1-A2.4)	(A2.1-A4.9)	8	0	0	<0.01	7	1	0	<0.03
e	(A2.1-A2.4)	(A2.1-A1.8)	2	5	1	>0.25	1	6	1	>0.25
f	(R2.1-A2.2)	(R2.1-R2.2)	2	5	1	>0.25	1	6	1	>0.25
g	(R2.1-A2.0)	(R2.1-R2.0)	1	6	1	>0.25	2	6	0	>0.25
h	(R2.1-A1.8)	(R2.1-R1.8)	3	4	1	>0.25	4	2	2	>0.25
i	(G2.7-A2.4)	(G2.7-G2.4)	3	3	2	>0.25	3	4	1	>0.25
j	(A2.1-R2.1)	(A2.1-G2.1)	0	3	5	<0.05	2	3	3	>0.25
k	(A2.1-R2.1)	(A2.1-B2.1)	0	2	6	<0.03	0	3	5	<0.05
l	(A2.1-G2.1)	(A2.1-B2.1)	1	4	3	>0.25	1	5	2	>0.25

* Sign test.

systematic change in apparent size. The apparent distance cha
change either in retinal size or in apparent size. These results a
with the conclusion of Kilpatrick and Ittelson (1953) that the inva
tionship between size and distance is restricted to special conditions an
not apply to those situations in which the field is poorly articulated.

Summary

The present investigation deals with visual perception when the entire visual field is uniform and when a small differentiated area is introduced into such a field.

The most representative description of the homogeneous Ganzfeld is that of close, impenetrable fog. The experience is a unique one, and most observers have difficulty in describing the field in terms usually associated with visual phenomena. In some instances, temporary cessation of visual experience is reported. Variations in wavelength rather than intensity of illumination alter the density and distance of the fog.

A differentiated area in the Ganzfeld changes its phenomenal characteristics. When the differentiation results from chromatic gradients alone, a distant, indefinite figure is reported, and modifications in the appearance of the fog are slight. Those situations involving dominant short wavelength seem more indefinite and distant than those involving dominant long wavelength. The addition of an intensive gradient to the chromatic gradient increases definiteness of the figure-ground segregation.

The effect of moderate differences in intensity is to produce a relatively definite separation of figure and ground. The density of fog is considerably reduced. Increased differences in intensity further separate figure and ground. The fog disappears. The figure is seen as closer than the ground. Their modes of appearance differ and a distinct boundary separates them. Those factors which increase the apparent distance of the field consistently decrease the apparent distance of the spot and the density of the fog.

The phenomenal characteristics of the Ganzfeld do not appear to be independently determined. Any change in the stimulus distribution that modifies one aspect of experience produces concomitant changes in the other phenomenal characteristics of the Ganzfeld. The distribution of stimulation rather than the nature of the local stimulus seems to determine what is experienced.

Maintaining a Figure

Cohen's observations suggest that an inhomogeneity is necessary for the maintenance of a stable and organized visual field. With that assumption in mind, we may proceed to inquire into the manner in which the visual system selects and holds a figure.

Early experiments by Rubin (1921) with a figure that could be seen in

ual system responds to the figure in one way,
d way (see Figure 3.2). Rubin demonstrated
ual system is dynamic; rather than respond
d segregation, the system remained receptive
s from all aspects, perceiving and organizing
ways. Upon this observation was based the hy-
:cludes change in any particular visual stimulus.
itself fails to exhibit change, then it is the visual
he change. In Rubin's tests the physical stimulus
om two faces to a vase; rather, the *perception* of
the ... unambiguous figures, change appears to be produced by minute ... vements causing the contours of the stimuli to fall
upon different areas of the retina. These rapid eye movements are involuntary and appear to be intrinsic to the visual system rather than learned.

If the visual stimulus presents no clear contours, the image will fade
as a result of prolonged stimulation. If the stimulus does not change and
the visual system can produce no change in the incoming stimuli, then perception and sensation appear to cease. Figure 3.3 shows such a figure without clear contours. If one fixates on the center dot, parts of the figure appear
to dissolve and fade.

Such observations of fading leads us to believe that if a stimulus were
presented to the same area of the retina for a prolonged period, fading
would occur. This possibility has also received attention in several experiments. As was the case with the Ganzfeld, the development of an experimental technique capable of presenting a stimulus to the same area of the
retina for prolonged periods of time proves to be a difficult task. Of the
several designs suggested, one of the best was developed by three Canadian
psychologists at McGill University: R. M. Pritchard, W. Heron, and D. O.
Hebb (*Canadian Journal of Psychology*, 1960).

Figure 3.2: Example of a reversible figure. The figure can be seen as a vase against
a dark background or as two profiles against a white background.

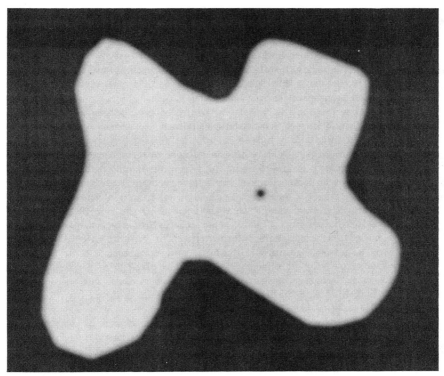

Figure 3.3: Stimulus configuration for the demonstration of fading. Fixate the dot in the center of the light figure at a distance of approximately ten inches. Maintain the fixation and observe how portions of the blurred borders appear to dissolve and disappear for short periods of time.

Visual Perception Approached by the Method of Stabilized Images

R. M. Pritchard, W. Heron, and D. O. Hebb

The present paper reports some preliminary experiments on the Ditchburn-Riggs effect which is obtained with stabilized images. Our results are such as to show that the original discovery, made independently by Ditchburn and Riggs and their collaborators about 1952, has opened a new and valuable avenue of approach to the analysis of visual perception.

In normal visual fixation, the image that falls on the retina is never really stable; "physiological nystagmus," the continuous tremor of the normal eye at rest, causes a slight but constant variation in the rods and cones that are excited. It is now known that the variation plays a vital role in perception, for it was shown by Ditchburn and Ginsborg (1952) and Riggs, Ratliff, Cornsweet and Cornsweet (1953) that stabilizing the image (experimentally eliminating variability of retinal excitation) leads rapidly to the disappearance of the visual object, followed by intermittent reappearance.

In their experiments, the target was projected on a screen after being reflected from a small mirror attached to a contact lens worn by the observer. Thus each slight involuntary movement of the "fixated" eye would produce a movement of the target. By having the subject observe through a complex optical system, it was possible to make the two movements correspond exactly: the angular extent and direction of the eye movement were matched by the movement of the target, cancelling out the normal tremor of the eye and producing a stabilized retinal image. In these conditions the line of demarcation between the two halves of a 1° field, separately lighted so as to give intensity ratios of up to 3:1, disappears intermittently for two to three seconds, at intervals of about one minute (Ditchburn and Ginsborg, 1952). Similarly, within a few seconds of stabilized viewing, a thin black line crossing a bright 1° field fades out; coarser lines are seen for longer periods, but still intermittently, the length of time the line remains visible being a direct function of its thickness (Riggs, et. al., 1953).

Later papers using this technique dealt with other aspects of the phenomenon, still with simple targets. Experimentally controlled movement of the image on the retina, as might be expected, restores the object to view, as does intermittent instead of continuous illumination (Cornsweet, 1956; Ditchburn and Fender, 1955; Ditchburn, Fender, and Mayne, 1959; Krauskopf, 1957). Krauskopf also showed that narrow bars need a higher intensity (higher contrast ratio) than broad bars to be seen 50 percent of the time; Fender (1956) and Clowes (1959), using coloured targets, showed that stabilization affects discrimination of hue as well as saturation and brightness.

Achieving stabilization by reflecting the image off the contact lens, however, has some limitations. The field that can be used is small, mainly because torsional movement is not controlled. The next step in the development of method was to attach the complete optical system to the eyeball itself (Ditchburn and Pritchard, 1956; MacKay, 1957; Yarbus, 1957). Since the optical system produces an apparently distant target, which is viewed with a relaxed eye, gross fluctuations of accommodation due to muscular fatigue could be ruled out as an explanation of fading. More important, larger and more complex figures could be used.

Ditchburn and Pritchard (1956) used interference fringes produced by a small calcite crystal between two polaroid sheets, and fastened by a stalk to a contact lens, to get a concentric ring pattern which covered a wide field and was in focus for a fully relaxed normal eye. With this method, it was found that the visual object is present for a very small fraction of the viewing time. Moreover, several observations of great interest were made (Pritchard, 1958; Pritchard and Vowles, 1960). It was found, in brief, that stimulation of other senses could affect the amount of time that the target was seen, and that when the subject's attention was directed to a particular part of the target, this part would usually remain in view longer. Also, it was shown that parts of interference fringes might appear and disappear independently of each other. These results led directly to the experiments which we now report.

Method

In the present investigation the method used to compensate for retinal-image motion produced by the involuntary eye movements is that described by Pritchard (1961). It consists, essentially, of a collimator device (one producing parallel rays of light), carried on a contact lens, as illustrated in Figure 3.4. The target to be viewed is maintained in the focal plane of a high-power glass lens and illuminated by a miniature surgical bulb attached to a diffusing screen. It is seen against a circular patch of light subtending 5°, while the rest of the diffuser is blackened to shield the eye from stray light. The assembly of lens, target, and light source is mounted by a ball-socket joint to a stalk carried on a contact lens, corrected for the subject's visual defects, if any. The lens is tight fitting and thus follows small eye movements accurately (Ratliff and Riggs, 1950; Riggs, Armington, and Ratliff, 1954). The target is easily changed by unscrewing the top of the collimator assembly and replacing one small circular target by another. When the top is screwed down again, the new target is immediately secured in the focal plane of the high-power lens and no additional focusing is necessary.

The targets are produced by photographing India ink drawings on white cards, or drawings in white ink on black cards. Then, 5 mm discs of the negative are viewed by the subject through the collimating lens and consequently are seen as if located at infinity. They are in focus, therefore, for the normal relaxed eye.

In the present study all the targets were presented within a central 2° field, in view of the earlier finding (Pritchard, 1958) of a marked difference between perception within this central region and more peripheral regions. All observations were monocular, the other eye being occluded. The luminance of the brightest parts of the target was maintained at approximately 25 milli-lamberts, with the experiment room in darkness during the viewing period.

The subject lay on a couch with his head supported, in a partly sound-proofed room or, in some of the observations, in an ordinary room at times when irregular auditory stimuli were at a minimum (see also Pritchard and Vowles, 1960). The target was then put in position by the experimenter, and a continuous recording was made of the subject's report. Control observations were also made, in which the subject viewed the same targets through the contact lens and collimator system, but without attaching one to the other, so that the image was not stabilized.

It is important to note that the subject must first be habituated to the viewing conditions, and for this reason reports obtained during the first three sessions, of approximately an hour each, were not recorded. For some subjects

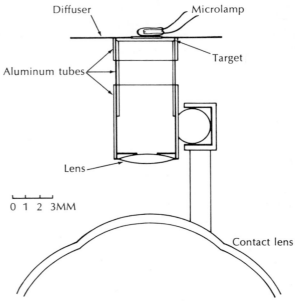

Figure 3.4:   The apparatus used to produce stabilized
images.

it is desirable at first to use a local anaesthetic to minimize sensations from
the contact lens, which tend to produce frequent blinking and jerky movements
of the eyeball, causing a slight slipping of the contact lens and loss of stabilization. But further, the visual phenomena themselves are so striking at first
that the subject inevitably tries to look at the object that has suddenly vanished
or equally suddenly popped into vision after having vanished, again destroy-
ing stabilization. Only when he has adapted to the phenomena themselves,
enough to be able to observe passively, does he begin to obtain the full range
of phenomena. When adaptation was achieved, in the present experiment, the
subject observed and reported on some fifty different visual objects.

The Phenomena

The phenomena of perception with stabilized images and complex targets seem
at first to have a bewildering variety, mostly without precedent in the subject's
previous experience, but signs of order begin to appear with continued observation. The phenomena described here are from the reports of four experienced observers; unless otherwise stated, each phenomenon has been independently confirmed at least once, a second observer simply being asked to
look at a new figure without being told what the preceding observer had found
of interest in it.

When the figure is first presented, it remains intact for a length of time which depends on its complexity. With a single line as target, the line fades and disappears, leaving the more dimly illuminated field only. Eventually this disappears also, replaced by a "rich" or intense black patch. Subsequently it regenerates. A more complex target may behave similarly or it may instead lose one or more of its parts, in ways that will be described.

The time of the first disappearance varies, perhaps because of different levels of attention in the observer or because of variations in the level of unfamiliar auditory stimulation (Pritchard and Vowles, 1960), but disappearance is quicker with simpler figures. Also, it has been possible to determine that a simpler figure such as a line is visible for about ten percent of viewing time, while a more complex figure such as an unconnected set of curlicues or a facial profile (Figure 3.5, boxes 2, 3) retains at least one of its parts for as much as 80 percent of the time. Such a comparison can be made directly by presenting two figures simultaneously (Figure 3.5, box 3); or the comparison may be quantified with repeated separate presentations, during which the observer presses a key whenever the figure is visible (Kader, 1960).

The greater time during which a more complex figure is present cannot be explained by assuming a random fluctuation of threshold in the different parts of the field. One might conclude, on such an assumption, that one or other part of the more complex figure remains visible only because the figure covers more of the field, and therefore is more likely to involve an area in which the visual threshold is, for the moment, lower than elsewhere. But, chaotic as the activity of the figure may seem at first, it still obeys some rules which relate to the form of the figure itself. It is these that we are now concerned with.

The "rules" may be summarized as follows. A meaningful diagram is visible longer than a meaningless one: an effect possibly related to the fact that attending to a diagram keeps it visible longer (Pritchard and Vowles, 1960). A straight line tends to act as a unit (to appear or disappear as a whole) even though it extends across the whole 2° field; if the line breaks up, the break is likely to occur at the point of intersection with another line. The several lines of a triangle, square, or such, act independently, with the exception that the activity of parallel lines in a figure is correlated. Jagged diagrams are more active, less stable, than rounded ones: a "good" figure (Koffka, 1935), is more likely to act as a complete unit than a "poor" figure, and there are occasional observations of completion or regularization of a figure. Finally, there are clearly marked field effects, in which the presence of a figure in one part of the field modifies the activity of parts of a neighbouring figure.

These results are illustrated in Figure 3.5, boxes 3 to 18. Box 3 shows two curves which are similar except that one is a recognizable profile of a face. When they are seen with the apparent fixation point midway between them, the left curve, without meaning, fades faster and is absent more frequently than the right. Box 14 combines three meaningful symbols: a "4," a "B" and a "3." Fading of the parts of this complex does not occur at random; almost all the time, when any part of the figure is present, it includes one or more of the symbols, complete. Similarly in Box 16: the meaningless superimposed

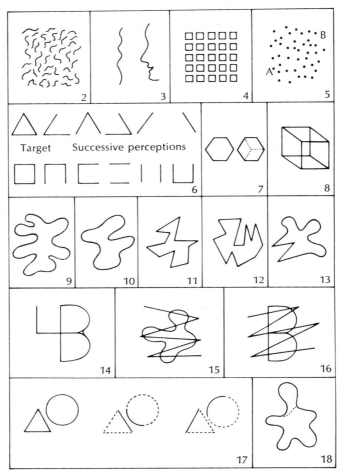

Figure 3.5:   Examples of visual stimuli used (boxes 6, 7, 17, and 18 also show successive perceptions).

lines, over the letter "B," act independently of it, and fade more frequently.

Boxes 4 and 5 are configurations which behave in such a way as to emphasize the importance of linear organization. This may be horizontal, vertical, or diagonal, but the horizontal is usually predominant. In box 4, whole rows of squares may disappear together, leaving one row intact; in box 5, a more or less random collection of dots, there is a strong tendency for the dots to organize themselves, so that a line of dots such as that running from A to B may take on unity and repeatedly remain in the field when the others have disappeared. For one observer, one of the rows of box 4 at times acquired a further unity which is hard to describe: the squares within the row remained fully distinct visually, but the row became one thing, separate from the other parts of the figure. Possibly this was one of the three-dimensional depth effects discussed below, but the observer could not be certain on the point.

With the diagrams of boxes 6, 7, and 8, the independence of separate straight lines making up a more complex figure is very striking. Box 6 shows two series of events which might occur with triangle and square respectively. Lines act as units. It is very seldom that an incomplete one is observed, except where a slight trace may occasionally remain at an intersection with another line. None of our data supports the assumption made elsewhere (Hebb, 1949) that it is the angle or corner that is a perceptual element. In these figures, again, the influence of parallel lines on one another is evident since opposite sides of square or hexagon (at the left in box 7) remain together too frequently for this to be explained as coincidence, whereas with the square it is rare for two adjacent sides only to remain. This parallel-line effect is most striking with the Necker cube; in addition, when the cube is seen in three dimensions (as it always is with the stabilized image), surfaces which are separate but in parallel planes act frequently together. The front and back of the cube may remain in sight, for example, while the other edges (the lines which connect the squares which constitute front and back faces) have disappeared. The parallel-line effect is not invariable, of course, and still less the parallel-surface effect: in addition to complete inversion of the cube (which occurs with the stabilized image as with normal vision) there may be a partial inversion, the same surfaces being seen at right angles to each other.

Our emphasis has been on the independent action of parts of a complex figure, but the figure can also—less frequently—act as a whole, appearing and disappearing as a single unit. The probability that it will do so is principally determined by its shape. A circle, or a diagram such as those of boxes 9 and 10, is relatively stable and quiet, whereas another, as in boxes 11 and 12, is quite unstable and likely to produce an effect of violent motion, as the separate parts appear and disappear in rapid succession. In general, the pattern composed of rounded curves is less active than a jagged one, and more likely to act as whole. The difference between smoothness and jaggedness appears dramatically in a single pattern such as that of box 13, in which the angular parts are likely to be active and unpredictable and the rounded parts to form a more stable unit or part figure. This effect is clearly related to the "good" figure of Gestalt psychology, but it must be said that even the circle, the good figure par excellence, frequently acts as though composed of separate perceptual elements (see discussion of box 17, below). We have in fact found no other extended figure than an uninterrupted straight line which reliably acts as a unit.

The behaviour of wholes is further illustrated by the diagrams of boxes 14, 15, and 16. We have already reported that box 14, containing three symbolic patterns, tends to break down in such a way as to leave one or more of the symbols intact. Here an effect of meaning and past experience is evident: similarly in box 16, where the "B" tends to remain for longer periods than the hatching lines, and even when they are present, the "B" is seen in a separate plane nearer the observer, as a separate entity. The diagram of box 15, however, shows that the effect can occur with a figure which lacks both meaning and goodness of form: the closed loop also tends to act as a whole though it is quite irregular.

Box 17 illustrates a field effect which has been observed repeatedly. There is a marked influence of one of the two figures on the other, seen in two ways. First, the parts of the triangle and the circle which are nearest to each other frequently remain visible while the other parts disappear (box 17, first example) and second, less frequently, a side of the triangle which remains is accompanied by an arc of the circle which is "parallel" to it (box 17, second and third examples). This, with the tendency of parallel lines to act together which was mentioned earlier, seems clearly to show the existence of an influence of a visual object which extends well beyond the actual area of stimulation.

The final illustration, box 18, concerns a completion phenomenon which occurs in several ways, including the special case of closure. When a diagram such as that of box 9 or 10 loses one of its limbs, we have obtained several reports of a transient closure, which is diagrammed in box 18. This appears to be a clear case of production of a better figure, and to it we may add the report of one observer that a slightly irregular hexagon became definitely regular. (On the other hand, a circle or other regular figure may be temporarily distorted, with an equally definite change of shape [one observer]. The effect is similar to the perceptual distortions reported by subjects who have just come out of "isolation" [Heron, Doane, and Scott, 1956].) A second example of completion is found in the hallucinatory addition of an eye to the profile of box 3 (one observer, but confirmed by a second observer with another profile figure).

Thirdly, a case which is perhaps equivocal as an instance of completion, but is of considerable interest and one which also brings us to our final topic, of depth effects. With the hexagon as presented in box 7, left, we have obtained reports of a "strong cube impression," the hexagon being perceived as the outline of a cube in three dimensions. The cube, also, is seen to reverse as the Necker cube does. The diagram at the right of box 7 shows how this may occur; the dotted lines do *not* appear in vision, but the figure acts in other respects as if they were present. In this sense, at least, there is completion.

Depth effects are ubiquitous. When the hexagon just referred to is seen as a two-dimensional figure instead of a cube, it is still clearly in a different plane from that of the background: nearly always above the surface, or closer to the observer. The effect is the same whether the figure is brighter than the ground or darker. The squares of box 4 have the appearance of a waffle iron, as protrusions from the surface (or, for one observer, occasionally as depressions); a row of circles of about the same dimensions looks like a row of craters of small volcanoes. The tridimensionality of the Necker cube is much more definite than with ordinary vision; with prolonged viewing it may deteriorate from the appearance of regular cube, but is still definitely in three dimensions, the interior connecting lines appearing like wires strung over and under each other.

Comment

The phenomena that have been described bear directly on two theoretical approaches to perception: Gestalt theory (Köhler, 1929; Koffka, 1935), and the theory of cell assemblies (Hebb, 1949; Milner, 1957) or trace systems (Lashley, 1958). On the one hand, Gestalt ideas concerning the phenomena of perception find further new support; on the other, an independent action of parts even of good figures demonstrates that an exclusively holistic treatment of the percept is not sufficient, so that the explanatory conceptions of Gestalt theory require modification. We believe that the data offer support to both approaches, and qualify them to a greater or less extent; it is too soon to go into detailed analysis, but we may say in general that the holistic ideas become more compatible with analytical ones than was evident previously.

The Gestalt closure that has been described (box 18) is most clear-cut and unambiguous, comparable only to what has been observed in cases of hemianopis (Fuchs, 1920; Lashley, 1941). There is clear evidence of the functional meaning of the conception of the "good" figure; of the functioning of the whole as a perceptual entity, distinct from part functions; and of groups as entities, and of similarity and contiguity as determinants of grouping. Finally, we have found evidence of marked field effects.

But with this we have found an extraordinary action of parts, independent of the whole. In the conditions of the experiment, this action tends to predominate over the whole in a way that never occurs in normal vision. The phenomena described, we believe, make inevitable the conclusion that perceptual elements (as distinct from sensory elements: Hebb, 1949) exist in their own right. In conformity with Gestalt ideas, these are organized entities, and the conclusion to be drawn here, perhaps, is not that Gestalt emphasis on organized wholes is erroneous but rather (a) that the wholes in question are often simpler ones than are usually discussed—that is, straight lines or short segments of curves—and (b) that the more complex wholes, such as square or circle, are syntheses of simpler ones though they may also function as genuine single entities. The earlier literature treated perception-by-parts and perception of wholes as antithetical, mutually exclusive ideas. In retrospect, one seems that a theoretical opposition is quite unnecessary, logically; and our data show that both conceptions are valid and complement one another.

The action of parts that has been described is also a very considerable confirmation of the theory of cell assemblies, in its main lines. As we have said above, the data show a need for revision, no support being provided for the idea that an angle or an intersection of lines is a perceptual element. Revision or development of the theory becomes necessary in other respects; for example, to account for the unexpected influence of continuity as such, seen with box 17 (see above). In general terms, however, the phenomena confirm the earlier analysis (Hebb, 1949) to a very surprising extent.

Today there are further data to support this approach. Apart from the present experiment, we may cite the auditory "holding" demonstrated by Broadbent (1956), and the phenomena of serial order in visual perception

(Mishkin and Forgays, 1952; Orbach, 1952; Heron, 1957; Kimura, 1959; and Bryden, 1960). All are intelligible in terms of a semi-autonomous activity of closed systems in perception but unintelligible when perception is regarded as a simple input system, and the concept of cell assembly or tract system becomes less remotely speculative than it may have seemed at first, and closer to the realities of behaviour. Further experiments of the kind we have reported, with the use of stabilized images, should make it possible to specify in more detail the properties of these closed systems and so provide a new understanding of the perceptual process.

Editor's Note: Metacontrast

In any discussion of the basic organization of perception, the phenomenon known as *metacontrast* deserves to be included. The original observation of this tendency of the visual system was made by Werner in 1935. He briefly presented a black circle and then removed it. After a pause of approximately 100 to 150 milliseconds (one millisecond, abbreviated msec, equals 1/1000 of a second), a second figure was presented. This second figure consisted of a ring, the inner border of which coincided with the outer border of the previously presented black circle. If the ring followed the circle within a period of no greater than 150 msec, only the ring was reported by the subject.

Werner's explanation of these observations involved the development of contour. He theorized that the perception of contour takes time. That is to say, after the presentation, a figure will only be seen as a figure if its contour is allowed to develop.

More recent research in the laboratory of Charles W. Eriksen at the University of Illinois has led to a reconsideration of this explanation of metacontrast. Eriksen and his collaborators have even shown that several phenomena have been lumped together under the single term metacontrast which in fact deserve separate attention.

The following paper, published in the *Journal of Experimental Psychology* in 1965, considers the temporal aspects of the masking effects of a stimulus on a previously presented or subsequent stimulus and offers several possible explanations for the phenomenon.

Backward and Forward Masking

Charles W. Eriksen and James F. Collins

If a briefly presented visual stimulus is followed by a second stimulation within a brief time interval, seldom longer than 1000 msec, there are circumstances under which the first signal will not be perceived by a subject even though the duration of its exposure was long enough for perception to have occurred had the second stimulus not been presented. Alpern (1952) provided a description of some of these phenomena and Raab (1963) has contributed a more recent review.

The backward masking, or as it is sometimes called, "metacontrast," has tended to be treated as a single phenomenon, but recent evidence has made increasingly clear that several phenomena are involved with different explanations or underlying processes (Eriksen and Collins, 1964; Eriksen and Hoffman, 1963). Eriksen and Hoffman (1963) have advanced an explanation for certain cases of masking in terms of a temporal luminance summation between the two stimulus fields with a resulting reduction in contrast ratio for the masked figure. The luminance-summation, contrast-reduction hypothesis has received strong support from several studies (Eriksen and Hoffman, 1963; Eriksen and Steffy, 1964; Steffy and Eriksen, 1965) and most recently Thompson (1966) has shown that an empirically determined function relating perceptual recognition of forms to contrast ratios, predicts quite precisely the recognition accuracy for forms masked by a succeeding second-field luminance where the effective contrast ratio for the form was computed, assuming luminance summation.

While the luminance-summation hypothesis seems to explain quite well certain instances of backward masking, there are other circumstances where masking is obtained that cannot be attributed to luminance summation and resulting contrast reduction. Kolers (1962) and Kolers and Rosner (1960) have reported masking effects on a disk stimulus followed by a second stimulus consisting of a ring under circumstances where the adapting and delay fields were illuminated at a level that would have reduced luminance summation and contrast reduction to minimal levels. Also Averbach and Coriell (1961), using quite bright adapting and delay fields, found impaired recognition for letters when the letter was circumscribed by a ring occurring later in time. Unfortunately the methodology employed in these studies was not very rigorous. The Kolers (1962) study was defective in the use of the duration of disk exposure as a dependent variable and along with the Kolers and Rosner (1960) experiment provided no control for shift in the subject's criterion of report (Swets, Tanner, and Birdsall, 1961). Indeed, Kolers and Rosner (1960) found that the probability of masking at a single delay interval *and identical stimulus conditions* varied from less than 20 to greater than 70 percent depending upon the range of delay intervals the subject was judging in that particular session. While the authors interpret this in terms of anchoring effects, it most likely reflects a changing criterion on the part of the subject correlated with the range of stimuli being judged. If the subject is making judgments over a long range of delay intervals, he experiences very little masking on presentations involving longer delays and is apt to adopt a very rigorous criterion for reporting the presence of the disk. When judging over a shorter range of delays, particularly over those intervals where masking is maximal, the subject is apt to adopt a more lenient criterion of disk presence since on none of the exposures does he get a very clear perception of the disk. The result is that any masking phenomenon is itself masked by a variable and unmeasured false-alarm rate.

In the present experiments we have attempted to remedy past defects in methodology by: (a) obtaining a more sensitive measure of masking through the use of a recognition criterion for forms; (b) the use of a forced-choice psychophysical procedure with confidence ratings on judgments; (c) a constant-stimulus exposure time adjusted to each subject's perceptual capability; and (d) observations of the effect on perceptual recognition when form stimulus and masking ring are presented concurrently.

Experiment I

The purpose of this experiment was to map the retroactive interference produced by a ring stimulus upon recognition of simple forms when the ring stimulus occurred concurrently with the form or at delay intervals as much as 250 msec after termination of the form stimulus. Two groups of subjects were run. The Group A subjects were run first at delay intervals designed to map the general outline of the interference function. On the basis of data obtained from Group A, Group B subjects were run at intervals designed to provide maximum information in the critical regions of the masking or interference function.

Method

Subjects. Ten adult college students volunteered to serve and were paid a fixed sum for the experiment. The five subjects in Group A contained four males and the five subjects in Group B one male. All subjects were trained over several practice sessions that involved perceptual recognition but not masking phenomena. All had normal or corrected to normal visual acuity.

Procedure. A three-field tachistoscope, previously described (Eriksen and Hoffman, 1963), was used to present the stimulus sequences. An adaptation field with a luminance of 0.572 apparent footcandles (ftc) contained a black H subtending 0.2° of angle which was used as a fixation point. Each of the two stimulus fields had a luminance of 0.200 apparent ftc. In order to minimize confounding from luminance-summation, contrast-reduction effects, the adaptation field remained on continuously and exposures of the two stimulus fields, F 1 and F 2, were superimposed upon the adaptation-field luminance. Thus, at all delay intervals between the two stimulus fields the adaptation-field luminance was present.

The stimulus forms consisted for the capital letters, A, T, and U, presented as black figures against a white ground and each subtending a maximum of 0.2° of angle. Previous research had found these letters to be approximately equally recognizable and equally confusable, one with another, in tachistoscopic presentations. The ring stimulus was also black on a white ground and had an outer diameter of 0.67° and an inner diameter of 0.30°. The ring was always presented in F 2 and so located as to center the form occurring in F 1.

Prior to beginning the experimental sessions each subject engaged in two practice sessions of approximately one hour each. During these practice sessions the subject's forced-choice recognition function for the three stimuli was determined when the letters were presented without the occurrence of the ring-masking stimulus. Instead only a blank white card was flashed at 0-delay interval in F 2 after presentation of a letter in F 1. From these practice judgments a base-level duration of exposure was determined for each subject that yielded approximately seventy percent forced-choice correct recognition. This base level was then used for this subject as the exposure duration for the forms in F 1. The mean value of this base-level duration was 44.0 msec. with a range from 27 to 57 for the 10 subjects. The ring stimulus when it occurred in F 2 always had a constant exposure time of 100 msec for all subjects.

Each subject served for five experimental sessions of approximately forty-minutes duration during which he made 108 judgments as to which letter had been presented. The subject was instructed before each stimulus sequence to fixate clearly the fixation point and when it appeared sharply and clearly to add pressure to the trigger which initiated the program.[1] After each trial subject reported whether A, T, or U had occurred along with a rating of his subjective confidence on a three-point scale. The subjects in Group A each made ninety judgments at each of five delay intervals (0, 68, 100, 130, and 250 msec) and ninety for the concurrent situation. The subjects in Group B differed only in that the delay intervals were: concurrent, 0, 10, 25, 50, and 250 msec. There were two kinds of trials for each delay interval as well as for the concurrent presentation. On half the trials, randomly selected, the letter form was followed by the ring stimulus after the appropriate delay (ring-present condition). On the other half, only a blank white card in the second field was flashed after the appropriate delay (ring-absent condition). By presenting half of the trials without the ring stimulus, a constant control was maintained on recognition accuracy without the presence of interference and also a control for a possible distracting effect of a flicker in the second stimulus field was provided. On the concurrent presentations the letter stimulus and ring were on the same stimulus card and were presented in F 1 followed at 0 delay by the 100-msec flash of the blank white card in F 2. The subjects made judgments at all delay intervals, and the concurrent situation during each experimental session and the order of delay intervals within sessions were counterbalanced across sessions and across subjects.

Results

The number of correct letter recognitions independent of subjective confidence level was analyzed by a three-way analysis of variance (ring present versus absent, delay interval, and subjects). Since different delay intervals were employed, a separate analysis was required for each of the two groups.

For both groups the effect of the ring-present-ring-absent conditions was

---

[1] We have found in past work (Eriksen and Hoffman, 1963) that this method of permitting subjects to initiate the sequence by manipulating the switch or trigger much as a rifleman squeezes off a shot, results in very stable recognition functions for tachistoscopically presented stimuli. It succeeds in eliminating variations in accommodation which account for considerable variability in tachistoscopic presentations.

significant beyond the 0.001 level and the effect of delay interval was significant beyond the 0.025 level. The interaction between ring-present-ring-absent and delay interval was also significant for both groups ($p < 0.025$). None of the interactions involving the subject variable were significant but there was a significant main effect attributable to difference in subjects ($p < 0.025$). This was anticipated due to inability to equate precisely all subjects at the 70 percent recognition point on base-level duration.

In Figure 3.6, percentage of correct recognition of the forms has been plotted for each of the two groups as a function of ring-present versus absent conditions and delay interval. The data points for the ring-absent condition have been fitted by a straight line of 0 slope. For the ring-present or masking condition the data points of 100-msec delay and less have been fitted to the shown curve by eye. The straight line of 0 slope fits the data for the ring-absent condition quite well suggesting that a flicker of the second stimulus field without the ring at the various delay intervals has little or no systematic effect upon recognition accuracy of the form presented in F 1. The data for the ring-present condition show a marked masking effect when the ring stimulus is presented after the form at delays under approximately 100 msec. The function appears quite flat from 0- to 50-msec delay, indicating uniform masking in this range, and it is important to note that the masking effect in this delay range is essentially the same as presenting the form with the ring surrounding it concurrently or on the same stimulus card.

Discussion

The data are quite clear in showing pronounced retroactive masking effect exerted by the ring stimulus for delay intervals under 50 msec and further that the masking effect is dissipated rather rapidly somewhere between 50- and 100-msec delay.

The data obtained from the two groups of subjects are in close correspondence where the delay intervals were the same. Perhaps the most significant finding with respect to the masking effect is that maximum masking appears to occur when ring and form are presented concurrently. This finding has major implications for the interpretation of the process underlying masking. In the past masking phenomena have been described in terms of erasure by the second stimulus of the first or displacement of the first stimulus by the second in perception. The finding that maximal masking occurs in the concurrent presentation argues against an erasure or displacement hypothesis. Rather, it suggests an interpretation in terms of visual or perceptual persistence and a lag time in the perceptual process itself.

The finding that perception of the letters A, T, or U is impaired when they are presented inside of a ring stimulus is rather easily understood. It suggests that the presentation of one of these letters in a clear white uncluttered field is an easier perceptual task for recognition than the perception of these letters inside of a black ring. Further, the finding that when the ring stimulus is delayed 50 msec after termination of the letter presentation, recognition impairment is almost as much as when the two stimuli occur concurrently suggests that the perception of the form had not been completed 50

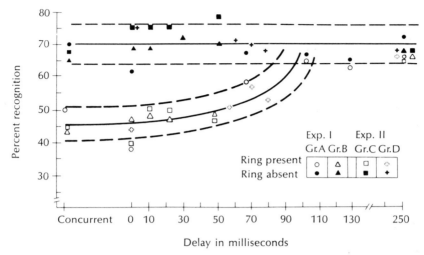

Figure 3.6: Recognition as a function of delay interval between the letter form and the ring stimulus or blank field (the dotted line curves indicate the +2o and −2o range around the solid line curves).

msec after termination of the stimulation. By the time perception does occur, ring and form appear to be present together requiring the perceptual task of distinguishing the form within the ring. In other words, the basis of the masking effect is that by the time perception occurs ring and stimulus, at short-delay intervals, are present together to form the percept.

Before speculating upon the perceptual-attentional processes that may underlie this phenomena, we deemed it wise to perform another experiment checking upon this interpretation of the basis of masking; namely, the simultaneous presence of the ring and form in the percept. If this interpretation of the impairment in perception is correct, then it would appear that proactive masking should have essentially the same results as retroactive masking. Presenting the ring stimulus prior to presenting the form should describe essentially the same masking function as when the ring follows the form. Either sequence should lead to the percept of the letter surrounded by the ring and thereby constitute a more difficult perceptual task for recognition. The persistence of the time relationships should be essentially the same for either forward or backward masking.

Experiment II

Method

Subjects.   Ten young adult college students (three males) served as subjects. Five were assigned to Group C (one male) and the remaining five to Group D. All subjects were paid a fixed sum for their services and had volunteered for the experiments. They were again given practice sessions on form recognition that did not involve masking arrangements. All had normal or corrected to normal visual acuity.

Procedure.   The procedure, stimulus materials, and apparatus were identical to those employed in Experiment I. The only difference was that under the ring-present conditions in this experiment the ring preceded the letter forms by the various delay intervals. The ring stimulus again was presented for a constant duration of 100 msec and the duration of the letter exposures was adjusted as before to the individual subjects base level. For the ten subjects the average base-level duration was 35 msec with a range of 19 to 55 msec. For the subjects in Group C the ring occurred concurrently and also preceded the form by lead times of 0, 10, 25, 50, and 250 msec. The corresponding lead times for the subjects in Group D were 0, 60, 70, 80, and 250 msec.

Results
Separate three-way analyses of variance (ring present versus absent, delay intervals, and subjects) were performed for the Group C and Group D data since some delay intervals were not shared in common by these groups. In both groups all three main effects were significant ($p < 0.01$) as was also the interaction between conditions and delay intervals ($p < 0.001$). The only significant interaction involving subjects was the subjects $\times$ condition interaction in Group C. Inspection of the data revealed that all five subjects showed an appreciable masking effect at delay intervals under 50 msec but two of the subjects showed a much more pronounced masking effect than did the other three.

To facilitate comparison between Experiments I and II the data from this latter experiment have also been plotted in Figure 3.6. Whereas in Experiment I the abscissa represents the delay in milliseconds by which the ring stimulus followed termination of the form, in interpreting the data from Experiment II delay interval represents the time between termination of the ring stimulus and presentation of the form. The dotted lines in Figure 3.6 represent the two sigma ranges bounding the designated curves. The sigma value is three and was obtained by averaging the error variances for the four groups in the two experiments. Examination of the Experiment II data in Figure 3.6 reveals that it corresponds quite closely with the data points from Experiment I. For both the ring-present and the ring-absent conditions, the data points for both experiments seem about equally well fitted by a straight line of 0 slope for the ring-absent condition and by the visually fitted curve for the ring-present condition.

Discussion
The results for both experiments are quite clear in demonstrating three important points. First, both forward and backward masking effects of a ring stimulus upon recognition of simple forms are found when improved indicator methodology is used, methodology that is relatively independent of effects that can be attributed to shifts in the subject's subjective criterion for report. Second, forward or backward asynchronies of the presentation of the form and

of the ring of approximately 50 msec or less produce an impairment in form recognition that is comparable in magnitude to the impairment obtained when ring and form are presented concurrently. And third, the masking effect of the ring appears to be symmetrical in time in that the forward masking effect is highly similar if not identical to the backward masking effect.

The finding that the maximum forward or backward masking effect is directly comparable to the amount of impairment in form recognition that occurs when ring and form are presented together most strongly suggests that the "masking" is attributable to greater difficulty in recognizing a form surrounded by a black ring than when the form is presented alone in an uncluttered field. In other words an exposure duration that yields 70 percent form recognition when the form occurs in any empty field is insufficient when the perceptual task requires recognition of the form surrounded by a circle or ring. This latter is a more complex stimulus and as ample evidence has shown, increased exposure durations are required for equal recognition accuracy of more complex stimuli (Hake, 1957).

This explanation of the "masking" effect poses other problems. Specifically, the question is raised as to how a ring stimulus that precedes or follows a form by intervals of 50 msec or more comes to be perceived as though the two stimuli had been presented together or concurrently?

Three possible mechanisms are suggested. The first is that the visual system is organized so that if a stimulus follows a previous stimulus within a critical lag, the transmission of the second stimulus through the end organs and the visual tracts is facilitated. Thus the second stimulus overtakes the preceding stimulus and they arrive together at the locus or loci in the central nervous system (CNS) where perception occurs. We have been unable to locate electrophysiological recording studies that bear directly on this issue, but techniques such as those employed by Lindsley and Emmons (1958) are capable of modification to shed light on this possibility.

A second possibility is that the visual-perceptual system is time gated. That is, visual perception occurs or is organized on the basis of chunks of sensory inputs of between 50 and 100 msec in size. This time chunking of sensory inputs need not be discrete in that successive 100 msec of inputs are successively organized. Rather, the process may be one where visual perception is organized on the basis of 100 msec of input but the successive chunks are greatly overlapping with the preceding and following ones. Similar conceptions of this time-ordering process have been proposed by White and Cheatham (1959) and by Callaway and Alexander (1960) in terms of their "neuronic shutter" theory. (Stroud [1956] has suggested a somewhat similar idea in his quantal theory of consciousness.) In addition to the evidence supplied by these investigators other suggestions that the visual-perceptual system deals or treats stimulation in such time chunks is found in the Bunsen-Roscoe law that holds for durations under 100 msec and in the recent work on the temporal luminance-summation, contrast reduction hypothesis (Eriksen and Hoffman, 1963; Eriksen and Steffy, 1964; Thompson, 1966). Also Ogle (1963) has shown that little impairment in depth perception occurs when disparity cues to the separate eyes are delayed by as much as 50 msec.

A third possible explanation may be found in attentional processes. Recent research in our laboratory has suggested that part of the time involved in perception can be attributed to an attentional focusing process. Broadbent's (1957) model of the attentional system provides for brief storage of sensory inputs before being attended, and recently Eriksen and Johnson (1964) have shown the feasibility of such a process in auditory perception. Ongoing research in our laboratory suggests that a finite time period is required for the attentional system to focus upon a sensory input and that the time required for focusing depends upon the level of discrimination required. The more complex or difficult the discrimination the longer the time required to focus to the necessary level. While this is highly speculative, the possibility does exist that the effective simultaneity of inputs differing by 50 msec or more may be due to the focus time of the attentional process. When the first input or stimulation arrives, the attentional process begins to focus upon it, but due to the latency and time involved in the focusing process, the second input or stimulation has arrived before focusing is completed. Thus when the input is attended both stimulations are effectively present together.

The choice between these three possible explanations or maybe others that have not been considered, cannot be made at the present time due to lack of adequate evidence. However, the results of the present experiments have moved the problem of masking to a new level where an explanation must be sought. The present data suggest quite clearly that the basis of masking is due to the more difficult discrimination required by the simultaneous occurrence of the form within a ring. The problem remaining now is to account for the mechanisms by which asynchronies of 50 to 100 msec are treated by this perceptual system as though they were simultaneous.

Before accepting the above conclusions note must be taken of some apparent conflicts between the data of the present experiments and results reported by other investigators. Averbach and Coriell (1961) presented a display consisting of sixteen letters in two rows of eight each. They report that when one of the letters was surrounded by a ring concurrently there was no impairment in the recognition of this particular letter. In fact, only slight impairment in ability to report the encircled letter was noted at 50-msec delay of the ring but by 100-msec delay, recognition of the letter was markedly impaired. This result would appear to be in marked conflict with that of the present study but the apparent contradiction can be quite simply resolved. While the duration of exposure of the stimuli in the present experiments was sufficient only for approximately 70 percent recognition for single-letter exposures, in the Averbach and Coriell study the display was exposed for 50 msec at a luminance of 70 footlamberts (ftl), a very strong stimulation and one well above that necessary for 100 percent correct single-letter identification. It was not of course sufficient for accurate report of all sixteen letters. However, if the display contained a circle or ring around one of the letters when it occurred, the effect of the ring would be to direct the subject's attention to that particular letter rather than the other fifteen, and since the duration of exposure was more than enough for perfect recognition of single letters, the subject could well report the letter even though the ring may have made it less legible or easily recognized than the other fifteen. The effect of the ring at 50 and 100 msec can be further understood in terms of their own data on visual persistence. With such an intense stimulation, well beyond that necessary for single-letter identification, visual persistence is still quite strong at 50 msec but the interference effect of the ring has become slightly more prominent due to some decay of the stimulus trace. By 100 msec the decay of the original input has now reached such a level that the occurrence of the ring constitutes effective interference in its recognition. Beyond 130 msec there is little indication in their data that masking is occurring. There is no evidence presented to show that recognition performance for a ring presented 130 msec or later differs significantly from the effect of the bar marker they employed in their other experiment that did not produce masking.

Kolers (1962) and Kolers and Rosner (1960) reported an essentially U-shaped masking function where masking of a disk stimulus by a succeeding ring was minimal at a few milliseconds delay, becoming maximal at about 50 msec and then disappearing in the region of 80 msec. The data from these studies are extremely difficult to compare to the present data or to any of the explanations examined, both due to the great differences in stimulus and task and to the very poor indicator methodology. No attempt was made to assess the subject's false-alarm rate or to assure that he maintained a given criterion not only within sessions but across sessions in different conditions. As was noted earlier the frequency with which the disk was reported masked varied over 50 percent for identical stimulus and delay conditions depending solely upon the range of delays a subject was judging within a session. (This 50 percent variation attributable to what the authors term anchoring effects is comparable in magnitude to the maximum masking effects obtained in their experiment.) It appears quite likely that the subject's criterion for reporting the presence of a disk at short delays of the masking ring was quite different than his criterion for reporting the presence of a disk at longer delays. In the absence of data on false-alarm rates it is impossible to interpret either of these experiments in terms of masking phenomena.

CHAPTER 4
Principles of Pereptual Organization

Various schools of psychology have developed around some fundamental principle or approach. The behaviorists, for example, base their system primarily on external, non-introspective behavior, while the structuralists specialize in consciousness and emotion. For the Gestalt school, which developed in opposition to American behaviorism, the study of perception provided the basic direction.

The Gestalt Movement

For the Gestalt psychologist, behavior is a complex process involving all contributing stimuli and response capabilities of the perceiving organism. The elements of behavior are integrated and organized into patterns which can only be understood in the context of their interrelationships. Knowledge of the functions of individual elements will not provide an adequate description of the integrated phenomenon. To know everything about hydrogen and everything about oxygen does not insure a knowledge of water. Rather than studying the individual contributing elements, the Gestalt psychologists choose to deal with wholes, with integrated phenomena. Their basic conception is to be found in the assumption that the whole is more than the sum of its parts.

The first Gestalt studies of perception centered around the question of perceptual organization. Psychologists of this school searched for and found conditions leading to the organization of sets of stimuli into wholes. They formulated factors describing the organization of figural elements into wholes, and attempted to describe all behavior along these lines or as functions of these factors.

The Gestalt school reached its peak of development under the leadership of Max Wertheimer at the University of Berlin in Germany. In 1912 Wertheimer won the attention of many psychologists with a paper on the subjective perception of movement. Some years later, two publications by Wertheimer outlined the basic ideas of Gestalt psychology. Today these three papers (Wertheimer, 1912, 1922, and 1923) are considered to be classic contributions to the study of the psychology of perception.

The third of these papers is perhaps the best known and provides the best insight into the Gestalt approach to perceptual organization. When it originally appeared in the German journal *Psychologische Forschung*, it was rather long, covering some fifty pages. Even today the German psychological publications tend to be rather lengthy (Murch and Wesley, 1966). It is not necessary to present a complete translation of Wertheimer's paper, since an excellent abridged version has been prepared by Michael Wertheimer, son of the late Max Wertheimer and an eminent psychologist in his own right. The abridged translation presented here first appeared in a book entitled *Readings in Perception* which was prepared by Beardslee and Wertheimer for the Van Nostrand Publishing Company in 1958.

Principles of Perceptual Organization

Max Wertheimer as abridged and translated by Michael Wertheimer

I stand at the window and see a house, trees, sky. Now on theoretical grounds I could try to count and say: "here there are . . . 327 brightnesses and hues." Do I have "327"? No, I see sky, house, trees; and no one can really have these "327" as such. Furthermore, if in this strange calculation the house should have, say, 120 and the trees 90 and the sky 117, I have in any event *this* combination, this segregation, and not, say, 127 and 100 and 100; or 150 and 177. I see it in this particular combination, this particular segregation; and the sort of combination or segregation in which I see it is not simply up to my choice: it is almost impossible for me to see it in any desired combination that I may happen to choose. When I succeed in seeing some unusual combination, what a strange process it is. What surprise results, when, after looking at it a long time, after many attempts, I *discover*—under the influence of very unrealistic set—that over there parts of the window frame make an N with a smooth branch. . . .

As another example, take two faces, cheek to cheek. I see the one (with, if you like, "57" brightnesses) and the other (with its "49"), but not in the division 66 plus 40 or 6 plus 100. Again, I hear a melody (17 notes) with its accompaniment (32 notes). I hear melody and accompaniment, not just "49"; or at least not 20 and 29.

This is true even when there is no question at all of stimulus continua; for instance if the melody and its accompaniment is played by an old music box, in short, separate little tones; or in the visual area, when figures composed of discontinuous parts (e.g., dots) become segregated on an otherwise quite homogeneous ground. Even though alternative organizations may be easier here than in the preceding cases, it is still true that a spontaneous, natural, normally expected combination and segregation occurs; and other organizations can be achieved only rarely, under particular conditions and usually with special effort and some difficulty.

In general, if a number of stimuli are presented together, a correspondingly large number of separate "givens" do not generally occur for the human; rather there are more comprehensive givens, in a particular segregation, combination, separation.

Are there principles for this resulting organization? What are they? One can try to determine and isolate the factors operating here experimentally, but a simpler procedure can be used in the presentation of the most critical factors: demonstration with a few simple, characteristic cases. The following is limited to the exposition of some essentials.

1. Given, in an otherwise homogeneous field, a row of dots with alternating distances, e.g., $d_1 = 3$ mm, $d_2 = 12$ mm.

● ●　　● ●　　　● ●　　　● ●　　　● ●　　　● ●　　　● ●

Normally such a row of dots is spontaneously seen as a row of small groups of points, in the arrangement ab/cd, and not, say, in the arrangement a/bc/de . . . . Really to see this arrangement (a/bc/de . . .) simultaneously in the entire series is quite impossible for most people. (If the constellation is composed of few dots, the opposing organization is easier to achieve and the result is more ambiguous. The situation is in general more labile. For instance, if the series above is decreased to ●　●　　　● ●　　　　● ●, the grouping a/bc/de/f is readily achieved.)

Of course a real *seeing* is meant here, not just conceiving some arbitrary combination; perhaps this will be clearer in dot series like the following:

You see a row of slanted groups (••), slanting from lower left to upper right, with the arrangement ab/cd/ef . . .; the opposite arrangement, a/bc/de . . ., with long slanted groups (•   •) is much more difficult to achieve. For most people it is impossible to achieve *simultaneously throughout the entire series* in such a constellation. It is difficult to achieve and when it does occur, it is much less certain—much more labile than the first, in relation to eye movements and changes in attention.

In other examples, such as

You see a row of small slanted groups (•), going from lower left to upper right. That is, if we label the dots as follows, you see

		c		f		i		l	
	b		e		h		k		etc.,
a		d		g		j			

the form abc/def/ghi/. . . . The opposite organization,

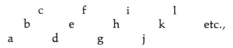

ceg/fhj/ . . ., is not seen, and is impossible to achieve simultaneously in the entire series for most people.

Or further, in

• • •   • • •   • • •   • • •   • • •   • • •

you see the triads abc/def/. . . and not one of many other theoretically possible groupings.

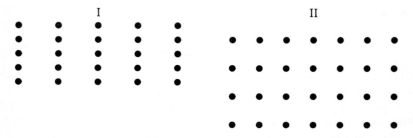

And in I, you typically see the verticals, in II the horizontals.

In all of these cases, a first simple principle emerges. The naturally resulting organization is the grouping together of the dots with small separation.

The organization of the dots with greater separation into groups either does not occur at all or occurs only with difficulty and artificially, and is more labile. As a tentative formulation: other things being equal, *grouping occurs on the basis of small distance* (the factor of nearness).

This principle has wider applications. It holds not only in vision and in spatial relations. Tapping continuously in the rhythm of our first example (● ●　　● ●　　　　● ● etc.) or the next to the last one (● ● ● ● ● ●　　● ● ●) demonstrates this effect in a very convincing way.

2. Given a constellation of dots with equal distances, with successive pairs different colors, in a homogeneous field—e.g., white and black in a gray field, in the following schema:

   a. ○ ○ ● ● ○ ○ ● ● ○ ○ ● ● ○ ○ ● ● ○ ○

Or better, a surface filled as follows:

   b. ○ ● ○ ● ○ ● ○ ●   c. ○ ○ ○ ○ ○ ○ ○ ○
       ○ ● ○ ● ○ ● ○ ●   ● ● ● ● ● ● ● ●
       ○ ● ○ ● ○ ● ○ ●   ○ ○ ○ ○ ○ ○ ○ ○
       ○ ● ○ ● ○ ● ○ ●   ● ● ● ● ● ● ● ●
       ○ ● ○ ● ○ ● ○ ●   ○ ○ ○ ○ ○ ○ ○ ○
       ○ ● ○ ● ○ ● ○ ●   ● ● ● ● ● ● ● ●
       ○ ● ○ ● ○ ● ○ ●   ○ ○ ○ ○ ○ ○ ○ ○

Or:

   d. ○ ○ ○ ● ● ● ○ ○ ○ ● ● ● ○ ○ ○ ● ● ● etc.

One sees the groups that are determined by similarity. In a, ab/cd/. . . ; in b, verticals; in c, horizontals; in d, abc/def/. . . ; to see the opposite organization clearly and simultaneously in the entire figure is usually impossible: a, a/bc/de/. . . ; b, the horizontals; c, the verticals; d, any of the arrangements, like cde/fgh/. . . etc.

If the number of stimuli is decreased, the other organizations also become possible, as in the first example of nearness as a factor; but generally they are still more difficult and more labile.

This leads to a second principle, which could tentatively be formulated this way: other things being equal, if several stimuli are presented together, there is a tendency to see the form in such a way that the similar items are grouped together (factor of similarity).

As before, the same holds true in continuous (not too slow) tapping rhythms in which loud and soft tapping are alternated. Analogous to a: . . ! ! . . ! ! . . ! ! . . ! ! etc.; analogous to d: . . . ! ! ! . . . ! ! ! . . . etc. In the first, you hear ab/cd/ef/. . . ; in the second, abc/def/ghi/. . . . To try consistently to maintain a different grouping is a task which requires considerable effort. Usually the natural (first) arrangement results soon all by itself, with the grouping as it were "tipping over."

Pitch operates the same way: analogous to a, for example, is c c g g c c g g c c g g; analogous to b, c c c g g g c c c g g g c c c.

In cases 2a and 2d just above, the conditions for the opposite organizations are not quite equivalent: aside from "leftovers," the rarer, or impossible, organization involves a change within the groups, a change in direction.

In 2a, ○ ○ ● ● ○ ○ ● ● ○ ○ ● ● ○ ○ ●, the b-c group is ○ ●, but the d-e group ● ○. Or in the rhythm . . ! ! . . ! ! . . ! ! . . ! !, b-c is weak→strong, but d-e strong→weak.

One can decrease this complication, e.g., by a continuation of the gradient: in the series of knocks, by following the first two weak ones by a stronger pair, these by a still stronger, etc., in the schema:

a.   ● ●   or b.   ● ● ●
                ● ●   ● ● ●
        ● ●   ● ● ●
  ● ●   ● ● ●   (With the ordinate

indicating intensity).

Analogously, in vision is the series (on a green background) white, white, light grey, light grey, medium grey, medium grey, dark grey, dark grey, black, black. Or with notes: a—c, c, e♭, e♭, f♯, f♯, a, a, c, c, . . . or b—c, c, c, e♭, e♭, e♭, f♯, f♯, f♯, a, a, a, c, c, c. . . .

The regularity indicated up to this point constitutes only a special case. Not only similarity or dissimilarity, but also greater and lesser dissimilarity operate in the same way, at least over a certain range. The note series a—c, c♯, e, f, g♯, a, c, c♯ . . . ; b—b, c, d, d♯, f, f♯, g♯, a, b, c . . . ; and c—c, c♯, d, e, f, f♯, g♯, a, a♯ . . . normally produce the organizations a—ab/cd/. . . , b—ab/cd/e. . . , and c—abc/def/. . . ; that is, they follow grouping according to minimal distances.

Analogous to corresponding simultaneous brightness and color series are the schemas:

d.   e.

If one confronts this principle of the size of the stepwise differences with that of nearness, there seems to arise the possibility of a more general principle which encompasses both of these and which would, in a certain sense, include spatial, temporal, and qualitative characteristics. If it should turn out that intensive and qualitative distance can be coordinated to a general spatio-temporal lawfulness, the instances discussed above could be considered instances of the principle of nearness. This must be carefully tested, but it can be experimentally studied.

Fields which were, previously, psychologically separate and heterogeneous could then be compared quantitatively in respect to the applicability of the same laws.

3. What happens, when two such factors are present together in such a constellation?

One can let the factors work together or against one another; for example, if the first produces the organization ab/cd/. . . ; the other can be set so as to enhance the same organization or to go in the other direction (. ./bc/de/. . .). One can weaken or strengthen an already-present tendency by changing distance relations as much as one can within the law of nearness.

For example, in series a (● ● ● ● ● ● ● ● ● ●) the factor of nearness produces ab/cd/. . . ; with this diminished number of stimuli this is not as unequivocally compelling as in a longer series; the organization a/bc/de/. . ., which occurs spontaneously very rarely, can yet be achieved by some, even though more difficult.

In series b (● ● ○ ○ ● ● ○ ○ ● ●) the factor of similarity also operates in the direction of the organization ab/cd/. . . ; achievement of the opposing arrangement, a/bc/de/. . . ; achievement of the opposing arrangement, a/bc/de/. . ., is much more difficult than in a and is impossible for most people.

In series c (● ○ ○ ● ● ○ ○ ● ● ○ ○ ●) the factor of similarity operates in a direction opposite to that of the factor of nearness; in spontaneous perception, a/bc/de. . . occurs more often than ab/cd/. . . ; aside from this, the series often looks typically "confused." The artificial achievement of the organization ab/cd/. . ., simultaneously in the entire series, is relatively difficult.

More clearly unequivocal relations, as in the following examples, may help to clarify this issue. However they must be exposed to observation one by one.

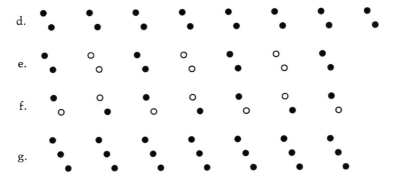

d.

e.

f.

g.

h.   i.   j.

● ● ● ● ● ● ○ ● ○ ● ● ● ● ● ●
● ● ● ● ● ● ○ ● ○ ● ○ ○ ○ ○ ○
● ● ● ● ● ● ○ ● ○ ● ● ● ● ● ●
● ● ● ● ● ● ○ ● ○ ● ○ ○ ○ ○ ○

In the initial series, d, the distance relations are such that the factor of nearness operates to some extent in the direction ab/cd. . . , but not as strongly as it would if the differences in distance were greater. As a rule, the short slanted lines ● ●, from upper left to lower right, result. The opposite organization (the long slanted lines ●   ●, from lower left to upper right) is clearly more difficult, less certain, and rarer.

In e, where nearness and similarity work in the same direction, the short slanted form is more unequivocal and more certain, and the opposite organization is in general impossible (or, at best, leads to confusion).

In f, where nearness and similarity are opposed, the factor of similarity is often victorious: one can see the long slanted forms ●   ●; however, grouping into the short slanted forms is possible for most people.

Series g shows the same thing as d.

In i, the verticals result (nearness and similarity cooperate) in j, the horizontals (the opposing factor of similarity is victorious).

Through a systematic variation of the distance relations in the initial series one could attempt to determine the region in which similarity wins out when it is added but works in an opposing direction. In this way one could also begin testing the strength of these grouping tendencies.

What has been demonstrated here in vision can also readily be shown in tones, varying time intervals, and pitch appropriately.

Further, the same relations with respect to the factors of nearness and similarity can be shown in experiments with stroboscopic movement. In both a and b, movement is typically perceived as occurring within the group,

            →   →   →   →
a.   ●   ●   ●   ●   ●   ●   ●   ●
     I   II   I   II   I   II   I   II
        →   →   →
b.   ○   ○   ●   ●   ○   ○   ●   ●
     I   II   I   II   I   II   I   II

determined in a by nearness and in b by similarity. Here again one could try to determine the relative strength of the two factors.

4. Given the following constellation, with its grouping clearly determined by nearness,

     ● ● ●   ● ● ●   ● ● ●   ● ● ●
     a b c   d e f   g h i   j k l

if, before his eyes, but without the subject expecting it, a change in the parts occurs, as, e.g., a sudden, small, vertical displacement of several of the dots upwards, two kinds of events are clearly distinguishable:

I. *Structurally reasonable* alterations, such as affect the groups already organized on the basis of nearness; e.g., shifting d, e, f upwards (or d, e, f and j, k, l).

II. *Structurally contrary* alterations, in which the common fate of the changed dots does not go along with the grouping that is already present; e.g., moving c, d, e upwards simultaneously (or c, d, e and i, j, k, or h, i, j).

Changes of this second kind do not go as smoothly as those of the first; while the first kind is readily taken in stride, the second usually produces a characteristic process. It is as if a special (much stronger) resistance existed against changes of this kind; there is a hesitation, sometimes a bewilderment, often a tipping over. The component parts affected by a common fate result in a grouping (in opposition to the influence of the factor of nearness). When c, d, e, i, j, k are displaced, the series is no longer in the form abc/def/. . . but is seen in the form ab/cde/fgh/ijk/l. (The threshold for the perception of such alterations also seems different in I and II.) We might designate this factor tentatively as that of "common fate"; the above cases are only special cases of its effects.

It is important to note that it is not only a question of equal alterations; similar things happen in changes that are, piecemeal, very different. For example, a slanting displacement of three of the dots in either the I or the II manner, or in "turning" c, f, i, l down and b, e, h, k upwards. (Qualitative changes operate similarly.) This principle also has a wide field of operation; how wide remains to be ascertained.

5. Imagine a series of rows, starting perhaps with the following row:

$$\bullet \quad \bullet \qquad \bullet \quad \bullet \qquad \bullet \quad \bullet \qquad \bullet \quad \bullet \qquad \bullet \quad \bullet$$
$$\text{a} \quad \text{b} \qquad \text{c} \quad \text{d} \qquad \text{e} \quad \text{f} \qquad \text{g} \quad \text{h} \qquad \text{i} \quad \text{j}$$

Let the distance between a and b, between c and d etc. (S_1) be 2 mm, and the distance between b and c, between d and e, etc. (S_2) be 20 mm; now construct a series of further rows, holding the position of a, c, e, g, i constant, and thus keeping $S_1 + S_2$ constant, but systematically varying the position of b relative to a and c (and the position of d relative to c and e, and so on) for example:

Row A	$S_1 = 2$ mm	$S_2 = 20$ mm	$S_1 + S_2 = 22$ mm
B	5	17	22
C	8	14	22
D	11	11	22
E	14	8	22
F	17	5	22
G	20	2	22

This is schematic; one must use a larger number of rows (with smaller steps of change). The number of dots (or groups) in a row can be varied as required.

Once one has constructed a larger number of such rows, one can now present them separately. The result is that one is not dealing with a multitude of psychologically equal steps. Three primary, distinct impressions emerge: the ab/cd/. . . form, clearest and most certain in the first rows; the /bc/de. . . form, equally clear in the last rows; and a third characteristic form, which is equally distinct from the other two forms and is produced by the middlemost row (row D in our example), giving an impression of uniformity, a "regular row."

Intermediate rows, lying outside these distinctive regions, often are ambiguous, not quite as precise; they easily appear more indeterminate, less clearly distinct, and can often be seen more easily in different ways.

Each of the three kinds of impressions are most distinct for certain ranges of stimulus values. Each has its field of application, thus, intermediate rows near D are typically seen as not quite regular, even when the distance differences are clearly supraliminal.

Another example can illustrate what is meant here: the series of angles from 30° through 150° (holding one side horizontal) is not simply a multitude of equals with a particular number of psychologically equal steps, as perhaps provided by just noticeable differences; but there are distinct primaries: the sharp angle, the right angle, the blunt angle. These three "qualities" emerge as more or less pure. The right angle, for example, has its "field": an angle of 93° appears typically as a more or less inadequate right angle. Intermediate steps have a characteristic lack of nicety or precision and can easily be seen as deviants from one or another of the original distinct steps; the number of significant steps—initially three—can increase with further experience with the forms, and new (intermediate) distinct steps can develop.

Significant here is that a form which is near a distinct step looks primarily like a "worse" form of the step; the 93° angle is not, above all, *that particular* angle (what a major change of the material would be necessary, to see such a form *as* characteristic in itself!), but is, psychologically, a "poor" right angle. That this is so can be shown clearly in an experiment, which shows the striking regularity of the tendency to the clear form. In tachistoscopic exposures, the subject just sees a right angle, an assimilation to the standard form, even when the stimulus is objectively quite deviant from a right angle. Other results indicate the same thing: with such forms near the particular step, one often gets the impression that the standard form is not quite right, somehow bad, "out of kilter," wrong, without being able to indicate in what direction the error lies.

In general, if one systematically varies materials in a stepwise manner— as in our example, the position of b between a and c—the resulting impressions are not psychologically equivalent, with each step having its own individual characteristics. Rather specific distinct steps occur, each with its range; the series shows discontinuities; intermediate forms typically appear as deviants from the category steps nearest to them. The same is true of the sequence from white to black and especially in the series of chromatic colors.

6. If one views the series of rows in Section 5 successively, one after the other in order, a new factor soon becomes clear: the factor of *stimulus-determined set*. If one begins with A and proceeds successively through G (or inversely from G to A), the original form character (ab/cd/. . . in the former case, bc/de/. . . in the latter), persists, often past the middle of the series,

until finally, often not until the last rows, it "tips over" into the opposite organization. (In experienced subjects, and under good experimental conditions, this tipping over can be a useful quantitative index.) Thus a constellation, row C for example, appears different if preceded by A, B, than if preceded by G, F, E, and D. In short, if such a row is a part of a sequence (in general, part of a whole), the sequence plays a determining role. A constellation which in one sequence appears one way looks specifiably different in a different sequence. In other words, a constellation which, taken by itself, would not give unequivocal results and would be less clear and less distinct achieves a lawfully determined form when placed in a sequence.

This factor of stimulus-determined set is very strong: even constellations which, by themselves, typically result in unequivocal organizations can be turned into a different form by this factor. It should be noted that, in addition to such a successive stimulus-determined set, simultaneous stimulus sets can also operate; and, more generally, certain field conditions play an essential contributory role.

7. If one computes the distances among all dots (relative to every single dot), theoretically Figure 4.1 would result in the following according to the factor of nearness: the dots of the left half of the horizontal line (group A) are in any case closer to the dots of the vertical line (B) than to those of the right half of the horizontal line (C); similarly, the dots of C are geometrically nearer to those of B than those of A. As a rule the result is "a straight line with a vertical standing on it," that is, (AC)B. The theoretical situation is not simple in Figure 4.1; according to the distances among the dots, (AB) and (BC) are equally favored relative to (AC); but in Figure 4.2, without a doubt (BC) is favored, relative to (AC) as well as to (AB); in spite of this, the spontaneous organization is as a rule not A(BC) but (AC)B—horizontal with slanting line.

Similarly favored according to nearness is the organization (BC) in Figure 4.3, yet typically (AB)C occurs—a long slanting line with a short horizontal.

This is stronger and still more distinct in constellations like Figure 4.4. Geometrical consideration of the separate distances among the dots would result, here in (CD) as favored above (BC), (FG), above (EG); yet typically one sees (ABDEGH . . .) and C and F, and not (DC), (FG); a long straight line with short slanting lines.

We could also substitute an objectively continuous line for the dot constellations. This does not alter the theoretical issue (Figure 4.5).

What is involved in these cases? The continuous straight line is favored, the *group with a direction*. But is it just a continuous straight line that is favored in this way? No; one can replace a straight course with many others (Figures 4.6 to 4.11).

Figures 4.6 and 4.7 typically are organized (AC)B, not (AB)C or A(BC); Figure 4.8 is organized (AD)(BC), not (AB)(CD); Figure 4.9 (AC)(BD), not (AB)(CD); Figure 4.10 (AD)(BC), not (AB)(CD); in Figure 4.11, try to see the organization (abefik . . .)(cdghjl . . .) as against the natural one (acegij . . .) (bdfhk . . .)!

One might think that angle relations at the critical place of crossing are all that is involved: 180° is more favorable than an acute or obtuse angle; certainly

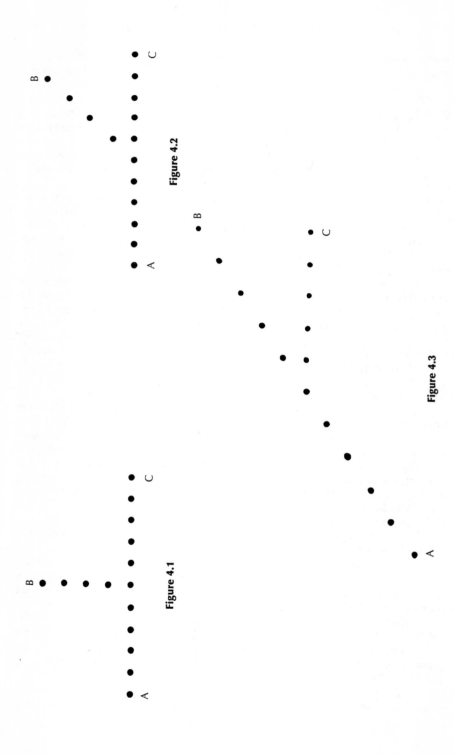

Figure 4.1

Figure 4.2

Figure 4.3

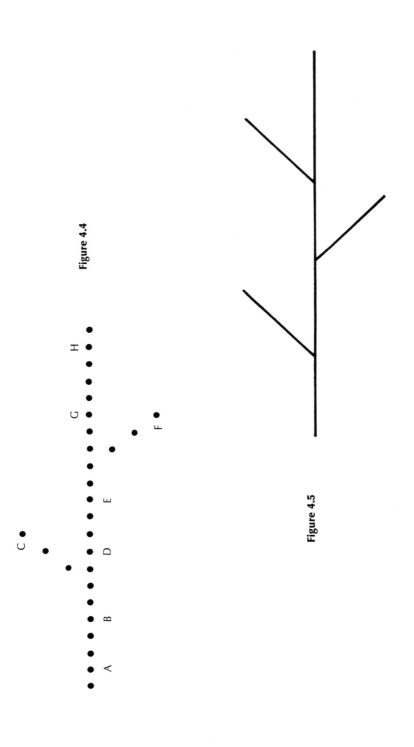

Figure 4.4

Figure 4.5

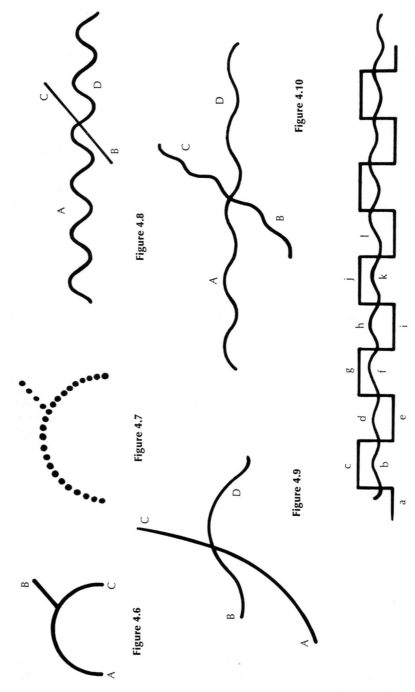

Figure 4.6

Figure 4.7

Figure 4.8

Figure 4.9

Figure 4.10

Figure 4.11

such an "angle" often appears as an inhomogeneity in the course of the line, but this factor also still misses the essential point, as the following figures indicate (Figures 4.12 to 4.15):

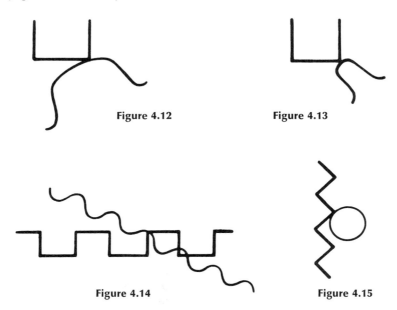

Figure 4.12   Figure 4.13

Figure 4.14   Figure 4.15

All kinds of experimental possibilities arise here; one could systematically vary the parts of such figures and see under what conditions one organization occurs, under what conditions another. In such variations, certain cases stand out as distinctive steps which are especially clear; there are other, intermediate cases which produce less clearcut results. For example (Figures 4.16 to 4.19):

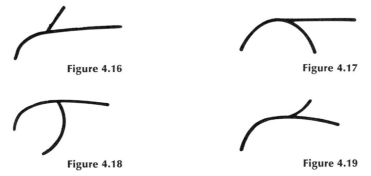

Figure 4.16   Figure 4.17

Figure 4.18   Figure 4.19

In constructing such designs, it soon becomes clear what is involved. One might tentatively formulate it this way: what is crucial is a good continuation, an appropriateness of the curve, an *inner belongingness*, a resulting in a *good whole* or *good configuration* which exhibits its own definite inner requirements.

Clearly this is but a very tentative formulation. As will be seen below, several techniques are available for increasing the precision of this statement so that it comes closer to a truly scientific form. I might remark at this juncture that this principle does not imply a mathematical "simplicity" in every sense of the term; it does not include just any arbitrary piecemeal regularity. The mathematical formula defining the figure can be quite complex; it is much less a matter of the simplicity of the smallest parts than of a simplicity relative to the larger parts (subwholes), in relation to the qualities of the whole. Such qualities of wholes play an extremely significant role here, characteristics like closure, symmetry, and inner balance. Further study is necessary to increase the precision of these formulations; it is clear that certain purely mathematical problems must be considered, especially the problem of characteristics of the whole as against mere piecemeal regularity.

The following cases illustrate a further factor, that of closure (Figures 4.20 to 4.22):

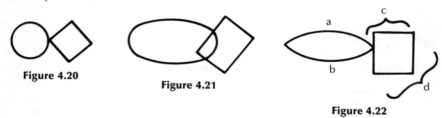

Figure 4.20

Figure 4.21

Figure 4.22

Given A, B, C, D, if AB/CD provide two closed processes and AC/BD two open ones, AB/CD is favored. As further examples (Figures 4.23 and 4.24):

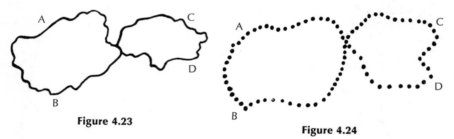

Figure 4.23

Figure 4.24

This factor of closure can be isolated from that of the good curve or of the good whole. Figures 25 and 26 are each typically not seen as three closed forms, but rather are determined by the factor of the good curve; the factor of the good curve wins over that of closure. This victory is still more decisive if the lines and curves are continued beyond the places where they meet one another at the ends (Figures 4.25 and 4.26):

Figure 4.25

Figure 4.26

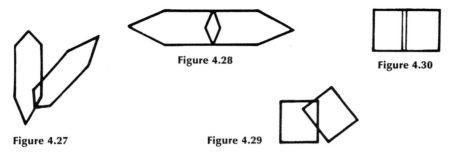

Figure 4.28

Figure 4.30

Figure 4.27   Figure 4.29

It is instructive to try to determine, in this connection, which constellations of two-line figures produce an impression of the duality of the figures, which do not, and which result typically in something entirely different, a kind of new unity. Comparing Figure 4.27 with Figure 4.28, and Figure 4.29 with Figure 4.30 clearly shows the tendency to the good whole configuration.

The following provides further examples of this tendency; in general, it is instructive to determine what additions are capable of altering the configuration. It soon becomes clear that the way to achieve such alterations is to complete subparts of the figure into good subwholes, preferably using a structurally contrary, poor division of the subparts. And this is central, for other additions (whether, in a piecemeal sense, quantitatively larger or smaller) do not have this consequence. A part (Figure 4.31) appears different (in Figures 4.32 to 4.36) when it is included in one constellation than when it is included

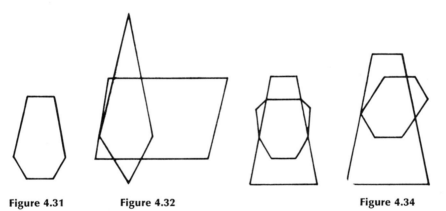

Figure 4.31   Figure 4.32   Figure 4.34

in a different one. Subjected to this technique, a person, thoroughly familiar with a given constellation presented alone, can be made quite blind to it. This implies consequences for recognition and for perception in general.

One might object that what has been meant by "good curve" in the last paragraphs could be readily apparent in the relations among the separate pieces ("elements") of the constellation. But this is not the case; variations quickly show that the exact position of individual dots or points is not essential. The sweeping course of events, characteristics of the constellation seen from above,

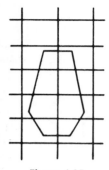

Figure 4.35

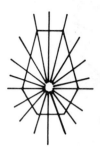

Figure 4.36

from the whole, main directionalities, characteristics of the whole, are crucial—even when the details, the form of the lowest parts is irregular and haphazard.

8. A further factor which produces certain integrations and divisions is *habit*, or *experience*. The principle, in simplest formulation, states that if AB is habitual, and C is habitual, but BC is not (perhaps due to still other associations such as names), or, again, if AB/C fits with past experience but A/BC does not, there is a tendency, given ABC, to see AB/C, the frequently repeated, learned, trained arrangement. It is characteristic of this principle that, in contrast to the principles in the preceding paragraphs, there is no involvement of the contents of the constellation, of their relations, of their characteristics. The resulting organization depends principally only on external extrinsic, arbitrary habit or drill.

For example, Figure 4.37 will not be organized as in Figure 4.38, but as *jump*. 314 cm is organized abc/de, not ab/cde or abcd/e; that is, 314 cm, not 31/4 cm or 314 c/m.

jump

Figure 4.37

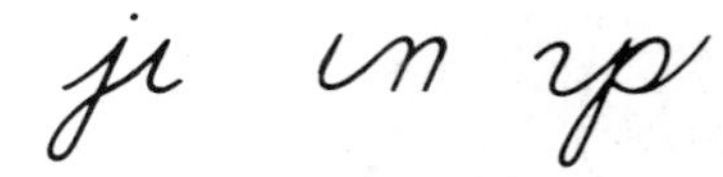

ju un zp

Figure 4.38

Doubtless this happens; to a great extent (how great, is an interesting question), arbitrary materials can be organized in arbitrary ways through a sufficient amount of drill. Whether, even in these cases, the process actually is simply due to arbitrary things happening to have occurred together or to have been seen together is still a question. Some scientists, with very strong theoretical orientations, will be inclined to view all the preceding, and especially the material in Section 7, as simply due to a factor of "past experience," and think they have solved all of the problems by the glib use of this magic word.

One might say, for instance: Are not organizations to which we have become accustomed the ones that are favored? Are not the straight line, the right angle, the smooth curve, the square, all familiar from past experience? Are we not accustomed to seeing divisions between units? Consider that words in print are close together, while there are spaces between words, thousands of trials in one's past experience. Does not past experience drill into us to see equal colored areas as belonging together?

All of this sounds, on the surface, quite obvious. But it by no means solves the problems. It is the duty of the doctrine of past experience to demonstrate concretely for each of these cases and for each of the factors the actual past experiences and times of drill that are involved. It must be shown concretely that the less appropriate organizations actually had not been previously experienced or had been experienced less frequently, and that for the acquisition of experience the assumed "arbitrariness" is actually valid. As soon as one examines this problem seriously, it becomes clear that it is nowhere near as simple and smooth as the answer first seems to suggest. This is even true in areas which at first seem quite clear—to mention but one example: the right angle. Does not the child, in thousands of instances, experience it—think but of tables, cupboards, windows, corners of rooms, houses? This seems self-evident; and yet, is the child's environment filled only with such man-made objects? Are there not in nature many—and very different—other "angles," in tree branches for example, which certainly are very frequent in one's experience (and these relative frequencies would of course have to be quantitatively estimated)? But still more important: is it really true that, in the sense of piecemeal experience, the cupboards, table, etc. present thousands of right angles to the child? In terms of retinal stimulation, no. Only in the extremely rare case of a direct frontal-parallel orientation is there a right angle on the retina. In the remaining, far more frequent cases, when the child looks at the table or the cupboard, the stimulus-experience is not that of a right angle at all. If one does not want to consider the literal stimulus situations, but phenomenal percepts, the problem simply repeats itself.

But whether or not one views the factors as somehow based on experience, the question still remains: in these factors, *are there or are there not some basic regularities, some basic principles? And if there are, what are they?* Precisely what are these principles, these regularities? These are the research problems that cannot be solved through the word "experience." As an example, take a case where, on the basis of past experience, we would see abc and def; placing these together, into abcdef, do we *always* see abc/def? To make this concrete, I will choose an area in which we have a tremendous amount of past experience (Figure 4.39).

This is nothing but a familiar M and a familiar W placed together; yet typically it is seen as a quite unfamiliar form: a curved unit between two symmetrical curves on the right and left. If the W is composed of parts abc and the M of def, one typically sees not abc/def but ad/be/cf, with /be/ between /ad/ and /cf/. Or, further, Figure 4.40 is composed of a "b" and a "q" (or a "d" and a "p"), Figure 4.41 of a written capital L and capital J, Figure 4.42 of p's and q's.

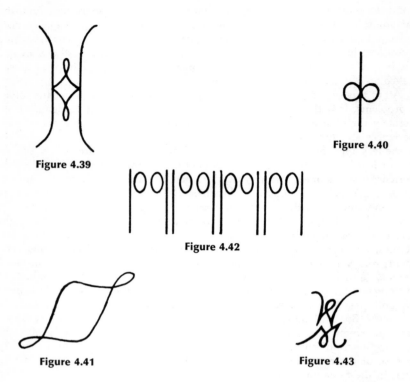

Figure 4.39

Figure 4.40

Figure 4.42

Figure 4.41   Figure 4.43

One might object that in the case of Figure 4.39, we are not familiar with a placement of one above the other, even though we may be familiar with the M and the W separately. But we could place them in the arrangement of Figure 4.43, quite as unfamiliar as the arrangement in Figure 4.39, and yet the M and the W emerge clearly.

9. To summarize, all of these factors and principles point in a single direction: perceptual organization occurs from above to below; the way in which parts are seen, in which subwholes emerge, in which grouping occurs, is not an arbitrary, piecemeal and summation of elements, but is a process in which characteristics of the whole play a major determining role.

Editor's Note: Research on Perceptual Organization

Wertheimer's insightful description of the factors that appear to affect perceptual organization provided the basis for additional empirical research by the Gestalt psychologists themselves and by many independent researchers in the United States.

Wertheimer stressed two important factors of perceptual organization at the outset of his presentation: the factors of proximity or nearness of figural elements, and the similarity of figural elements. From an intellectual point of view, Wertheimer's examples of these factors would tend to convince us of the validity of proximity and similarity as determining sources of influence on the organization of the perceptual field. Questions concerning the interrelation and interaction of these two factors can only be answered, however, in a more experimental manner.

In the perceptual laboratories of Cornell University Julian Hochberg and A. Silverstein developed a method to assess the interaction between factors of proximity and similarity. The primary discussion of their method was presented in the *American Journal of Psychology* in 1956.

A Quantitative Index of Stimulus Similarity: Proximity vs. Difference in Brightness

J. E. Hochberg and A. Silverstein

The problem of defining or measuring "similarity" has long been important in perception, in learning, in thinking, and in concept formation. The operational indexing of similarity has been attempted in the fields of human learning and performance, verbal meaning, and discriminative learning of animals. In perception, however, little has been done. A method of indexing is reported here, with a brief consideration of its limitations and difficulties.

A score for stimulus-similarity is obtained along one restricted dimension by setting the "organizational" effects of similarity into conflict with those of stimulus-proximity; proximity being directly measurable. Consider a matrix of black dots on a white background, with the distances a between rows, b between columns 1 and 2, 3 and 4, 5 and 6, and c between columns 2 and 3, 4 and 5. If $a = b = c$, the dots are equidistant horizontally and vertically. Except for "space errors" or visual anisotropy, the dots should not be organized into vertical arrays (columns) any more than into horizontal arrays (rows). If we hold a constant and decrease the ratio b/c (move columns 1 and 2, 3 and 4, 5 and 6 closer together, columns 2 and 3, 4 and 5 further apart), beyond some transitional point, the subjects will see the dots arranged in vertical double-column arrays (1 and 2, 3 and 4, 5 and 6), by the operation of the 'law of proximity.' There will in general be a threshold-ratio for this perceptual transition, $b/c = L_o$. Let us assume that the strength of this factor toward vertical organization, for any ratio L_i, is some function, s, of the difference $L_i - L_o$, that is, $s(L_o - L_i)$.

If we now so change the matrix of dots that the alternate rows, a_1, a_3, a_5, differ along some dimension, relevant to perceptual organization, from the intervening rows, a_2, a_4, a_6, it is no longer the case that the subjects should be as likely to see vertical as horizontal arrays at the previous transitional point: the difference (or departure from similarity) between rows $a_{1,3,5}$ and $a_{2,4,6}$ should, as it increases past come threshold value D_o, generate horizontal single-row arrays, $a_{1 \ldots 6}$, by the operation of the "law of similarity." Let us assume that the strength of this factor toward horizontal organization, for any stimulus-difference, D_i, is some function k of the magnitude of the difference $D_i - D_o$, i.e. $k(D_i - D_o)$.

Thus, with $b/c = L$, but at some $D_i > D_o$, the subjects should no longer report the transition to vertical organization; instead, the ratio b/c would have to be reduced further, to some value L_i such that $s(L_o - L_i) > k(D_i - D_o)$. As we decrease the similarity between alternate rows, we must therefore increase the factor of proximity in order to shift perceptual organization from horizontal to vertical arrays, and proximity can therefore be used to measure at least certain aspects of similarity.

Procedure

To test this hypothesis, the following apparatus was constructed (Figure 4.44): an upright white card (12 inches long $\times$ 10⅝ inches high) bore alternate

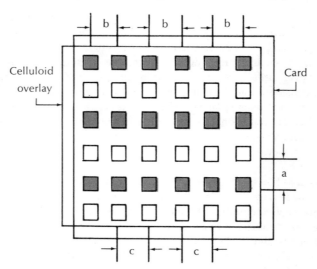

Figure 4.44: Apparatus used to vary the arrays.

columns 1, 3, and 5, 42 mm apart horizontally, each composed of squares (6 mm square) of black (Hering gray paper No. 48) alternating, one beneath the other, 18 mm apart vertically, with squares of gray (in Condition 1, No. 17; in Condition 2, No. 6), for a total height of eight squares in all. Identical intervening columns 2, 4, and 6 are so placed on transparent celluloid overlays atop the card that the ratio b/c, between these columns and those (1, 3, and 5) on the card, can be varied. For each of the two degrees of dissimilarity between dots (Condition 1: black, No. 48 vs. gray, No. 17; Condition 2: black, No. 48 vs. gray, No. 6; conditions presented in balanced order), eleven subjects using a reduction screen found the transitional points by the method of adjustment (10 points in each condition, 5 in each direction) between horizontal and not-horizontal arrays (L_h) and between vertical and not-vertical arrays (L_v). The results appear in Table 4.1.

Results

The results indicate clearly that the use of proximity to score some aspect of similarity (or dissimilarity), along the dimension of brightness, is possible. Certain limitations should, however, be pointed out:

(1) This technique can index similarity along only those dimensions which will affect perceptual grouping (and thereby discover which stimulus-dimensions are involved in this kind of perceptual organization).

(2) Although there is obviously at least gross ordinal agreement with a jnd index of similarity for the values tested (the Hering Gray numbers), we do not know the relationship between the present index and other possible indices.

(3) In some cases, an additive approach to interacting variables, such as simultaneous contrast, will probably not work: for example, if we were to attempt to scale similarity of form by this method, differential 'good continuation' between adjacent shapes, and over-all patterning, would probably prove completely inextricable.

Despite these limitations, the technique may prove a useful one for direct application, as employed here. Perhaps more fruitfully, it can provide a quantitative baseline against which the broadest range of stimuli may be scaled indirectly by providing anchorage points for the more flexible 'esthetic methods' of ranking, e.g., triads.

Editor's Note: Figural "Goodness"

Wertheimer described several determinants of perceptual organization that have been shown experimentally to influence the perception of figures in a field. The underlying force which the Gestalt psychologists believed responsible for figural perception was described as a tendency to organize the field into units which caused a minimum of stress. That is to say, the elements of a figure were perceived to belong together as a result of a force set up

Table 4.1

Subjects	Condition 1		Condition 2		Differences I_h Cond. 2 − Cond. 1	I_v Cond. 2 − Cond. 1
	L_h	L_v	L_h	L_v		
1	4.2	3.3	4.9	4.2	0.7	0.9
2	8.8	6.2	12.1	6.9	3.3	0.7
3	2.4	0.6	3.7	2.6	1.3	2.0
4	3.2	0.4	4.8	2.4	1.6	2.0
5	3.8	0.0	4.3	1.3	0.5	1.3
6	4.4	4.1	5.2	6.8	0.8	2.7
7	2.8	0.2	8.5	1.4	5.7	1.2
8	1.4	1.3	3.8	1.7	2.4	0.4
9	4.6	−0.4	11.1	1.0	6.5	1.4
10	1.6	0.8	2.5	1.4	0.9	0.6
11	7.1	−0.7	10.0	0.3	2.9	1.0
				Mdiff.	2.42	1.29
				t	3.98	5.86

between such elements. Identifying the nature of this force proved, however, to be a problem. Koffka (1935), one of the leading proponents of the Gestalt school, deemed this force "goodness." In his words, the perceptual "organization will always be as 'good' as the prevailing conditions allow" (page 110). But what did Koffka mean by "good"? Although this question has remained unanswered for a number of years there have been several attempts to develop more quantitative descriptions of figural goodness. Rather than rely on such a subjective concept as "goodness," later experimenters have sought a more objective means of describing the forces operating upon the organization of the perceptual field.

One such attempt utilizes the principles of *information theory*, which has been developed in the area of communication and has found rather widespread application in the description of diverse psychological processes. Information theory deals with the coding of information to be transmitted from a stimulus source (output) to a responding organism (input) and the subsequent encoding of the information by the responding organism.

Perception can be considered a process enabling the responding organism to assimilate information about its external or internal world. The information or output of stimulus elements is received and encoded or organized by the responding organism. Fred Attneave of the University of Oregon has outlined this information theory approach and has presented several examples of its application to the problems of perceptual organization. His paper, which follows, was first published in the *Psychological Review* in 1954.

Some Informative Aspects
of Visual Perception

Fred Attneave

The ideas of information theory are at present stimulating many different areas of psychological inquiry. In providing techniques for quantifying situations which have hitherto been difficult or impossible to quantify, they suggest new and more precise ways of conceptualizing these situations. Events ordered in time are particularly amenable to informational analysis; thus language sequences are being extensively studied, and other sequences, such as those of music, plainly invite research.

In this paper I shall indicate some of the ways in which the concepts and techniques of information theory may clarify our understanding of visual perception. When we begin to consider perception as an information-handling process, it quickly becomes clear that much of the information received by any higher organism is *redundant*. Sensory events are highly interdependent in both space and time: if we know at a given moment the states of a limited number of receptors (i.e., whether they are firing or not firing), we can make better-than-chance inferences with respect to the prior and subsequent states of these receptors. The preceding statement, taken in its broadest implications, is precisely equivalent to an assertion that the world as we know it is lawful. In the present discussion, however, we shall restrict our attention to special types of lawfulness which may exist in space at a fixed time, and which seem particularly relevant to processes of visual perception.

The Nature of Redundancy in Visual Stimulation:
a Demonstration

Consider the very simple situation presented in Figure 4.45. With a modicum of effort, the reader may be able to see this as an ink bottle on the corner of a desk. Let us suppose that the background is a uniformly white wall, that the desk is a uniform brown, and that the bottle is completely black. The visual stimulation from these objects is highly redundant in the sense that portions of the field are highly predictable from other portions. In order to demonstrate this fact and its perceptual significance, we may employ a variant of the "guessing game" technique with which Shannon (1951) has studied the redundancy of printed English. We may divide the picture into arbitrarily small elements which we "transmit" to a subject in a cumulative sequence, having him guess at the color of each successive element until he is correct. This method of analysis resembles the scanning process used in television and facsimile systems, and accomplishes the like purpose of transforming two

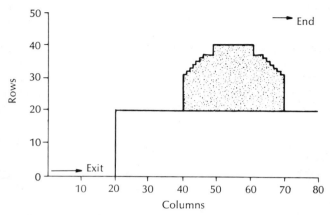

Figure 4.45:   Illustration of redundant visual stimulation.

spatial dimensions into a single sequence in time. We are in no way supposing or assuming, however, that perception normally involves any such scanning process. If the picture is divided into 50 rows and 80 columns, as indicated, our subject will guess at each of 4,000 cells as many times as necessary to determine which of the three colors it has. If his error score is significantly less than chance $\frac{2}{3} \times 4,000 + \frac{1}{2}(\frac{2}{3} \times 4,000) = 4,000$, it is evident that the picture is to some degree redundant. Actually, he may be expected to guess his way through the figure with only fifteen or twenty errors. It is fairly apparent that the technique described, in its present form, is limited in applicability to simple and somewhat contrived situations. With suitable modification it may have general usefulness as a research tool, but it is introduced into the present paper for demonstrational purposes only.

Let us follow a hypothetical subject through this procedure in some detail, noting carefully the places where he is most likely to make errors, since these are the places in which information is concentrated. To begin, we give him an 80 × 50 sheet of graph paper, telling him that he is to guess whether each cell is white, black, or brown, starting in the lower left corner and proceeding across the first row, then across the second, and so on to the last cell in the upper right corner. Whenever he makes an error, he is allowed to guess a second and, if necessary, a third time until he is correct. He keeps a record of the cells he has been over by filling in black and brown ones with pencil marks of appropriate color, leaving white ones blank.

After a few errors at the beginning of the first row, he will discover that the next cell is "always" white, and predict accordingly. This prediction will be correct as far as Column 20, but on 21 it will be wrong. After a few more errors he will learn that "brown" is his best prediction, as in fact it is to the end of the row. Chances are good that the subject will assume the second row to be exactly like the first, in which case he will guess it with no errors; otherwise he may make an error or two at the beginning, or at the edge of the "table," as before. He is almost certain to be entirely correct on Row 3, and on subsequent rows through 20. On Row 21, however, it is equally certain that he will erroneously predict a transition from white to brown on Column 21, where the *corner* of the table is passed. Our subject's behavior to this point demonstrates two principles which may be discussed before we follow him through the remainder of his predictions. It is evident that redundant visual stimulation results from either (a) an area of homogeneous color ("color" is used in the broad sense here, and includes brightness), or (b) a contour of homogeneous direction or slope. In other words, information is concentrated along contours (i.e., regions where color changes abruptly), and is further concentrated at those points on a contour at which its direction changes most rapidly (i.e., at angles or peaks of curvature).

Evidence from other and entirely different situations supports both of these inferences. The concentration of information in contours is illustrated by the remarkably similar appearance of objects alike in contour and different otherwise. The "same" triangle, for example, may be either white on black or green on white. Even more impressive is the familiar fact that an artist's sketch, in which lines are substituted for sharp color gradients, may constitute a readily identifiable representation of a person or thing.

An experiment relevant to the second principle, i.e., that information is further concentrated at points where a contour changes direction most rapidly, may be summarized briefly. Eighty subjects were instructed to draw, for each of sixteen outline shapes, a pattern of ten dots which would resemble the shape as closely as possible, and then to indicate on the original outline the exact places which the dots represented. A good sample of the results is shown in

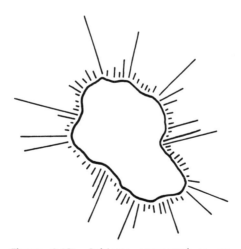

Figure 4.46: Subjects attempted to approximate the closed figure shown above with a pattern of ten dots. Radiating bars indicate the relative frequency with which various portions of the outline were represented by dots chosen.

Figure 4.46: radial bars indicate the relative frequency with which dots were placed on each of the segments into which the contour was divided for scoring purposes. It is clear that the subjects show a great deal of agreement in their abstractions of points best representing the shape, and most of these points are taken from regions where the contour is most different from a straight line. This conclusion is verified by detailed comparisons of dot frequencies with measured curvatures on both the figure shown and others.

Common objects may be represented with great economy, and fairly striking fidelity, by copying the points at which their contours change direction maximally, and then connecting these points appropriately with a straightedge. Figure 4.47 was drawn by applying this technique, as mechanically as possible, to a real sleeping cat. The informational content of a drawing like this may be considered to consist of two components: one describing the positions of the points, the other indicating which points are connected with which others. The first of these components will almost always contain more information than the second, but its exact share will depend upon the precision with which positions are designated, and will further vary from object to object.

Let us now return to the hypothetical subject whom we left between the corner of the table and the ink bottle in Figure 4.45. His errors will follow the principles we have just been discussing until he reaches the serrated shoulders of the bottle. (A straight 45° line would be represented in this way because of the grain of the coordinate system, but we shall consider that the bottle is actually serrated, as it is from the subject's point of view.) On the left shoulder there are thirteen right angles, but these angles contain considerably less than thirteen times the information of an angle in isolation like the corner of the table. This is true because they fall into a pattern which is repetitive, or redundant in the everyday sense of the term. They will cease to evoke errors as soon as the subject perceives their regularity and extrapolates it. This extrapolation, precisely like the subject's previous extrapolations of color and slope, will have validity only over a limited range and will itself lead to error on Row 38, Column 48.

At about the same time that he discovers the regularity of the stair-step pattern (or perhaps a little before), our subject will also perceive that the ink bottle is symmetrical, i.e., that the right contour is predictable from the left one by means of a simple reversal. As a result he is very unlikely to make any further errors on the right side above Row 32 or 33. Symmetry, then, constitutes another form of redundancy.

It should be fairly evident by now that many of the Gestalt principles of perceptual organization pertain essentially to information distribution. The *good Gestalt* is a figure with some high degree of internal redundancy. That the grouping laws of *similarity, good continuation,* and *common fate* all refer to conditions which reduce uncertainty is clear enough after the preceding discussion and we shall presently see that *proximity* may be conceptualized in a like manner. It is not surprising that the perceptual machinery should "group" those portions of its input which share the same information: any system handling redundant information in an efficient manner would necessarily do something of the sort. Musatti (1938) came very close to the present point

Figure 4.47: Drawing made by abstracting thirty-eight points of maximum curvature from the contours of a sleeping cat and connecting these points appropriately with a straightedge.

when he suggested that a single principle of homogeneity might subsume Wertheimer's laws of special cases. All of our hypothetical subjects extrapolations have involved some variety of homogeneity (or invariance), either of color, of slope, or of pattern.

The kinds of extrapolation that have been discussed certainly do not exhaust the repertory of the human observer. For example, if the brightness of a surface were changed at a constant rate along some spatial extent, an observer could probably extrapolate this change with a fair degree of accuracy (given an appropriate response medium, such as choosing from a set of Munsell color patches). Likewise, we may reasonably suppose that a contour, the direction of which changes at a constant rate (i.e., the arc of a circle), could be extrapolated. Any sort of physical invariance whatsoever constitutes a source of redundancy for an organism capable of abstracting the invariance and utilizing it appropriately, but we actually know very little about the limits of the human perceptual machinery with respect to such abilities. A group of psychophysical studies determining the accuracy with which observers are able to extrapolate certain discrete and continuous functions of varying complexity must be carried out before we can usefully discuss any but the simplest cases.

A troublesome question arises in this connection: where does perception leave off and inductive reasoning begin? The abstraction of simple homogeneities from a visual field does not appear to be different, in its formal aspects, from the induction of a highly general scientific law from a mass of experimental data. Certain subjective differences are obvious enough: thus reasoning seems to involve conscious effort, whereas perception seems to involve a set of processes whereby information is *predigested* before it ever reaches awareness. When extrapolations are required of a subject in an experimental situation, however, it is difficult or impossible for the experimenter to be certain whether the subject is responding on an "intuitive" or a "deliberative" basis. I do not know any general solution to this problem, and can only suggest that a limited control may be exercised by way of the establishment of a desired set in the subject.

The Abstraction of Statistical Parameters

Although Figure 4.45 presents a situation much simpler, or more redundant, than the visual situations which ordinarily confront us, the reader need merely look around the room in which he is sitting to find that the principles illustrated apply to the real world. Further, it may be argued on neurological grounds that the human brain could not possibly utilize all the information provided by states of stimulation which were not highly redundant. According to Polyak's (1941) estimate, the retina contains not less than four million cones. At any given instant each of these cones may be in either of two states: firing or not firing. Thus the retina as a whole might be in any one of about $2^{4,000,000}$ or $10^{1,200,000}$ states, each representing a different configuration of visual stimulation. Now, if by some unspecified mechanism each of these states were to evoke a different unitary response, and if a unitary response consists merely of the firing of a single unique neuron, then $10^{1,200,000}$ of such response-neurons would be required. The fantastic magnitude of this figure becomes somewhat apparent when one calculates that only about 10^{54} neurons could be packed into a cubic light year. The fact that the number of *patterns* of response-neurons might plausibly equal the number of retinal configurations simplifies matters only if there are certain one-to-one connections between cones and response-neurons, in which case the response is to some degree merely a copy of the stimulus.

We may nevertheless ask: how *would* an observer respond to a situation in which the retinal receptors were stimulated quite independently of one another? This situation would be in practice very difficult to achieve (even more difficult than its diametric opposite, the *Ganzfeld*), particularly if we demanded that the stimulation at a given moment (which might be supposed to have a duration of about 100 msec (see Attneave and McReynolds, 1950) be entirely independent of the stimulation at any other moment. In an effort to get some notion of what such a random field would be like, Figure 4.48 was constructed. Each of the $140^2 = 19,600$ small cells of the figure was either filled or not filled according to the value of a number obtained from a conversion of Snedecor's (1946) table of random numbers from decimal to binary. If the figure is viewed from a distance such that the angle subtended by a cell is of the order of the "minimum separable" (about 1′), it illustrates roughly how a small portion of the random field suggested above might look at some particular instant. Perhaps the most striking thing about the figure is the subjective impression of *homogeneity* that it gives: the left half of the figure seems, at least in a general way, very much like the right half. This is remarkable because we have previously associated homogeneity with redundancy, and Figure 4.48 was constructed to be completely nonredundant. Now, in psychological terms, it is fairly clear that the characteristic with respect to which the figure appears homogeneous is what Gibson (1950) would call its *texture*. In physical terms, two invariant factors may be specified: (a) the probability (0.50) that any cell will be black rather than white, and (b) the size of cells. Both of these factors probably contribute to perceived texture, which is un-

Figure 4.48: A "random field" consisting of 19,600 cells. The state of each cell (black versus white) was determined independently with a p of 0.50.

doubtedly a multidimensional variable, though the latter may be somewhat the more important. If the figure is viewed from a sufficient distance, these two parameters become identifiable with (a) the central tendency, and (b) the dispersion, of a continuous brightness distribution in two dimensions.

It appears, then, that when some portion of the visual field contains a quantity of information grossly in excess of the observer's perceptual capacity, he treats those components of information which do not have redundant representation somewhat as a statistician treats "error variance," averaging out particulars and abstracting certain statistical homogeneities. Such an averaging process was involved in drawing the cat for Figure 4.47. It was said earlier that the points of the drawing corresponded to places of maximum curvature on the contour of the cat, but this was not strictly correct; if the principle had been followed rigidly, it would have been necessary to represent the ends of individual hairs by points. In observing a cat, however, one does not ordinarily perceive its hairs as individual entities; instead one perceives that the cat is *furry*. Furriness is a kind of texture; the statistical parameters which characterize it presumably involve averages of shape and direction, as well as size, of elements. The perceived contour of a cat (the contour from which the points of Figure 4.47 were taken) is the result of an orthogonal averaging process in which texture is eliminated or smoothed out almost entirely, somewhat as if a photograph of the object were blurred and then printed on high-contrast paper.

The sense in which a surface of a particular texture may be said to provide redundant stimulation has perhaps been adequately indicated. This sort of redundancy might be demonstrated by the guessing-game technique, with a suitable modification in the level of prediction required, i.e., by increasing the unit area to be predicted and requiring the subject to select from a multi-dimensional array of samples the texture (i.e., the statistical parameters) which he believes the next unit will have. In view of Gibson's (1950) convincing argument that a physical edge, or contour, is as likely to be represented in vision by an abrupt texture change as by an abrupt color change, I have considered it important to show how texture may be substituted for color without materially altering the principles derived from Figure 4.45.

Perception as Economical Description

It is sometimes said that the objective of science is to describe nature economically. We have reason to believe, however, that some such process of parsimonious description has its beginnings on a fairly naive perceptual level, in scientists and their fellow organisms alike; thus the difficulty, mentioned earlier, of distinguishing between perception and inductive reasoning. It appears likely that a major function of the perceptual machinery is to strip away some of the redundancy of stimulation, to describe or encode incoming information in a form more economical than that in which it impinges on the receptors.

If this point of view is sound, we should be able to generate plausible hypotheses as to the nature of specific perceptual processes by considering rational operations which one might deliberately employ to reduce redundancy. The approach suggested, as it applies to the perception of a static visual field, is equivalent to that of a communications engineer who wishes to design a system for transmitting pictures of real things over a practically noise-free channel with the utmost economy of channel time and band width, but in a manner designed to meet standards such as human observers are likely to have. Some of the reduction principles which he might usefully employ in such a system are listed below. It will be found that these principles serve to summarize and integrate ideas which have been developed somewhat informally in the foregoing sections, as well as to introduce new considerations. The principles may be grouped according to the forms of redundancy with which they are concerned: thus 1–4 deal with varieties of continuous regularity; 5 and 6 with discontinuous regularity, or recurrence; 7–9 with proximity; and 10 with situations involving interaction.

1. An area of homogeneous color may be described by specifying the color and the boundaries of the area over which it is homogeneous. (It is assumed that limits of error tolerance on relevant dimensions have been agreed upon, e.g., that there is some definite number of colors from which the receiving mechanism may be directed to choose.)

2. Likewise, an area of homogeneous texture may be described by specifying the statistical parameters which characterize the texture and the boundaries of the area over which these parameters are relatively invariant. Thus, if

Figure 4.48 represented a part of the upholstery of a sofa, it would probably be satisfactory simply to instruct the receiving mechanism to reproduce the texture by filling in cells of a certain size from any table of random numbers. It is true that this process would result in the complete loss of 19,600 bits of information; the essential point is that we are dealing here with a class of stimuli from which such a huge information loss is perceptually tolerable.

3. An area over which either color or texture varies according to some regular function may be described by specifying the function and the boundaries of the area over which it obtains (cf. Gibson's [1950] *texture gradient*). This principle actually implies both 1 and 2 as special cases.

4. Likewise, if some segment of an area boundary (contour) either maintains a constant direction or varies according to some other regular function, it may be described by specifying the function and the loci of its limiting points. Figure 4.47 illustrates a special case of this principle.

5. If two or more identical stimulus patterns (these might be either successive portions of a contour, or separate and discrete objects) appear at different places in the same field, all may be described by describing one and specifying the positions of the others and the fact that they are identical (compare *similarity* as a grouping law).

6. If two or more patterns are similar but not identical, it may be economical to proceed as in 5, in addition specifying either (a) how subsequent patterns differ from the first, or else (b) how each pattern differs from some skeleton pattern which includes the connumalities of the group (cf. the "schema-with-correction" idea discussed by Woodworth [1938]; also Hebb's [1949] treatment of perceptual schemata).

7. When the spatial loci of a number of points are to be described in some arbitrary order, and the points are arranged in clusters or proximity groups (as in Figure 4.49), it may be economical to describe the points of each group with respect to some local origin (0′ or 0″), transmitting as a separate component the positions of the local origins with respect either to each other or to some arbitrary origin, whichever is required. Since the points occupy a smaller range of alternative coordinates on the local axes than on arbitrary axes, less information is required for their specification. If the amount of information thus saved is greater than the amount needed to specify the positions of the local origins, a net saving will result. What is redundant in the present case is the *approximate location* of points in a cluster: this component is isolated out when a local origin is described (cf. the concepts of "within" and "between" variance). The local origin principle may also be used in conjunction with some regular scanning procedure if the order in which the points are to be specified is not predetermined (but see also 9, below). The relevance of these considerations to *proximity* as a perceptual grouping law is evident.

8. The preceding principle may be generalized to apply to dimensions other than spatial ones; e.g., brightness, coarseness of texture, etc. A "local origin" on such a continuum would appear to have essentially the characteristics of Helson's (1947) *adaptation-level*, in terms of which constancy phenomena and a variety of other psychophysical findings may be accounted for. This generalized principle is closely similar to 6 above, the chief difference

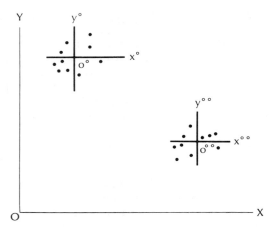

Figure 4.49: A functional aspect of proximity grouping is illustrated. The loci of clustered points may be described with choices from a smaller set of numbers if local origins are used.

being that 6 is applicable to combinations of discrete variables, or to situations of ambiguous dimensional organization.

9. If the loci of a number of points are to be described, and the order in which they are taken is immaterial, they may be arranged in a sequence such that the distances between adjacent points are minimized, and transmitted with each point serving as origin for the one following it. This procedure will result in some saving if the points are clustered, as in Figure 4.49, but it is most clearly applicable when the points are "strung-out" in some obvious sequence. In the latter case, a further economy may be achieved by the use of special coordinates such as distance from a line passing through the two preceding points (or from an arc through the three preceding points, etc.; cf. 4 above).

10. Certain areas and objects may be described in a relatively simple way, by procedures of the sort suggested above, if they are first subjected to some systematic distortion or transformation. Consider the case of a complex, symmetrical, two-dimensional pattern viewed from an angle such that its retinal or photographic image is not symmetrical. It will be economical to transmit a description of the pattern as if it were in the frontal plane, and thus symmetrical (eliminating the redundancy of symmetry by means of 6a), together with a description of the transformation which relates the frontal aspect described to the oblique aspect in which the pattern is viewed. Koffka (1935) and other Gestalt psychologists have held that many objects have some "preferred" aspect, and that this aspect has the characteristics of a "good Gestalt." The present principle supports this view on functional grounds, since the perceptual transformation of a figure to an aspect in which similarities among parts are maximized may be interpreted as the initial step in an efficient information-digesting process. It should be clearly recognized, however, that an over-all economy is achieved only if the amount of information required to

describe the transformation is less than the amount of information saved by virtue of the transformation; thus a transformation must be relatively simple to be considered useful, at least by the present criterion.

Let me indicate briefly how these considerations may be integrated with others of a more general nature. Interdependencies among sensory events may exist either in space or in time, or they may cut across both space and time. In studying the redundancy of spoken English, for example, one is dealing with interdependencies which may be considered purely temporal. The present discussion has been restricted, quite arbitrarily, to relationships in space: to forms of redundancy and information-distribution which may obtain in the visual field at a particular instant, and which a computer of conceivable complexity might evaluate from a photograph. The extension of the visual field in time, which I propose to discuss in a subsequent paper, introduces new varieties of redundancy involving the temporal continuation or recurrence of spatial configurations which may be nonredundant at any instant considered in isolation. Any individual learns a great deal, over his life-span, about what-goes-with-what. Thus, if an ear is disclosed in a situation like that illustrated by Figure 4.45, the observer can predict that a mouth, nose, eyes, etc. are also present and approximately where they are. This sort of redundancy is spatiotemporal in its basis; predictions are not possible merely on the basis of the present visual field, but depend also upon previous fields which have contained faces. Principle 6 above suggests the approach to economical description which might be extended to such cases. Further, as Brunswik (1947, 1952, 1953) has pointed out in some detail, ecological principles of very broad generality may be derived from experience. For example, the frequency with which an observer has encountered symmetrical objects in his past may certainly affect the point at which, in predicting successive cells of Figure 4.45, he "assumes" that the ink bottle is symmetrical. Likewise in terms of economical encoding: each of the varieties of spatial redundancy suggested above will itself occur with some determinate frequency over any given set of fields (e.g., the set of pictures which a computer-transmitter might have been required to handle over some period of past operation), and a knowledge of this and related frequencies may be used in determining the optimal assignments of actual code symbols. As a result of factors such as these, spatial and spatiotemporal redundancy (or entropy) are difficult to separate empirically, but the distinction remains a conceptually convenient one.

The foregoing reduction principles make no pretense to exhaustiveness. It should be emphasized that there are as many kinds of redundancy in the visual field as there are kinds of regularity or lawfulness; an attempt to consider them all would be somewhat presumptuous on one hand, and almost certainly irrelevant to perceptual processes on the other. It may further be admitted that the principles which have been given are themselves highly redundant in the sense that they could be stated much more economically on a higher level of abstraction. This logical redundancy is not inadvertent, however: if one were faced with the engineering problem suggested earlier, he would undoubtedly find it necessary to break the problem down in some manner such as the foregoing, and to design a multiplicity of mechanisms to perform operations of the sort indicated (some principles, e.g., 6, would require further breakdown for this purpose). Likewise, the principles are frankly intended to suggest operations which the perceptual machinery may actually perform, and accordingly the types of measurement which are likely to prove appropriate in the quantitative psychophysical study of complex perceptual processes.

CHAPTER 5
Space Perception

The external visual world is perceived as having three dimensions: the vertical plane, horizontal plane, and distal plane. External stimuli, then, are perceived as being located at a specific point in space, defined on the basis of these three dimensions.

One can judge the verticality of a pole without great difficulty by utilizing, as his frame of reference, the horizontal and vertical planes of the physical environment in which the pole is located. But the frame of reference is not the only source of information. The position of the observer's body in relation to the gravitational pull of the earth also affects perception: a blind-folded subject, seated in a chair which is tilted to one side, can maneuver the chair, via a controlling mechanism, into an upright position without great difficulty. Obviously, since he cannot see and therefore is unable to use the physical planes, he is relying on a second system—namely, the gravitational pull of the earth.

An assessment of the importance and the relative contributions of each of these two cues of spatial position provides a challenging task for experimental study.

Solomon Asch of Swarthmore College and Herman Witkin of Brooklyn College collaborated in studying the vertical frame of reference (*Journal of Experimental Psychology*, 1948). This publication also elucidates the questions to be queried on the perception of the upright or vertical and provides an excellent discussion of previous research on the topic.

Studies in Space Orientation: Perception of the Upright with Displaced Visual Fields

S. E. Asch and H. A. Witkin

Introduction

The experiments to be reported in the present series of papers are concerned primarily with the process of orientation toward the upright in space.

Our experienced space has the vertical and horizontal directions prominently represented within it. All objects in our surroundings are perceived as having a definite orientation: they are upright, or tilted in varying degree, or horizontal. Further, the perceived direction of an object is usually strongly indicated, and cannot be changed at will. Indeed, in a given field, the direction of an object remains constant when head or body is tilted, and seems generally independent of body position. Perception of the upright is an important function in man; we depend upon it continuously in our practical relations with objects and in our body movements. It is also an extremely broad function, involving the interaction and cooperation of visual, kinesthetic, and labyrinthine experiences.

That orientation has not been explored more intensively despite its fundamental importance seems due to a highly significant characteristic of orientation itself: the perception of the vertical and horizontal is achieved so effortlessly that it fails to become conspicuous. Under ordinary circumstances everyone is able to establish the vertical and the horizontal correctly, quickly and without deliberation. The conditions of orientation are so highly constant that disturbances are hardly ever encountered. They do, however, occur under more unstable conditions, of which the airplane is a notable example. In the plane, disorientation may be so severe that the person can be upside down and perceive himself and the plane as upright, or suddenly see the sky where he believes the earth should be, and so on. Disturbances such as these lead to an appreciation of the marked stability and orderliness which normally characterize our orientation in space, and at the same time point up the need for a closer understanding of this function.

Aside from throwing light on a central psychological function, a study of orientation should contribute toward the clarification of several significant theoretical issues. Because the visual field is involved in orientation in a comprehensive and direct way, it should provide further evidence concerning the role of field factors in perception. More specifically, since orientation involves the employment of a frame of reference in a literal sense, its investigation furnishes an excellent opportunity to establish the role of varied and changing frames of reference. In view of the increasingly significant role of the "frame of reference" as a systematic concept in the most diverse regions of psychology, a further investigation of it in an area where it is perhaps most simply represented should prove fruitful.

Orientation also provides an important instance of perceptual constancy. When, for example, the head is tilted or the person is inclined to one side, a correct perception of the upright is retained. Under these conditions the specific visual stimulation, represented by the angle at which the projected main lines of the field intersect the retinal coordinates, as well as bodily sensations, is markedly changed. This stability in the experience of the upright, despite marked changes in proximal stimulation, indicates the presence of a constancy phenomenon analogous to that found in the perception of size, shape, color, and brightness.

Of unusual interest in the study of orientation is the fact that it involves the manner in which the person relates himself to the world about him. As he perceives the position and direction of other objects, so does each person also perceive his own position and direction. To what extent is the body localized as other objects are and to what extent does its special relation to the subject play a role? The exploration of this question may cast light on the relation of perceptual functions to features of personality organization. It would appear promising to seek such relations first in functions as central and comprehensive as orientation.

The investigations to be reported in this series are concerned with the following questions: How do visual and postural experiences cooperate in orientation, and what are their respective contributions? How do changes in the frame of reference affect the perception of the main directions of space? What conditions are responsible for constancy of the perceived upright, and under what conditions does constancy fail? Are there individual differences in the adequacy of orientation and in mode of orientation? If such differences are present, how consistent are they, and what is their origin? Do they relate to the individual's characteristic way of coping with his surroundings, even possibly in their social aspects? How can the adequacy of orientation be improved?

The first task set for investigation was that of establishing the role and relative importance of the principal sources of orientation, namely, the visual and postural experiences, and of determining the manner in which they interact in perception of the vertical and horizontal. It is therefore necessary to preface our investigations with a brief account of what is at present known about the sensory basis of orientation.

Orientation depends on two major sources of experience, the visual and postural. Through vision we perceive a space which is clearly articulated and which is organized into a framework-like structure, the main axes of which are the horizontal and vertical directions. In addition to this visual basis, there is a fund of information proceeding from the experience of our own bodies. The latter data, which arise in the course of bodily adjustment to the downward pull of gravity, include kinesthetic sensations from muscles, tendons, joints, and viscera, as well as excitations from the labyrinth.

Yet, while orientation depends on these distinct sources of information, we do not have in our experience distinct conceptions of the upright, one visual and the other postural. Our experience of spatial orientation is unitary. The final processes to which both visual and postural factors contribute produce the experience of a single upright. Indeed, there is ordinarily a close coincidence between the two systems: visually upright objects are also gravitationally upright.

This intimate and orderly relation between visual and postural factors creates a difficulty when the object is to establish their respective roles in orientation; for whether a given judgment of the upright is based on visual data or on the felt position of the body, the result is exactly the same. The role of the two systems can be studied only by means of techniques which permit their separation and variations in the relation between them. By tilting the visual field while the body remains upright, visual and postural factors may be separated. Further, by excluding the visual field it becomes possible to observe the characteristics of orientation when based on postural factors alone. Such procedures have been used in prior studies and also will be the basis of the investigations to be reported.

The role of visual and postural factors in orientation has been the object of investigation of systematic theory. Koffka (1935) has presented the view that the main directions of visual space constitute the perceived vertical and horizontal. The visual field, according to Koffka, creates its own framework; the main lines within it assume the function of vertical and horizontal. It would follow that if our visual surroundings were to be tilted, our perceived vertical and horizontal would shift toward the new main directions. We would then perceive the new framework as upright, and the orientation of all objects within it would be perceived in relation to it.

In formulating this view, Koffka based himself on the classical mirror experiment of Wertheimer (1912). In that experiment the subject looked through a tube into a tilted mirror which displaced the image of a room by 45°. By this procedure the visual coordinates were separated from the postural coordinates and displaced by a definite amount. It therefore became possible to determine whether a given judgment of the upright was made in terms of the visual framework, or with reference to the body position, or by a compromise between the two. Wertheimer found that upon first looking into the tilted mirror the subjects perceived the scene as tilted. A bouncing ball was seen to fall at an angle, a person walking across the room appeared to be falling to one side, and so on. However, with continued inspection, the mirror scene came gradually to look upright and everything within it acquired a normal aspect. The interval required for the righting of the scene was believed to be consumed in a gradual "wearing off" of the framework of the outer world. This acceptance of the new framework Wertheimer interpreted as evidence of the importance of visual field factors as against postural factors.

A fundamentally different emphasis concerning the basis of orientation is found in the work of Gibson and Mowrer (1938). While these writers acknowledge the importance of visual factors and their effect upon postural data, they believe that our orientation in space is anchored mainly to postural factors. The latter are decisive in situations of conflict and are genetically primary. Visual stimulation, they assert, cannot be a basis for orientation unless postural orientation is already presupposed. Indeed, they go as far as to claim that the primacy of postural factors is a logical requirement, that the visual framework develops in the context of maintaining the postural equilibrium in response to the pull of gravity.

We cannot here consider the full basis of evidence for the formulation of Gibson and Mowrer. Of more immediate relevance are the observations made by Gibson when he repeated the mirror experiment of Wertheimer with results that he claimed to be different. Gibson's subjects looked through a tube into a tilted mirror, the images of which were displaced approximately 30°. They perceived the tilt from the start and also reported a lessening of the tilt with continued observation. However, the scene did not fully right itself. Only with a special effort could the subjects momentarily feel themselves in the room. Generally, however, they did not feel themselves part of the tilted room, the position of the body remaining "an omnipresent factor in the seeing of the room." In opposition to Wertheimer, Gibson concluded from these observations that judgment of the upright is anchored mainly to the body.

It is clear that in order to establish the respective roles of the visual and postural systems in orientation it is necessary to clarify the apparent contradiction between the reports of Wertheimer and Gibson. This was attempted in the present study, where the mirror experiment was repeated with a large number of subjects and under several different conditions.

Experiment

The top of a 48″ × 40″ mirror was tilted back by 15° from the vertical. The scene which it provided had, therefore, a tilt of 30°, or twice that of the mirror. The result was equivalent to placing the subject in front of a visual field tilted backward by 30°. The subject was brought into the laboratory blindfolded, and placed in a standing position in front of, and slightly to one side of the mirror. A circular cardboard tube, two feet long and nine inches in diameter, through which he was to view the mirror scene, was placed over his face. This tube was tilted downward by approximately 30°, in order to include a view of the floor of the scene, and the farther end of the tube was eight inches from the mirror surface. The subject remained blindfolded for a period of three minutes. Before the blindfold was removed, the experimenter read the following instructions: "When you open your eyes, you will be observing a scene. Try to describe what you see of the room and the objects in it." The subject was not informed that he was facing a mirror and he was not questioned at all about the tilt of the scene until the observation period was over. Upon opening his eyes the subject saw the reflection of a portion of a large laboratory, including tables, chairs and apparatus. A great part of one wall and of the floor of the room, and of the scene outside one of the windows, were also visible. The view excluded the reflection of the subject, the tube and the mirror edge.

After he had described the scene for a period of two minutes, the subject's perceived vertical was measured. For this purpose, a rod two and one-half feet long, pivoted at its center, was used. The stand on which the rod was mounted was placed on a table which was parallel to the visible wall of the scene. The rod was capable of rotation in a plane parallel to this wall—that is, toward the subject or away from him. The rod stood twelve feet to the back and fifteen feet to the left of the subject so that in the mirror it appeared to be in front and to the left of him. Since the plane in which the rod moved was to the left, it was slightly oblique to the subject. There was no difficulty, however, in seeing the plane clearly. A square cardboard mounted on the side of the table toward the subject excluded from view the stand and a protractor fixed to the stand in back of the rod. Before the measurements were taken the experimenter read the following instructions: "You see the rod on the small table. The experimenter is going to move the rod gradually. We want you to tell us when the rod is perfectly upright, that is, when it is parallel to your body. As the experimenter moves the rod, you will say 'now' when it reaches this position. We will take a few measurements."

During the observation period the rod had remained perpendicular to the floor. It was now moved to a near-horizontal position. The experimenter then moved it slowly in steps of 2° until the subject indicated that it had reached the vertical. Four successive measurements of the vertical were taken with the rod returned to a near-horizontal position on each trial. On the first and third trials the rod was moved in a counterclockwise direction from its initial position; on the second and fourth it was moved clockwise.

When the measurements had been taken the subject was told to close his eyes and led to an adjoining room. He was then questioned in detail regarding his observation of the tilt. After this he was returned to the experimental room with eyes open and placed directly in front of the tilted mirror without the tube. It will be noted that the subject was now much nearer to the mirror than in the first test with the tube. From this position the subject saw the reflection of the room in the mirror, but he also saw the mirror, its edges, and his own reflection. He was specifically cautioned to align the rod image with his body and not with the image of his body. Four measurements were taken in the manner described above.

It will be noted that both with and without the tube the instructions explicitly directed the subject to align the rod with the felt position of his body. This was done to insure maximum attention to the body as a basis for judgment. Also, to fail to instruct the subject in this way would have left the task ambiguous.

A word of explanation should be given concerning the readings obtained with the rod. If the subject accepts the tilted mirror scene as upright, in making the rod image upright he will adjust it to the axes of the scene. The rod image will therefore deviate from his body position by 30° or to the extent of the tilt of the scene. At the moment, of course, the rod is objectively upright, and the reading on the protractor is therefore 0°. The position of the subject's perceived vertical, which is 30° off the true vertical, is found by subtracting zero degrees from 30°. At the other extreme, if the subject takes full and proper account of the tilt of the scene, he will bring the rod image to the true upright. The rod image will therefore deviate from his body position by 0°, or will be at a 30°-angle with the vertical axis of the scene. In this case, the rod itself is objectively tilted by 30°, so that the protractor reading will be 30°. To obtain the position of the subject's perceived vertical, which is at 0°, it is necessary to subtract this value from 30°.

In brief, by subtracting the protractor reading from 30°, the position of the perceived upright may be determined. In cases where the protractor reading is negative, indicating that the rod image has been displaced even farther than the tilted scene, a value of 30° is added to the reading. In any case, the larger the value obtained, the farther has the perceived upright been shifted, under the influence of the tilted visual field. All results will be given in terms of the deviation of the rod image from the true upright, or from the position of the body.

Subjects, all college students, were used in this experiment.

Results

Figures 5.1 and 5.2 present for the with-tube and without-tube conditions, respectively, the distribution of the deviations of the subject's perceived vertical from the upright position of his body. The score of each subject is based on four measurements.

The following are the principal results of the experiment:

1. When the subjects viewed the mirror scene through the tube, the perceived upright deviated toward the axes of the tilted mirror world to a remarkable degree. The average setting of the rod for the group of forty-nine subjects was 21.5° from the true vertical. In short, the perceived vertical was very much nearer to the mirror axes than to the position of the body. An appreciable number of subjects accepted the tilted scene either as completely upright or as almost completely upright.

2. Even more striking are the results obtained when the subjects stood directly in front of the mirror and looked at the tilted scene without a tube. Although the subjects now knew that they were looking at a mirror (something of which most subjects were unaware when looking through the tube), they localized the vertical far nearer to the axes of the tilted scene than with the

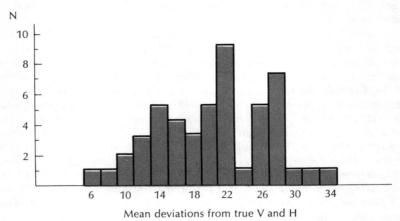

Figure 5.1: Distribution of individual scores when the rod was adjusted with the tube. N is 49.

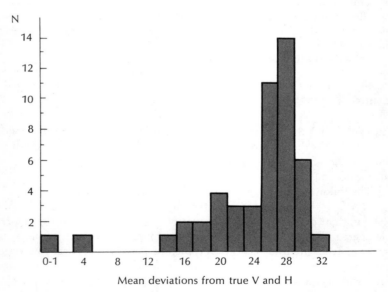

Figure 5.2: Distribution of individual scores when the rod was adjusted without the tube. N is 49.

tube. Now the average deviation of the perceived vertical from the true upright was 26.4°, or less than 4° from the main axis of the mirror world.

3. Under both conditions of observation the range of individual differences is great, extending over nearly the entire region between the true upright and the 30°-tilt of the mirror scene. In a few cases, in fact, scores greater than 30° were obtained. (See Figures 5.1 and 5.2.) When looking through the tube, one subject at one extreme compensated for the tilt of the visual surroundings to an extent where he succeeded in bringing the rod to within an average of 6° of the true upright. On the other hand, fifteen out of the total of forty-nine subjects gave deviations of 26° or more. Without the tube, though there is a greater concentration of cases toward the upper end of the distribution, the range of individual differences persists. At the one extreme is a subject who compensated completely for the tilt of the scene so that his deviation was 0°; while thirty-two subjects at the other extreme gave deviations of 28° or higher.

In the course of the experiment a number of qualitatively different reactions were obtained which will now be described.

Six subjects reported that the scene which they saw through the tube was perfectly upright. Two of these continued to perceive the mirror room as upright when they viewed it without the tube. This group of six was clear in asserting that the scene appeared upright throughout the period of observation, and were amazed when they subsequently saw the mirror. In the case of the subject the mirror was turned to the upright while his eyes were closed. When asked subsequently to report what changes he observed he replied: "New objects have come into view," but he insisted that the scene was as level earlier as it was now.

In general, these subjects expressed deep surprise when they saw the mirror upon removing the tube from the face. One subject reported: "I am astounded. I didn't think it was possible to make such a mistake." Another asserted: "I was completely absorbed in the picture. It seems hard to believe that the room was tilted; everything appeared perfectly straight." Another subject reported: "No, this is not what I saw before. The whole thing is slanted now. It seems to have shifted. I didn't know I was looking into a mirror." One of the subjects, when returned to the scene said: "The scene looked perfectly straight before. The floor looked level; I felt I was looking at an extension of the room." The mean deviation of the perceived upright from the true upright for this group of six subjects was, with the tube, 28.5°. The 1.5° displacement from the tilt of the mirror scene was probably within the experimental error of measurement. Without the tube, five of these subjects set the vertical at 29.5° from the true upright or within half a degree of the vertical of the mirror scene.

The greater number of the forty-nine subjects, forty-three, perceived the scene as tilted when viewed through the tube. (The frequency with which the tilt was perceived was very likely increased by the initial instructions, which specifically directed the subject to align the image of the rod with the felt position of the body.) The reports of these subjects, however, reflect considerable differences in emphasis, which may be important for subsequent investigation.

First, six of these subjects perceived the scene as tilted when viewed through the tube, but attributed it to their own position. In the words of one subject: "I seemed to be at an angle: I was the one off." It is of particular interest that this subject, whose vertical deviated from the true value by 19°, felt that the real vertical was that of the visual field, and that in taking his body position into account he was departing from the true value. An almost identical statement was obtained from another subject: "The room looked all right to me; it seemed as if I were standing at an angle. The true upright was that of the room." Another subject reported: "I had the optical impression that I was at an angle myself." Still another subject said: "I feel I am leaning backward." The following report is also of interest: "The room had a queer appearance, its perspective was strange but I was not aware except at moments that it was tilted. Sometimes it was as if I were looking at the scene from a somewhat peculiar point of vantage."

The remaining thirty-seven subjects in this group of forty-three who reported the room to be tilted, spoke of the room as actually appearing tilted. This they often ascribed to the position from which they observed the scene rather than to the scene itself. In their comments some tended to speak of the tilt in terms of the relation between their position and that of the room, rather than in terms of a tilt either in the visual surroundings or in their body position.

Those subjects who perceived the tilted scene as upright placed the vertical, as described above, in alignment with the vertical axes of the mirror-room. Equally extreme results were also obtained with subjects who did perceive the tilt. This was most notably the case when subjects stood directly in front of the mirror without the tube. Under these conditions nineteen subjects gave deviations which were within two degrees of the tilt of the scene. Of these, two saw the scene as upright. The remaining seventeen subjects saw the scene as tilted, but, despite this, adjusted the vertical essentially to the mirror-room axis. These latter subjects were aware, or they were made aware, that, since the surroundings were tilted and their position upright, the rod as they placed it could not be parallel with the upright body. Despite this knowledge, they could not find another position in the mirror-scene that fulfilled this requirement. One subject fully conversant with the problem reported: "I see the room as tilted, and the rod as vertical (at a deviation of 30°), even though the table nearby appears tilted. Any position of the rod away from this appears as distinctly tilted. This is the only possible vertical in the scene." Another subject commented: "This is virtually impossible. . . . I will say it is vertical now (at a deviation of 30°) but I don't think I'll ever get it right. It will never achieve the position at which I am standing." Another subject reported: "I can't tell when I think the rod is vertical in relation to my body because I'm always relating it to the walls."

There were a few subjects who in an attempt to take the body into account, tilted the rod farther than the scene itself. One subject tilted the rod once 40° from the position of his body, another 35°. When these subjects attempted to relate the position of the body to the visual vertical they became entirely confused and the error in judgment of the upright became greater than it would have been if the body position had been completely neglected.

Of particular interest is the difference in results obtained with the tube and without it. It would have been plausible to predict that the visual vertical would be less affected by the tilted scene when the subject had full knowledge that a mirror was being used and was actually able to see the tilt of the mirror. Yet the opposite was the case. In thirty-one out of forty-nine cases the deviations in the direction of the tilted scene increased when the tube was eliminated. (Only differences greater than 2° were considered significant.) Further, the increases in the deviation of the vertical were often large, reaching, in one case, 21.5°. In contrast, there were only five subjects whose deviations were greater without the tube than with it. Often, after having adjusted the rod without the tube, the subject would change it, in the direction of smaller deviations from the true upright, when the tube was restored.

The greater effect of the tilted visual scene when the subject looked into the mirror without the tube seems to be due primarily to the more lifelike quality of the scene under the latter conditions. The subject now perceived a far wider expanse in contrast with the previously more restricted and somewhat more artificial view. Also, the scene was far richer in objects and details and, though extending only to the space in front of him, it seemed also to surround him. Despite his more accurate knowledge of the true conditions, the subject found it far more difficult to isolate a single line from the surroundings and to relate it to his body position.

The reports also indicate that the tube helped many subjects considerably in determining the vertical. Often the subject would take note of how the image of the rod cut the circular opening of the tube. At other times the subject would relate the rod to the position of his face, or more particularly, to the line joining the eyes. In effect, the vertical was in these cases established by a process of isolation. The image of the rod was divorced from the surroundings of the room and its position estimated with reference to the face and tube. While in using this approach the subjects were not always wholly successful, many were able to reduce the extent of the deviations considerably. At the same time there were considerable individual differences in this regard. There were subjects who could not separate themselves from the visual scene, and indeed became confused when they attempted to relate the vertical to the position of the body.

Though the problem of the righting of the tilted scene was not studied systematically, three subjects who in the with-tube condition initially perceived the scene as tilted reported after continued observation that it became less tilted, or that the tilt disappeared completely. One subject whose initial deviation (based on four determinations) was 8.5° from the true upright or 21.5° from the mirror, came to see the room as perfectly upright. A new set of four measurements was taken, yielding an average deviation of 28.2° from the upright or 1.8° from the mirror. In the words of one subject: "At the beginning it (the floor) was at an angle. Then it straightened itself. Later it (the tilt) completely disappeared." Another subject reported: "It is beginning to look as if it were level. Now I see the room as perfectly straight."

Discussion

The present experiment has provided striking evidence of the predominance of the visual framework over postural factors in perception of the upright. Since the body remained erect while the visual field was displaced, the visual and postural systems were brought into conflict. It was found with this technique that the perceived upright was always much closer to the visual than to the postural vertical. In the first experimental condition, where the tube was used, the perceived upright was displaced by an average of 21.5° from the true upright—that is, from the position of the body—or by only 8.5° from the upright of the mirror scene. In the second condition, where the tube was removed and the subject brought closer to the mirror, the results were even more striking, with the perceived upright now deviating by an average of 26.4° from the true upright, or by only 3.6° from the upright of the mirror. Under each condition, not only did nearly all subjects perceive the upright primarily in terms of the coordinates of the visual field, but an appreciable number adopted these coordinates completely. These results were obtained though the subjects were emphatically directed to take the postural system as their standard. It is also to be noted that the technique employed gave full play to the gravitational factors. The subject was outside the tilted field; moreover, because he stood erect he had the optimum opportunity to determine the position of his body accurately, and to involve his body in judging the upright.

Equally important is the finding of large individual differences. Both with the tube and without it, the range of the subjects' determination of the upright was great, covering the greater part of the region between the true upright and the upright of the tilted visual field (see Figures 5.1 and 5.2). Under each condition, many subjects were markedly affected by the visual field; their body position seemed virtually without effect. Indeed, some subjects became confused and their errors increased when they attempted deliberately to refer to their bodies. At the other extreme there was a much smaller number of the subjects who perceived the vertical primarily with reference to the position of the body.

The results indicate that perception of the upright is also clearly affected by the specific structure of the visual field. When the view was more articulated and lifelike, as was the case when the subjects looked into the mirror without the tube, the effect of the visual coordinates was markedly strengthened. This observation is particularly significant since the changed structure of the visual field acts on a strictly perceptual rather than on a cognitive basis. Though without the tube the subject had full knowledge of the tilt of the field, and of the extent of the tilt, this knowledge proved ineffective in the perception of the vertical. Indeed, despite the knowledge, the visual field exerted a greater influence upon perception than when this knowledge was not available, as was the case when the tube was used. It is indicated that under the given field conditions the subject perceives the upright in a determined way; he cannot alter its direction, not even when he possesses the knowledge that would suffice to provide the necessary correction.

The present findings, based on a more intensive study and on a larger number of subjects, help to settle the apparent contradiction between the observations of Wertheimer and Gibson. Contrary to Gibson's conclusion that under conditions of conflict between visual and postural factors the shift of the perceived vertical toward the visual coordinates is slight, in the present experiment most individuals showed a very marked shift in the perceived vertical. Also, the conclusion of Gibson that the visual field does not right itself under the given conditions is not in full accord with the results obtained here. While the effect of prolonged observation of tilted visual fields was not investigated systematically in the present experiment, a substantial number of subjects accepted the tilted visual framework as upright from the very outset, indicating that full righting of the field may even occur at once, without the need for prolonged observation. The results of the present study demonstrate that the visual framework plays a much more decisive role in establishing the upright than postulating by Gibson. In this regard they tend to support the conclusions reached by Wertheimer. It is indicated by some of our findings that a possible reason for the difference between Gibson's and our own results may lie in the smaller number of cases employed in Gibson's study. It has been established here, by using a large group of subjects and testing them with a quantitative technique, that there are important individual differences in the mode of perceiving the upright. Consequently, if a small group of subjects is employed in a given condition, the results obtained may not represent the general situation. It is accordingly possible that because he used a small group, Gibson may have been tapping one segment of the population. Because Wertheimer also used a small number of subjects in his study, it is possible that selective factors in the group used may similarly account for the difference in observations between Wertheimer and Gibson.

For the reasons mentioned the more general assumptions of Gibson and Mowrer concerning the genetic and indeed the logical primacy of postural factors will require reexamination. Such a comprehensive evaluation must be reserved until the results of further investigations have been reported.

Summary

In this first of a series of studies on space orientation, an effort was made to determine the relative importance of visual and postural factors in perception of the upright. Since these two systems normally function together, it was necessary to separate them in order to establish the specific contributions of each. For this purpose, the mirror technique, employed by Wertheimer in some of his investigations, was used. By requiring the subject to look into a tilted mirror scene while his body remains erect, we have essentially a situation where the visual coordinates are displaced while the postural upright remains unchanged. With this technique it was possible to determine whether the perceived upright is based mainly on the axes of the visual field or on the position of the body. In an experiment with forty-nine subjects striking evidence was found of the primary importance of visual factors in perception of the upright, and of the secondary role of postural determinants. Though most subjects were greatly influenced by the tilted visual field in making their judgments, there were found significant individual differences in this regard. Some subjects accepted the tilted field entirely, perceiving it as fully erect, while others, at the opposite extreme, were able to make full allowance for the tilt of the scene, and in their judgments succeeded in approximating the true upright. Experiments in which the tilted scene was viewed with a tube and without a tube have demonstrated that the specific structure of the visual field affects the manner of perceiving the upright in a specific way. Some of the differences in conclusions between Wertheimer and Gibson, derived from this same mirror technique, are considered in light of the results of the present experiment.

Depth Perception

The information on the spatial position of objects in the visual world is transmitted to the retina along two dimensional coordinates. An object can be represented on the retina only as up or down and left or right. As the retina itself is a two-dimensional surface, only these dimensions can be utilized in space perception. Yet we easily locate objects relative to a third dimension. This feat is accomplished via several properties of the visual system and on the basis of learned relationships of the characteristics of near and far objects.

Three biological cues, intrinsic to the visual mechanism, have been identified: binocular disparity, convergence, and accommodation. Binocular disparity provides by far the most information on the third dimensional location of an object. The light reflected by the distal object to each retina differs somewhat, because of the separation of the two eyes. The disparate image presented to each retina, when fused by the brain, provides a good cue of the distance of the perceived object, so that the nearer the object is, the more disparate are the two retinal projections. The child's Viewmaster® utilizes this technique by photographing a scene from slightly different angles and then presenting a different picture to each eye with retinal congruency, so that a single, fused, and focused image is perceived. Convergence refers to the inward movement of the two eyes, as they focus on nearer objects, and also to the outward (away from the nose) movement as they focus on more distant objects. In accommodation the shape of the lens is modified to focus the light from more distant objects upon the retina. In each case, kinesthetic feedback from the muscles carrying out these movements may relay information as to the spatial location of the perceived object to higher centers of the brain.

The number of environmental or learned cues of depth is much larger than the three biological depth cues. Approximately twenty-five such environmental cues have been identified. The following list represents some of the more important cues:

1. Visual angle: Objects which are nearer are perceived by looking downward at a greater angle than those located at greater distances.

2. Brightness: Objects which are nearer appear to be brighter.
3. Texture gradients: Objects extending into the distance take up less retinal space as distance from the observer increases. The texture of the surface is more dense at proximal points than at distal points.
4. Interposition: If one object partially blocks a second object, the second object is perceived as more distant.
5. Clearness: Clear and distinct objects are perceived as nearer.
6. Proximal size: Smaller objects are perceived as farther away.

The last of these cues deserves further consideration. Objects of known size project a smaller retinal image when viewed from a distance; that is, the amount of retina stimulated increases with nearness of the object viewed. Further, the size of an object is reduced on the retina as the object moves away from the observer and is increased as the object moves toward him. Since the observer knows from experience that most objects maintain their size, he perceives the change in size as a change in the spatial location of the object, relative to the dimension of depth.

Observers are able to judge the size of objects from various distances, on the basis of *size constancy*. The question then arises: If the observer actually perceives the object as retaining its size, how can the object's size serve as a depth cue? The answer is that the observer interprets what he actually sees; that is, what he may choose to report may not be the same as what he actually sees. Although the object appears phenomenally smaller, he reports it as maintaining its size because of his previous experience in viewing distal objects. It would appear plausible that the report of perception given by the observer would depend upon how he were asked to relate his observations or how he perceived the task with which he was confronted.

Leibowitz and Harvey at Penn State University have undertaken a number of studies on the effect of different instructions in a size-judging task. The results of their study are presented in terms of ratios, named after the Viennese psychologist who developed the ratio. The Brunswick ratio (BR) relates the following aspect of the perceptual task to one another:

$$BR = \frac{P - R}{C - R}$$

P = judged size of the distal object

C = objective or actual size of the distal object independent of distance

R = size of the projected retinal image of the distal object

If the subject reports the distal object as maintaining its size irrespective of the distance of the object from the observer, then the judged size (P) will equal the actual size (C). The ratio of $P - R/C - R$ will remain near 1.0. If the subject relies on the size of the retinal image the value of P will become smaller as the distance of the object to be judged increases and the ratios of $P - R/C - R$ would approach zero.

The Effects of Instructions, Environment, and Type of Test Object on Matched Size

H. W. Leibowitz and Lewis O. Harvey, Jr.

The phenomenon of size constancy refers to the observation that the "perceived" size of objects at different distances does not change as much as one would predict from the dimensions of the retinal image. Experimental investigations have, in general, confirmed such observations. A large number of studies have reported empirical functions relating matched size to distance which tend to agree with a prediction based on invariance of perceived size as a function of distance. It is becoming clear, however, from recent experimental studies that there is no unique function relating matched size to distance. Rather, there are families of functions, the parameters of which are determined by a number of experimental variables.

The most effective of these variables are the instructions given to the subject in a size-matching experiment (Carlson, 1960; Jenkin and Hyman, 1959; Leibowitz and Harvey, 1967). In general, instructions which emphasize the permanent qualities of objects such as "objective" instructions, produce larger size matches than instructions which stress visual angle relationships—"retinal." Instructions which emphasize phenomenal size, usually referred to as "apparent" instructions, produce intermediate matches.

Another important variable is test-object familiarity. Most size-matching studies in the literature, in order to insure that the subject's responses are determined by stimulus parameters present in the experimental situation, utilize test objects such as circles, triangles, or sticks which have no definite size and can logically assume a wide range of dimensional values (Gibson, 1950; Holway and Boring, 1941). It is clear, however, that knowledge of the nature of the test object is relevant to an estimation of its size (Bolles and Bailey, 1956; McKennell, 1960). For example, Leibowitz and Harvey (1967) carried out a size-matching study using a highly familiar test object, a human being, under three sets of instructions—objective, apparent and retinal—in a cue "rich" outdoor environment. The results, compared with those of Gilinsky (1955) who used the same instructions (except apparent) but with triangular wooden test objects, suggest that the unfamiliar test objects are overestimated relative to the familiar test objects under the same conditions.

These conclusions are only tentative since the magnitude of size matches is affected by a large number of variables which may in turn be sensitive to particular experimental conditions. The purpose of the present study is to attempt to clarify the effects on size-matching behavior of instructions, object familiarity, and environment. To this end, three experiments have been carried out. Experiment I represents an extension of the Leibowitz and Harvey (1967) study using unfamiliar test objects (boards) instead of human beings. Experiment II investigates the effects of environment by obtaining size matches in a situation with obvious and conspicuous depth cues (railroad tracks) as compared with matches obtained in an outdoor situation providing minimal cues (open field). Experiment III was designed to clarify some of the relationships obtained by combining all of these variables into a single experimental design.

Experiment I

The purpose of this experiment was to provide a direct test of the differences previously obtained between Gilinsky (1955) and Leibowitz and Harvey (1967). The specific issue in question is whether the larger matched sizes obtained by Gilinsky were the result of the fact that she utilized "unfamiliar" or "neutral" wooden triangle test objects as compared to the human-being test objects of Leibowitz and Harvey. Experiment I replicates the Leibowitz and Harvey study but utilizes unfamiliar test objects consisting of vertical boards. Matches were made under three sets of instructions at distances ranging from 340 to 1,680 feet.

Method

Subjects.   The subjects in all phases of this study were undergraduates at the university enrolled in elementary psychology classes who served in the experiment to satisfy one of the requirements of the course. They were aware of the purpose or nature of the experiment, had normal vision with or without correction, and observed binocularly. Sixty such subjects served in Experiment I.

Procedure.   The three sets of instructions used in this study were identical to those used in the Leibowitz and Harvey study. The objective and retinal instructions were identical to those used by Gilinsky (1955) except for minor modifications to correspond to the specific testing situation. These instructions are as follows:

OBJECTIVE INSTRUCTIONS

"I am going to give you very specific directions as to what you are to do. It is important that you do exactly as I tell you. Suppose I were to place the rod on the left (comparison object) beside the board (test object); how big would the rod have to be so that it would be exactly the same size as the board? I am going to set the rod at various heights and I want you to judge which would be taller if they were placed side by side, the rod or the board."

APPARENT INSTRUCTIONS

"I am going to give you very specific directions as to what you are to do. It is important that you do exactly as I tell you. I am going to set the rod on the left (comparison object) at various heights and I want you to judge which appears taller, the rod or the board. Please disregard any knowledge you may have about the real height of the object, and base your judgment on the way it appears."

RETINAL INSTRUCTIONS

"I am going to give you very specific directions as to what you are to do. It is important that you do exactly as I tell you. As you know, the farther away an object is from you, the smaller is its image. The moon and the stars, thousands of miles away, look very tiny but we know that they are actually very large. Now imagine that the field of view is a scene in a picture or a photograph. Every image in the picture is fixed in size. If you were to cut the fixed image of the board and paste it on the image of the variable rod, how big would the variable rod have to be so that the two images would be exactly the same size? I am going to set the rod at various heights and I want you to judge which photographic image would be larger, the rod or the board."

After the instructions were read to the subject, he was questioned to insure that they were understood. It was often necessary to give further operational examples before we were satisfied.

Matches were obtained for three instructions and two test-object conditions: (a) boards which were six feet high and one foot wide painted a highly visible (0.90 reflectance) "fluorescent" red to maximize contrast with the light background; (b) the same boards with a person, a graduate student approximately six feet in height and dressed in typical summer clothing, standing next to them. For both conditions, the subject was instructed to match the size of the board alone. These test objects were viewed one at a time in the middle of the Mall on the University campus at distances of 340, 680, 1020, 1360, and 1680 feet. These boards remained hidden from the subject's view behind trees until they were placed on the Mall by assistants. The subject did not observe the boards being carried onto or being removed from the Mall. He stood on the steps of the Library facing the Mall and alternately viewed the test object and the comparison object, a wooden surveyor's leveling rod, two inches wide, which protruded vertically from behind a wall 51 feet from the subject and 90° to his left: The base of the visible portion of the rod was level with the subject's feet. The sixty subjects were randomly assigned to six groups of ten each. Each subject was tested under only one experimental condition. The experiment was arranged in a three-by-two factorial design.

The order of presentation of distances was determined by a Latin square design. A modified method of limits procedure as followed by Leibowitz and Harvey (1967) was employed. No time limit was placed on the subject who completed his observations in approximately thirty minutes. All observations were made in good weather in the summer of 1966.

Results. To facilitate comparison with the other phases of the study, Brunswik ratios (BR) are used to indicate the extent to which subject's matches are in accordance with veridical size matching (Brunswik, 1933). A BR of 1.0 indicates that the data are in agreement with a prediction based on the true physical size of the test object (the law of size constancy) while a

BR of zero indicates agreement with a prediction based on the visual angle.

An analysis of variance indicated that there were no significant differences between the two test-object conditions: between the boards alone and the boards with a human standing next to them, $F(1,299) = 1.72$. Apparently instructions to match the size of the board effectively eliminate any influence of the person. Therefore, these two groups of data are combined and are plotted in Figure 5.3 as the mean BR as a function of distance for the three instruction conditions (dashed lines). The significant effect of instructions reported in the previous study (Leibowitz and Harvey, 1967) is confirmed by the present data, $F(2,299) = 46.9$, $p < 0.001$. Objective instructions produced the highest size matches, retinal instructions gave the lowest matches, with the apparent instructions falling between these two extremes. Also as before, objective size matches are independent of distance while both apparent and retinal size matches decrease significantly in magnitude with distance [$F(4,299) = 14.3$ $p < 0.001$].

The solid lines in Figure 5.3 represent the data for the human objects alone (Leibowitz and Harvey, 1967). It will be observed that for each instruction condition, the unfamiliar test object (boards) resulted in higher size matches than did the familiar test object (humans). These results are consistent with our interpretation of Gilinsky's (1955) study that the demonstrated overestimation of the true size of the test object with objective instructions results from the use of unfamiliar test objects.

Experiment II

The purpose of the study was to explore further the effect of different environments on size matching. An environment with obvious cues to depth was provided by standard gauge railroad tracks. An environment which was chosen to minimize conspicuous cues was provided by a 10-acre athletic field. The test object consisted of a 1⅛–inch diameter aluminum tube five feet long painted the same fluorescent red as the boards in Experiment I. This rod was placed perpendicular to the subject's line of vision, either symmetrically across the railroad tracks, or on the surface of the athletic field at distances of 100, 200, 300, 400, and 500 feet from the subject. The comparison object was a similar tube which could be extended from behind a black box to a length of twelve feet. This comparison object was placed 53 feet from the subject and 90° from his line of sight to the test object. The sixty subjects were all drawn from the same population and met the same criteria as those in Experiment I.

A modified method of limits was used with the order of presentation of the various distances being determined by a Latin square design. The subjects were randomly assigned to six groups of ten each, and placed in a three-by-two factorial design. No time limit was placed on the subject who usually completed the matches within fifteen minutes. All observations were made binocularly in good weather during the fall of 1966.

Results.   The data are presented in Figure 5.4 as the mean BR as a function of distance for the two experimental environments under objective, appar-

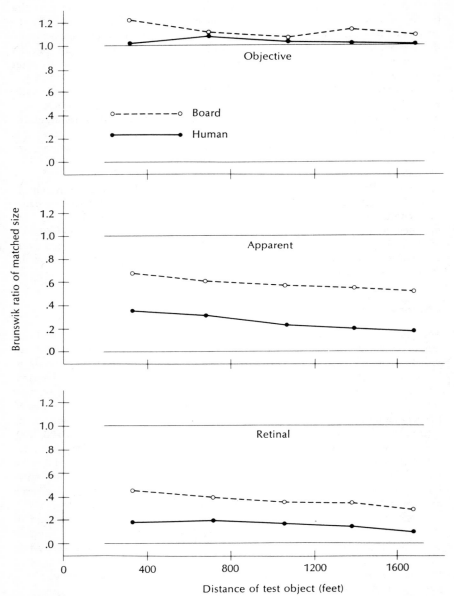

Figure 5.3: BR of matched size (percentage of constancy) as a function of distance under three sets of instructions for familiar (human being) and unfamiliar (board) test-objects in an outdoor environment.

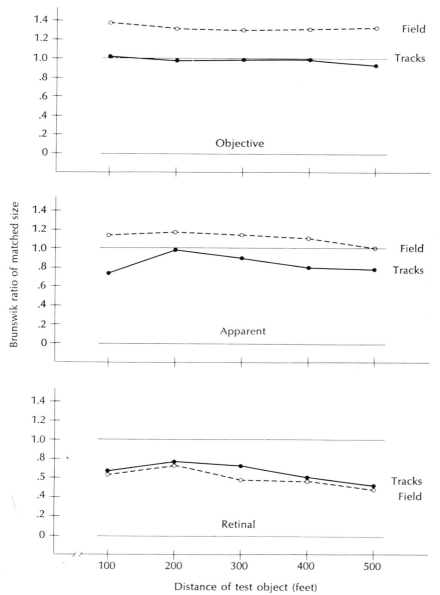

Figure 5.4: BR of matched size (percentage of constancy) as a function of distance under three sets of instructions for a horizontal bar test-object viewed in a cue "rich" (railroad tracks) and cue "poor" (open field) environment.

ent and retinal instructions. Analyses of variance indicated that environment had no significant effect on size matches made with retinal, $F(1,99) = 0.34$, or apparent instructions, $F = 3.35$. With objective instructions, however, the matches made in the open-field situation were significantly higher than those made on the railroad tracks, $F = 6.7$, $p < 0.05$.

Experiment III

Experiment I demonstrated that the size of the unfamiliar test object is overestimated relative to that of a familiar test object (Leibowitz and Harvey, 1967) of equal physical size. In addition, the results of Experiment II suggest that the nature of the environment can influence matched size and that this effect interacts with the instructions given to the subject. Experiment III was designed to combine all of these variables (environmental setting, familiarity of test objects and instructions) in one experimental design. Matches were obtained on the railroad tracks and an open field, with both human being test objects and boards, and with the three instructions used in Experiments I and II. It was hoped that this study would clarify the relationships among the nature of the test object, the experimental environment and the instructions.

Procedure. The 180 subjects were drawn from the same population and met the same criteria as in the other phases of the study. The subject sat in a chair and observed alternately either the test object, located at one of five distances in front of him, or a white vertical comparison strip, four inches wide and of variable height, located 90° from the line of sight of the test object and fifty feet from the subject. The strip was a loop of canvas belt, the bottom half of which was painted white and the top half black. The belt passed over two pulleys located at the top and the bottom of a black board eight feet high and four feet wide. Only the front half of the loop was visible against the black board as the background, since the rear half of the loop passed in back of the background board. One of the pulleys was driven by a reversible electric motor so that the subject was able to control the visible amount of white strip by means of a switch.

Twelve groups of ten subjects each were used in a three-by-two-by-two experimental design. The same three instructions were employed as in the previous experiments. The two experimental environments were the railroad tracks used in Experiment II and an open athletic field. The test objects were either boards, five feet high and one foot wide, painted a highly visible fluorescent "rocket red" or a human being, a female graduate student five feet six inches in height, who wore a white laboratory coat. The test objects were presented at distances of 100, 200, 300, 400, and 500 feet with the order of presentation being determined by a Latin square design. Only one human test object was used at the five test distances, since Leibowitz and Harvey (1967) showed that there were no differences between size matches made on one person at five different distances and matches made on five different people at those same distances.

Three additional groups of ten subjects each were tested in both experimental environments with the board test objects while viewing monocularly through a reduction screen. This reduction screen condition was introduced as a control to evaluate any anticipated differential effects of the two testing environments. The reduction screen was produced by a vernier microscope stage to which was attached an "L" shaped piece of aluminum. This "L" shaped piece could be precisely positioned in relation to a second rectangular cutout in an aluminum plate so as to produce a rectangular opening of varying dimensions. This vernier apparatus was mounted at the far end of a piece of plastic pipe six feet in length and four inches in diameter. The entire apparatus was securely attached to a tripod which held it at the proper viewing height. The subject viewed monocularly through a two-inch opening at the near end of the tube. The vernier was calibrated to produce openings corresponding to the five visual angles subtended by the boards at their respective distances. The precision with which this reduction screen was constructed, plus the unusually great distances between the eye and the reduction slit minimized motion parallax and blur of the slit edge.

The method of adjustment was used throughout to obtain size matches. The subject matched the comparison strip to the test object by manipulating the switch which electrically raised and lowered the visible portion of the white comparison strip. No time limit was placed on the subject who completed observations within approximately fifteen minutes. All observations were made in good weather during the spring, summer, and fall of 1967.

Results.   The results are plotted in Figure 5.5 as the mean BR as a function of distance for the three test-object conditions under the three instructions. Since statistical analysis demonstrated no significant differences between size matches made under apparent and retinal instructions, data from these two groups have been combined in Figure 5.5. Further analysis showed that the size matches made on the railroad tracks did not differ significantly from those made in the open field situation, so that these two groups of data were also combined. Statistical analysis confirms the impression that the unfamiliar test object consistently produced larger size matches than the familiar test object $[F(1,38) = 20.7$ for objective, 14.8 for apparent, and 13.5 for retinal instructions, $p < 0.001]$. The boards, when viewed through the reduction screen, produced lower size matches than when viewed with unrestricted binocular vision. This difference was not significant for retinal instructions $[F(1,38) = 3.5]$, reached the 0.05 level for apparent instructions $(F = 4.7)$ and the 0.001 level for objective instructions $(F = 17.67)$. There were no statistical differences between the two experimental environments for any of the test-object conditions with any of the instructions. These results, for a vertical test object, contrast with the data of Experiment II for a horizontal test object in which matches made in the open field were higher, under objective instructions only, than those made on the railroad tracks. As in the previous experiments, size matches decreased significantly as a function of distance with apparent $[F(4,152) = 14.9, p < 0.001]$, and retinal instructions $(F = 37.7, p < 0.001)$ but not under objective instructions $(F = 1.23)$.

Table 5.1 presents the mean standard deviations across the five test distances for each experimental condition. It may be noted that the variability of the data under objective instructions is less than that under apparent and retinal instructions. It will also be observed that the variability is much greater with the reduction screen than without it.

Discussion.   The results of this study confirm the conclusions drawn from previous experiments (Carlson, 1960, 1962; Gilinsky, 1955; Leibowitz and Harvey, 1967) that the functions relating matched size to distance can and do assume a wide range of values depending upon the specific experimental conditions, with instructions being a very important parameter. In quantitative terms, the effect of instructions is of greater magnitude than any other variable and as such, the influence of instructions must play a significant role in any theoretical account of size-matching behavior.

It should be made clear that perceived size as a conscious phenomenon is not being investigated directly. Rather, we are quantifying size-matching behavior whose relation to perceived size is particularly sensitive to instructions. The instructions chosen are not independent of one's particular systematic approach. For example, objective instructions correspond most closely to the theoretical concepts implied in Gibson's "visual world" (Gibson, 1950). Apparent instructions are most appropriate to the phenomenological approach followed by the Gestalt psychologists and their philosophical predecessors. Retinal instructions are most compatible with the objectives of the introspective

Table 5.1

Standard deviations (mean of five distances)

Railroad Tracks Test Object *Instructions*	*Human*	*Boards*	*Reduction Screen*
Objective	0.067	0.117	0.304
Apparent	0.225	0.232	0.302
Retinal	0.281	0.239	0.445

Field Test Object *Instructions*	*Human*	*Boards*	*Reduction Screen*
Objective	0.193	0.114	0.349
Apparent	0.205	0.299	0.322
Retinal	0.292	0.186	0.286

Note: The same 10 subjects were tested at each of five distances. The standard deviations (S.D.) are the mean of the five S.D.s obtained at each of the five distances.

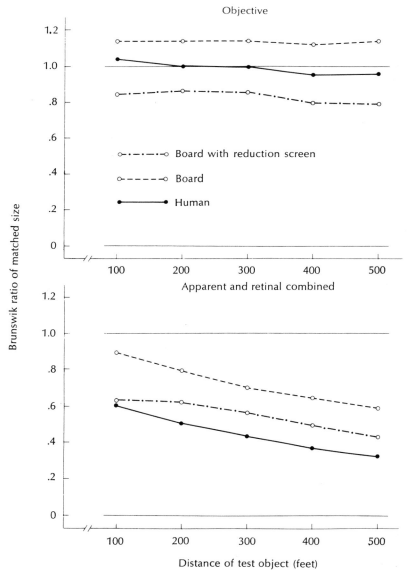

Figure 5.5: BR of matched size (percentage of constancy) as a function of distance under three sets of instructions for familiar (human beings) and unfamiliar (board) test objects, and for the board test object viewed through a reduction screen.

method espoused by the structural psychology of Wundt and Titchener (without, of course, meeting the criterion of valid data within their system). Whatever one's theoretical approach, it would seem highly desirable, in view of the magnitude of the empirical effect of instructions, to introduce multiple instructions in any study of size-matching behavior.

The present data shed light on the frequently reported finding that matched size may be greater than the true size of the test object, "overconstancy." This overestimation has been reported in a number of studies and has been a source of theoretical speculation and interest in the size-matching literature (Wohlwill, 1963). The results of the present study demonstrate that overestimation of matched size is favored by the use of unfamiliar test objects and an environment such as an open field in which few depth cues, other than texture, are present. In the present study, the data obtained with a tube-test object in an open field (Experiment II) resulted in overestimations of the true object size by as much as 40 percent. The same test object when viewed on the railroad tracks produced matches in close agreement with the true size of the test object (with objective instructions). In both Experiments I and III, the size of the familiar human-being test object was accurately matched, with objective instructions, while the size of the unfamiliar board test object was overestimated. For the other instructions the same trend was observed in that the unfamiliar test object was always judged larger than the familiar one. These results suggest that overestimation (overconstancy) represents an error in size matching which is favored by a lack of cues. Thus, under rich cue conditions, objective instructions result in veridical size matches while the lack of cues produces over- rather than underestimation of matched size. A clue to why overestimation occurs is suggested by the results obtained with retinal instructions.

It will be observed in all of the functions obtained in the present and previous studies that none of the subjects' matches was ever in accord with a prediction based on the visual angle. Even with explicit retinal image instructions, subjects are unable to accurately match retinal size but consistently overestimate it. Indeed, visual angle matches have been reported only under the most extreme conditions of cue restriction (Lichten and Laurie, 1950). It is clear that matched size consistently tends to be larger than the visual angle size. This finding might provide a partial explanation of the overestimation of unfamiliar test objects with objective instructions as follows: size-matching behavior is based in part on the size of the retinal image. When the subject views an unfamiliar object, he has fewer cues on which to base his size judgment, and this lack of cues, in turn, forces the subject to rely more heavily on the size of the retinal image itself (instead for example, on cognitive knowledge about the test object). But since the retinal image size is consistently overestimated, to the extent that the subject bases his objective size matches on the retinal size, his objective size matches will also be overestimated. When viewing a familiar object, the subject relies less upon the actual size of the retinal image and makes more accurate size matches. A comprehensive explanation for the overestimation of retinal image size will probably be rooted in the evolutionary history of the perceptual mechanism.

It should also be noted that matches made under objective instructions are independent of distance, while those made under apparent and retinal instructions tend to decrease with distance, although not as rapidly as one would predict from the diminishing size of the retinal image. Thus, instructions affect not only the general position of the matched size-distance functions, but also affect their slopes. Theoretically, decreasing slope implies a greater influence of stimulus cues, while a zero slope implies independence from such cues and greater reliance on cognitive factors.

The results obtained with apparent instructions in Experiment I and II were quite close to those obtained under retinal instructions. In Experiment III, there were no significant differences between size matches made with the two instructions. This finding allows us to express our dissatisfaction with the apparent instructions. Often subjects, when given these instructions, would express confusion and would ask for further clarification about the meaning of the word "appear." Our findings indicate that in the face of this ambiguity, most subjects probably assume retinal instructions or in any case make size matches based on the fact that the test object's image grows smaller with increasing distance. From the subject's point of view, the objective and the retinal instructions are far more satisfying because they are based on operations which can be specified clearly and a criterion of "right" and "wrong" established. Apparent instructions have no such operational clarity and are thus a source of confusion. Their use in an experiment as an experimental manipulation is not invalidated by this lack of clarity, but the theoretical interpretation of size matches made with apparent instructions is quite difficult.

Particular attention should be paid to the magnitude, or rather the lack of magnitude, of the effect induced by the use of the reduction screen. On the basis of previous studies, it is assumed that the use of reduction produces matches which are close to a prediction based on the law of the retinal image (Boring, 1946; Holway and Boring, 1941; Katz, 1935). The present data, to our knowledge, are the first obtained with reduction in an outdoor environment and at ranges exceeding 100 feet. In this situation, the effects of reduction are considerably less than those typically reported in the literature. This discrepancy between the data obtained at close distances in an indoor laboratory, as compared to those obtained in an outdoor environment over greater ranges, emphasizes the difficulties inherent in generalizing from limited ranges and experimental conditions.

The results of this study both contribute to and identify deficiencies in our theoretical understanding of size-matching behavior. It is clear that instructions have a profound effect on the magnitude of size matches, although the mediating mechanisms are not understood. It is also apparent that both knowledge of the test object as well as the retinal image dimensions influence size matches and that the relative importance of these variables depends, in turn, on the instructions, the type of test object, and the experimental environment. The classical overconstancy phenomenon is seen to depend empirically on the lack of either cognitive or physical cues, but the basis for the overestimation error is still a matter of theoretical speculation. Most importantly, the present results reemphasize the essential requirement that our understanding of even relatively "simple" phenomena such as size matching demands a comprehensive series of functional relations obtained over wide ranges of experimental conditions and parameters.

Summary.   Objective instructions in outdoor settings consistently produced the highest magnitude size matches when compared with apparent and retinal instructions and were veridical when the test object was familiar and the environment contained conspicuous depth cues. Overconstancy is favored by the use of unfamiliar test objects and an open-field environment. The magnitude of size matches decreases with distance under apparent and retinal instructions, but remains constant under objective instructions. The effect of reduction is much less than previously reported in the literature for experiments conducted in an indoor environment. It should be emphasized that there is no unique function relating matched size to distance, but rather a family of functions whose parameters are particularly sensitive to variables such as instructions, the nature of the test object, and the environment.

Auditory Space Perception

The ability to localize an object in space is not confined to the visual mechanism of perception. An individual also is able to localize objects via the auditory system, although a great deal of dependency upon visual cues is still necessary for accurate localization. Auditory—like visual—space localization depends in part on the physiological characteristics of the hearing organs and in part on the organism's previous experience with the stimuli.

The basic empirical observations were made quite early by a number of different experimental psychologists. Used in typical experiments were various models of a sound stage with a blindfolded subject seated in the center. Located around the perimeter of the sound cage were small loudspeakers or other devices through which a click sound could be presented. Subjects presented with click sounds almost invariably could indicate whether the sound source was to the right or left. Distinction between sounds located up or down or between those located in front or in back of the subject was much more difficult. In the absence of other cues, subjects were unable to make accurate judgments over the entire medium plane. Whereas they correctly identified sound source to the right or to the left, the subjects made many errors in assigning the sound an up-down or back-front position. These observations have led Woodworth and Schlosberg (1954) to term the medium-plane localization difficulties the "cones of confusion."

On the basis of such observations, several theories of sound localization were presented. Each theory specified auditory characteristics which were considered important in sound localization. The first and most obvious cue discussed in most of the theories is the relationship of the two ears to each other. A sound located to the left will reach the left ear sooner than the right ear. The difference in time of arrival would reveal the sound's location to the perceiver. The greater the interval, the farther the sound is displaced towards the ear receiving it first. The second cue, which would appear to be important, is intensity; a sound originating from the left varies in intensity when it reaches the left ear and when it reaches the right. Since intensity diminishes as a function of traveled distance, localization of the sound source should be possible. Widescreen movies, by the way, utilize the differences in time of arrival and intensity in order to make it appear that the sound is coming from the source depicted on the screen. In one system, speakers are located at the four corners of the screen. If the sound is supposed to come from the upper left, then the upper left speaker is somewhat louder and starts the presentation of the sound a fraction of a second sooner. The source of the sound can be localized, then, by increasing or decreasing the time and intensity difference between the left and right speakers.

Despite the difficulties encountered by the subjects in sound cages, most individuals in real life circumstances experience little difficulty in locating a sound along the medium plane. This fact depends in part on our experiences with sounds and the use of visual cues to aid in localization. Upon hearing the noise of a car, one looks toward the nearest street and subsequently "hears" the sound from that position in space. If the sound is known, as that of a barking dog, for instance, one looks for and localizes the source of sound (front or back) upon perceiving the dog. Also, certain sounds come from characteristic directions (airplanes in the air, dogs on the ground). Even when the source of the sound is presented in a position quite divergent from the apparent visual origin, one adapts and tends to localize the sound in accord with the visual cues. For example, someone in a drive-in movie is aware that the sound comes from the speaker hung in the window, located left or right, rather than from the direction of the screen. After a short period, however, he tends to perceive the sound as coming from the screen and is no longer disturbed by the discrepancy. Furthermore, placement of the speaker in the back seat solves the problem created by "cones of confusion" and no further difficulty is experienced in "hearing" the sound from the screen.

Of the early studies in sound localization, several have won the position of classical experimental studies in the psychological literature. One such study was conducted by Paul Thomas Young in 1927 during his stay at the University of Berlin. The experimental studies lent credulence to the speculative explanations of the mechanism of auditory space localization which were presented above. Beyond this, however, Young's insightful and narrative style of presentation provides enjoyable reading matter in itself. In the experimental psychology of today, lack of space and de-emphasis of subjective observations have all but destroyed the literary aspects of psychological reports. Further, special note should be given to the "control group" listed in the first footnote. All of these individuals continued in psychology and contributed a great deal to our knowledge of behavioral processes. The original report appeared in the *Journal of Experimental Psychology* in 1928, after Professor Young had returned to the University of Illinois. The present writer has made some minor editorial changes and abridged the original forty-page manuscript.

Auditory Localization with Acoustical Transposition of the Ears

Paul Thomas Young

If a master surgeon could transplant the right inner ear to the left side of the head, stretching the eighth nerve without disturbing any of the neural connections, and at the same time transplant the left inner ear to the right side of the head, one would expect sound localizations to be reversed as regards right and left. Right-left reversal would be expected from the standpoint of any one of the leading theories of auditory localization.

Although such an operation is out of the question the same result can be brought about acoustically in a relatively simple manner. The right auditory meatus can be extended over the head by means of a sound-proof tube which is connected to an artificial pinna in the region of the left ear; and by a similar device the left auditory meatus can be extended to an artificial pinna near the right ear.

The Pseudophone. An apparatus called a pseudophone after Thompson (1879) for transposing the ears acoustically is shown in Figure 5.6. The olive-shaped earpieces, right and left, are so made as to fit into the corresponding auditory canals. Each earpiece is connected by a rubber joint to a soundproof tube which passes over the head to a receiving-trumpet on the opposite side. These trumpets are made of hard rubber and are taken, in fact, from an instrument designed for persons hard of hearing. All parts are fastened to a light frame which rests snugly upon the head and which exerts a weak pressure on the earpieces, thus holding the entire apparatus in place. The receiving trumpets are placed immediately in front of the natural pinnae and each is turned slightly forward at an angle corresponding to the natural angle of the pinna.

The tubes of the apparatus are precisely equal in length and are symmetrical in every respect so that the time consumed by a sound wave in passing from the right trumpet to the left ear is equal to that consumed by a wave passing from the left trumpet to the right ear. Hence the apparatus reverses the normal time-difference between stimulation of right and left ears. It can easily be shown that the apparatus also reverses the phase difference between right and left ears, and further that it reverses the binaural intensive ratio. Consequently right-left reversal of localization is to be expected from the standpoint of any one of the leading localization theories.

The chief practical difficulty with the pseudophone was the prevention of sound leakage between the earpieces and the auditory meatus. The slight tension of the apparatus against the ears helped to prevent leakage; but this tension produced headaches (and so had to be reduced) and eventually it made the auditory canal quite sore through friction and rubbing. The earpieces were fitted to the writer's ears and when in use they were smeared with thick Vaseline®. Despite the Vaseline® there was some sound leakage; but by far the greater part of energy reaching the ears came through the apparatus. When properly adjusted a watch held so close that it touched the skin of the ear was not heard on the same side but was sometimes weakly heard on the opposite side. This watch test was used every time the pseudophone was adjusted and whenever leakage was suspected.

A question which naturally arises is whether the pseudophone modified the characteristics of the stimulus. All sounds heard through the instrument appeared noticeably louder than normal, and this is probably explained by the size and shape of the receiving-funnels which were designed for the deaf and so collected more sound energy than the natural pinnae. Sounds heard through the pseudophone were accompanied by a faint humming noise similar to that heard when listening to a hollow cavity, and this effect is doubtless due to resonance of the tubes for frequencies of a particular range. The timbre of sounds was also changed by the apparatus; but the modification was slight and did not disturb the observations. With adaptation all of these peculiarities ceased to be noticed.

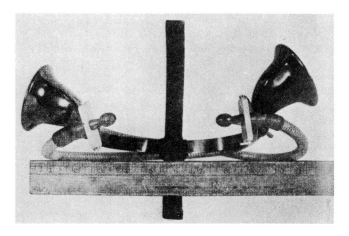

Figure 5.6:   The reversing pseudophone.

Experimental

The problem. The experiment started from the assumption that acoustical transposition of the ears would also transpose sound localizations and thus produce a basic discrepancy between visual and auditory spaces. The original problem was twofold; (1) What are the characteristics of sound localization with the ears transposed? and (2) Does habituation bring back to normal initial disturbances in auditory localization?

First Observations

The experiments described in the following account were made mainly by the writer, although a group of nine subjects was used for purposes of control.[1] The observations were made under conditions of everyday life on the streets of Berlin and in the house. Experiments were also made in the laboratory under controlled conditions. In the latter case localization was made by pointing to the source of the sound. Various sources were used such as rapping on wood, ticking of a clock or metronome, whistling, and the voice.

First observations of the writer are given in part below. On May 12 the pseudophone was worn about the laboratory for twenty minutes. Disturbances in localization were recorded at the time of their occurrence.

While writing in my notebook the creaking of a door was heard directly behind and then a laboratory assistant was seen entering the door immediately in front (180° reversal). A few minutes later this same assistant stood beside his desk on my left and dictated a letter. His voice seemed louder than normal and it had an unfamiliar timbre. When I looked at him the localization of his voice was entirely normal. The same door opened a second time. At first the creaking sounds were heard in the rear but when I looked at the man entering the room the localization of these sounds changed to front.

The noise of rain pattering on the window pane across the room at my left was distinctly localized off to the right and at the same time a watch seen on a table on my right was heard ticking at the left (double simultaneous reversal). The assistant who stood in front of the window spoke and his voice was normally localized but at the same time the rain pattering on the window was heard on the opposite side (simultaneous normal and reversed localization).

On May 14 I stood before an open window of the Institute and listened to the street sounds in front and a few feet below. The tread of horses on the pavement, auto horns, street-car bells, and the hum of motors, seemed to be normally localized. Once a horse came from the left to the median plane. The sound of the tread was normal in localization. When the horse reached the median plane I closed my eyes. Then the horse was distinctly heard to recede

---

[1] The control group consisted of Fl. T. Dembo, Dr. K. E. Zener, Herr K. Duncker, Herr Dr. K. Gottschaldt, Herr F. Hoppe, Mr. N. Maier, Mr. J. F. Brown, Dr. C. R. Griffith and Herr Dr. K. Lewin.

in the direction from which he came. A moment later the eyes were opened and when the horse was again seen the localization of the tread quickly became normal.

On May 18 a metronome was placed head-high in a quiet room and started at the rate of ninety-two strokes per minute. When I stood directly in front of the metronome and looked at it there was no disturbance in localization. When I turned my right side towards the metronome bringing the source roughly in the binaural axis the clicks were localized at the left despite the fact that I saw the metronome indirectly at the right. Similarly, when I turned my left side toward the metronome the ticking was distinctly on the right. The localization was clear-cut and definite and there was an unmistakable discrepancy between visual and auditory localizations of the metronome-object. I walked around the source in a circle of about 1.5-m radius keeping my right shoulder towards the beating metronome. The sound was localized to the left and it moved around the room as I walked. The sound seemed to come from a phantom source upon the wall. I turned my left side to the metronome and walked in a circle in the reverse direction. The sound was distinctly on the right and it moved about the room as I walked.

On May 26 the metronome experiment was repeated. I discovered a curious illusion in which estimations of distance and of direction were incompatible. When my right trumpet was directed towards the metronome the ticking was localized at the end of the room to my left. Keeping my right trumpet towards the source I moved sidewards in the direction of the sound. When I walked towards the sound the intensity became less and less and when I walked away from the sound the intensity grew louder and louder. When I moved towards the sound I appeared to be going in the right direction but at the same time to be getting always farther and farther from the supposed source. When I moved away from the sound I appeared to be coming nearer and nearer to the source. The experience was paradoxical. When I deviated from the direct path I found that the sound was no longer at that end of the room but had changed to some other place. When I walked around the room parallel to the walls the phantom sound moved with me and was always away from the center of the room. The task of approaching and "finding" the phantom sound-object on the basis of auditory cues was impossible, a will-o'-the-wisp chase.

After the above observations an assistant studied my localizations made with closed eyes. He reported that in the region of the binaural axis, localization was misplaced by about 180° but in the region of the median plane another type of right-left reversal was generally made. This second type may be described as right-left reversal without front-back reversal. For example, if the source were 15° to the right of the median plane in front, the localization would be 15° to the left of the median plane in front, and vice versa. The latter type of right-left reversal was also noticed with the control subjects but the conditions of its occurrence have not been investigated.

Definitions.   The first observations gave rise to a distinction between normal and reversed localization. *Normal localization* is placing the sound where its objective source exists. This occurs with and without the pseudo-phone. *Reversed localization* is placing the sound at the subject's left when the source exists at his right and placing the sound at the subject's right when the source exists at his left. Apparently there are two or more types of reversal and these will be considered later. Throughout the following study the terms "normal" and "reversed" localizations will be used as here defined.

Preliminary Experiments

(A) **Binaural Intensive Ratio.** The sensitiveness of a trumpet may be reduced by stuffing it with cotton. The amount of cotton and the tightness with which it is packed regulate roughly the amount of sound energy passing through a trumpet to the opposite ear. Control of the binaural intensive ratio in this manner gave an interesting and unexpected result.

Sound localizations were thrown towards the more sensitive trumpet. For example, when I stood with my right trumpet turned towards the metronome the clicking was heard at the left. When I stuffed cotton in the right trumpet without changing any other condition the localization remained at the left and was even more definite and distinct than before the reduction of "sensitivity." When I removed the cotton and stuffed it in the left trumpet without changing any other condition the first effect was to make localization vague, diffuse, indefinite, and this was followed by unmistakable normal localization of the sounds.

This tendency for localization to be on the side of the open trumpet was strikingly demonstrated by the following method. The right trumpet was plugged and the body moved so that at one moment the open left trumpet was turned towards the source and at another moment the open trumpet was turned away. This procedure brought about distinct changes from normal to reversed localization since the localization tended to be on the side of the open trumpet. In rotating the body localization was in one position definitely normal and in another position definitely reversed, but between these two regions were transitional places of indefinite localization.

The observations were repeated at widely separated intervals throughout the entire experiment and always with the same result. As a check the pseudo-phone was put on backwards so that the right earpiece fitted into the left ear and both trumpets were directed towards the rear instead of towards the front. A clock was used instead of a metronome. In this case the result was the same; localization tended to be thrown towards the open or more "sensitive" trumpet.

One very important fact needs to be considered. The above observations were made by the writer alone and with complete knowledge of conditions including the position of the source. One or two tests with control subjects failed to confirm the result when eyes were closed and the subject was ignorant as to which trumpet was stuffed and ignorant of the position of the source. There is need for further experimentation upon this curious phenomenon.

(B) Localization with a Single Trumpet and Ear.   Observations upon monaural localization were made by removing one of the earpieces and stuffing the ear with cotton smeared with Vaseline®. It was found that the index finger covered with Vaseline® and held in the ear practically eliminated external sounds.

Repeated observations gave the same result. A few excerpts have been made for purposes of illustration.

> "Right ear plugged and right trumpet connected to left ear. I am actually hearing with the right trumpet. When the trumpet is turned towards the clock the ticking is louder and clearer than when the trumpet is directed to other places and also the sounds are localized *there* where I see the clock. When the trumpet is turned away from the clock localization is indeterminate. The sounds are nowhere, indefinite, or perhaps they are vaguely placed where the source is. A watch placed next to the right trumpet gives ticking in or next to the left ear."

On another day:

> "Left ear plugged and left trumpet connected to right ear. When the trumpet is directed towards the source localization is wholly indeterminate. Once I thought it was reversed, but I'm not sure of that."

In general, the results indicate that normal localization is possible with a single trumpet connected to the opposite ear. Normal localization was easy, definite, certain when the clock was located in front of the trumpet. Under present experimental conditions a left trumpet appears to function as a left pinna despite the fact that it leads to the right ear, and a right trumpet appears to function as a right pinna despite the fact that it leads to the left ear.

The above observations were made by the writer with complete knowledge of conditions including the position of the source. On two successive days following these observations, experiments were made without knowledge. The writer was seated and kept his eyes closed. An assistant held the clock in the plane of the head at a distance of about ½ m. Localization was indicated by pointing to the source. The assistant estimated that localizations were objectively wrong in about 80 percent of the trials. There were some right-left confusions. I found myself observing the loudness and timbre of the ticking sounds and noting how these characteristics of the sound changed when I moved the head. Objectively correct localizations were made on the basis of these cues.

The total experiment shows that knowledge of the position of the source may determine monaural localization; and that experiments with knowledge and without knowledge may give wholly different results.

(C) Observations with Two Pinnae on the Same Side of the Head.   On four successive days of the experiment the left earpiece was removed so that the auditory meatus was unobstructed and at the same time the left trumpet was connected to the right auditory meatus. The arrangement gave two pinnae —one natural and one artificial—on the same side of the head, and none on the opposite side. The trumpet was a bit in front of the natural pinna and 5 to 7 cm removed from its peripheral ridges (see Figure 5.6). A similar arrangement gave two right auricles.

A few excerpts from the record follow.

"When the two left pinnae were directed towards the source localization was normal and surprisingly definite. The field of definiteness extended to the median plane and well around to the right in front and in back. When the right side of the head was turned towards the source the localization was indefinite and uncertain and at times localization was lacking. Twice in this case when the head was about a meter from the clock the localization was reversed. I tried repeatedly to find the conditions of reversal but failed to do so."

"With two right pinnae localizations are normal in all places around me but at the left there is a region of indefiniteness. Sounds from the left region are voluminous, space-filling, unlocalized, and relatively weak in intensity. Occasionally localizations are reversed when the source is at the left and then the sounds have a different *Klangfarbe* from that of normally localized sounds."

Observations were made by the writer with complete knowledge of conditions including the position of the source.

(D) Right Trumpet to Right Ear and Left Trumpet to Left Ear.   Following a suggestion of Dr. M. Wertheimer a control experiment was made with modified pseudophone. The apparatus was changed so that the right trumpet connected through the sound-proof tube to the right earpiece and similarly the left trumpet connected to the left earpiece. Observations were made without knowledge of conditions; the writer localized and an assistant served as experimenter.

Right and left were never confused but in the median plane front and back were sometimes interchanged. Some of the localizations were made by means of deliberate head movements and observing the changes in intensity and timbre in relation to these movements. When the source was directly in the central axis of the right trumpet localization was due right, although actually this axis pointed somewhat to the front of due right (see Figure 5.6). The same was true on the left side. Positions in front of the trumpet's axis were confused with positions behind the axis.

The Main Experiment

The aim of the main experiment was (1) to determine the characteristics of sound localization with the ears acoustically transposed and (2) to study the effect of habituation when the ears are transposed.

During the experiment the pseudophone was worn for a period of eighteen consecutive days. For the first nine days the pseudophone was worn an hour daily (11 to 12 A.M., June 10–18). For the following six days the period was lengthened to two hours (10 to 12 A.M., June 19–24). Most of this time was spent upon the streets of Berlin in the region of the Kurfürstendamm, observing the localization of various street sounds.[2] Finally the pseudophone was worn continuously for three complete days. At night during the latter period the pseudophone was removed and the ears were plugged with *Ohropax* (a commercial product) and Vaseline®. The time (June 25–27) was spent on the street, in the house under everyday conditions and in the psychological laboratory. During the main experiment the pseudophone was worn for a total of fifty-eight hours. From first to last in the present investigation the writer observed with the pseudophone approximately eighty-five hours.

(I) Characteristics of Sound Localization with the Ears Acoustically Transposed

In the following sections each paragraph contains material taken from a single experimental day. Within each section the chronological order has been preserved, but a few sample reports cannot indicate temporal relations nor the frequency with which each type of experience occurred.

(A) **Dissociation of Visual and Auditory Localizations.**   The term "dissociation" is here used to describe a type of experience in which a well-known source is seen in one place while the sound, known to be associated with the source, is heard in another place.

> A mechanical pavement-breaker was making a very loud noise pounding and breaking the rocks on the street. As I approached the machine the sound was clearly and unmistakably transposed in locality. The noise remained reversed regardless of whether my right or left side was turned towards the source. I sat on a bench 150 feet away from the pavement-breaker but the localization was still reversed. By looking steadily at the source and thinking about its position I could get a normal localization but I could not get a sharp and definite placing of the sounds at the place of the source.

> While thinking out a problem and paying no attention to the auditory experiment I noticed that the clock on my left was heard ticking distinctly on my right and this continued after the abnormality was noted. I was in a state of abstraction.

(B) **Right-Left Reversal of Auditory Localization.**   There were a good many cases in which definite localization was made and subsequent investigation proved that the localization had been reversed. Some examples follow.

> I heard a dog barking distinctly to the left-front. Quite automatically I looked towards the spot and saw some shrubbery but no dog. After a random visual search the barking dog was found to the right-back of my original position.

---

[2] When the pseudophone was worn on the streets it was covered by a large, loose-fitting cap which left the trumpets and earpieces uncovered. The apparatus had the appearance of a rather freakish instrument for a Schwerhörer. It was more or less embarrassing to be seen on the streets with the outfit.

I stood with my back towards the street, looking in a store window. An auto passed behind me from left to right and the localization was normal. The horn tooted unexpectedly first on the left (which was heard right) and then on the right (which was heard left). A small cue such as reflection of objects in the plate glass was enough to give knowledge of actual conditions.

(C) Changes from Reversed to Normal Localization and Vice Versa.   In a great many cases the reversed localization changed to normal when the position of the source became known. This was frequently the case with continuative noises. Shifts from normal to reversed localization were relatively infrequent but occurred when a source passed out of view and was no longer attended to.

I stood before an open window facing the street which was a bit below. A horse, motorcycle, or truck would be heard approaching, for example, from the right and I would expect to see the source appear at the right. Despite expectation the source regularly appeared at the left. When I fixated the source visually and followed it across the field the sounds were normally localized; but after the source had disappeared at the right the sounds were frequently heard receding at the left. Several times there was dissociation: I saw a team walking away to the right and heard a phantom auditory team going away to the left. I closed my eyes and followed the auditory movements by pointing. An assistant said that pointing was consistently opposite to the actual movements of the source. For example, when a vehicle moved from left to right the pointing was from right to left.

An assistant in the laboratory tested my localizations as I sat on a chair with eyes closed. Unmounted tuning forks of the following frequencies were used: 100, 150, 250, 500, 600 d.v. When a fork was in front of the trumpet localization was on the opposite side. When a fork was moved from right to left localization shifted from left to right. After this I opened my eyes and held a fork near the right trumpet; localization was to the right. I moved the fork to the left; localization was to the left. Rotating the fork gave the customary maxima and minima of intensity without changing the localization.

(D) Reversal of the Localizing Reaction.   Not only were the sounds transposed in localization but also bodily movements were occasionally reversed. Bodily movements seem to be secondary processes in the sense that localization does not depend upon them.

While walking along the sidewalk I heard the voices of two ladies and their steps approaching and overtaking me from behind on the right. Quite automatically I stepped to the left making more room for them to pass. I looked back and found that I had stepped directly in front of them. My automatic reaction as well as the localization was reversed.

(E) Deliberate Correction of the Localizing Reaction.   Reversals of bodily reaction generally occurred during the early part of the experiment. On the third day deliberate movements were made on the basis of knowledge and not on the basis of the sensory localization.

I found myself deliberately correcting known reversals. I heard a pedestrian overtaking me from behind on the right. Knowing that the person was actually on the left, I stepped aside to the right to let him pass. Once I heard a team of horses drawing near on a side street to my right. Deliberately I looked to the left and saw the team there, and at the same time the localization of the sound shifted.

I heard a pedestrian overtaking me on the left. As the sounds came nearer I expected the person to pass on the right but the sounds were still heard left. For a moment there was an interplay between sensory expectation (left) and intellectual expectation (right). Then I *heard* the pedestrian on the right at the moment he appeared there in indirect vision.

(F) Normal Localizations.   One of the most interesting features of the present experiment is the occurrence of normal localizations despite the transposition of the ears. The preliminary experiments showed that, at the very start, fixation of the source, or attention to it, sometimes brought about normal localization. This occurred repeatedly at all stages of the present experiment. Thousands of cases were not recorded.

Sixteenth day: "The ordinary house sounds were normally localized—closing of doors, foot-steps, running water, etc. After an hour on the street I had the impression that practically all sound localizations were normal. When an object was seen the sound localization was normal without any thought about it; when not seen but attentively followed localizations were usually normal. Very probably there were undiscovered reversals. . . . When I entered my room the clock was ticking in its normal place regardless of whether right, left, front or back, provided I looked at it or attended to its position. I rested on a couch for half an hour. The clock was ticking at my right and normally localized throughout. Then I put the clock on a table in the center of the room at the height of the head and walked around it. With my left trumpet towards the clock the localization was reversed and the ticking moved around the wall. The reversed type of localization soon gave way to the normal type. When the right trumpet was turned there was at first uncertainty and then normal localization. When I stood with the clock in front the ticking was in back but soon became normal and remained normal. Thus after relaxing on a couch there was at first reversed and uncertain localization and then an appreciable recovery of the normal type."

(G) Atypical Auditory Localizations.   The record contains three cases of confusion between front and back—two on the left side and one on the right. For example:

An auto was seen to pass on the left. When in front two toots of an auto horn were heard in back on the left. There were no other autos in sight so the case was probably a confusion of front and back on the left side. The localization was immediate.

The record also contains three cases of normal localization made on a purely auditory basis when the source was not in view.

(H) Double Localizations.   Several types of double localization occurred. (1) When stimulation was relatively intense localization was sometimes in or at the opposite ear while at the same time a second localization was out in space at the place of the source. (2) When a source moved across the median plane in back there were sometimes two localizations—one to the right and one to the left of the median plane. Both sounds were out in space. (3) When two characteristically different sounds originated at about the same place the sound attentively observed was normal while the other was transposed. This was noticed in the first observations.

> The hum of a motor was normally localized and at the same time the hum was also heard on the opposite side. It is hardly correct to say that I heard two hums—one right and one left—for the experience had a unitary character. It would be more nearly correct to say that one and the same motor hum was heard simultaneously in two places.

> I sat on a bench with my back towards the street. There were two simultaneous localizations which spread out from the median plane in opposite directions. For example, the sharp sounds made by a horse-tread gave the impression of a horse moving from the median plane to the left and at the same time of a horse moving from the median plane to the right. I followed a team attentively from right to left and checked up visually to make sure that the actual team had passed from right to left. I heard the noises pass normally from right to left. When the team was directly behind there were double localizations. A ghost-like sound which I regarded as an auditory mirror-image moved in a direction opposite to the main sound.

> Seventeenth day: I stood in my room with a clock in the median plane about a meter in front of me. I noticed two types of localization: (1) With eyes open, head and eyes fixated upon the clock, an observational set to hear the clock where it is—the ticking was localized in an entirely normal manner. The ticking was *there* in front and there was no other localization. (2) With eyes closed, with a very slight oscillatory movement of the head and with an observational set directed towards the rear, the ticking was localized in the rear. It was unmistakably *there*. The timbre of the sound was different in the two cases. Under the second conditions the sound had a metallic character which was rich and full when compared with the sound heard under the first conditions. Ordinarily there was either one or the other localization but at times both were present together and when this occurred the ticking was heard simultaneously front and back and also there was an unmistakable difference in timbre. The rich metallic ticking was in back and the other ticking was in front.

(J) Unlocalized Sounds and Indefinite Localizations.   When a sound was definitely and precisely localized it was referred to a small spot—whether the localization was normal or reversed. There were times, however, when this spot was large and when the auditory image was poorly defined. There were also times when the localization was merely off-at-the-right or off-at-the-left and the sound seemed to be diffuse and voluminous. Frequently localization was entirely lacking but the loudness, timbre, pitch, and temporal relations of the sound were still definitely recognizable. Unlocalized sounds were very diffuse and sometimes appeared to surround the body indefinitely in all direc-tions. Diffuseness or space-filling character seems to vary inversely with the precision of localization.

> I tapped on the pavement and on fence posts with a cane. The localization was not reversed nor was it normal. The sounds belonged *there* at the tip of the cane or on the pavement but there was no clear-cut sensory localization of the sounds. The sounds were referred in thought to the source but they were not heard there. They were not heard anywhere.

> Sixteenth day: Once a rumbling sound was heard at the left. The localization was very indefinite. The sound was clearly on the left and it was spread out diffusely in space. Then an auto was vaguely sensed in indirect vision at the right and the localization shifted to the right but it remained indefinite. It was diffuse, in no particular place, but certainly off at the right. Then the auto passed and localization became definite and normal. The sound of the motor was exceedingly loud. . . .

(II) The Effect of Habituation

On the afternoon of the last day of the experiment an assistant tested the writer's localizations. Eyes were closed and localizations were made by point-ing. Every trial gave a right-left reversal! This indicates that habituation to the extent of about 58 hours did not disturb the right-left reversal of localizations made on a purely auditory basis.

Throughout the main experiment when a sound came suddenly, un-expectedly, or from an unknown position the localization was reversed. When, in other words, localization was made on a purely auditory basis reversal was the usual thing at the close of the habituation period. The total record contains only three cases of objectively correct localization made under everyday condi-tions on a purely auditory basis. If one considers that a chance predisposition may account for these three cases, it becomes likely that habituation to pseudo-phonic localization gave no indication of a return to normal. From first to last purely auditory localizations were reversed.

The case is different when the influence of vision is considered. At the very start of the experiment localizations were occasionally normal when the source was seen or when its position was attentively fixated. This was reported by every one of the nine control subjects who, incidentally, gave reversed localization when tested with closed eyes.

For the writer normal localizations usually occurred when the source was fixated visually or when an attentive adjustment was made to its position. As the experiment progressed a casual glance at an object was sufficient to check up the fact that its sound was normally localized. With habituation all of the sounds in a complex situation were normally localized without any thought about the matter. On a busy street, for example, with a street-car *here* and a man talking *there* and an auto passing *yonder*, all sounds were normally local-ized and the total visual-auditory experience was as it is in everyday life with-out the pseudophone. And not only this! When a source passed out of view its localization remained normal when I paid any attention to the matter. In other words, at the start vision sometimes determined the localization and with habituation there was increasing dominance of vision until finally a stage was reached indistinguishable from normal. There was increasing and finally complete visual dominance in determining sound localizations but, as noted above, this did not extend to auditory localizations lacking a visual cue.

Dissociation of visual and auditory localization was more apt to occur during the first ten or fifteen minutes of the experimental period than at other times. Several of the control subjects also noticed at the start a wholly confused and disorganized visual-auditory world. This does not mean that the occurrence of visual-auditory dissociation was limited to the early part of the experiment. Dissociation was apt to appear at any stage of the experiment when the sounds were loud. It appeared once when I was in a condition of abstraction, and at the close of the experiment dissociation could be brought about through the control of observational attitude when the source was in the binaural axis. But the impression remains—although it is only an impression—that disorganization between visual and auditory worlds was present more frequently during the first than during the latter part of the hour. Moreover, dissociation was more prominent during the first days of the experiment than during the last days. At the close of the experiment it was possible to go for hours without noticing any case of visual-auditory dissociation.

One interesting change with habituation refers not to the place-character of the sound but to the bodily movements. During the first two or three days localizing reactions—moving the head so as to fixate a source, gross movements of the body corresponding to the sound—were occasionally right-left reversed. When this was discovered movements were made deliberately so as to correct the disturbance. Then I practically ceased depending on auditory cues and relied largely on vision. Before crossing a street there was much looking here and there. Habituation led to increased reliance upon vision in the regulation of bodily movement. Perhaps, however, realization of the unreliableness of auditory cues, combined with the warning of friends that the experiment involved real danger if I were careless, had something to do with this increased reliance upon vision.

The pseudophone was removed at 5:30 P.M. on the eighteenth day of the experiment. There was at first a refreshing calm about the entire world of sounds and this lasted at least ten or fifteen minutes. Doubtless this quiet should be regarded as an adaptation effect. The pseudophone, being made of trumpets for the deaf, increased the intensive level of all sounds and added resonance of its own in a certain frequency range. For three days I had been adapted to this and ceased to notice it. Then sudden relief came and gave the impression that all sounds in the laboratory and on the street were quiet and "soft." Upon removal of the pseudophone localizations were immediately normal and no subsequent disturbance in localization was noted.

The experiment leads to the distinction between two types of sound localization, definable in terms of their conditions; (a) auditory and (b) visual-auditory. Habituation developed the second type to a point indistinguishable from normal life without changing the first type.

Summary and Discussion

Effect of the Pseudophone upon Auditory Localization. The present experiment started from the assumption that auditory localization depends upon a difference of stimulation between the right and left ears. The physical nature of this difference has not been considered: it may be a difference of time, phase, amplitude, wave-form, or a combination of these conditions. Whatever the essential physical basis of localization may be, the acoustical interchange of the ears may be expected to give a right-left reversal to sound localizations.

The theoretical expectation has been abundantly confirmed. When localizations were made with closed eyes and without knowledge of the position of the source there was a consistent and unmistakable right-left reversal of localizations. This was the case with a control group of nine subjects. With the writer, reversed localization persisted after the pseudophone had been worn about eighty-five hours. With the acoustical interchange of the ears a source on the left was placed with great regularity on the right and vice versa. The few exceptions to this rule can be explained by reference to extraneous experimental conditions.

The exact effect of the pseudophone upon auditory localization has not been studied, and it is clear that a thorough quantitative investigation is needed to clear up the matter. In general, two types of right-left reversal were noted.

(A) The most frequently noticed disturbance was a right-left reversal of about 180°. When the source was 60° from the median plane in the right-front quadrant, Figure 5.5, the localization was 60° from the median plane in the left-back quadrant. When the source was 90° left the localization was 90° right and vice versa.

The relationship is not exactly one of 180° as will be seen from the following observation. Let S represent a source, O an observer, and L the position of the localized sound.

If the relationship between source and localized sound were exactly 180° in every case, rotation of the body of O would not change the apparent position of L. The experiment was made several times by the writer. In four critical positions the 180° relationship was seemingly exact; when the source was due right or due left and when it was in the median plane in front or in back of O. Between any two of these positions the sound was displaced to the right or to the left; in two quadrants it moved to the right and in two quadrants to the left. This observation is given to indicate that the relationship is not exactly one of 180° and that the matter needs to be investigated quantitatively.

(B) On several occasions an assistant tested the writer's localizations. He reported that when the source was, for example, 10° to the right of the median plane in front the sound was localized 10° to the left of the median plane in front. The same relationship was found near the median plane in the rear.

A clock was carried in a circle around the head of one of the control subjects who had been instructed to follow its motion by pointing. When the source was 30° right-front he pointed 30° left-front (see Figure 5.7); when the source was 60° right-front he pointed 60° left-front; when 90° right he pointed 90° left; when 60° right-back he pointed 60° left-back, and so on for several complete revolutions. This was rare for most frequently he and the other subjects pointed to a position 180° from the source.

The median plane presents a special case. When the source is due front it is generally localized as due back. When the source is due back it may be localized in front but most frequently it is localized in back. In other words, localizations in the median plane tend to be thrown towards the rear. This suggests the normal tendency to throw localizations forward.

The above statements are not intended to represent final conclusions but rather to indicate problems in need of further study. Right-left reversals should be studied in relation to such conditions as the distance between the trumpets, the direction in which the trumpets face, the binaural intensive ratio.

Visual Dominance. Acoustical transposition of the ears introduces a basic discrepancy between sound localization and visible source. When, however, a source is fixated visually or merely attended to without fixation the sounds originating from the source may be localized normally. This was observed repeatedly by the writer and verified by a group of nine control observers. Habituation to pseudophonic hearing made the normal localizations more frequent, certain, and definite until finally the visual-auditory integrations were indistinguishable from those of ordinary life. At the close of the habituation experiment the writer could remain on a busy street for an hour or more without noticing any lack of coordination between visual and auditory experiences.

In everyday life one does not have to search far to find situations in which vision dominates in determining sound localization. The ventriloquist speaks consistently in one voice when he moves puppet A and in another voice when he moves puppet B. The on-looker becomes gradually adjusted to the situation and then gets the well-known ventriloquist's illusion. The vitaphone (talking motion pictures) gives a further illustration of the same principle. The voice of a speaker in an auditorium may be indefinitely localized but fixation upon the speaker makes the localization more definite. Here are cases of visual-auditory localization!

Auditory and Visual-Auditory Localization. Although visual-auditory localizations developed so that the sight-sound coordinations were indistinguishable from those of normal life, auditory localizations remained persistently reversed till the close of the experiment. Both types of localization are stable and they are easily distinguished since one type gives reversed and the other type gives normal localization. Auditory localization depends upon some physical difference between the stimulation of right and left ears. Visual-auditory localization depends upon an adjustment of the organism with respect to a visible or known position in phenomenal space.

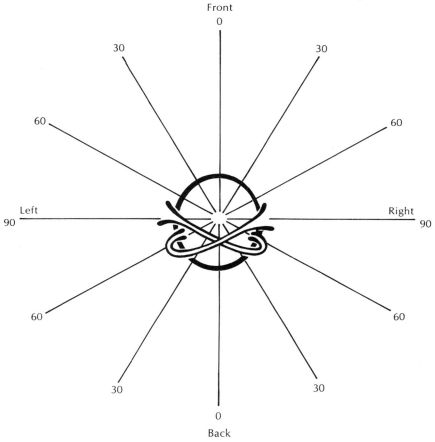

Figure 5.7

The experiment as a whole makes it necessary to distinguish between these two types of sound localization. And the distinction relates in an orderly way all of the facts revealed in the main experiment: dissociation of source and sound; right-left reversal of localization; shifts from reversed to normal localization and vice versa; reversed localizing reactions; normal localizations; double localizations. Indefinite localizations and a few atypical localizations can be explained as intermediate or transitional experiences.

Auditory-Motor Localization.   When a deliberate search is made for the source of a sound without the aid of vision and touch subjective changes in the loudness and timbre of the auditory experience in relation to head and gross bodily movements assume the leading role. Auditory-motor localization may lead to a correct judgment of the position of the source. It may also lead to an immediate normal localization despite the reversal of the pinnae.

How Are Sounds Localized?   The physical theories are doubtless correct in maintaining that sound localization depends upon some difference between the stimulation of the right and left ears; but these theories do not go far enough. They throw no light on the physiological and psychological processes of localization. They fail to take into account the possibilities of visual and auditory-motor localization.

Equally incomplete is the statement that sound localization depends upon "suggestion" and "knowledge." What is "suggestion"? and how does "knowledge" operate? We have already seen that sensory localization—the hearing of a sound as here or there—may not agree with the knowledge of the position of the source. Words cannot solve the problem as to how sounds are localized.

> Animals react to sudden noises by moving the body so that the source comes to be visually fixated. If a noise is made near a resting dog, the ears will be pricked up and the head moved so as to bring the source before the eyes. The writer recently saw a cat pass beside a basement window at a distance of about two meters. When the animal was directly opposite the window he tapped lightly on the pane. Instantly the cat stopped, turned her head towards the window, looked, and ran away. Münsterberg (1889) has pointed out that such localizing reactions have biological value since they bring the source before the eyes and under the nose of the creature.

Actual movement appears to be unnecessary for sound localization. I believe that the essential condition is a neuro-muscular set, a postural adjustment of muscles relative to some position in space or relative to the total situation. This set is the condition of movement when localizing movements do occur, but the set may persist without any explicit reaction.

What is meant by neuromuscular set may be demonstrated as follows. Let the reader pick out certain points in front, in back, and to the side; then with eyes closed let there be attentive fixation first on one point and then on some other. The kinaesthetic pattern in the region of the eyes and head will be felt to shift with change of attentive fixation. Doubtless the kinaesthetic patterns indicate changes in the tonus of muscles. In the early stages of the main experiment visual-auditory localization seemed to involve similar adjustments with reference to the position of the source.

Goldstein (1926) has noted that *Einstellung* may displace sound localizations in a non-conscious, physiological manner. He has also shown that localization should be regarded as a function of the total organism. Patients with cerebellar and frontal lesions showed disturbances in sound localization but they also showed similar disturbances in cutaneous and visual localization when the test was made by pointing. Localization depends upon muscle tonus.

The present experiment has made it clear that sound localization is not merely a function of the ear. It is an accomplishment of the organism as a whole involving muscle-systems common to both eye and ear. Under ordinary conditions auditory localization and visual-auditory localization bring about the same result—visual fixation of the source—and they bring about this result through the same muscles—those that move the eyes, head, trunk, etc.

With the pseudophone, auditory localization and visual-auditory localization became divorced and opposed in their demands upon the localizing musculature. The types remained distinct and the experiment gave no evidence that the auditory type is a derivative of the visual-auditory type. The probable explanation of this negative result lies in the fact that the two types of localization depend upon wholly different stimulus conditions. Auditory localization depends upon some acoustical difference between stimulation of right and left ears. Ordinarily the stimulation changes muscle tonus so that if movement results, the subject's eyes are directed towards the source. Visual-auditory localization, on the other hand, depends upon some visual cue which determines at the start the position of the source, and this cue may also determine the localization of the sound. The position of the source may be determined by touch and even by sound (auditory-motor localization). It is a neuro-muscular set or adjustment towards the source or the total situation which determines sound localization, and this set is describable as a pattern of muscular tonus.

If the above analysis is correct, there is no reason to expect that further habituation to visual-auditory localization with the pseudophone would eventually develop normal auditory localization. The former depends upon non-auditory cues and when these cues are removed there are left merely the acoustic conditions of localization and with the pseudophone these conditions result in reversed localization.

Whether repeated *auditory-motor* localization would eventually bring about normal *auditory* localization is a question which cannot be answered on the basis of present results.

Volume and Localization.   In the present experiment volume seemed to vary with the precision of localization. Sometimes a sound was heard precisely at a single spot. At other times the sound was larger and visualized as covering an area. Sometimes a sound was vaguely off-at-the-right or off-at-the-left and it appeared more diffuse than the definite localizations. Most interesting of all were the unlocalized sounds in which the pitch, intensity and timbre were about as always but the sounds had no particular place character. Sometimes they surrounded the body diffusely.

Unlocalized sounds appeared to be transitional between the two opposed localization types. A leak artificially made around the earpieces was found to make localizations indefinite, to give them greater outspread.

The observations suggest that volume and precision of localization are inversely related; the greater the volume the less precise the localization, and vice versa. In a good many unlocalized sounds, however, the volume was not observed.

I do not know what relation these observations may have to the views of Boring and Banister but I believe that volume should be more carefully studied in relation to localization.

Conclusions

1. Acoustical transposition of the ears by means of a pseudophone produced a right-left reversal of auditory localizations.

2. Despite the transposition of the ears, localizations of sound were normal when the source was seen or its position attentively fixated.

3. There are at least two distinct types of sound localization; (a) auditory localization and (b) visual-auditory localization.

4. Habituation up to fifty-eight hours did not modify auditory localizations and systematic practice up to thirteen additional one-hour periods gave no indication that normal auditory localization could be developed from the visual-auditory type.

5. Habituation to visual-auditory localization with the ears acoustically transposed developed the type until indistinguishable from normal.

6. Deliberate movements of search made with eyes closed in relation to observed changes in the loudness and timbre of sounds lead to objectively correct judgments of the position of the source and occasionally to immediately normal localizations, despite the acoustical transposition of the ears.

7. Localization is believed to be a function of the total organism, accomplished in various ways, but involving a neuromuscular adjustment with respect to a source or to a total spatial situation. The physiological conditions of localization are to be sought in pattern changes of muscle tonus.

CHAPTER 6
Context
and Perception

Perception depends on the situation in which it occurs, and stimuli can evoke a much different perceptual response when they appear in a different context. For example, a day of 65° weather, following a week of below-freezing temperatures, is perceived as being very warm, while another day with the same temperature seems rather cold, if it has been preceded by a week of 80° weather. A candle burning in a brightly lighted room appears rather dull, but the same candle in conditions of low illumination appears rather bright. In each case, the stimulus is perceived differently, while the sensory component remains the same.

Another situation, in which the sensory stimulus changes while the perceiver's definition of the stimulus remains unchanged, also is not uncommon. The shape of an object is recognized even when the object is presented from varying angles. A book, for example, first viewed straight on and then from an angle stimulates the retina quite differently in both cases. Yet the book is perceived as the same object. A young man recognizes his girl friend as the same individual despite differences in illumination, location, and even attitude.

The context in which a stimulus occurs may markedly affect perception, or perception of that same stimulus may remain constant in many different contexts. Situations exist in which both of these responses can be seen to occur. For example, in the perception of hue and brightness: an article of clothing, viewed first in an artificially lighted store, later may appear to possess a different hue or brightness in direct sunlight. On the other hand, the definition of hue and brightness of known objects remains unchanged even when the objects are viewed in varying degrees of illumination. Such objects are said to display *color constancy* and *brightness constancy*.

Hans Wallach of Swarthmore College studied extensively the conditions in which an object does or does not display constancy and published his now-classic report in the *Journal of Experimental Psychology* (1948). Although Wallach's description of the problems involved provides most of the background necessary to understand the results of his experiments, some explanations of terminology should be made. More recently perceptual psychologists have tended to use the term "color" in a somewhat different sense than utilized by Wallach in this paper. The psychological response, color, is considered to be composed of three dimensions: hue, brightness, and saturation. A color sensation displays some aspect of each of these three variables. "Hue" refers to the differential sensation evoked by light radiations of specific wavelengths. Brightness refers to the continuum extending from black through the various grays to white. Such achromatic colors contain no hues. "Saturation" refers to the pureness or number of wavelengths contributing to the sensation of color. Wallach uses the term "color" to refer to white, black, and gray tones (achromatic or opaque colors). In the present-day terminology, one refers to a variation in brightness rather than in color.

Furthermore, a brief description of the device known as an *episcotister* should make the following article easier to understand. The episcotister consists of a rotating disc with an opening of a given size or number of degrees. A constant light source of a set strength is passed through the rapidly rotating disc such that the light reaching a target surface is seen as constant rather than flickering. By varying the size of the opening in the disc, the strength of illumination of the target can be adjusted.

Brightness Constancy and the Nature of Achromatic Colors

Hans Wallach

Part I

The problem of brightness constancy arises through the following circumstances. The amount of light which is reflected by an opaque object and which stimulates the eye depends not only upon the color of the object but just as much upon the amount of light which falls on the object, that is upon the illumination in which the object is seen. When in spite of this, the seen colors are in agreement with the object colors, when a given object appears to have the same color in various illuminations, we speak of brightness constancy.

The majority of investigators who aim at all at functional explanations understand this problem to mean: How is illumination registered and in what way is it taken into account so that the experienced colors remain constant when the illumination is varied? In this version the problem is a difficult one at the outset, for illumination is never directly or independently given but is represented in stimulation only inasmuch as it affects the amount of light which is reflected by the objects. To be sure, we perceive illumination as well as surface color; a spot of light here, a shadow there, a brightly lighted region near the window or the dim light of dusk on everything. But the fact remains that both variables, object color and objective illumination, affect the eye through the same medium, the varying amount of reflected light. If the seen illumination were found to be in agreement with the objective illumination, in principle the same problem would arise which we face regarding the surface colors. There is only one stimulus variable to represent two objective variables each of which seems to have its counterpart in experience. Under these circumstances investigation has largely consisted in the study of factors by which illumination could be recognized and in the demonstration of their effectiveness in bringing about constancy.

The following observations suggested a radically different approach to the writer. They concern some variations of an experiment by A. Gelb which demonstrated brightness constancy in a most impressive way. Gelb's experiment (Ellis, 1939) is most conveniently performed by opening the door of a dimly lighted room and by suspending in the frame a piece of black paper. This paper is illuminated by a strong projection lantern which stands on the floor or on a low table and is tilted upwards so that the part of its beam which is not intercepted by the black paper passes through the open door onto the ceiling of the adjacent room where it is invisible to the observer. In the light of the strong lantern the paper may look white instead of black. When a piece of paper is held up in front of the black paper so that it too reflects the strong light of the lantern, the black paper assumes a black color. According to the usual interpretation it looks first white because no cues for the special strong illumination are available when this illumination affects only one visible surface. With the introduction of the white paper into the beam a special brilliant illumination becomes visible and constancy is restored: the two papers are perceived with their real color.

The arrangement of Gelb's experiment lends itself to a still more impressive demonstration. When the black paper is presented alone, reducing the intensity of the lantern light by small steps to zero causes the perceived color of the paper to vary all the way from white through gray to black. Every change in illumination is accompanied by a corresponding change in the perceived color. However, when a larger white paper is fastened behind the black paper so that the latter is seen surrounded by white, the same changes in illumination do not at all affect the seen colors which remain white and black throughout. Paired in this way the colors are immune to changes in illumination and remain "constant." It is rather a change in the perceived illumination which now accompanies the change in the objective illumination.

The question arises: what determines the color with which the black paper is seen at a given intensity of the lantern light when the paper is presented alone? Do we deal in this situation with an absolute relation between the intensity of the light which stimulates a portion of the retina and the resulting perceived color? In considering this question we have to remember that there is another variable in the situation, the dim general illumination of the room. When this is varied it becomes immediately clear that this general illumination also affects the color of the black paper. When, with a high intensity of the lantern light, the general illumination is raised, the color of the black paper changes from white to gray, and this in spite of the fact that the paper too now reflects light of a somewhat higher intensity than before. Only *relatively*, that is in relation to the light which comes from other surfaces, has the light reflected by the black paper become less intense.

Such dependence of the perceived color on the *relative* intensity of the perceived light should be demonstrable in a much simpler form, and this is the case.

In a dark room a white screen is illuminated by the light of two slide projectors. In one of the projectors an opaque card with a circular hole of ½-inch diameter is inserted, and the bright image of the hole is focused on the screen. The slide for the other projector consists of a blank glass covered with an opaque card with a circular hole of one-inch diameter and with a one-half inch cardboard disk which is pasted concentrically into the hole. Focused on the screen this slide produces a bright ring. The two projectors are so adjusted that this ring surrounds the image of the one-half inch hole so that the edge of the latter coincides with the inner edge of the ring. The light intensity of the projectors can be changed by running them on variable transformers or by letting their beams pass through episcotisters.

We have then on the screen a circular region (disk) and surrounding it a ringshaped region which reflect light intensities that can be separately controlled. When the intensity of the disk is kept constant and that of the ring is widely varied, the color of the disk may change all the way from white to dark gray. The disk looks dark gray when the light reflected from the ring is of high intensity and it becomes white when the brightness of the ring is greatly lowered. When the light intensity of the disk is varied and that of the ring is kept constant, the color of the disk, of course, undergoes similar changes. Again it is quite clear that the color which appears in one region, namely in that of the disk, depends on the relation of the light intensity of this region to that of its surroundings. This is true also of the ring. It can be shown in corresponding fashion that its color depends on the relation of the intensity of the ring to that of the disk.

When the ring is altogether omitted so that the disk is seen in completely dark surroundings, it ceases to look white or gray and assumes instead a luminous appearance similar to that of the moon at dusk. Lowering the intensity of the disk greatly does not change this mode of appearance, provided the rest of the room is really dark; the disk looks merely dimmer. The same observation can be made with the ring when it is presented without the disk, or with both the ring and the disk when they are placed far from each other on the screen. Opaque colors which deserve to be called white or gray, in other words "surface colors," will make their appearance only when two regions of different light intensity are in contact with each other, for instance when the ring surrounds the disk or when two oblongs have the longer edges as their common border.

The importance of a close contact for the emergence of surface colors becomes strikingly clear in the following observation. The intensity of the disk is adjusted to be one quarter that of the ring, which makes the color of the disk a medium gray. An opaque object is moved from the side into the beam of the lantern which projects the ring so that part of it is blotted out by the shadow of that object. When this happens the gray color disappears almost simultaneously from that part of the disk which is adjacent to the shadow. It looks as if the dense gray there were dissolving leaving the screen transparent to let a light behind it shine through. Brought about in this fashion, the change from surface color to a luminous appearance is quite impressive. That side of the disk which is still well surrounded by a brighter ring continues to show the gray color, and between it and the luminous side the disk shows a steady gradient in the density of the gray.

These observations make it clear that, at least under these conditions, surface colors occur in our experience when regions of different light intensity are in contact with each other and that the particular surface colors which come about depend on the relation of these light intensities. They are apparently the product of nervous processes of limited scope, for close spatial contact between the regions of different light intensity is required for their emergence. Moreover, the degree to which surface color is present in a certain region depends on the intimacy of the contact between this region and its partner. This is easily demonstrated by the following observations.

No matter what the brightness relation between ring and disk be, the ring will always show a less dense surface color and have more of a luminous appearance than the disk. This becomes quite clear when two pairs of such regions are presented for comparison which are so chosen that the intensity of the ring in one pair equals that of the disk in the other one, and vice versa. Even the region of lower light intensity in each pair, which is perceived as a gray, has a more luminous appearance where it occurs in the ring than where it occurs in the disk. The most obvious explanation for this difference in the mode of appearance is that the disk is more under the influence of the ring than vice versa, inasmuch as the disk is completely surrounded by the ring, whereas the ring is in contact with the disk only on one side. This explanation agrees well with the observation reported earlier that the elimination of part of the ring rendered that part of the disk more luminous which was then no longer enclosed by a region of different light intensity.

This influence under which surface colors emerge is clearly a mutual one. Though less so, the ring does display surface color. There is a great difference in the mode of appearance between a ring which surrounds, for instance, an area of higher intensity and an equal ring presented in an otherwise dark field. Whereas the latter looks merely luminous, the former shows in addition to some luminosity a distinct gray.

The mutual influence on which the emergence of surface colors depends must also account for the fact that the particular colors which come about depend on the relation of the stimulating light intensities. It is probably best conceived of as some kind of interaction which takes place as part of the nervous process which underlies color perception.

It will be remembered that the dependence of the perceived colors on the relative intensities of the stimulating light was also evident in the variations of Gelb's experiment which were first reported. It remains to be added that the transition from surface color to a luminous mode of appearance can be demonstrated with Gelb's set-up in the following way. At first the special illumination of the black paper and the general illumination of the room are so adjusted that the black paper looks white. When now the general illumination is further reduced, the paper becomes more and more luminous, and it ceases altogether to look white when the rest of the room is completely dark. Luminosity of the paper can also be produced by excluding the general illumination from its immediate neighborhood. By such measures a rather luminous gray, not unlike that appearing in the ring, may also be achieved. Thus it is not only in projected rings and disks that luminosity appears as an alternative to surface colors when adequate differences in intensity are lacking or when the contact between those regions is diminished. Clearly discernible segregated objects as for instance a suspended piece of black paper function in the same fashion.

Part II

So far, we have become acquainted with the way in which surface colors come into existence and with the manner in which they depend on the stimulus situation. They depend on the relation of stimulus intensities on the retina which are so located with regard to each other that the subsequent nervous processes interact. Now the question arises what bearing this has on the problem of brightness constancy.

In order to answer this question, some clarification of the nature of brightness constancy is needed. One may say that brightness constancy prevails when a perceived color is in agreement with the corresponding object color. Object color is a persistent physical characteristic of a surface, the property to reflect a certain proportion of the light which falls on that surface. For instance, a surface which looks black under constancy conditions reflects about four percent of the illuminating light, and a white one about 80 percent. This property, called reflectance, is not conveyed to the eye as such. It is rather represented to the eye by light of a given intensity. This fact constitutes the problem of brightness constancy, for the intensity of the reflected light depends to the same degree on the color of the reflecting surface as on the strength of the illumination. If in our environment illumination were always and everywhere the same, the fact that our visual sense is not directly affected by reflectances but only by the reflected light intensities would not raise a problem in perception, for the reflected light could represent the object colors unequivocally. But illumination varies widely, even between different parts of the same visual field, and often very different light intensities come to represent the same reflectance to the eye and, in constancy, produce the same color in the observer's experience. When, for instance, a medium gray which reflects 20 percent of the illuminating light is presented once in an illumination of an intensity 100 and again under light of an intensity 300, the intensities of the reflected light are 20 and 60 respectively; if complete constancy prevails, both stimulus intensities lead to perception of the same medium gray. Similarly the white background on which the gray samples are shown will reflect light of the intensity 80 in the weaker illumination and of the intensity 240 where it is in the stronger illumination, and the two differently illuminated parts of the background will probably both be judged as white. At first glance no orderly connection between stimulus intensity and perceived color seems to exist.

There is, however, one feature in the stimulus situation which remains the same when the illumination is varied. The intensity of the light reflected by the gray in the weaker illumination (20) stands in a ratio of 1:4 to that reflected by the white in the weaker illumination (80), and the same ratio exists between the intensities reflected by the gray and the white in the stronger illumination (60 and 240). It is easy to see that in the case of any given set of object colors the ratios of the intensities of the reflected light remain the same for any change in illumination which affects all of them. Thus, if the perceived colors were to depend on the ratios of the intensities of the reflected lights, they would remain unchanged when a given set of object colors were presented in changed illumination, and constancy would be assured. A medium gray may serve again as an example. Although it affects the eye with different light intensities when the illumination is changed, it would be perceived as the same color because the ratio of the intensity that it reflects to the intensity of the light reflected by the surrounding white would remain the same, for a change in illumination affects the latter in the same proportion.

At this point we have to consider the observations reported in Part I. They suggested that the perceived surface colors depend on the relation, not yet quantitatively defined, of the light intensities in interacting regions. But we now find that constancy would result, if our visual perception functioned in such a fashion that the perceived colors depended on the ratios of the intensities of the reflected light.

Thus, we merely have to make the assumption that the relation on which surface colors depend is one of simple proportionality to give the observations of Part I a direct bearing on the problem of brightness constancy. If this assumption were correct brightness constancy would find its explanation in the very process by which surface colors come about.

This assumption can be tested by simple experiments. If it is correct, the particular colors which are perceived in a pair of ring and disk should depend on the ratio of the intensities of the two regions, and only on that ratio. In other words, no matter what the absolute intensities of ring and disk may be, the same colors should be seen in the case of any pair of intensities which happen to stand in the same ratio to each other. This is, in close approximation, the case, as the following report of quantitative experiments shows.

Two pairs of ring and disk were used, in order to permit simultaneous comparison. The intensity of each of these four regions could be varied independently.

> Four identical projections lanterns equipped with 500-watt bulbs were used for this purpose. They were arranged in two groups and each group produced on the screen a pair of ring and disk as described in Part I. They were all so adjusted that they gave their respective regions the same light intensity. This was done in the following way. First a pair of ring and disk was formed with one lantern from group I and one from group II, and the intensity of one of them was varied until the contour between the ring and the disk disappeared because of brightness equality. Then these two lanterns were restored to their respective groups and similar adjustments were made within each group by varying the light intensities of the not yet equated lanterns.
>
> The intensity variations required by the experiments were brought about with the help of episcotisters through which the lantern beams had to pass before reaching the screen. This technique has the advantage that the episcotister apertures are a direct measure of the relative intensities in the various regions.
>
> Measurements were made by the method of limits. Ring and disk of one pair and the ring of the other pair were kept at constant intensities, and the intensity of the remaining disk was varied in suitable steps until the subject judged the colors of the two disks as equal.

In the first experiment one of the rings was given the full illumination of its lantern and the disk inside it received half of the intensity, for its light beam passed through an episcotister of 180° aperture. The light for the ring of the other pair was cut down to one-eighth of full intensity by passing it through an episcotister of 45° aperture. The aperture for the disk of the latter pair was varied in steps of 2°. The following are the means of one upper and one lower limit for each of five subjects: 24, 26, 24, 23, 24° with a total mean of 24.2°. This result means that, on the average, a light intensity in a disk corresponding to an episcotister aperture of 24.2° when it is surrounded by a ring of an intensity of 45° aperture brings about in the subject's experience the same gray as does a disk of an intensity of 180° aperture inside a ring of an intensity of 360° aperture. There is only a small deviation from the value of 22.5° which with 45° forms the same ratio as does 180° with 360°. Comparing the grays in the two disks was not difficult for the subjects. The great difference in absolute intensity between the two pairs of ring and disk (8:1) made the less intense pair look much dimmer, but that did not affect the distinctness of the disk's color. However, it made the rings look very different; though both were white, the more intense one was by far more luminous. This latter observation which was also made in most of the following experiments seems to be important, for it corresponds to a fact which can be observed in real constancy situations. When identical sets of object colors are placed in different illuminations and appear approximately the same, the set in the stronger objective illumination is often also *seen* to be more strongly illuminated. Perceived illumination and the different degree of luminous appearance which was frequently observed in our experiments seem, functionally speaking, to be closely related experiences. A detailed discussion will be presented in a later publication.

In another experiment a disk of 90° intensity was shown in a ring of 360° intensity. This combination which forms an intensity ratio of 4:1 brings about a much darker gray in the disk. In the other pair, the disk whose intensity was varied was surrounded by a ring of 180° intensity. The proportionate value for the disk is here 45°. The averages of two upper and two lower limits for each of four subjects were 46, 52, 45, 44° with a mean of 47°.

In the following experiment the disk of the brighter pair was varied and a ratio of 3:1 between ring and disk was used. In the darker pair, the ring had an intensity of 180° and the ring one of 60°, and the variable disk was surrounded by a ring of 360° intensity. Five upper and five lower limits were determined for each of three subjects. The means were 113, 115, 121°. The proportionate value is here 120°.

It will be noted that so far all deviations from the proportionate values were in one direction. They all imply that, where they occur, a disk of proportionate intensity in the dimmer pair looks darker than the disk in the pair of higher intensity; *viz.*, in the first two experiments the disk in the less intense pair had to be given a slightly higher than proportionate intensity to give a color match and in the last experiment the disk in the more intense pair had to be made objectively darker. Thus, although these deviations are small, they deserve our attention. Experiments with an improved technique were made to find out how significant they are.

To facilitate measuring a variable episcotister was used for the determination of the limits. This device permits changing the aperture by definite amounts while it is spinning. Only when the subjects had given a judgment of equality was the episcotister stopped and its angle measured with a protractor.

It has been described above how the intensities of the four lanterns were equated at the outset of the experiments. These equations are likely to contain subliminal errors which could affect our measurements. In the experiments which follow the episcotisters were interchanged between the groups of lanterns after half the number of limits had been determined for a given subject, so that the group which during the first half of an experiment produced the brighter pair of ring and disk were made to produce the dimmer pair during the second half, and vice versa. Thus, any error in the original lantern adjustment which would affect the measurements during the first half of the experiment in one direction would in the second half affect it in the opposite direction. In this manner such an error will appear in the scatter of the limit values but will not affect their mean.

The first experiment (I) done with this improved technique was one with a small difference between the brighter and the dimmer pair. The former had a ring of 360° intensity and a disk of 180°, and the other pair had a variable disk in a ring of 180°. Four subjects took part in the experiment. For each one four upper and four lower limits were determined. Table 6.1 presents the means of these limits. The proportionate value is here 90°. It will be noted that the small deviations from this value are in a direction opposite to those previously reported, for they would imply that a disk of proportionate intensity in the dimmer pair is perceived as a slightly lighter gray than the disk in the more intense pair.

This is not so with the results of the following experiment (II) in which a still lighter gray was produced and in which the intensity of the dimmer ring was only one quarter of that of the brighter one. In the dimmer pair the ring had an intensity of 90° and the disk was variable, while in the brighter pair the ring had 360° and the disk 240° of light. The results are given in Table 6.2. With the subjects Mo. and Cr., ten upper and ten lower limits were determined, with Ke. and Cy. only six. Individual differences are larger in this experiment. For two of the subjects there was a marked deviation from the proportionate value of 60°, which implied that for them a disk of 60° intensity in the dimmer pair showed a slightly darker gray than the disk in the brighter pair.

Ten subjects were employed in an experiment (III) in which the variable disk was surrounded by a ring of 360° of light and the dimmer pair consisted of a ring of 90° and a disk of 30° intensity. Six upper and lower limits were determined for each subject, except for subjects Mo. and Cr., who again supplied ten pairs of limits each. The average of the individual means as shown in Table 6.3 was 106°, a clear deviation from the proportionate value of 120°. It implies that the gray in the disk of low intensity looks somewhat darker than a disk of proportionate value in the brighter pair.

The direction of the deviations from proportionate values encountered in the last two experiments was such that they could be regarded as the effect of a slight influence of the absolute stimulus intensities on the color process which otherwise could be conceived as functioning according to a proportional law. The question arose whether these deviations reflected intrinsic properties of the color process or whether they were introduced by incidental experimental conditions. An answer cannot yet be given and must be left to further detailed

Table 6.1

**Episcotister settings in degrees for disk
within ring of 180° in comparison
with disk of 180° within ring of 360°**

Subjects	Ad.	McN.	Ba.	Cl.	
Upper limit	88	86	85.5	90	
Lower limit	84	84	79.5	84.5	
Mean	86	85	82	86	Grand mean: 85

investigation. However, an experiment which was performed with this question in mind will be reported below, because it will add the data of still another combination of intensities.

It was suspected that the presence of the brighter pair of ring and disk in the visual field when the gray in the disk of the dimmer pair developed was responsible for the fact that this gray looked a trifle too dark. If the high intensities of the brighter pair had an influence across the spatial interval on the colors which emerged in the dimmer pair, this is what should have happened. Such an influence can be avoided by presenting the pairs successively. This was done in the following experiment (IV). The intensities in the brighter pair were 360 and 180°, the ring in the dimmer pair was 90° and the disk was varied. Table 6.4 shows for four subjects the means of four upper and four lower limits. Ordinarily, with an intensity ratio of 4:1 between the rings the deviation under discussion was to be expected. It did not appear. The slight deviation from the proportionate value of 45° was in the opposite direction.

In another experiment, however, successive presentation failed to eliminate completely the deviation under discussion. Experiment III was repeated with three further subjects who did the experiment twice, once with successive and once with simultaneous presentation. The limits listed in Table 6.5 are the averages of four determinations each. Although successive presentation reduces the deviation from the proportionate value of 120°, it does not eliminate it.

These deviations from proportionate values appear rather insignificant when one compares them with the remaining effect of the proportional law. For example, in experiment III which showed the largest deviation, a disk of

Table 6.2

**Episcotister settings in degrees for disk
within ring of 90° in comparison
with disk of 240° within ring of 360°**

Subjects	Mo.	Cr.	Ke.	Cy.	
Upper limit	61	62	73	74	
Lower limit	62	64	68	67	
Mean	61.5	63	70.5	70.5	Grand mean: 66.4

Table 6.3

Episcotister settings in degrees for disk within ring of 360° in comparison with disk of 30° within ring of 90°

Subjects	Ca.	Ga.	Hs.	Ht.	Lu.	Ro.	Mo.	Cr.	Ke.	Cy.	
Upper limit	104.5	91	117.5	116.5	113	130	128	107.5	105	113	
Lower limit	92.5	91	99.5	98.5	103	112	100	103	97	95	
Mean	98.5	91	108.5	107.5	108	121	114	105	101	104	Grand mean: 106

Table 6.4

**Episcotister settings in degrees for disk
within ring of 90° in comparison
with disk of 180° within ring of 360°**

Subjects	Ad.	McN.	Ba.	Cl.	
Upper limit	43	42	41	44	
Lower limit	41	40	42	44	
Mean	42	41	41.5	44	Grand Mean: 42

an intensity of 30° aperture had on the average the same color as one of an intensity of 106° aperture, that is, an intensity 3.5 times as high. The deviation from the proportionate value of 120° amounts only to 12 percent.

It should be mentioned at this point that such experiments can also be done with a less elaborate set-up. Two color mixers and one projection lantern suffice for a crude demonstration of the proportional law. With the help of a large color wheel of black and white disks and a small one fastened on top of it to the same mixer one can obtain a ring-shaped and a circular region in which the intensities of the reflected light can be varied independently. On one mixer, e.g., the large wheel can be set to show a sector of 90° white and the small one a sector of 45° white. To the other mixer are fastened a small wheel with a white sector of 180° and a large wheel of 360° white. When the mixers spin in general room illumination, one sees a dark gray disk surrounded by a medium gray ring on one mixer and a light gray disk in a white ring on the other one. However, when the mixers are placed in separate strictly local illumination they look quite different. That illumination can be provided by a lantern equipped with an opaque slide which has two circular holes a good distance apart. It projects two narrow beams of light of equal intensity. When the mixers are placed each in one of the beams at such a distance from the projector that their wheels are covered by the light almost to the outer rim and the rest of the room is entirely dark, both color mixers show a white ring and a light gray disk much alike in color. The reason for this change is easy to understand. Under local illumination the two color mixers provide exactly the

Table 6.5

**Episcotister settings in degrees for disk
within ring of 360° in comparison with disk
of 30° within ring of 90°**

Subjects Presentation	Cl.		He.		Be.	
	Sim.	*Succ.*	*Sim.*	*Succ.*	*Sim.*	*Succ.*
Upper limit	110.5	121	99	108.5	104	112
Lower limit	99.5	99	97.5	99	94	104
Mean	105	110	98	104	99	108

same pattern of stimulus intensities as the set-up in experiment IV, and thus the same colors develop as in that experiment. In general illumination, on the other hand, the pairs of ring and disk are surrounded by regions of other intensity, e.g., the light reflected by the wall of the room, which cooperate in determining the colors which come about in the pairs. If, for instance, light reflected by a white wall forms the stimulus intensity of the surrounding region, that intensity stands to the intensity of the dimmer ring in a ratio of 4:1, and in this relation the ring should assume a medium gray color, as indeed it did.

It was explained above how the assumption that the achromatic colors depend on the ratios of the pertinent stimulus intensities accounts for brightness constancy. On that occasion complete constancy was shown to follow from this assumption. However, complete constancy has hardly ever been demonstrated experimentally. An object color presented in reduced illumination usually looks somewhat darker than another sample of that color in full illumination, though not as much darker as the difference of the reflected light intensities would warrant if there were no constancy. Yet complete constancy would follow from a direct application of the proportional law. Deviations from proportionality which occurred in our experiments are by far too small to account for the usual lag in constancy. The difficulty resolves itself when it is realized that the proportional law cannot be applied so simply to this situation. Here the two pairs of regions, the sample and its background in full illumination and the other sample with background in reduced illumination, are not as completely separated from each other as the corresponding regions in our experiments, for the regions of different illumination are in contact with each other and the brighter one can have an influence on the dimmer one. In other words, we have here a case where three or more regions of different intensity interact. Such processes have not yet been sufficiently investigated, and no report can be made at this time. It seems, however, quite likely that a full investigation will furnish the rules for the prediction of the lag in constancy in individual experiments.

This report may so far have given the impression that, apart from the small deviations discussed, the proportional law permits prediction of color equations if the pertinent stimulus intensities are known. However, this is so only with important qualifications. To a certain extent also the geometrical arrangement of the regions of different intensity has an influence on what colors come about in these regions. Some brief experiments which permit a first appraisal of the importance of these conditions will be reported below.

In the measuring experiments so far reported the width of the ring was five-eighths of the diameter of the disk so that the area of the ring was four times as large as the area of the disk. A reduction of the width of the ring to one-fourth of the diameter of the disk so that its area was about the same as that of the disk did not affect the color in the disk as the following experiment shows, in which the colors in two disks were compared which were surrounded by rings of different width. Both rings were given the same intensity of 120° aperture; the disk in the narrow ring had an intensity of 15° and appeared as a very dark gray; the disk in the ring of standard width was variable. The mean of two upper and two lower limits for a single subject was also 15°. A number of other observers were satisfied with that equation.

The width of the narrow ring was further reduced so that it amounted to only one-sixteenth of the diameter of the disk. The same constant intensities as in the last experiment were used. The averages of two upper and two lower limits for each of two subjects were 37 and 37°. This result means that a disk of 15° intensity inside the very narrow ring looked as light as a disk of 37° intensity inside a ring of standard width. The outcome of this experiment was so striking that we repeated it with another combination of intensities. The intensity of the two rings remained the same, but the disk in the very narrow ring had an intensity of 60°. Again a higher intensity was needed for an equation in the disk inside the standard ring. The averages of two upper and two lower limits for the same two subjects were 87 and 86°. However, with this intensity ratio of 120:60, which produces a light gray, the effect of making the ring very narrow was not so great. It amounted only to 45 percent, whereas in the case of a ratio of 120:15 which normally produces a very dark gray the disk in the standard ring had to be made 145 percent more intense. On the whole it looks as if the very narrow ring which has only one-quarter of the area of the disk cannot make the disk color as dark as does a ring of sufficient width.

As just reported, no difference in the effect of a ring which has about the same area as the disk and of one which has four times the area of the disk has been found. Two further measurements were made with a much wider ring. Its width was 1.5 the diameter of the disk and its area fifteen times that of the disk. In one experiment the intensity ratio between the wide ring and its disk was again 120:15. In the disk of the standard pair the averages of four upper and four lower limits for the two subjects were 17 and 16°. When a ratio of 120:60 was used, averages for two pairs of limits were 66 and 63°. The deviations from 15 and 60° respectively are probably incidental. At any rate, they are not in the direction which would indicate an enhancement in the effectiveness of the ring with increased width. It seems that, once the ring has an area equal to that of the disk, any further increase in its width does not affect the resulting color of the disk.

It was reported in Part I that a ring looks more luminous than a disk of the same intensity in another pair in which the intensities of ring and disk are the same as in the first pair but interchanged. The question arises whether such a reversal of intensities also causes a color difference in the regions of equal intensity. Two pairs of disk and ring in which the area of the ring was the same as that of the disk were presented and the lights were so arranged that in one pair the lower intensity was in the ring and in the other pair in the disk. The two higher intensities in the two pairs amounted both to 360°, the ring of lower intensity was kept at 45°, and the disk of lower intensity was variable. Measurements were made with four subjects. The means of three upper and three lower limits were 54, 71, 83, 86°. These figures indicate that for the same intensity ratio the lower intensity appears as a lighter gray when it is given in the ring than when it is given in the disk. A rather dark gray results from a ratio of 360:45°. In the case of smaller ratios which give rise to lighter grays the differences in color which result when the intensities of ring and disk are interchanged are very much smaller. For an intensity ratio of 2:1 only a difference in luminosity can be discerned.

Summary

It was found that opaque achromatic surface colors are perceived when light of different intensity stimulates adjacent areas on the retina. The achromatic color which is seen in a particular region must be regarded as the result of stimulation received from that region *and* of stimulation from neighboring regions. Although these colors are qualities which are perceived in a given region, they are products of an interaction process, which depends on difference in stimulation in at least two areas. In the absence of a suitable difference in stimulation a color of an entirely different mode of appearance is seen. A single bright region in an otherwise dark field, for instance, looks luminous instead of white, and reducing the light intensity in that region fails to make it look gray; it continues to appear luminous and merely becomes dimmer.

The first steps were taken to investigate quantitatively the rules of this dependence in the simplest case, that of two regions of different intensities of stimulation where one region surrounds the other. The colors which come about under these circumstances depend in close approximation on the ratios of the intensities involved and seem independent of the absolute intensity of local stimulation. The region of higher intensity will assume the color white and that of lower intensity will show a gray (or a black) which depends on the intensity ratio of the two regions. The greater the difference in intensity the darker will be the gray which appears in the region of the lower intensity.

It can be shown that a dependence of perceived colors on the ratios of stimulus intensities accounts for the constancy of achromatic colors under varying illumination. Complete constancy would follow from this rule of interaction of two intensities. The fact that measurements of brightness constancy rarely give results which denote complete constancy presents no difficulty for this explanation. These experiments involve interaction between more than regions of different stimulus intensity.

Figural After-Effects

Some of the most striking effects of context upon perception have been described as *figural after-effects*. In general, figural after-effects refer, as the name implies, to the effects of a prior figural stimulus upon the subsequent perception of a figure. J. J. Gibson of Cornell University was the first to describe the phenomenon of figural after-effects. In a number of experiments, subjects viewed curved lines for varying periods of time and under various conditions of stimulation. For example, in one study subjects viewed a curved line for ten minutes, then were shown a straight line. They reported that the straight line appeared curved somewhat in the opposite direction as the preceding curved line.

The figural after-effects are sometimes confused with another perceptual phenomenon with a similar name: *figural after-images*. Despite the similar terms, the two phenomena appear to be rather different. The most common of the after-images is the so-called *negative after-image*. If a subject views a square red card for about sixty seconds, then immediately looks at a medium gray background, usually he will report seeing a blue-green square superimposed on the gray background. The after-image is the complementary color of the preceding stimulus color. If the background has a hue, the complementary after-image will mix with the background color following the laws of additive color mixture. For example, a red square followed by a greenish-yellow background would induce a green after-image. After-images appear to be the result of certain retinal properties of the visual system: when the red square is viewed by one eye and the background color is viewed by the other eye, no after-image results. With figural after-effects, on the other hand, the contrary condition seems to exist; in Gibson's experiments, when the curved line was viewed by one eye and the straight line by the other eye, an after-effect still occurred. The mechanism of figural after-effects is evidently located at some higher visual center, beyond the point of binocular mixing of incoming information.

In summary, then, figural after-images are chromatic sensations resulting from color stimulation and are limited to the stimulated eye. Figural after-effects, then, are changes in the appearance of figures caused by viewing a preceding figure, and they are transferred from the stimulated to the opposite eye.

Although Gibson was the first to investigate the figural after-effects, the most thorough study was made by Wolfgang Köhler and Hans Wallach, at that time associated with the Department of Psychology of Swarthmore College. In an 88-page article in the October, 1944, issue of the *Proceedings of the American Philosophical Society*, they described in detail their studies and developed a theory explaining their observations in relation to the more encompassing *Gestalt Field Theory*. Since the entire document exceeds the scope of this introduction to perceptual research, we are presenting only the first section, in which a variety of figural after-effects are described. Several sections of this part of the report also have been deleted.

One reason for not including the latter sections, dealing with the theoretical explanation of the observations, is the controversial nature of the theory. It attempts to explain the experimental results with a neurophysiological model, described in psychological rather than neurophysiological terms. An alternative explanation, also presented in neurophysiological terms, has been published by Osgood and Heyer (1951). More recently, a third explanation has been presented by Ganz (1966), who attempts to relate figural after-effects to the broader category of the simultaneous illusions. As can be seen by the appearance of several alternative theories, the original presentation by Köhler and Wallach not only presented a variety of interesting experimental results, but also severed the critical function in psychology of arousing interest for new research and theoretical development.

Figural After-Effects:
An Investigation
of Visual Processes
Wolfgang Köhler and Hans Wallach

Introduction

The concept of figural after-effects is just emerging from its formative stage. About ten years ago remarkable instances of such effects were discovered by J. J. Gibson.

Gibson reported his first discovery in 1933. His subjects observed that during prolonged inspection slightly curved lines gradually became less curved. When afterwards straight lines were shown in the location and orientation of the curves, such straight lines appeared curved in the opposite direction. Their distortion could be measured. Gibson did not restrict his experiments to the case of visual curves. He asked blindfolded subjects to move their fingers along a convexly curved edge and to repeat this movement for several minutes. They reported that the curve gradually appeared less convex. Afterwards a straight edge felt definitely concave. In vision he found that not only curves gave clear after-effects but also lines which were bent at the middle into an obtuse angle. When the apex of the angle had been fixated for some time, straight lines of the same location and orientation appeared bent in the opposite direction. A further phenomenon was observed and measured by Gibson (1933, 1934, 1937), M. D. Vernon (1934), and Gibson and Radner (1937). When their observers inspected a straight line which was moderately tilted with regard to the vertical or the horizontal, afterwards the objective vertical or horizontal appeared tilted in the opposite direction. Moreover, when the position of the vertical (horizontal) was thus altered the horizontal (vertical) tended to turn in the same direction.

Several other observations were made. In the *first* place it was found by Gibson that the after-effects were fairly closely restricted to the locus of the inspection figure. Here the term locus is to be understood in reference to the visual sector of the nervous system, because an effect which was caused by inspection of a figure in one place would show on an appropriate test object elsewhere as soon as the eyes were turned into the right position relative to this object. *Secondly*, however, Gibson observed that when only one eye was used during the inspection period an after-effect of a somewhat smaller amount could clearly be observed in the corresponding part of the other eye's field. *Thirdly,* long inspection times, although desirable for certain purposes, proved not to be necessary for noticeable after-effects. When Gibson and Radner measured the "tilted line" effect after varying periods of inspection they found that it was unmistakably present after five seconds, and about maximal as early as one or two minutes later. With such inspection times the curve of the development tended to become parallel to the abscissa. Particularly impressive is the *fourth* observation. Once a strong figural after-effect had been obtained it often persisted for many minutes. As a matter of fact, with one of Gibson's subjects the after-effect did not disappear within twenty-four hours when by a proper device the inspection of vertical curves had been continued for several days. But, *fifthly,* individual differences as to the amount of the after-effects were quite conspicuous, although only Bales and Follansbee (1935) found them entirely absent in some subjects.

We agree with most factual statements made by Gibson and by the authors who continued his work. But we do not believe that Gibson's interpretation of his data is correct. He assumes that it is deviation of inspection objects from "norms," like straight lines in general and verticals or horizontals in particular, which leads to figural after-effects. Actually, figural after-effects are not restricted to such special instances. It will soon be seen that, as a matter of principle, inspection of any specific entity in a visual field can cause figural after-effects. Gibson's discoveries will therefore have to be re-interpreted within the larger body of facts which is now at our disposal.

The existence of figural after-effects in a more general sense was first inferred from the behavior of reversible figures. Some data concerning the spontaneous reversals of such figures under conditions of prolonged inspection have been given elsewhere (Köhler, 1940). Here we will repeat merely that the speed of those reversals tends to increase as fixation is continued, that then the figures will still be unstable after rest periods of several minutes, and that for this reason their instability can be enhanced in a sequence of separate inspection periods. This fact of summation or accumulation suggests that prolonged presence of a figure in a given location tends to operate against further presence of this figure in the same place. It may be concluded that the presence of a figure in the visual field is associated with a specific figure process in the visual sector of the brain, and this process gradually alters the medium in which it occurs. In a reversible figure a redistribution of the figure process seems to occur when that change has reached a certain level.

It follows from these assumptions that a figure which has become unstable in its original location must again appear more stable when it is shown in a new position. Such a recovery can actually be demonstrated.

Preliminary Experiments

For a first observation an outline figure, an oblong or a circle, is drawn with india ink on a white screen, and a fixation mark is added on one side (see Figure 6.1). The outline ought not to be too thin. On a second white screen the same drawing is prepared in the same position relative to the fixation mark, but on the other side of this mark, and symmetrically, an identical figure is here added. The subject first fixates the mark on the former chart for, say, five minutes and from a distance of two yards. If he then fixates the mark on the second chart he will find that its two objectively equal figures have not the same appearance. The figure which coincides with the previously inspected object will be pale or gray in comparison with its black partner, it will seem to lie farther back in space, and it may look a trifle smaller. Depending upon the individual subject one or another of these facts will appear more conspicuous. For instance, some subjects report at once that the two objects have not the same size, while others do not mention this difference spontaneously. A few may even deny its existence. More convincing results are generally obtained with oblongs than with circles.

The following experiments differ in two respects from the above-mentioned design. The test objects are no longer equal to the inspection objects, and consequently the outline of the former does not, or does not throughout, coincide with that of the latter. It will be seen that this change does not obliterate the after-effects.

1. In Figure 6.2 the inspection object is an outline circle. The subject fixates a mark on the periphery of the circle. The test object is an oblong divided by a curve into approximately equal parts. This curve is congruent with the corresponding part of the circle and bears a fixation mark where that of the circle lies. In Figure 6.2 the inspection object (I-object) and the test object (T-object) are united; actually the T-object is shown when the I-object is no longer visible. After an inspection period of several minutes all subjects report that the right side of the T-oblong is larger, particularly higher, than its left side. It will surprise every observer to find that after a sufficient inspection period the horizontal contours of the oblong are actually broken so that it assumes the shape indicated in Figure 6.3. A depth effect is no less obvious. Normally the convex part of the oblong tends to appear in front of the concave part. After the inspection period just the opposite is true; the concave part now lies "upon" the convex half; in other words, the figure-ground relationship is reversed. Obviously in the interior of the I-figure the figural after-effect is stronger than it is immediately outside its contour.

The I-object need by no means be a circle. When the observation is repeated with a rectangle and therefore with a T-object divided by a straight line it gives precisely the same result.

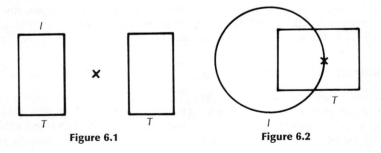

Figure 6.1   Figure 6.2

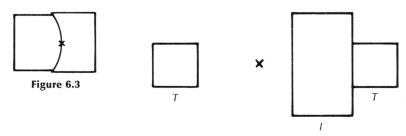

Figure 6.3

Figure 6.4

2. When experiment 1 of this section was first performed the outside part of the T-object appeared so "intense" that for a moment the following interpretation seemed possible. Inside the figure area prolonged inspection causes an effect of "depression" while just outside the figure the opposite holds. Actually this is not the case. When a T-object just outside an I-figure is compared with a second one which lies at a great distance, the former will be found to show all symptoms of "depression." This can be demonstrated with the arrangement shown in Figure 6.4. (In this figure the I- and the T-objects are again united while actually they are shown in succession.) After the inspection period the T-square on the right side will look considerably smaller; it will also lie farther back in space and be pale in comparison with its partner. It follows that the after-effect extends beyond the area of the inspection object, and that its symptoms are here the same as they are within the figure. In experiment 1, therefore, the outside part of the T-object seemed particularly "intense" only in comparison with the more strongly affected inside part.

3. In a further experiment a figural after-effect is demonstrated when the outline of the affected T-object has no point in common with the outline of the I-figure (Figure 6.5). After an inspection period of several minutes no subject will miss the striking difference in the appearance of the T-squares. The square above the fixation point will appear smaller than the other T-object; it will also lie farther back in space. Under the conditions of this experiment, therefore, the after-effect pervades the whole interior of the I-object.

Within limits the particular nature of the T-object may be varied. If the squares are replaced by pairs of horizontal lines, one pair within the circle, the other symmetrically below the fixation point, the after-effect remains just as striking. Within the area of the circle the T-lines appear gray, not black; they lie back in space, and are probably nearer one another; they are also clearly shorter.

4. There are no figures without outlines or contours. It is, therefore, a plausible assumption that in some way contours are responsible not only for the existence of figures as such but also for any after-effects which are established when figures are shown for some time in a constant location. In Figure 6.6 the broken lines of the I-square on the right side of the fixation mark "surround" the right T-object more completely than the two inner verticals surround the left T-object. The distance of these verticals from each other has

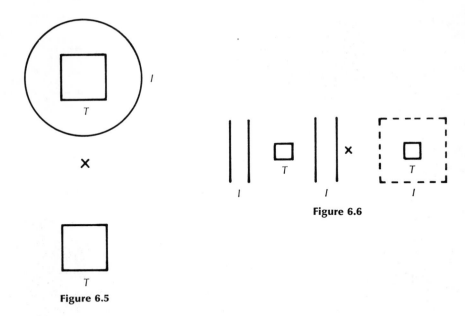

Figure 6.6

Figure 6.5

the same length as the edge of the *I*-square on the right side. But in terms of actual contour each edge of the square is only two-fifths of each continuous vertical on the left side. The total actual contour of the square is, therefore, in this measure eight-fifths while the length of the two continuous lines is two, or ten-fifths. In other words, the total length of actual contour is twenty-five percent greater in the case of the two continuous lines. Moreover, on the left side two more verticals are added on both sides of the *T*-object. Distances of the *I*-contours from the *T*-objects are in this pattern directly comparable, because the broken lines of the square have the same location relative to the right *T*-object as the inner continuous *I*-lines have to the left *T*-object. Thus the experiment can decide whether, apart from the amount of contours in the neighborhood of a *T*-object, the particular configuration of these contours plays a part in determining the after-effect.

The answer is perfectly clear. The *T*-object on the left side appears larger and, for most observers, also nearer. It follows that the strength of an after-effect depends upon the specific configuration in which the *I*-contours are given in the neighborhood of a *T*-object. Mere quantity of contour at a given distance is surely not the only decisive factor.

5. Experiments 1, 3, and 4 have proved that the interior of a figure is in an altered condition when this figure has been for some time in the same place. It seems, however, equally relevant to know to what extent the effect extends into the environment of a figure. In experiment 2 we have found that a *T*-object which lies just outside the figure is clearly "depressed." The next experiment shows that this influence of the *I*-figure is not restricted to *T*-objects in an immediately adjacent position.

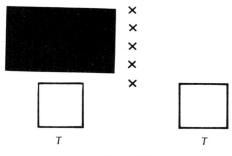

Figure 6.7

Figure 6.7 is to be interpreted as follows: The *I*-object, a solid black oblong, is shown with the lowest of the five crosses as a fixation mark. After prolonged inspection the two *T*-squares are compared when the eyes fixate either the same or one of the higher marks. (These higher marks are given only on the *T*-chart, not during the inspection period.) The higher the mark lies which is fixated in the test the greater will be the distance between the area previously occupied by the *I*-object and the left *T*-square. Thus a number of tests with varying distances can be made with the same *T*-chart. Short inspection periods between successive tests will keep the after-effect at a high level if inspection has been sufficiently long in the beginning. Our subjects observed from a distance of about two yards, a distance which was used in most of our experiments.

All observers reported that the left *T*-object was affected when they fixated the first, the second, or the third mark from below. With some subjects the limit was not reached at this point. Since the fixation marks were two-fifths of an inch distant from one another, and the first one-fifth of an inch distant from the nearest contour of the *I*-object, this observation means that in the present experiment the after-effect extended for all subjects at least one inch beyond the area of the *I*-figure. Again we found variations as to the particular symptom which seemed to impress individual observers most. One subject would stress the comparative paleness of the left *T*-object, another its smaller size, again another the fact that it lay back in space. Frequently a fourth symptom was mentioned, a displacement of the left *T*-square. We prefer to discuss this new fact in another section.

As preliminary evidence this observation will suffice. Although it is quite true that figural after-effects are centered about the locus of the *I*-figure they are by no means strictly limited to this place. Therefore it does not seem entirely relevant to ask whether or not these effects are "localized." Their center has a very definite location; but from this center the temporary disturbance extends considerably into the environment.

From this fact we can draw an important conclusion. It will not be denied that the prolonged presence of a figure in a given area is the cause of the after-effects. This can mean only that continued occurrence of a specific figure process in a given location changes the state of the medium in which this process occurs; that in the changed medium 'the figure processes of T-objects are altered; and that as a consequence the visual characteristics of these T-objects are affected. But from this point of view the extension of the after-effects in space will roughly correspond to the extension of the figure processes by which they are established. It follows that, although the color processes of a given figure are limited to the area of the figure as such, in some way the figure must act beyond this restricted area. Otherwise no after-effects could be observed outside and at a distance from the I-figure. In this sense, then, a figure has a "field" by which it is represented in the environment.

At this point a terminological remark becomes necessary. We have to distinguish between two facts. A figure process, it appears, tends to alter conditions within the medium in which it occurs, and when the figure disappears the medium seems for some time to remain in its changed condition. This is a state of affairs for which, apart from the medium itself, only the figure process of the I-object is responsible. Suppose now that a T-figure is shown in the affected region. Generally speaking, not all parts of this region will be equally affected. Consequently any alterations which the process of the T-figure may suffer will depend upon the particular position which this T-figure has in the affected zone. Furthermore, the particular size and shape of the T-figure will also influence such after-effects. Hence, within a region which has been affected by inspection of a given figure not one but several after-effects will be demonstrable. Under these circumstances it would be confusing if both the alteration of the medium as such and the various effects of this alteration upon specific T-objects were given the same name. We propose to call only the alterations of T-objects "figural after-effects" and to refer to the affection of the medium as "satiation." This name is not meant to have any particular implications beyond the fact that the prolonged presence of a given figure causes the "depressed" condition of the medium. As soon as the nature of this depression becomes sufficiently known the term satiation may of course be replaced by a better defined concept.

The observations above refer to a few particular patterns. From this one should not infer that inspection only of special objects causes satiation and figural after-effects. It has been shown that both solid and outline figures can be used. But we obtained equally strong effects with grid-like patterns. Furthermore, a simple straight line suffices as an I-object. In the arrangement of Figure 6.8 the two squares are T-objects. After inspection of the line for several minutes the left square will show the now-familiar symptoms of depression. The direction of the line and correspondingly the location of the T-squares may of course be varied. Again, the effects are not restricted to the locus of the line itself.

Figural after-effects, we have seen, are no less revealing as to the nature of the figure process per se than they are interesting on their own account. With the following examples we wish to demonstrate the sensitivity of figural after-effects to apparently minor changes of the I-pattern, and therefore of the figure process.

Figure 6.9 needs no explanation. The outline of the lower circle is inter-

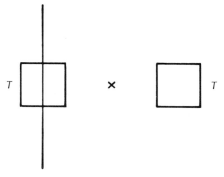

Figure 6.8

rupted on one side; the angular size of the opening amounts to 60°. We found that after the inspection period the lower T-square appeared nearer and just a trifle larger than its partner.

Even objectively equal I-figures may cause slightly different after-effects if their spatial orientation is varied. In Figure 6.10 the pairs of parallel lines on both sides of the fixation mark are identical. Nevertheless their after-effects were found to be perceptibly different: the left square lay back in space. It seems to follow that the figure process between the vertical parallels is not

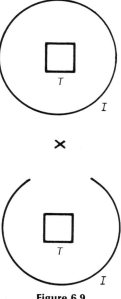

Figure 6.9

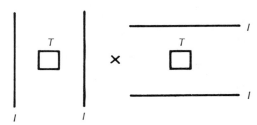

Figure 6.10

quite the same as that between the horizontals, that it is more intense between the verticals. Our pattern represents a special instance of the so-called Vertical-Horizontal illusion. Visually the vertical lines are longer than the horizontal lines. For the same reason the horizontal distance between the vertical lines is visually shorter than the vertical distance between the horizontal lines. It remains to be seen whether these facts are related to the present observation.

We subjected a second so-called illusion to the same procedure. Figure 6.11 shows the Müller-Lyer pattern together with two *T*-objects which were presented after prolonged fixation of the mark in the center. Our subjects agreed that in this instance the observation was particularly convincing. The left square lay clearly behind the right square, and the former was smaller than the latter. This result was to be expected if the intensity of the figure process, and therefore satiation, was greater in the more closed area on the left side. But it seems curious that just the part of the figure which contains the stronger process appears as shorter.

Just as prolonged inspection of countless objects causes satiation and figural after-effects, so the *T*-objects need not be squares or other very simple figures. It seems particularly important that in strongly affected areas *distances* between such objects are changed just as are the sizes of the objects themselves. If a *T*-object lies within an affected zone it tends to appear smaller. Similarly, if two *T*-objects are shown in such a region they will lie nearer each other than they do in a less affected region.

In Figure 6.12 the oblong is the *I*-object. The four squares are the *T*-objects. After inspection of the oblong the left *T*-squares will show the usual symptoms of depression; they will appear to lie back in space, to be paler and smaller. But quite as striking will be the fact that the left side of the *T*-pattern is shortened in the vertical direction. In other words, the *T*-pattern as a whole will appear as a trapezoid, not as a square or an oblong.

Is this influence upon the distance between two *T*-objects a secondary consequence of changes which the size of these objects themselves suffers?

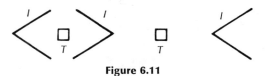

Figure 6.11

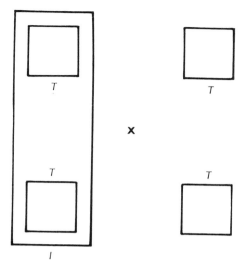

Figure 6.12

One might be inclined to believe that as these objects become smaller the over-all extension of the pair in the vertical direction must decrease, and that it is this decrease which appears as a reduction of their distance. That more than this is involved can be shown with the arrangement of Figure 6.13. Here the *T*-objects are four thin horizontal lines the width of which cannot be appreciably altered when they lie within an affected area. None the less after inspection of the oblong the distance between the lines on the affected side is reduced. In this respect the free zone between two separate *T*-objects does not seem to differ essentially from the objectively empty interior of a closed outline object. Just as this area of a closed *T*-object appears smaller when the object is shown within an affected region, so an area which is only partly enclosed by two *T*-objects will shrink under the same circumstances.

In the further development of our investigation *T*-patterns like the four squares of Figure 6.12 proved to be extremely useful. Figural after-effects of many kinds can be tested with the same simple arrangement. We may add a few more instances which demonstrate the decrease of distances between separate *T*-objects.

In the first place, the effect is the same if we test a *horizontal* distance. After inspection of the oblong in Figure 6.14 the pattern of squares is no longer symmetrical; its lower horizontal distance is shortened. Secondly, if the *I*-object itself consists of two separate objects as it does in Figure 6.15, *T*-objects which are presented within the areas of these *I*-figures appear again too near one another. On the face of it the present effect does not seem to differ very much from the one in which two *T*-squares lie within the area of one *I*-object.

Again with the same *T*-pattern we can show that within an *I*-object the alteration of the medium need by no means be uniform. After inspection of the

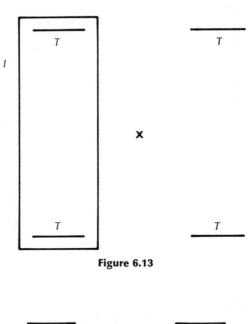

Figure 6.13

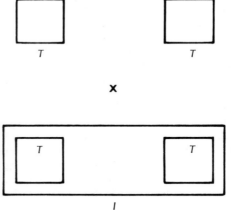

Figure 6.14

large square in Figure 6.16 the four *T*-objects do not appear as a symmetrical pattern; the vertical distance on the right side, which lies nearer the contour of the *I*-object, is clearly shorter. It follows that within a sizable *I*-object satiation is more intense in the neighborhood of the contour than it is in more central regions.

Distances between *T*-objects decrease also if these objects lie in a strongly affected region *outside* the area of a previously inspected figure. After inspection of the solid oblong in Figure 6.17 the vertical distance of the *T*-objects on

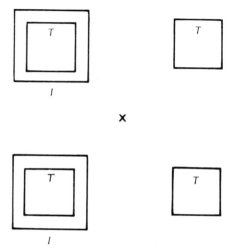

Figure 6.15

the right side appears much shorter than the distance of those on the left side. This effect, too, will be found to extend considerably into the environment. In the arrangement of Figure 6.18 the distances cc and c_1c_1 remain equal. At such distances from the I-figure satiation must either be absent or have but a weak gradient. On the other hand, the distance bb is clearly shortened although less so than aa.

Nobody will operate for long with such T-patterns without being surprised

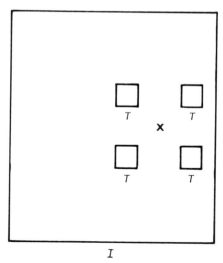

Figure 6.16

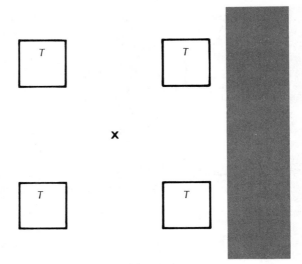

Figure 6.17

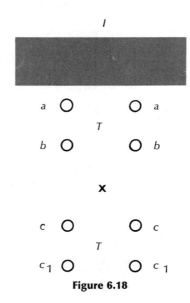

Figure 6.18

by a curious phenomenon. In the first experiment in which the pattern of four squares was used the two squares on the left side appeared nearer each other than the squares on the right side because the former fell into a strongly affected area. But Dr. R. Crutchfield who was then one of our observers remarked at once that this distortion of the T-pattern was not symmetrical: the distance on the left side was shortened more by a displacement upward of the lower T-object than by an opposite change in the position of the higher object. Ever since this first observation the same fact has impressed us in practically all experiments in which the nature of the test permitted its occurrence. With regard to satiation, just as in other respects, the visual field clearly constitutes an anisotropic medium. Not only are figural after-effects generally stronger in the lower half of the field, they also appear here earlier. After a very short inspection period, therefore, subjects may report distortions only in the lower half of the T-pattern. We shall soon find that the same rule holds for patterns and after-effects which have otherwise little resemblance with the present observation. For instance, Gibson's "curved line" effect often shows only in the lower half of the T-line when inspection has been restricted to ten or fifteen seconds. On the other hand, no such asymmetry seems to exist in the horizontal dimension. If within an evenly affected area a horizontal distance is shortened this distortion is to our knowledge always symmetrical. So it appears at least if the objective pattern itself is placed symmetrically with regard to the median vertical.

Obviously, the asymmetry of figural after-effects is unrelated to the nature of the patterns which serve as I-figures and as T-objects. These objects may be perfectly symmetrical above and below the equator of the visual field; and yet their lower parts will be more easily and more strongly affected. This can mean only that the median in which visual figure processes occur is anisotropic in the vertical dimension.

Editor's Note: Adaptation Level

A discussion on contextual effects in perception would be incomplete without mention of the research led by Harry Helson of Kansas State University on *adaptation level*. One might consider adaptation-level theory as the continuation and extension of figural effects to a broader basis of perceptual response tendency. The level of adaptation of an organism refers to the state of balance or equilibrium maintained in response to stimuli from the environment. That level is determined by all preceding environmental stimuli experienced by the organism. If the organism has been living in an average temperature of 32°, he experiences warmth during a day of 65°. After a week of 80°-weather, one day of 65° is perceived as cool. The organism was adapted to the cooler weather in the first case and to the warmer weather in the second condition. Whether the temperature would be perceived as high or low depends upon the prevailing temperature conditions prior to the introduction of the new temperature. The increased or decreased temperature disrupted the equilibrium of the adaptation level, causing the organism to perceive the new temperature as high or low. At the same time, the new stimulus causes the adaptation level itself to become sufficiently modified that a second day of the same new temperature would not be perceived as unusually warm or cool.

Knowledge of the stimulus conditions affecting the adaptation level makes it possible to predict the organism's response to a new stimulus. The new stimulus then modifies the adaptation level. Adaptation level as a concept of behavior regulation represents a dynamic system of interaction between the sensory responses, perceptual tendencies of the organism and all stimuli of the internal and external environment.

One of Helson's first studies, published in 1938, may help to demonstrate this concept. Subjects sat in a small enclosure which was illuminated by a light of a single wavelength. The walls of the enclosure and a table located in front of the subject were covered with a medium-gray paper insuring uniform reflectance of the light. Upon entering the enclosure, the subject reported perceiving everything as quite red, blue, or green, depending upon the wavelength of the light source. After fifteen minutes he adapted to the light and the experiment was begun. A total of nineteen cards ranging in steps, which appeared to be equal, from white through black were to be judged—according to a special scale—on hue, brightness, and saturation. All subjects had previously rated the cards under daylight conditions on the scale. To illustrate the basic observations made, let us consider a situation in which a red-light source was used during the adaptation period. According to Helson, the red-light stimulus established an adaptation level for red. The brighter cards, that is, those ranging from medium gray towards white, were judged to be red, whereas the gray cards, those darker than the walls, appeared to be green. The medium grays, which were the same color as the walls, appeared to be neutral. Green is the complement of red and is the usual after-image produced when a neutral stimulus card is viewed after prolonged presentation of a red stimulus. In a following session, subjects were presented with the same test. This time, however, the walls were covered with white paper creating an even higher red stimulation. The adaptation level established for red visual stimulation would be higher after such stimulation. This time, the lighter grays were judged to be red with numbers 3 and 4 of the nineteen cards appearing neutral. Cards 5 through 19 appeared in varying degrees of green. With the use of black paper on the walls of the enclosure, a very low adaptation level for red could be established in which cards 1 through 17 appeared red. The prior stimulation with red established the subject's adaptation level and determined his subsequent perception of the gray cards.

In the ensuing thirty years, a great deal of research has been carried out on this concept, extending from visual adaptation through all other sensory modalities into such areas as learning and social behavior. In 1964, Harry Helson was asked by the American Psychological Association to prepare a paper on the current directions of research on adaptation level

(*American Psychologist,* 1964). The paper has been reproduced here in its entirety, with the exception of the section on reinforcement theory, which, in the opinion of this author, exceeds the limitations set for these readings.

Current Trends and Issues in Adaptation-Level Theory

Harry Helson

To discuss current trends and issues in adaptation-level theory I shall have to limit myself to a few of the highlights in selected areas that range from psychophysics to social psychology. This discursive treatment is not due to personal choice but is dictated by the fact that the theory has found application in widely separated areas.

Let me begin by recalling an episode in the early 1930s when I gave a demonstration before the Optical Society of America of the inadequacy of the CIE (Commission Internationale de l'Eclairage) method of color specification. In this demonstration, although the stimulus qua stimulus did not change with change in surround, its color could be made anything we pleased by appropriate choice of the luminance and hue of the background color. In the discussion that followed, the late Selig Hecht, perhaps the leading worker in science at that time, arose and said: "Why do you complicate the problems of color vision by introducing background effects? Why can't you wait until we have solved the simpler problems before we go on to the more complicated ones?" Had my co-workers and I taken this advice the principle of color conversion, which accounts for the Bezold-Brücke phenomenon and the Land colors (Judd, 1951, 1960), would not have been formulated in 1938; we would not have shown that with proper choice of background all the psychological primaries can be seen in mono-chromatic illumination (Helson, 1938); we would not have found that neutral backgrounds induce chromatic changes as well as lightness contrast in object colors; and we would not have devised formulae predicting the colors of objects in non-daylight sources of illumination (Helson, Judd, and Warren, 1952; Helson, Judd, and Wilson, 1956). In all these cases adaptation, conceived as something more than mere loss of sensitivity from long-continued stimulation, was found to be the key concept in our attempts to understand and predict experimental findings.

For the past decade or so we have been faced with essentially the same situation in the field of psychophysics which existed in the field of visual science during the early 1930s. Workers in the tradition of classical phychophysics have tried to establish pure scales relating physical and psychological magnitudes by ruling out series, anchor, and order effects. In this approach each sense modality is presumed to have its own fixed sensitivity predetermined by the nature of the receptor mechanism. Each scale is supposed to have unique constants giving rise to negatively or positively accelerated functions. According to this view the organism acts only as a meter or transducer of energy; any variations due to series, contextual, background, or residual stimuli are considered errors that must be gotten rid of at all costs.

In contrast to the classical approach, adaptation-level theorists believe that complex factors determining psychophysical judgments must be taken into account, and a broader base must be incorporated in psychophysical laws. Contrasted with classical psychophysics, or the psychophysics of stimuli, is the psychophysics of classes, or frame of reference psychophysics. In this approach stimuli are regarded not as isolated events but as members of classes, and interest centers in the way stimuli are ordered in the classes to which they belong. Each class of stimuli is judged with respect to internal norms which can be objectively and quantitatively specified. Judgments are relative to prevailing norms or adaptation levels. Thus a four-ounce fountain pen is heavy, but a baseball bat to be heavy must weigh over forty ounces. What is called heavy or light cannot be attributed merely to a change in scale modulus or to semantic set or to judgmental relativity because different bodily members, different sets of muscles, and a different stance are used to swing a baseball bat and to write with a fountain pen. Even within the same sense modality different scales have to be used for different classes of objects if they are referred to different internal norms. Thus a single scale will not suffice for judging the sizes of rectangles or cubes under laboratory conditions, and judging the sizes of houses. A large house is judged according to a different internal norm from that used in judging large rectangles. Functional considerations also influence internal norms: A house that is large for a family of three is small for a family of eight. Psychophysics cannot ignore the role of internal norms except at its own peril. By internal norms we refer to the operationally defined concept of adaptation level.

The concept of adaptation level may be defined by at least three different sets of operations:

1. Adaptation levels appear as neutral or indifferent zones in bipolar responses. The bipolar nature of behavior has been recognized in almost all systems of psychology, e.g., by Lewin (1951) in his positive and negative valences; by Pavlov (1927) in his concept of facilitation and inhibition; by Koffka (1935) in his concept of the "demand" character of objects which Boring (1936) put into behavioral terms as "that which attracts or repels us"; by N. E. Miller (1959) in his concept of approach-avoidance gradients; and in the concepts of positive and negative reinforcers used by learning theorists. Descriptively, we find positive and negative after-images in sensory processes, and pleasant and unpleasant feelings in the domain of affects. If we measure bipolar properties of behavior on continua, then it is immediately evident that there are neutral zones between opposite qualities and opposed modes of behavior. Operationally, the stimuli or conditions eliciting neutral responses furnish a measure of prevailing levels. Long ago (1924), Hess pointed out that the earthworm, *Lumbricus terrestris*, avoids certain intensities of light above a certain level, approaches weaker intensities, and remains quiescent at some

intermediate intensity. In the most primitive responses objects are grossly dichotomized into approach-ignore-avoid, good-indifferent-bad, pleasant-neutral-unpleasant. This is the simplest form of categorizing or scaling, and all scaling methods, whether they require the use of language or some other type of response, are fundamentally bipolar rating scales in which the neutral or zero is fixed by the organism. Adaptation levels are revealed in all forms of behavior whether they are sensory, motor, or cognitive verbal in nature.

2. We may deduce the concept of adaptation level (AL) from a set of assumptions regarding the nature of psychophysical judgments as was done by Michels and Helson (1949) in reformulating the Fechner law. Less strict than the derivation of AL by logicomathematical reasoning is the incorporation of a parameter in empirical equations to make the organism's functional zero the zero of psychological continua. In such cases the best values of AL can be determined from all judgments of a set of stimuli by curve fitting, linear interpolation, and so on. This has been done both by means of the reformulated Fechner law and also in using other types of equations, in the determination of the loci of achromatic points in strongly chromatic illuminances (Helson and Michels, 1948).

3. We may arrive at the concept of AL in the time-honored way found so fruitful in mathematics, physics, and chemistry—by definition. There are many advantages in defining a concept besides the important one that we then know what we are talking about. AL as a weighted log mean derives much of its value, like many concepts in physics, in being defined so that constants appropriate to specific cases can be determined. Like the general differential equation relating resistance, capacitance, and inductance in electrical circuits, which can be used to solve any number of specific problems, so the definition of AL as a weighted mean can be used to obtain quantitative answers to many different questions.

This definition has provided a number of deductions such as the pooling or integrative nature of most types of responses, the decentered position of stimuli eliciting neutral psychophysical judgments, the nonlinearity of stimulus-response functions, and AL as the moving zero of psychophysical and other functions. In addition it has accounted for such experimentally determined facts as the tendency of organisms to match level of output with level of input, variability of response with constant stimulation, and effects of anchors, context, and residual factors in perception and judgment.

We have found that the weighted log mean definition of AL is the best approximation to the neutral or indifferent region for sensory magnitudes. In estimates of the averages of series of numbers, Parducci, Calfee, Marshall, and Davidson (1960) have stressed the role of mid-, median, and end points of the series in determining AL. I prefer the weighted log mean because it brings in all the stimuli, not just the mid- and end stimuli, because of its greater theoretical power and greater generality, and because this definition requires fewer arbitrary constants than any other definition so far proposed. As an example, let us consider a recent application by Bevan, Barker, and Pritchard (1963) of this definition to handle an effect Stevens has called hysteresis, which means "lagging behind." These writers point out:

When one asks what it is that lags, the concept of adaptation level presents itself for consideration. According to this point of view, the apparent difference in magnitude between two successively presented stimuli depends not simply upon a difference between the intensive processes representing the first (standard) and the second (variable), but upon the difference between an internal norm evolved from a combination, on the one hand, of all of the relevant prior inputs including the standard and, on the other, the process representing the variable. If a sequence of inputs is non-random (i.e., ascending or descending), then we may expect that there will be a lag in the shift of the internal norm in contrast to the shift in standard stimuli. If the norm evolves from successive presentations of an ascending series, it may be expected that the bowing will be upward; if a descending series is used, the expected bowing is downward (pp. 103–104).

Using lifted weights, Bevan, Barker, and Pritchard obtained concave upward curves in light-to-heavy order and concave downward curves in heavy-to-light order. Stevens' assumption (1957) that bowing is due to poorer discrimination at the higher end of the scale, resulting in greater use of upper categories, cannot, they show, explain positively accelerated curves because in these cases discrimination is better at the high than at the low end of the continuum. Hence this argument can apply only to *negatively* accelerated curves. Excellent fits were obtained to experimental data by taking as the effective stimulus not the physical value of the stimulus being judged, but the difference between the stimulus judged and the adaptation level, calculated as a weighted log mean of preceding stimuli, with the immediately preceding stimulus as standard. On this basis upward bowed curves were obtained for ascending series and downward bowed curves for descending series. No new assumptions had to be made in this application of the weighted mean definition to explain upward and downward bowing with ascending and descending orders of stimulus presentation.

Let us now turn to some other studies that reveal current trends and bear on fundamental issues in adaptation-level theory:

1. *Anchoring effects of subliminal stimuli.* In this connection it was found by Black and Bevan (1960) that experimental subjects judged a set of five electric shocks ranging from 1,500 to 2,700 μa (microampere) as more intensive following a subliminal anchor shock than did a control group which received the five supraliminal shocks without the subliminal anchor. Since the subliminal shocks were not detected by GSR (Galvanic Skin Response) measures it appears that a behavioral measure, judgment, may be more sensitive to the influence of stimulation than a widely used physiological indicator. Similar results were found by Goldstone, Goldfarb, Strong, and Russell (1962) in judgments of shock with subliminal anchors, and by Bevan and Pritchard (1963) with sound stimuli. As shown in Figure 6.19, subjects given a subliminal sound anchor preceding each series stimulus reported higher loudnesses than did a control group not given the subliminal anchor. Reinforcing effects of 2,300 μa shocks were found by Bevan and Adamson (1960) to be most effective when the preadaptation electric shock was below 2,300 μa, least effective when the preadaptation shock was above, and intermediate in effectiveness when the

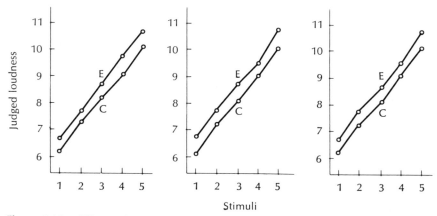

Figure 6.19: Effects of a subliminal sound stimulus in raising judged intensity of series stimuli. (The control group, C, was not given the subliminal stimulus. The three plots are for subliminal sound introduced at varying intervals between successive stimuli. (*Bevan and Pritchard, 1963.*)

preadaptation shock was the same as in the learning series. These findings were replicated with rat subjects in a subsequent study by Black, Adamson, and Bevan (1961) using running speed to escape shock as the criterion. It is difficult to believe that rats are subject to semantic sets, judgmental relativity, or change in scale modulus, as proposed by Stevens (1958) as alternatives to adaptation-level theory. It seems simpler to assume that shocks following preadapting weak shocks are effectively more intense, and shocks following preadapting strong shocks are effectively less intense because of their effects on prevailing adaptation levels.

2. *Residual effects of anchors in memory and recall.* Using a null method that did not require judgment in terms of language responses, Steger and I (unpublished study) have found that effects of anchors persist over a period of time and influence recall as well as conditions during immediate impression of stimuli. In the first study four groups of subjects judged a series of black squares on white background during the impression or learning series. The squares ranged from 1.0 to 3.82 inches on a side and were judged in terms of a rating scale from very, very small to very, very large. The initial conditions for the four groups were as follows: (a) without anchor stimulus; (b) with an anchor at the geometric center of the series (1.96 inches); (c) with a 9.0-inch anchor; and (d) with a 0.30-inch anchor. The average size judgments are shown in Figure 6.20 and are in line with expectations from known anchor effects: The squares were judged smallest with the largest anchor, largest with the smallest anchor, and intermediate with the anchor at the center of the series and with the no anchor condition. One week later subjects were called back to the laboratory and asked to identify the smallest, middle, and largest stimuli in the series from a much more extended series that ranged from 0.10 inch to 14.56 inches on a side presented in ascending and descending orders. As shown in Figure 6.21, the residual effects of the anchors in the impression trials are

evident after one week: The 9.0-inch anchor group picked the smallest set of three; the 0.30-inch group picked the largest set of three; while the two control groups picked sets intermediate in size between those of the other two groups.

The first experiment was replicated and extended in a second experiment with four new groups of subjects to determine the relative potency of anchors as residuals, anchors given during the impression phase. Two control groups were not given anchors during the impression phase but were exposed to the 0.30- and 9.0-inch anchors during the recall phase. One experimental group was given the 9.0-inch anchor during the impression phase and the 0.30-inch anchor during the recall phase; conversely, the other experimental group was given the 0.30-inch anchor in the impression session and the 9.0-inch anchor in the recall session. The results again show expected effects of anchors as seen in Figure 6.22 where the stimuli recalled with the 9.0-inch anchor present were smaller (curves coded V and VIII in Figure 6.22) than stimuli recalled with 0.30-inch anchor (curves coded VI and VII in Figure 6.22). Comparison of the curves for Groups VI and VII show that the 0.30-inch anchor during recall was more effective if it followed 9.0-inch anchor during the impression phase one week earlier than if no anchor was present during the impression phase. However the 9.0-inch anchor in the recall phase following 0.30-inch anchor in

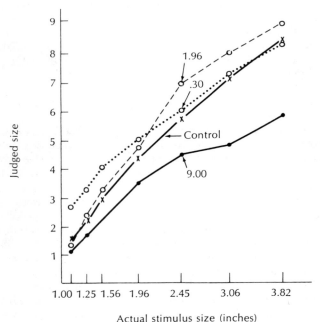

Actual stimulus size (inches)

Figure 6.20: Judged size of stimuli in the impression phase showing expected anchor effects with small (0.30 inch), intermediate (1.96 inches), and large (9.0 inches) anchors and under the control condition in which no anchor was employed.

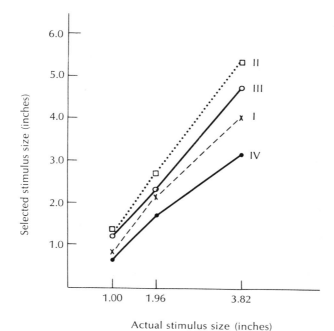

Figure 6.21: Smallest, middle, and largest stimuli of the
series recalled one week after initial presentation.

the impression phase did not yield significantly lower recall choices than under
the control condition (Groups V and VIII).

The clear effects of earlier levels operative later in recall argue against
semantic set or judgmental relativity as an explanation since a matching-from-
memory technique rather than verbal response was employed in these experiments. It is usually agreed that null or matching methods are freer from higher-
order biases than are any other psychophysical methods and indeed are regarded by many physicists and engineers as the only valid psychophysical
methods. In this study the most stringent psychophysical criterion was employed to rule out higher-order involvements. The basic nature of anchor and
contextual effects in recall seems amply established.

3. *Series effects with an absolute, extraexperimentally anchored language.*
Still further evidence against the theory of judgmental relativity comes from a
study by Campbell, Lewis, and Hunt (1958) in which subjects rendered judgments of pitch of tones in low and high contexts by identifying them on a
simulated piano keyboard after having been made acquainted with the pitch
of middle C. In high context, pitches were designated lower than in low context
as we would expect. These authors concluded that the shifting judgments of a
common tone in different contexts was independent of the specific semantic
details of the usual method of single stimuli assessment, since the response
language was anchored outside the experiment and hence was not relative to

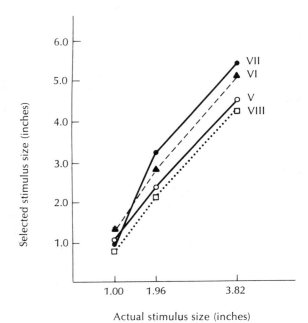

Figure 6.22: Smallest, middle, and largest stimuli recalled one week after initial impression with large
(small) anchor if small (large) anchor was employed
during the impression phase.

the situation. Furthermore, the response language, they pointed out, was absolute in that it referred to invariant aspects of the stimulus, thus disposing of
the explanation of shifts in scale values of stimuli in different contexts in terms
of judgmental relativity.

4. *Neutral zones in unexpected places.* For the benefit of those who may
feel that the concept of adaptation level does not have as wide a range of
application as some of us have claimed for it, I would like to cite the discovery
of neutral points in an unsuspected area. In a study of reaction time (Helson
and Steger, 1962) we found that when a second light followed the primary
light signal at intervals ranging from 10 to 170 msec the reaction time was
significantly lengthened as shown in Figure 6.23 with maximum inhibition in
the neighborhood of 100 msec. What is difficult to explain in this finding is
how stimuli coming so long after the primary stimulus, when the reaction is
presumably almost complete, can nevertheless delay the consummatory response. When asked by one of my students what relation this phenomenon
might have to adaptation-level theory, I was obliged to answer that I did not
see any relation although I secretly felt that it would indeed be extraordinary
if a neutral set of stimulus conditions did not exist for this phenomenon also.
Later work, using heteromodal stimuli, confirmed my belief. Using a light
stimulus followed by a tone, or a tone stimulus followed by a light, we found

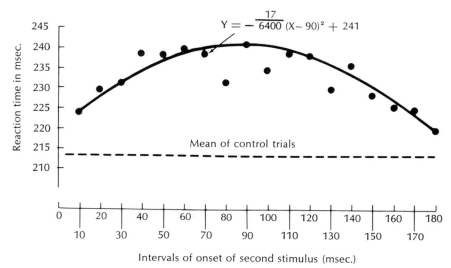

Figure 6.23: Showing increase in reaction time to a light stimulus when it is followed by a second light at intervals ranging from 10 to 180 msec. (*Helson and Steger, 1962.*)

that from simultaneous presentation of the two stimuli up to about 25–35 msec, response to the first stimulus was facilitated, quickened, and at 50 msec up to about 175 msec response to the first stimulus was inhibited, slowed (cf. Figure 6.24). The neutral or equilibrium condition in which the second stimulus neither facilitated nor inhibited response to the first stimulus proved to be in the region of 25–35 msec. We have thus demonstrated the bipolar nature of simple spot reactions and the presence of neutral zones of stimulation in this area. Added to the difficulty of finding a physiological explanation of how a stimulus following an earlier one can lengthen reaction time, we now have to explain the neutral intervals during which a later stimulus neither facilitates nor inhibits response to an earlier one. We seem to have here a tool for the investigation of phenomena of central facilitation, equilibrium, and inhibiton.

5. *Assimilation and contrast in sensory and social-judgmental processes.* It has been maintained by a number of workers that there are two independent processes at work both in judgments of sensory stimuli (Sherif, Taub, and Hovland, 1958), in judgments of social issues (Sherif and Hovland, 1961) and in judgments of clinical materials (Campbell, Hunt, and Lewis, 1957), one of which results in assimilation or greater likeness, and the other results in contrast, or greater difference in judged stimuli. Perhaps the most striking examples of assimiliation in the field of sensory processes are the von Bezold designs in which *white arabesques lighten* and *black arabesques darken* chromatic backgrounds. It has been maintained by these workers that while contrast effects may follow from adaptation-level theory, assimilation effects do not. In a series of studies (Helson, 1963; Helson and Joy, 1962; Helson and Rohles, 1959) we have been able to show that far from being mutually exclu-

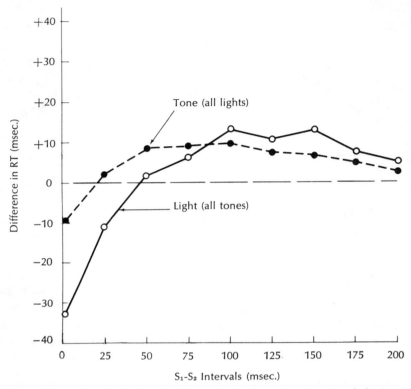

Figure 6.24: Showing facilitation (shortening) of reaction time to a light (tone) when followed by a tone (light) up to about 25 msec, with little or no effect between 25 and 50 msec, and inhibition (lengthening) of reaction time from 75 msec to 175 msec.

sive processes, assimilation and contrast lie on a single continuum and are complementary in nature. Instead of using the artistic designs of von Bezold and others, we resorted to straight, ruled black and white lines on gray ground which give as striking assimilation effects as the von Bezold figures. By using straight lines it is possible to vary the width of the lines and to vary the ratios of line width to width of intervening gray. Systematic variation of line width and width of medium gray area shows (see Figure 6.25) that assimilation is found up to about 10-mm line widths with all line separations. Then, as the black and white lines become wider, assimilation gives way to contrast: The gray areas between the white stripes are darkened and between the black stripes are lightened in accordance with expectations from classical contrast. In Figure 6.26 are shown the conditions that yield assimilation on the one hand and contrast on the other. The line separating the two regions denotes the

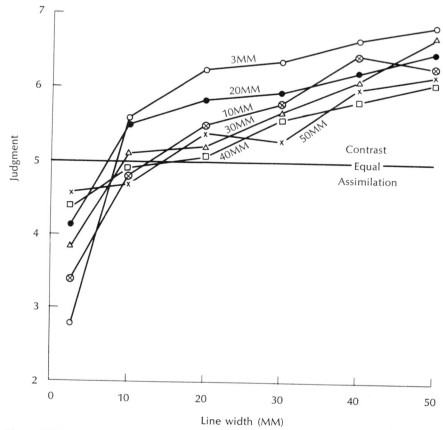

Figure 6.25: Contrast and assimilation as a function of line width for various separations. (*Helson and Joy, 1962.*)

conditions under which neither contrast nor assimilation appears. It is therefore evident that assimilation and contrast are complementary processes which plot on a single continuum separated by a neutral zone in which white and black lines neither lighten nor darken intervening gray areas.

Had we stopped our investigations after using the middle gray background we would not have realized that our generalizations were valid only for this condition because in a subsequent study (Helson, 1963), using near-white and near-black (very light and very dark) backgrounds, only assimilation was found as shown in Figures 6.27 and 6.28. This finding follows from a physiological hypothesis I advanced to account for assimilation and contrast (Helson, 1963) which was as follows: Small differences in excitation in neighboring areas (either in the retina or the brain) summate to produce assimilation while larger differences result in inhibition of the weaker impulses to produce contrast. It follows at once there are intermediate differences in excitation which

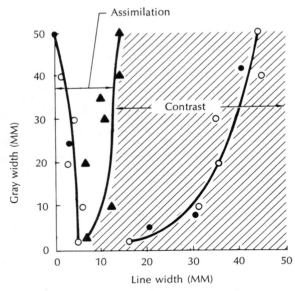

Figure 6.26: Domains of assimilation and contrast. Each point in the plane represents the combination of line width and line separation that yields either assimilation or contrast. (*Helson and Joy, 1962.*)

give rise neither to summation (assimilation) nor inhibition (contrast). This consequence of the theory was verified experimentally. Only one additional assumption is needed to handle all cases: We assume that area functions for luminance in such a way that larger areas are equivalent to higher luminances. This assumption explains the cases where assimilation gives way to contrast as the white and black lines are widened relative to the intervening gray areas. The failure of contrast to appear with near-white and near-black backgrounds is easily explained on the basis that the differences in excitation between the white lines and light backgrounds, on the one hand, and the black lines and the dark backgrounds, on the other, are small and therefore summate, giving rise to assimilation. It is immediately apparent that for contrast to be perceived the adaptation level must have a value *between* contiguous areas; for assimilation to be perceived AL must be *below* or *above* the neighboring areas.

With a satisfactory account of assimilation and contrast at the sensory level we have a model with which to envisage these phenomena at the social-judgment level. In social judgments small differences in items from an individual's own position are minimized (assimilation), while larger differences are magnified (contrast) (Sherif and Hovland, 1961). Suffice it to say here it does not now seem necessary to regard contrast and assimilation as opposed, independent processes. Their complementary nature appears as clear in the field of social judgments as in the field of sensory processes. Plots of scale values of

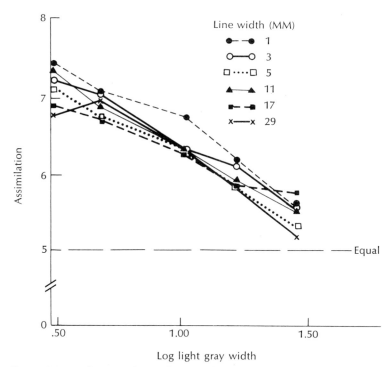

Line width (MM)

●– –● 1
○—○ 3
□····□ 5
▲—▲ 11
■– –■ 17
x—x 29

Log light gray width

Figure 6.27: Showing that only assimilation is found with backgrounds of high (80 percent) reflectance. (Assimilation is shown as a function of line separation—width of white.)

lifted weights (Figure 6.29) as a result of the introduction of extreme anchors are similar to the plots of scale values of statements concerning attitudes toward the Negro by those having moderate and extreme pro- or anti-Negro biases (Figure 6.30, from Hovland and Sherif, 1952). The complementary nature of assimiliation and contrast in social judgments arises from the fact that in finite scales if some scale items are spread apart (contrast), others will be crowded together (assimilation). By taking neutral or indifferent zones into account in attitude scaling we find there are two kinds of contrast: In the first type an item on one side of the scale (the favorable side) moves to the other side (unfavorable), thereby involving a change in *sign* or *quality* in the attitude. In the second type of contrast which was stressed by Sherif and Hovland, separations in scale values of items are increased without changing from posi- tive to negative or vice versa and are therefore matters of *degree*. The differ- ence between changing an individual's position from pro to con, or vice versa, and creating a more favorable or more unfavorable attitude can be very great and may have considerable practical significance, for example in changing voters' attitudes or consumer preferences.

6. *The methodological importance for social psychology of studies leading to functional relations between variables.* In applying the AL paradigm to

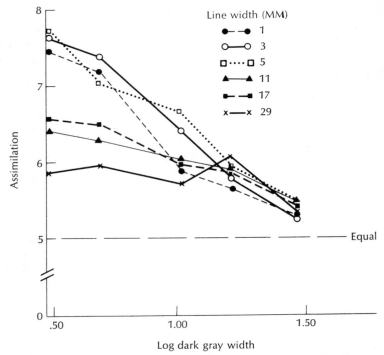

Figure 6.28: Showing that only assimilation is found with background of low (14 percent) reflectance. (Assimilation is shown as a function of line separation—dark gray width.)

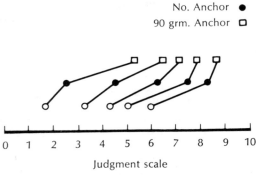

Figure 6.29: Assimilation and contrast effects in judgments of lifted weights when extreme anchors are introduced.

social phenomena we hoped to show that it is possible to establish functional relations between intensity of stimulation and magnitude of response. Most of the basic information in the quantitative sciences is contained in equations expressing the variation in magnitude of dependent variables as functions of independent variables. In the study of personality and interpersonal interactions most studies have been concerned with correlations of responses to various tests or response-response correlations, rather than with the establishment of functional relations between situational and behavioral variables through variation and control of the intensity of stimulation. In the studies with Blake and our colleagues on the effects of social pressures on expression of attitudes and on other types of response, we varied the intensity of stimulation in accordance with the paradigm shown in Table 6.6. By combining weak, moderate, or strong focal stimuli with negative, neutral, or positive background stimuli, we were able to study behavior as a function of as many as nine "intensities" of stimulation.

Systematic variations of intensity of social stimulation revealed that with strong social pressures to conform, most individuals conform; with strong pressures against conformity, most individuals do not conform; and with intermediate pressures, frequencies of conforming and nonconforming reactions divide about equally. Thus in Table 6.7 it is seen that when a weak request is

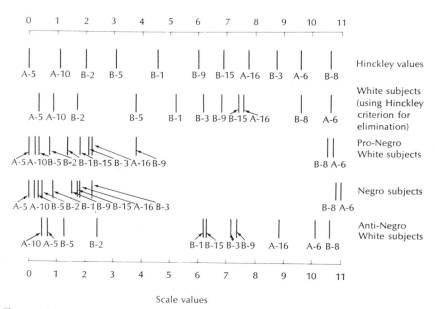

Scale values

Figure 6.30: Contrast and assimilation effects as shown by shifts in scale values of attitude items by those holding extreme positions. (Effects of extreme positions with respect to social issues are formally similar to shifts in judgments of lifted weights when extreme anchors are introduced.) (*Hovland and Sherif, 1952.*)

Table 6.6

Paradigm of strengths of focal and background stimuli acting upon subjects in the Texas action studies

Background Model	Strength of Focal Stimuli		
	Strong	*Moderate*	*Weak*
Agrees	+ +	0 +	− +
Absent	+ 0	0 0	− 0
Refuses	+ −	0 −	—

Note—Code: + indicates strong condition; 0 indicates moderate condition; − indicates weak or negative condition.

made for volunteers to take part in a psychology experiment, and a planted subject is heard to refuse, almost everybody refused. As the stimulating conditions were intensified with stronger requests to volunteer, and when planted subjects responded positively, more individuals agreed to take part in the experiment. In what was designed to be the neutral condition, the group split as near 50-50 as was possible with an odd number of subjects (Rosenbaum, 1956).

It is also possible to determine the role of personal factors in behavior as shown in a study of petition signing by Helson, Blake, and Mouton (1958). When subjects were asked to sign popular or unpopular petitions just after other (planted) individuals agreed or refused to sign, it was found that those who signed also had higher submissive scores on the Allport-Allport A-S reaction study than did those who refused, the difference between scores of the two groups being highly significant ($p < 0.01$). Submissive subjects, as judged by the A-S reaction scores, were also found to yield to group pressures to a greater extent than ascendant subjects, in reporting number of metronome

Table 6.7

Volunteering as a function of stimulus and background factors

Social Background	Stimulus Strength								
	High			Moderate			Low		
	Yes	No	W	Yes	No	W	Yes	No	W
Positive	12	3	(9.4)	12	3	(9.1)	6	9	(9.5)
Neutral	12	3	(9.1)	7	8	(7.4)	0	15	(4.6)
Negative	11	4	(8.6)	1	14	(5.5)	1	14	(5.3)

*Note—*Numbers in parentheses are average ratings on a scale from 0 to 15 of willingness to participate in the task (from Rosenbaum, 1956).

clicks, giving answers to arithmetic problems, and in expressing attitudes toward statements concerned with war and peace.

One of the advantages of performing experiments with systematic variation of conditions is that we not only find what we may have been looking for, but often something unexpected turns up which may be more interesting than the initial hypotheses. Thus in the study of expression of attitudes under social pressures previously referred to, we found, as shown in Figure 6.31, that the more frequently individuals were influenced by the group, the greater was their agreement with the group and conversely, the more frequently subjects differed from the group, the greater was their disagreement. There is thus a a functional relation between frequency and extent of conformity to social pressures.

I must confess that the methodological importance of systematic variation of situational conditions does not seem to have been conveyed to social psychologists by the studies that Blake and I, and our colleagues, did at the University of Texas, for the number of publications reporting response-response or test-test correlations has not diminished. Granting the value of such studies for some purposes, it is my belief that we shall not develop a *science* of personality or interpersonal relations until we have laws expressing the degree to which variation in one variable, whether situational or personal, is related to

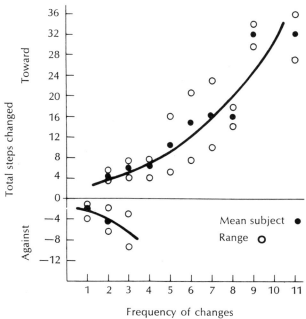

Figure 6.31: Extent of movement toward or against group position as a function of frequency of yielding to, or resisting, group pressures. (*Helson, Blake, Mouton, and Olmstead, 1956.*)

variation in other variables. When this happens we shall have a truly experimental social psychology and an experimental, as contrasted with a test, approach to personality and clinical psychology.

Last but not least among the current trends are investigations by Bevan and his co-workers (Behar and Bevan, 1961) of cross-modal judgments, applications to Rorschach testing by Block (1964), to TAT tests by Dollin and Sakoda (1962), effects of context on scaling traits by Young, Holtzman, and Bryant (1954) and Podell (1961), and investigations by Goldstone and his co-workers (Goldstone and Goldfarb, 1964) in their experimental-psychophysical approach to psychiatric disorders.

While much has been accomplished, I believe that much more remains to be done both in refining present applications and in extending AL theory to new areas. I have great faith in the value of experimental-quantitative approaches to psychological problems. Perhaps the chief value of AL theory has been its encouragement of such approaches in the areas where it has been applied.

CHAPTER 7

Learning and Perception

It is difficult to assess the role of learning in perception. All of the organizational tendencies described thus far are—at least in part—the result of the organism's previous experiences. Perhaps one could say that perception is based on learning, whereas sensation represents the organism's intrinsic responsiveness to specific stimuli. To sense a stimulus requires only that the stimulus have specific characteristics. Perception, however, requires previous experience and learning.

The perceptual processes and learning are so interrelated that we are often oblivious to the dependency of our responses upon prior experiences and learning. Almost every object perceived is perceived in the light of our experience with that object. The "chair" is much more than a conglomerate of wood and paint; it is an object whose function is recognized from previous experience.

The objective study of experience and perception is nearly impossible. At best, we can observe response tendencies of the organism and draw tentative conclusions about the experience variables which led to the organism's development of these tendencies. In the case of humans, the past history of each organism is so varied that comparison is difficult. In the case of lower animals, however, it is possible to control the environmental experience to a greater degree and then to observe the perceptual tendencies of the organism as a function of the experience. Even under ideal conditions, however, it remains difficult to assess the degree to which sensory experience has been controlled.

One approach has been to deprive the animal of some aspect of sensory experience which would occur in normal development. The perceptual response tendencies of these animals are then compared to animals raised in normal environments in which the sensory experience being studied occurred. If a modified perceptual response pattern is observed in the deprived animals, in comparison with the normal animals, the tentative conclusion can be drawn that the deprived sensory experience was responsible for the development of that particular response pattern. Emphasis must be placed on the *tentative* nature of the conclusion; it may well be that the sensory deprivation itself and the experience of developing under abnormal conditions is responsible for the deviation. In a study of the effects of sensory deprivation, Riesen (1950) raised a chimp in total darkness. At the end of the test period the animal was unable to learn simple form discriminations. The incapability, however, was caused by defects in the visual system and was not a result of the failure to experience form. Evidently some sensory stimulation is necessary for the normal development of the visual system. Animals receiving only 1½ hours of diffuse illumination daily showed normal development of the visual mechanism.

Such questions as those about the development of form perception are representative of how the relationship between learning and perception has been queried. Cues such as size, shape, and color are utilized by the normal individual to distinguish between objects. Is the utilization of such cues an innate property of the visual system, or must each individual learn to use these cues? An adult organism can make fine form discriminations between objects differing in only minute aspects. Such a capability may be the result of the sum total of experience with objects and forms gathered by the organism during his life-span, or it may be due to the biological nature of the responding organism, or both.

Arthur Siegel, during his stay at New York University, undertook the study of the development of form discrimination. The subjects were a group of animals allowed to develop without ever having the opportunity to perceive form while at the same time undergoing normal development of the visual system. Through a clever experimental technique, Siegel was able to accomplish this difficult task (*Journal of Comparative and Physiological Psychology*, 1953).

Deprivation of Visual Form Definition in the Ring Dove: Discriminatory Learning

Arthur Siegel

Introduction

Deprivation of visual function throughout life is of interest to psychologists because of the relevance of the effects of this deprivation to theories of visual perception.

The method of deprivation heretofore employed has involved rearing the experimental animals in complete darkness from birth to time of testing. This method of rearing has been criticized because of the possibility that visual brightness deprivation in addition to visual form deprivation may initiate either retinal or central nervous structural changes. This objection has been partially confirmed by some findings of Riesen (1950).

The usual method of dark-rearing was therefore modified in the present experiment so as to allow the retinas of the experimental animals to be continually stimulated during daylight hours by diffuse light, while, at the same time, perception of visual form was prevented.

Subjects

The subjects were thirty-six ring doves from the colony maintained by the Department of Animal Behavior of the American Museum of Natural History. Of these, twenty-four experimental birds were reared without visual form definition, and twelve control birds were normally reared.

Apparatus

A modified Lashley-type jumping apparatus was used in the training situation. Essentially this apparatus consisted of a perch so built that a bird upon it could "see" both stimuli located twenty inches subrostrally. The stimulus plates were so arranged that when a bird jumped down to the negative stimulus, the platform holding the stimulus collapsed, causing the bird to fall into a net eighteen inches below. The stimuli were a frosted-glass triangle and a frosted-glass circle of equated area, both of which were on black backgrounds. The central area of each of these was illuminated from below by a ten-watt incandescent electric bulb. The walls of the jumping apparatus were painted flat black, and inasmuch as the experimental work was carried out in a darkened

room, the only "figures" visible were the uniform fields of the circle and triangle. In the mid-line, posterior to the perch, the plunger apparatus of a pinball
machine was set so that a jump could be forced on any bird which failed to
jump in the time allotted for each trial. The inner edges of the stimuli were
separated by one and one-half inches. Thus, it was impossible for the birds to
make mid-line landings. The jumps were focalized and confined to the stimulus
fields by having the front and sides of the apparatus flush with the edges of
the stimuli, and by having the back of the apparatus as close to the perch as
possible. Into the door, located at the top of the apparatus, was cut a small,
rectangular observation window.

Method

The general sequence of operations in this experiment was as follows: *rearing*
under conditions of visual definition deprivation; *preliminary training* in
jumping from a perch to the horizontal; *training* on a circle versus triangle
discrimination; *testing* for visual acuity, and vestibular responses and the
checking of indices of the general health of the birds.

Conditions of Rearing

Because the eyes of the ring dove open when the bird is four to five days old,
the experimental birds were hooded at three days of age with a plastic (vinyl)
translucent head covering. This allowed the retinas of the squab to be stimulated henceforth by a diffuse uniform field of light, but at the same time prevented form perception.

The transmission characteristics of the material out of which the hoods
were cut were examined by two independent observers on a Bausch and Lomb
constant-deviation spectrometer. Both observers agreed that the material was
nonselective. All wavelengths passed through. There was no absorption even
at the ends of the spectrum, where absorption most frequently takes place.

The hood was fitted by hand and so designed that it allowed the beak
of the young dove to extrude. This permitted feeding and breathing, while,
at the same time, it prevented all specific form perception. The hood was also
constructed so that it could be loosened, without ever being removed, to allow
for growth of the bird. Hoods were inspected twice daily, and appropriate
adjustments were made as needed. The hood was constructed so that it did
not press against the corneas of the squab.

Owing specifically to the deprivation of visual definition, the doves did
not develop pecking responses. Therefore, from the time of rejection by their
parents until the termination of the experiment, the doves were fed and given
water by hand. The same formula of mixed grain given to the normally reared
doves (control animals) in the museum colony was fed by hand to the hooded
birds. The feeding was accomplished by grasping a dove by the beak with one
hand and inserting the food into its mouth with the other hand.

The control animals were reared normally in the museum colony. No experimental or control bird was younger than eight weeks of age, nor was any older than twelve weeks of age when started on the preliminary training.

Preliminary Training

In advance of their use in training and tests, all experimental and control birds were given experience in jumping from a perch to a table top. This experience was essential for participation of the hood-reared birds in the training proper owing to their diminished "life style." It was observed that the hood-reared birds did not move about as much as did the normally reared birds, did not fly unless forced to do so, and when first unhooded as adults, were apt to fly only erratically and with definite errors in space orientation.

This pretraining was accomplished by use of a perch of adjustable height. Each bird was first forced to jump twenty times from a perch two inches above a surface. On the following day, the height of the perch was increased to three inches, and the birds were given twenty trials at this height. This procedure was repeated daily. That is, each day the birds received twenty more trials, and the height of the perch was increased one inch. At a height of twenty inches, two days' training (or forty jumps) was given. The total number of pretraining jumps each bird received, therefore was 400.

Training

Following the pretraining, a window the size of the lower halfeye was fixed in the mask of each experimental bird, thus allowing monocular vision. (For one group, trained using both eyes, two openings were cut.) Between experimental sessions this window was thenceforth covered with masking tape. Images of objects located subrostrally to the birds would impinge on the upper retina. Images of objects located suprarostrally would impinge on the lower retina. The experimenter's aim in covering the upper half-eye and locating the images subrostrally was to confine images to the upper retina. Hence, when the terms "uncovered eye" or "eye" alone are used in this paper, it should be kept in mind that images were confined to the upper hemiretina. This restriction was not pertinent to the present experiment, but was introduced for the purposes of a further experiment with the same experimental birds.

Specifically, each experimental session for each bird involved the following routine. The bird was taken from a home cage in a blacked-out room and the appropriate aperture fixed for the eye to be uncovered during the experimental session. The bird was then placed in a blacked-out cage. Five minutes later the bird was taken from this blacked-out cage and was placed, via the door located at the top of the jumping apparatus, on the perch of the blackened apparatus. Before this, the stimuli had been set in place, and when the subject seemed comfortably perched, the stimuli were illuminated.

If the subject made the correct choice (responded by jumping to the positive stimulus), the apparatus was immediately darkened, and the bird was then replaced in the blacked-out cage. Necessary adjustments, such as transfer of the position of the stimuli, were then made, and after an interval of five minutes, the bird was replaced in the apparatus, as above, for his next trial.

If the subject made the wrong choice (responded by jumping to the negative stimulus), the stimuli were immediately darkened, and the bird was left in the net while necessary adjustments were made in the position of the stimuli. Immediately following these adjustments, the bird was replaced on the perch for its next trial. Hence, the subject was kept in the apparatus until the correct choice was made. Avoidance of the fall and return to the blacked-out cage following reaction to the positive stimulus thus constituted reward, and the fall following reaction to the negative stimulus constituted punishment.

If any bird failed to jump after three minutes in the situation, the plunger apparatus was released, forcing the subject forward and off the perch, down to the stimuli.

Each bird received thirty trials per day. On completion of thirty trials, the hole in front of the eye used in training was covered with the masking tape and the bird returned to its home cage. The normally reared birds were treated in exactly the same manner in the experimental situation. However, the normally reared birds, for purposes of adaptation, wore hoods for three days in their situation, as well as during all experimental situations.

The arbitrary criterion of having learned the discrimination was nine out of ten consecutive jumps toward the positive stimulus on any one day of the training session. According to this criterion, if a bird jumped to the positive stimulus for its last eight trials on one day, it was still required to make nine out of ten consecutive jumps toward the positive stimulus on the following day.

Eighteen of the experimental birds were trained using their right eyes (Group A), and six were trained using their left eyes (Group B). Six of the normally reared birds were trained using their right eyes (Group C), and six were trained using both eyes (Group D). The number of subjects in Group A was greater than the number of subjects in the other groups because Group A is a composite of birds used also in an additional experiment. Likewise, Group D, not a direct control for the present experiment, is included because of its relevance and interest as an indirect control.

Feeding of the birds of all groups took place after the daily experimental session.

Precautions and Controls

Visual Acuity and Ophthalmoscopic Examination. Visual acuity was tested by taking advantage of the optokinetic reaction. When a drum consisting of black and white stripes is rotated in the visual field, doves and many other animals show nystagmic movements of the head. In testing visual acuity, the method of limits was used. That is, the width of the black stripes was decreased by 1 mm steps until the optomotor reaction disappeared (upper threshold). Then, starting at a point below this, the width of the stripes was increased until the reaction reappeared (lower threshold). Three decreasing and three increasing series were given to each bird tested. The absolute threshold was defined as the mean of the three upper and three lower thresholds. Eight randomly chosen hood-reared birds and four randomly chosen control birds were so tested for visual acuity.

Six randomly selected birds, three normals and three controls, were examined ophthalmoscopically to ascertain the condition of their retinas.

General Controls.   To exclude the possibility that some animals might learn from the manner in which they were placed on the perch or in dependence upon the noise made by the shifting of stimuli, the same kind of noise was made between trials whether the stimuli positions were changed or not, and the experimenter attempted to place the subject on the perch in exactly the same position and manner for each trial.

Varying the position of the positive and negative stimuli from right to left, following Gellermann's (1933) series, controlled positional habits and the possibility that animals might react to relative distances of the stimuli from the side of the apparatus. For one-half the birds, the circle was the positive stimulus; for the other half, the triangle was positive. This evenly distributed over the data any innate propensity of the birds for either the circle or triangle, and also reactions made on the basis of brightness per unit area. This last factor was further controlled by varying, in a prearranged manner, the brightness of the positive and negative stimuli over four different levels as soon as a bird had made four out of four, or four out of five, reactions to the positive stimulus. Thus, each stimulus was brighter than the other for a portion of the last five or six jumps prior to the reaching of the criterion. This variation was continued until the bird either reacted twice toward the negative stimulus, or reached the criterion of mastery. If either the criterion of learning was reached or two incorrect jumps were made, the ten-watt intensity level was reinstated.

Animals may sometimes react to some minute aspect of the stimulus, rather than to the form of the stimulus. In order to control any cues, subliminal for human beings, to which the birds may have reacted, three different triangles and three different circles, all of the same dimensions, were used successively in a random manner in all experimental conditions for each bird.

Results

In order to test the significance of the difference between the number of trials taken by the normally reared and hood-reared birds, Cochran's procedure recommended for use when there is suspected heterogeneity of variance was followed. The *t*'s (t-tests) derived from this method of treatment are presented in Table 7.2, and the means and sigmas for each group are shown in Table 7.1. The results indicate that in the four possible comparisons between hood-reared and normally reared groups in the initial training, the hood-reared groups took

Table 7.1

**Trials for initial discriminatory learning,
experimental and control groups**

Group	N	Eye Used	Mean	Sigma
A	18	right	126.0	20.2
B	6	left	127.6	18.5
C	6	right	72.3	13.4
D	6	both	83.1	16.3

significantly more trials to reach the criterion than did the normally reared groups.

On the other hand, between the results for the two normally reared groups no significant differences are found. Similarly, between the two hood-reared groups, there are no significant differences. Therefore, the scores for the hood-reared birds were combined into one inclusive group. The same was done for the normally reared birds. This gave an inclusive mean of 126.8 jumps to reach the criterion (sigma, 24.9) for the hood-reared birds. The inclusive mean obtained for the normally reared birds was 77.7 (sigma, 15.9) trials. This difference is significant below the 0.01 level.

No statistically significant difference was shown between the visual acuity of those hood-reared and those normally reared birds tested. Here we follow the general assumption that the optokinetic test is valid for appraising visual acuity. This statistical comparison was confirmed by postexperimental observation of the hood-reared birds.

Ophthalmoscopic examination indicated a limited opacity of the fluid media of the eyes of the hood-reared birds as compared with the normally reared birds.

No gross behavioral differences to rotary acceleration and deceleration were noted between the experimental and control groups.

Discussion

Several alternative explanations may be submitted for the larger number of trials taken by the hood-reared birds to reach the criterion of learning the visual discrimination used in this experiment.

In view of the ophthalmoscopic data, it is possible that diminished visual acuity in the hood-reared birds operated to cause the increase found. The present author tends to reject this as the crucial variable because the visual-acuity data of the hood-reared, as compared with the normally reared, birds did not support this, and because the postexperimental hood-reared behavioral emergences, which depend upon a functional visual substrate, were not such as to support this explanation. For example, fifteen hours after having been

Table 7.2

Comparison of *t*'s between experimental and control groups

Normally Reared	Hood-Reared	
	A	B
C	6.97	5.30
D	4.87	4.04

unhooded, the hood-reared birds demonstrated coordinated pecking at small grains of food. Various other explanations in terms of central nervous changes, retinal degeneration, and photochemical imbalance, are also rejected in view of the demonstrated visual function of the hood-reared doves. Specifically, it does not seem that these chemical or physiological changes, if present, would reverse themselves within the time that the above-mentioned coordinated responses, which depend upon functional visual system, emerged. Attributing the discriminatory learning shortcomings of the hood-reared birds to some motor or structural deficit imposed by hood rearing seems also unacceptable on the grounds that close observation of the hood-reared birds brought out nothing to support this explanation, and also on the grounds that pretraining to jumping seems to have controlled this variable. The essential motor response, jumping from a perch to the horizontal, seems to have been established in the habit repertoire of the hood-reared birds by the pretraining. Moreover, the hood-reared birds were able to fly nonerratically after a period of one to two days in a cage permitting flight in spite of the diminished "life style" imposed by hood rearing. This would indicate not only a healthy, mature motor substrate, but also a visual substrate that could function in terms of an adequate perception of objects after the appropriate learning had taken place. That the pretraining may have been differentially effective for the normally reared as compared with the hood-reared birds also seems unacceptable on observational and operational grounds. It can be stated that the conditions of learning during the pretraining, as well as during the training and testing sessions, were as equivalent as possible for the hood-reared and normally reared animals. To the criticism that unrevealed qualitative differences may have existed in the effectiveness of the reward for the experimental and control groups, the investigator can only point to a too-slender evidence regarding the role of differential effect in the early stages of perceptual-motor learning. If there actually was a differential effect from falling on the development of the perceptual processes in our experimental and control cases, further investigation is required to demonstrate it.

We therefore interpret our results as supporting theories which emphasize experience as a prerequisite to normal adult function in visual perception. The crucial variable would seem to have been the visual inexperience of the experimental animals.

Summary and Conclusions

Twenty-four ring doves were reared to the time of investigation without experience in visual-form definition and were so maintained between training jumps and sessions. The number of trials taken by these birds, as adults, to learn a visuomotor perceptual task was then compared with that of twelve normally reared birds. The birds reared without visual form definition took significantly longer to reach the criterion of learning than did the normally reared birds. This finding is interpreted as being in conformity with perceptual theories which maintain that a change in the neural substrate, dependent upon previous visual experiences, is a prerequisite for normal adult visual function.

Editor's Note: Differential Experiences

Sensory-deprivation represents only one approach to the study of the role of experiences in perception. A second popular method is to present the organism with specific sensory experience above and beyond the level of normal experience. Such studies have the obvious advantage of allowing the sensory mechanism to develop in the normal manner.

One approach toward differential-sensory experience was introduced by Hymovitch (1952). Groups of rats were raised under differing environmental conditions. The first group lived in a large box, which provided a wide variety of sensory experience, as well as contact with other animals. A second group, raised in individual mesh cages, also enjoyed varied sensory experience, but its contact with other animals and amount of motor activity were restricted. The third group grew up in small stovepipes, which restricted both motor activity and sensory experience. The fourth and final group developed in an enclosed activity wheel, which allowed adequate motor activity but restricted sensory experience. After six weeks all animals were tested in a maze-learning situation. Groups one and two, those enjoying the sensory experience, showed greater learning ability than groups three and four did. Restricted motor activity, on the other hand, appeared not to be a major factor, as groups one and two did not differ in their maze-learning performance.

This approach to the problem of learning and perception presents several problems, one of which relates to exploratory behavior. The animals raised with little sensory experience tended to be more timid in the maze than those raised in stimulus environments. While the lack of experience, itself, may contribute to the failure to learn, it also may have contributed to individual behavioral differences. Those animals raised without sensory experience might have been more restricted generally.

Another approach to learning and perception has been used at Cornell University. Animals were raised in environments containing specific forms and later trained to utilize these forms in a discrimination-learning task in an attempt to demonstrate whether previous sensory experiences enhance subsequent learning behavior. An example of this procedure was published by Eleanor J. Gibson and Richard D. Walk (*Journal of Comparative and Physiological Psychology*, 1956).

The Effect of Prolonged Exposure to Visually Presented Patterns on Learning to Discriminate Them

E. J. Gibson and R. D. Walk

Recent literature on the development of discrimination has shown an increasing trend toward acceptance of empiricistic explanations. That ability to discriminate visually presented patterns develops with the experience and environmental reinforcement of the growing animal may be the case, but the evidence for this view is still inconclusive. Early studies by Lashley and Russell (1934) and by Hebb (1937) on the rat favored a nativistic interpretation of the differentiation of visual qualities, but later comparable studies with the chimpanzee and pigeon apparently favored an empiricistic explanation. Recent experiments by students of Hebb have employed an "enrichment" technique, with results which appear to favor a learning hypothesis. These studies attempted to provide a generally "rich" environment and used as criteria tests of a rather general type. If opportunity to view a varied and patterned environment is important in the differentiation of visual qualities, we do not know how general or how specific the relevant experience must be.

The experiment to be reported proposed to investigate the dependence of visual-form discrimination in adult rats on a specific variation in visual stimulation during growth. To this end, an experimental group of animals was raised from birth in cages which exhibited on the walls circles and triangles identical in form with ones later to be discriminated. The control group was raised under the same standard conditions but without opportunity to see these forms before the discrimination learning began. If the opportunity to view specific forms favors development of the ability to differentiate them in a later discrimination-learning problem, the experimental animals should learn faster and show a higher proportion of subjects reaching the criterion than the control group.

Method

Rearing. The subjects were albino rats reared from birth in identical one-half inch wire-mesh cages measuring $15 \times 13 \times 9$ inches. The cages were placed next to each other in a small, softly lighted empty room. Each cage was surrounded by white cardboard walls on three sides, several inches from the wire mesh, and a blank wall of the room on the fourth side, four feet from the mesh. At the top seven feet from the mesh was the ceiling of the room. Visible within the cage were only the cage mates, a water bottle on one wall, and food.

On the walls of the cages of the experimental animals were fastened four black metal forms, two equilateral triangles, and two circles. The circles were three inches in diameter and the triangles were 3½ inches on a side. These patterns were changed in position occasionally to assure a random relationship to food and water. All during the experiment, stimulus patterns were left on the sides of the cages of experimental group animals.

A total of four groups was used, two experimental and two control. These will be numbered as follows: E_1 (experimental, litter 1), E_2 (experimental, litter 2), C_1 (control, litter 1), and C_2 (control, litter 2). Litters E_1 ($n = 8$) and C_1 ($n = 2$) were the first born. These litters were born five days apart and, because of the long interval between litters, not split. E_2 ($n = 10$) and C_2 ($n = 9$) were born within a day of each other, and litters were split when the pups were one or two days old. The young were weaned at four weeks of age, and at eight weeks sexes were divided so that males and females were in separate cages. The experiment was begun when the animals were approximately ninety days old.

Apparatus.   The apparatus was a modification of one described by Grice (1948). Two V-shaped discrimination compartments were joined together and a false floor constructed. The two stimulus patterns were side by side at the ten-inch–wide end of both choice chambers. The 4⅜ inch × 4⅜ inch metal stimulus holders slid into grooves between the 1¾ inch center partition and the side of the apparatus. Masonite doors fitted into grooves one-fourth inch in front of the stimulus holders. The apparatus was painted a flat black, and each section was covered by glass. A 25-watt bulb mounted 25 inches above the floor furnished the only illumination. The stimulus holders were first painted a flat white, and a black circle and triangle were painted on the white background. The circle was 2¾ inches in diameter and the equilateral triangle three inches on a side. The stimulus holders and 1⅛ inch square doors in them, and the animal obtained food by pushing open the door in the center. There were four separate stimulus holders, one with the circle and one with the triangle, for each discrimination box.

Training Procedure

Pretraining.   Animals were placed on a 24-hour feeding cycle for approximately one week prior to the start of experimentation. They were given three to four days' training in obtaining a small quantity of wet mash from the stimulus holders by pushing open the door in the center. The stimulus holders were painted flat black for this pretraining. The door on only one side of the discrimination box was raised at a time. As soon as the animal obtained the food from the food cup, the experimenter lowered the door in front of the stimulus holder. The door between the two discrimination boxes was then opened for the next trial, and the animal secured food by pushing its nose against the black stimulus holder at the opposite end. The animal ate ten times from the cup in the holder in the following order: RLLRRLLRRL.

Table 7.3

**Number of days trained and errors
for the experimental and control groups**

	Experimental Group				Control Group		
Animal	No. Days Run	Initial Errors	Repetitive Errors	Animal	No. Days Run	Initial Errors	Repetitive Errors
LE₁ 30 ♂	12*	39	44	LC₁ 2 ♂	14*	25	11
LE₁ 31 ♂	7*	22	34	LC₁ 20 ♀	15	68	52
LE₁ 32 ♂	11*	28	19	LC₂ 4 ♀	15	50	44
LE₁ 33 ♂	5*	11	9	LC₂ 6 ♀	15	59	30
LE₁ 35 ♀	15	32	21	LC₂ 7 ♀	15	67	18
LE₁ 37 ♂	14*	40	41	LC₂ 12 ♀	15	60	28
LE₁ 40 ♂	7*	24	29	LC₂ 15 ♀	15	80	80
LE₁ 41 ♂	8*	24	24	LC₂ 11 ♂	15	66	72
LE₂ 44 ♀	7*	23	28	LC₂ 5 ♂	15	68	80
LE₂ 47 ♀	10*	25	16	LC₂ 13 ♂	15	74	117
LE₂ 62 ♀	15	70	73	LC₂ 14 ♂	15	84	92
LE₂ 63 ♀	9*	23	16				
LE₂ 64 ♀	12*	39	50				
LE₂ 43 ♂	15	57	51				
LE₂ 45 ♂	13*	28	12				
LE₂ 46 ♂	10*	25	16				
LE₂ 60 ♂	9*	30	23				
LE₂ 61 ♂	10*	37	34				
Mean	10.50	32.06	30.00		14.91	63.73	56.73

* Indicates that animal reached criterion; the criterion day's trials are included in number of days run.

Discrimination training.   During discrimination training both Masonite doors on the choice side of the apparatus were raised, exposing the two stimulus patterns side by side. Both stimulus holders were baited. As soon as the animal pushed against one stimulus door, the Masonite door in front of the opposite stimulus was closed. If the choice was correct, the animal was allowed to eat the wet mash in the food cup. After sixty seconds, the door between the two compartments was opened and the animal proceeded to the opposite end, where the next choice was made. If it was incorrect, a modified correction procedure was followed. Both doors in front of the stimulus holders were closed. After sixty seconds the animal was allowed to make a choice in the opposite discrimination box. Animals were allowed up to three errors per trial. Following the third error the door in front of the correct stimulus figure remained open, and the animal was allowed to eat from it. This procedure meant that the animal ate equally often on each side of the apparatus. Ten trials were given each day with a maximum of three errors per trial.

The positive stimulus was presented in the following order: RLRRLLRLLR; LRLLRRLRRL; RRLLRRLRLL; LLRRLLRLRR. The order was repeated every four days. For half the animals in each group the circle was the positive stimulus, and for half the triangle. Animals were run until they attained a criterion of eighteen out of twenty correct responses, with the last ten consecutive responses correct (one day's run), or until they were run in the experiment for fifteen days (150 trials). After the experimental session animals were allowed to eat food pellets for one hour. The hunger drive was a function of approximately 22½ hours deprivation. Each of the two experimenters ran one-half of the experimental and one-half of the control animals.

Results

The number of days of discrimination training and the errors (initial and repetitive) are presented in Table 7.3 for both groups of animals. In the table are indicated the sex and litter of each animal. The second litters (LE_2 and LC_2), it will be remembered, were split at birth and thus provide a somewhat better controlled population. It is obvious from the table that there is a difference between experimental and control groups. Out of the control group, only one animal reached the criterion during fifteen days of training. But fifteen of the eighteen experimental group animals did. By the chi-square test, this difference is significant at better than the 0.001 level of confidence. If we calculate the chi square for animals of the split-litter groups only, using Fisher's exact test, the significance of the difference is between 0.002 and 0.001. The errors, both initial and repetitive, reflect the same trend.

A further check on differences in the population studied is possible by testing males against females. When this comparison is made, the chances are exactly 50 in 100 that there is any difference between sex groups.

Figure 7.1 shows the learning curve for experimental and control groups. Percentage of correct responses is plotted against days of training. The animals that reached the criterion are included in the percentages on the assumption that they would continue at their final level of performance. The curves show that the groups begin to diverge by the third or fourth day of training and diverge increasingly thereafter until the tenth day, when a majority of the experimental group has learned.

Discussion

The results presented show conclusively a difference in ease of learning a circle-triangle discrimination between the group reared with these forms exhibited on the cage walls and the control group. Since the control group had the same conditions of training (and pretraining), the same living conditions, and, in our second litters, the same heredity, the difference must be attributed to some advantage arising from the opportunity to look at the forms. This advantage could be something specific which happens early in the animals'

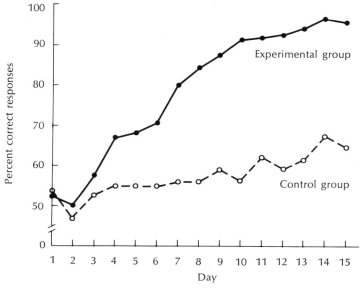

Figure 7.1: Learning curves, in percentage of correct responses per day, for the experimental and control groups.

development, analogous with "imprinting" or with Hebb's (1949) postulated development of reverberating neural circuits. On the other hand, a learning theorist who favors "hypotheses" as a factor in learning a discrimination might suggest that seeing the forms on the cage walls favors formation of the correct hypothesis. Since the forms were left on the walls during the learning period, it is not possible to conclude that early experience in viewing the forms is the basis of the effect. Suitable controls are at present being run to clarify this point.

Since research in discrimination learning has centered round the continuity hypothesis in recent years, it might be asked whether the present results tend to confirm or deny this hypothesis. The animals in the experimental group profited, in the discrimination task, from an opportunity to view the two forms without any differential reinforcement of them. Nondifferential reinforcement in viewing these could have occurred, since the animals ate and drank in their presence. Spence's (1936) article suggests that some degree of positive excitatory potential, irrespective of differential reinforcement, would be consistent with faster learning when differential reinforcement is introduced. On the other hand, the values selected for his analysis are purely arbitrary, so it cannot be concluded that effective nondifferential reinforcement either confirms or refutes his statement of the hypothesis. Bitterman and Elam (1954) concluded that perceptual differentiation occurs in the course of sheer experience with test stimuli, despite lack of differentiation reinforcement. But this conclusion is beclouded by their further finding that there is a general retarding effect of nondifferential reinforcement. The present results seem to demonstrate clearly the positive transfer from experience in viewing the test stimuli, without the complications introduced by specific application of reinforcement.

Further research on the problem described will investigate whether there is an optimal or critical time for the visual experience, and the relative specificity of the resulting facilitation of discrimination learnng.

Summary

This experiment sought to determine the effect of early and continued exposure to certain forms, presented visually, on the ease with which an adult animal learns to discriminate them. Two groups of animals were raised from birth in well-illuminated cages surrounded by white cardboard. Animals of the experimental group also had mounted on the walls of their cages black circles and triangles, from birth throughout the duration of the experiment. When the animals were approximately ninety days old, both experimental and control groups learned a circle-triangle discrimination. Animals of the experimental group reached the criterion significantly faster and made fewer errors than the control group. It was concluded that visual experience with the forms to be discriminated, even in the absence of differential reinforcement, facilitated the discrimination learning.

Human Learning and Perception

The two preceding experiments have demonstrated that experience extensively affects perception in lower animals. Obviously, adequate deprivation studies would be impossible with human subjects, and studies in which individuals are temporarily deprived of certain kinds of sensory stimuli are handicapped by insufficient information about the individual's prior experiences. That a modification of perception does take place under conditions of deprivation has been demonstrated. Individuals deprived of food for prolonged periods show marked modifications in perceptual responses. The exact nature of the modifications, however, is so dependent upon the individual's previous experiences that it cannot be predicted.

A few observations of children reared in conditions of severe deprivation have been recorded, although the cause of deprivation and the actual conditions have been rather difficult to assess. Such children are usually retarded in mental development and physically underdeveloped. Again, the mental retardation or physical structure of the child may have been the reason for, rather than the result of, the imposed deprivation.

Clinical observations of individuals deprived of sensory experience during early life, who achieved normal sensory functioning at some later date, have not been numerous enough to warrant valid conclusions. Von Senden (1932) described the perceptual tendencies of individuals deprived of visual experience during early life, who regained their sight after an operation. Senden's report was based on medical reports of clinical observations over the time-span of 1695 to 1928. Most of the reports were very poor and provided at best anecdotal indices of the effects of visual deprivation on human perception.

Because of these difficulties, then, the relationship between learning and perception at the human level has been assessed more on assumption than on empirical evidence. The few studies which have attempted actually to observe and describe the relationship mostly have dealt with the effects of learning upon perception. These involve experimental situations in which prior experiences of the subject dictate the way an event is perceived. Adelbert Ames, Jr., of the Institute for Associated Research in New Hampshire, designed a wide variety of such demonstrations (see Ittelson and Kilpatrick, 1951, and Ames, 1951). One of the most popular of the Ames's demonstrations, known as the *Rotating Trapezoidal Window,* has been utilized in a variety of experimental situations. In the *Scientific American* (p. 55) in 1951, Ittelson and Kilpatrick described the window as follows:

"By means of a piece of apparatus called the "rotating trapezoidal window" it has been possible to extend the investigation (of human learning) to complex perceptual situations involving movement. This device consists of a trapezoidal surface with panes cut in it and shadows painted on it to give the appearance of a window. It is mounted on a rod connected to a motor so that it rotates at a slow constant speed in an upright position about its own axis. When an observer views the rotating surface with one eye from about ten feet or more or with both eyes from about twenty-five feet or more, he sees not a rotating trapezoid but an oscillating rectangle. Its speed of movement and its shape appear to vary markedly as it turns. If a small cube is attached by a short rod to the upper part of the short side of the trapezoid, it seems to become detached, sail freely around the front of the trapezoid and attach itself again as the apparatus rotates."

The perception of the oscillating rectangle appears to the naive observer to be quite natural. If the subject is allowed to view the apparatus from above, he is able to ascertain the true motion. However, after the subject is shown the true rotating movement, and he again views the window under the original experimental conditions, he still sees it as oscillating.

The role of learning in perception, then, is demonstrated by showing how the subject's previous experience with windows and their shape caused him to experience modification of reality—to see the movement as oscillatory rather than rotating. In order to maintain the constant window shape, such a movement is necessary; otherwise we would need to see the window changing its shape.

These observations opened an interesting possibility for an experimental study of previous experience and perception of the rotating window. If individuals who had not seen windows or square shapes could be found, they probably would be able to perceive the window's true motion. This possibility was explored in a study by Gordon W. Allport and Thomas F. Pettigrew (*Journal of Abnormal and Social Psychology*, 1957). The subjects in the study, Zulus, were living in an environment with few windows or square shapes; their experience with square shapes was, at least, much less than that of members of our society. In the following presentation, several paragraphs have been deleted from the original paper.

Cultural Influences on the Perception of Movement: The Trapezoidal Illusion among Zulus

Gordon W. Allport and Thomas F. Pettigrew

Traditionally, theories of the visual perception of movement—with which the present study deals—have been divided into two classes: 1. The *nativistic,* theories emphasizing the role of retinal and cortical functions relatively unaffected by learning, habit, experience, or meaning; and 2. The *empiricistic,* theories giving primary weight to the role of experience and learning.

For our purposes it is essential to subdivide empiricistic theories into two groups:

Cumulative habit.   Stressing the effects of many types of early, remote, and generalized experience which by transfer or cross conditioning become a major determinant of the perception of movement. Toch and Ittelson (1956, p. 199) state that "contemporary empiricism" favors this type of approach, offering its explanations of perceived movement in terms of "weighted averages of experiential sediments of all kinds acting inseparably."

Object connotation (meaning).   Explaining perceived movement largely in terms of familiar objects. One sees continuous wing motion in an electric sign representing a bird in flight, although the stimulus actually occurs discontinuously in two or in three fixed positions. This theory would hold that our familiarity with birds in flight causes us to fill the gaps with perceived motion. A good statement of this theory of stroboscopic movement may be found in James (1890). This author insisted that "perception is of definite and probable things." In explaining illusions, James leaned heavily upon their resemblance to familiar objects. In so doing he was merely rendering more concrete and specific Helmholtz's theory of "unconscious inferences" and Wundt's "assimilation" theory.

The Cross-Cultural Approach

To gain light on this dispute psychologists have often asked, "How about primitive peoples?" If we can find a tribe or a culture where relevant past experience can be ruled out, we could then determine whether the perception resembles that of western peoples. If it does so, then the argument for nativism is presumably stronger. The first extensive attempt to apply this test was made by W. H. R. Rivers (1901) during the Torres Strait expedition in 1898. Rivers presented to the island natives a whole array of visual illusions and compared their reports with western norms. For some of the illusions there were no appreciable differences; for others, the natives seemed on the whole less susceptible than westerners. While Rivers himself does not make the point clearly, his results seem to show that illusions involving object connotation (e.g., a European street scene) are far less compelling to the natives than are illusions having no such object connotation (e.g., the rotating spiral).

It is not easy for Western psychologists to visit primitive tribes, nor to conduct among them adequately controlled experiments. The present article, however, deals with one such attempt. But before we describe it, the theoretical point at issue should be made entirely clear: *We do not claim to be testing the merits of the nativist or empiricist positions directly.* For reasons that will appear in the course of our discussion, we do not believe that comparative perceptual studies on Western and on primitive peoples can solve this particular riddle. *We claim only to have illuminated the part played by object connotation (meaning) in the perception of motion as over and against the part played by either nativistic determinants or cumulative habit.* Our experiment is *not* able to distinguish between the role of these last two factors.

The Rotating Trapezoidal Window.   Before the days of Gestalt psychology it was customary to regard visual illusions as oddities, as exceptional experiences to be accounted for either in terms of nativistic or experiential constraints. Today, however, we make little distinction between illusions and veridical perceptions, since no illusion lacks veridical elements and no veridical perception is devoid of subjective shaping. So-called illusions are simply instances of perception where the discrepancy between impression and knowledge (whether the knowledge be the subject's or the experimenter's) is relatively striking. It is in such "looser" conditions of perception that theorists often seek to obtain light on the relative weight of factors entering into the normal perceptual process. The reasoning is not unlike that which leads psychologists to study exaggerated functions in psychopathology in order to obtain light on the same but less exaggerated functions of the normal mind.

Our experiment follows this logic, making use of the rotating trapezoidal window described by Ames (1951)—a device that has been called "a dramatic masterpiece of ambiguous stimulation." The window (Figure 7.2) is so proportioned that as it rotates, the length of the longer edge is always longer on the retina than is the shorter edge (even when the shorter edge is nearer). The resulting perception is normally one of oscillation or sway; the observer apparently tending to keep the longer edge nearer to him. Instead of seeming to rotate, as it actually does, the window is seen to sway back and forth in an arc of 90 to 180°.

An appended cube and rod add great interest to the illusion, since the perceived *rotating* of these objects conflicts sharply with the perceived *sway*

Figure 7.2:   The experimental situation.

of the window. In consequence, the cube is usually seen to detach itself and swing without support in a ghostly fashion in front of the window (for that period of time when the shorter edge, to which it is attached, is in fact nearer to the subject). Similarly, the rod bends, twists, or "cuts through" the mullions in order to accommodate itself to the phenomenal oscillation. The observer finds the bizarre effect both amusing and inexplicable.

The window used in the present experiment is smaller than the original Ames window; length thirteen and one-fourth inches, height of the long side twelve and one-half inches, height of the short side nine inches. Ames demonstrated that within limits the ratio of the sides of the trapezoid to one another cannot affect the illusion. The optimum speed of rotation Ames reports as three to six rpm. Our own motor-driven window ran slightly less than 2 rpm. The original Ames window had mullions dividing it into fifteen frames; ours had six frames (probably more normal for a "window"). For certain comparisons, we employed also a true rectangular window, 12 × 10½ inches.

The explanation Ames gives for the illusion maintains (a) that the observer, owing to familiarity with rectangular windows assumes *this* window to be rectangular; and (b) that owing to long experience with doors, windows, and similar objects, the observer has learned to interpret longer retinal stimulations as coming from nearer objects. Hence, the longer edge of the window is interpreted as being nearer, and the window is seen to oscillate rather than to rotate.

Ames (p. 14) gives a clearly empiricistic explanation with a leaning toward the object connotation version:·

"In his past experience the observer, in carrying out his purposes, has on innumerable occasions had to take into account and act with respect to rectangular forms, going through doors, locating windows, etc. On almost all such occasions, except in the rare case when his line of sight was normal to the door or window, the image of the rectangular configuration formed on his retina was trapezoidal. He learned to interpret the particularly characteristic retinal images that exist when he looks at doors, windows, etc., as rectangular forms. Moreover, he learned to interpret the particular degree of trapezoidal distortion of his retinal images in terms of the positioning of the rectangular form to his particular viewing point. These interpretations do not occur at the conscious level, rather, they are unconscious and may be characterized as *assumptions* as to the probable significance of indications received from the environment."

It should be added that Ames does not insist that object connotation ("windowness") is the sole determinant of the illusion. He himself employed a variety of trapezoidal figures and discovered that even a plane surface of trapezoidal shape arouses the illusion of sway, though to a much less degree than does a "window frame."

The Hypothesis. In order to test the "object connotation" theory, we studied various groups of Zulu children (ten to fourteen years old) in Natal whose own culture is virtually devoid not only of windows, but, to a surprising extent, of angles, straight lines, and other experiential cues that would presumably "cause" the illusion if it were wholly a product of experience. Our hypothesis therefore is:

Zulu children, provided they are unacculturated (amabinca) *will report the illusion of sway in the trapezoidal window* less *often than will urbanized acculturated Zulu children* (amabunguka) *or than white ("European") children.*

The Zulu Culture. Zulu culture is probably the most spherical or circular of all Bantu cultures, possibly the most spherical of all native African cultures (though it would be difficult to prove this contention). The word *zulu* means heavens or firmament, and the aesthetic ideal of round rather than angular styles affects native art, architecture, and speech.

Huts are invariably round (*rondavels*) or else beehive shaped, whereas in other Bantu tribes they are sometimes square or rectangular. Round huts arranged in a circular form with round stockades to fence in animals, constitutes a typical African homestead (*kraal*). Fields follow the irregular contours of the rolling land, and never seem to be laid out in the neat rectangular plots so characteristic of Western culture (see Figure 7.3).

The typical Zulu hut has no windows, and no word for such an aperture exists. In the more primitive beehive grass huts, doors are merely round entrance holes; in the round mud huts doors are amorphous, seldom if ever neatly rectangular. Cooking pots are round or gourd shaped. In his studies among Zulus, L. Doob (1957) finds that the less acculturated natives, relative to westernized natives, show a statistically significant preference for circles over squares when they are asked to choose between designs drawn in these shapes (personal communication to the authors).

Figure 7.3: Circularity in the Zulu environment.

It is commonly said in Natal that Zulus fresh from reserves cannot plow a straight furrow and are unable to lay out a rectangular flower bed. Such inability is of course overcome with experience and training, but the initial defect would seem clearly related to the circularity that is characteristic of life on the reserves and to the lack of familiarity with straight layouts.

Linguistically, the same bias towards circularity is seen. While it is possible to say "round" in Zulu, there is no word for "square." There is a word for "circle" but not for "rectangle." To speak of window, of square, or of rectangle at all, a Zulu is forced to borrow these terms from Afrikaans or from English —provided he is able to do so.

The Subjects.   The experiment required the use of two contrasting groups of subjects: those who had lived all or most of their lives in Western culture, and those who were unacculturated. Even in the Bantu reserves or in Zululand itself it is not possible to make certain that a resident does not know what a window is like. While schools, churches, and health centers are few and far between, they are nevertheless within the possible range of visitation by most native inhabitants, even children. Our experiments at Polela and Ceza took place in health centers, at Nongoma in a court house. The subjects, to be sure, were brought in from remote parts of the reserves by lorry, or came on foot; but they had at least this one-time acquaintance with a rectangular building and windows.

Still, it is possible to say that the experiment dealt with two widely contrasting groups in respect to the degree of experience they had had with Western architecture and ways of life. Some members of the more primitive groups, for example, may never have seen windows with rectangular panes of glass prior to the actual experimental situation.

By using herd boys as subjects—mostly between ten and fourteen years of age (few of them knew their age exactly)—we were able to make certain that they had never been off the reserves and had never attended school. Boys of the same age comprised our urban control groups: one group of European boys at Greyville Community Center; another group of Bantu boys at the Lamontville Community Center in Durban. Most of these urban boys were attending school.

Our major experiment thus involved the following groups:

Group A	Urban European boys	(20 cases)
Group B	Urban African boys	(20 cases)
Group C	Polela Rural Africans	(20 cases)
Group D	Nongoma Rural Africans	(20 cases)

A rough indication of the cultural differences between the rural and urban groups lies in answers to the question asked at the end of the experiment about the rectangular window, "What does this look like?" The percentage saying "window" or "window frame" among the urban children was 88; among the rural, 45.

Procedure.   The procedure involves four conditions, varying two factors bearing on the perception of the illusion: monocular versus binocular viewing and distance from the stimulus object. Each subject saw first the rectangular, and then the trapezoidal window in at least three full revolutions under each of the following conditions.

First trial:	ten feet	binocular
Second trial:	ten feet	monocular
Third trial:	twenty feet	binocular
Fourth trial:	twenty feet	monocular

It was thought that this order would impose the "hardest" condition first and therefore minimize the effects of suggestion. One might fear that if at twenty feet with one eye a subject easily perceived the illusion he might become accustomed to expecting oscillation in the trapezoidal window at closer distances and under binocular conditions. Conversely, of course, it might be argued that a subject who cannot perceive the illusion at ten feet binocularly would form an expectation that might prevent his obtaining it under easier conditions. We shall refer later to a control experiment (starting at twenty feet monocularly) designed to check on any suggestive effect that might arise from our order of presentation.

The experimenter required the assistance of a second psychologist who kept records of the subjects' reports, also of an interpreter with all African subjects. Care was taken to prevent subjects who had finished the experiment from communicating with subjects who had not.

After being put at ease, the subject gave his age (if he knew it) and his degree of education (if any). The subject then sat in a chair placed at the proper distance from the window and was told to watch carefully the movement that he would see. After approximately three revolutions the experimenter asked, "How does it seem to you to be moving?" Often the subject spontaneously used his hands to indicate the motion until the experimenter was satisfied whether a full rotation or a fluctuation was intended. The use of hand motion by the subject proved to be fully convincing, for when he reversed the hand at precisely the right moment for the illusion to occur there could be no question concerning his experience. This device gave a useful check on the accuracy of the translator's report of the subject's verbal statements.

After obtaining a report for the rectangular window in each of the positions, the trapezoidal window was inserted in place of the rectangular, and the same method of report employed. In addition, the subject was asked to tell whether the motion of the trapezoidal window was "like" that of the first window. This procedure served as a further check on the verbal description and hand report. In nearly all cases it was possible to record a clear and unequivocal judgment of the subject's perception. Less than three percent of all judgments were listed by the experimenter as "uncertain."

Whenever the illusion was reported for the first condition, the bar was inserted and the subject asked, "How does the bar move?" and "Does the bar stay straight?" On occasional trials when the subject had reported both the sway of the window and the bending of the bar, the cube was attached and the subject asked to describe its motion. In these cases there was usually laughter (as with American subjects) and considerable confusion and difficulty manifested in describing so unreal and "spooky" a motion. Because of the difficulty of communicating concerning these complex phenomena we make no further systematic use of the cube and rod in the present study.

At the conclusion of the experiment, the subject was asked what the rectangular window "looked like." He also stated his preference for one of two geometrical drawings presented to him in pairs (a circle, square, trapezoid). He then received a slight payment for his services (usually one pound of sugar or a candy bar and sixpence).

Results

General Results.   Table 7.4 gives the results for the two unacculturated groups (Nongoma and Polela Reserves) and for the two districts within metropolitan Durban, African (Lamontville), and European (Greyville).

Combining all four conditions, there is a very significant tendency for the urban groups to report the illusion more often than the rural groups (correct 2×2 $X^2 = 15.34$; $p < 0.001$). This difference is most marked with the first condition (corrected 2×2 $X^2 = 12.38$; $p < 0.001$). There is also a significant trend with the second condition (corrected 2×2 $X^2 = 4.80$; $p < 0.05$) and a slight tendency with the third condition (corrected 2×2 $X^2 = 1.87$; $p < 0.20$) for the rural children to observe the illusion less often than the urban children. Virtually no difference exists with the fourth, twenty feet and one eye condition.

Table 7.5 expresses the results in an alternative way. Since four conditions of presentation were used we can determine in how many of these four conditions on the average each of the cultural groups reported the illusion. For

Table 7.4

Number reporting illusion
(boys 10–14 years of age, N = 20 in each group)

Condition	Nongoma Rural			Polela Rural			African Urban			European Urban		
	Yes	No	Uncertain	Yes	No	Uncertain	Yes	No	Uncertain	Yes	No	Uncertain
First condition (10 ft., both eyes)	3	17	0	4	14	2	13	7	0	11	9	0
Second condition (10 ft., one eye)	14	6	0	16	4	0	19	1	0	19	1	0
Third condition (20 ft., both eyes)	8	12	0	17	1	2	16	3	1	16	4	0
Fourth condition (20 ft., one eye)	18	2	0	17	2	1	18	2	0	19	0	1
Totals	43	37	0	54	21	5	66	13	1	65	14	1

Table 7.5

Distribution of scores

	Number of Yes's					
Sample	*4*	*3*	*2*	*1*	*0*	Average
Nongoma	2	4	10	3	1	2.15
Polela	4	10	3	2	1	2.70
Urban African	12	4	2	2	0	3.30
Urban European	11	5	3	0	1	3.25
Total (*N* = 80)	29	23	18	7	3	2.85

the two unacculturated groups combined, the illusion is reported in 2.425 of the four conditions, while for the acculturated groups the average is 3.275. This mean difference has high statistical significance ($t = 3.51$; $p < 0.001$).

It is evident from Tables 7.4 and 7.5 that city dwellers, whether Zulu or European, find the illusion somewhat more compelling than do rural ("primitive") natives. This tendency is especially pronounced at ten feet with binocular vision—a condition when binocular cues of true depth (in this case, true rotation) are most plentiful. The reader will also note that the results for Polela (rural) stand somewhat between those for the city children and those from Nongoma (rural). At ten feet binocularly, they resemble those of Nongoma; at twenty feet binocularly, those of the city boys. Polela is, in fact, one hundred miles closer to Durban than is Nongoma which lies in the heart of Zululand. There is no doubt that the children in Polela have somewhat more familiarity with Western architecture (specifically with windows) than do the children of Nongoma. The results (Table 7.5) correspond to a continuum of cultures: city children having a maximum of familiarity with Western architecture, Nongoma children the least.

Preference for Circles. Following the experiment, all subjects were shown drawings of a square, a trapezoid, and a circle (in pairs), and asked to express a preference. Table 7.6 indicates that those who expressed a preference for the circle (at least once in the two pairings) tend in the African groups to report the illusion *less* often. This tendency holds for all experimental conditions for all three African groups. The relationship is statistically significant, however, for only the binocular conditions. Circle-preferring Zulu children report the illusion significantly less often than the angle-preferring Zulus in Conditions 1 and 3 (corrected 2×2 $X^2 = 3.89$; $p < 0.05$), but the difference in the monocular, second and fourth, conditions is not significant (corrected 2×2 $X^2 = 0.18$, n.s.). There are no differences approaching significance between the circle and noncircle-preferring European subjects.

Let us assume that the aesthetic preference for circles may provide an index of the subjective closeness of the individual to Zulu culture (since it is, as we have seen, overwhelmingly a circular culture). If we do so we may say

Table 7.6

Percentage of cases reporting illusion among subjects preferring and not preferring circle

Condition	Combined African Groups N = 60		European Group N = 20	
	Pre- ferring Circle N = 39	Not Pre- ferring Circle N = 21	Pre- ferring Circle N = 12	Not Pre- ferring Circle N = 8
10 feet, binocular	28	43	58	50
10 feet, monocular	79	86	100	88
20 feet, binocular	59	86	83	75
20 feet, monocular	87	90	100	88
All conditions	63	76	85	75

that this subjective closeness seems to predispose the subject to resist the illusion. Stated in terms of transactional theory, rectangles and trapezoids have less functional significance for him. His perception of the window's rotation is accordingly more frequently veridical.

We have noted that this influence is significant only in the conditions involving *binocular* perception. A reasonable interpretation would be that cultural effects cannot easily change the basic demand character of the illusion monocularly perceived, but may do so when binocular conditions leave more latitude for choice and for interpretation among a greater number of cues.

This result then, so far as it goes, lends some weight to the contention that "cultural significance" is playing an appreciable part in determining the results.

Illusion with Rectangle.   Before viewing the trapezoidal window, every subject in all four conditions first saw the rectangular window rotating. The purpose was to make sure that the sway (oscillation) reported for the trapezoid was judged to be *different* from the motion of the rectangular window. In most cases, indeed, the subject was able to make the distinction clearly, indicating by gesture and by words that the rectangular window went "round and round" whereas the trapezoid oscillated.

There were cases, however, where the rectangular window was reported as oscillating. In fact, nearly one-third of the eighty subjects reported such a phenomenon at one or more of the four conditions. The actual percentage reporting sway in the *rectangular* window at each of the four conditions is:

First condition	0
Second condition	8
Third condition	16
Fourth condition	28

It is inconceivable that this curious and somewhat unwelcomed finding may be a result of a "suggestive" order of presentation. Thus, no subject seeing the rectangle before the trapezoid under the first condition (ten feet binocularly) reported the phenomenon. And, with the exception of three cases, no subject reported the rectangular illusion in the second, third, or fourth condition *unless* he had previously reported the trapezoidal illusion. Altogether, eighty-one percent of our subjects reported the illusion monocularly at twenty feet for the trapezoidal window, but only twenty-eight percent did so for the rectangular window under the same condition. In virtually all these cases the subjects had grown accustomed to seeing oscillation at some previous stage with the trapezoid.

Pastore (1952), however, finds that more than half of his fifty-eight American college subjects reported sway with the rectangle during a three-minute exposure, and at considerable distance from the window (where the retinal angle subtended by the two shapes may be subliminal). He does not tell whether the subjects had grown accustomed to the sway of the trapezoid before they reported sway in the rectangle. We must leave this problem for the time being unsolved.

A Control Experiment

In order to determine whether unwanted suggestive effects, caused by our order of presentation, were influencing the results at the optimal stage for the trapezoidal illusion (viz., twenty feet monocularly) we simplified our procedure with entirely new subjects. Urban and rural Africans served as before. To secure the latter, we visited the Ceza Medical Mission in Zululand, approximately twenty miles from Nongoma. Both Ceza and Nongoma are in the deepest part of the native reserves, over 200 miles north of Durban. Polela, as we have said, lies about 100 miles west of Durban and has more European influence (European-style architecture). This fact, we repeat, seems to explain why, as Tables 7.4 and 7.5 show, the Polela subjects report the illusion somewhat more frequently than do subjects at Nongoma or Ceza.

In the control experiment, the subject was asked to cover one eye. Sitting at twenty feet from the rotating trapezoidal window he then described its motion (both in words and by hand motion). Later he was seated at ten feet from the object and using both eyes described the motion, comparing it with the previous motion. Finally he was, as in the other groups, asked his preference for the circular, square, or trapezoidal figures. None of these herd boys had ever been to school.

For an urban control group we used a fresh population of Lamontville boys of the same age range.

Results

Table 7.7 gives the results.

These data are practically identical with those of the Nongoma and urban

Table 7.7

Number reporting illusion in control experiment

| | Ceza (Rural) N = 24 | | | Lamontville (Urban) N = 21 | | |
Condition	Yes	No	Uncer-tain	Yes	No	Uncer-tain
First condition						
(20 ft., monocular)	22	2	0	20	0	1
Second condition						
(10 ft., binocular)	2	18	4	14	7	0

African samples cited previously. Again, the rural Zulu group reported the illusion significantly less often than the urban Zulu group in ten feet binocular condition (corrected $2 \times 2\ X^2 = 11.53$; $p\ 0.001$), but no differences appear at the twenty feet monocular condition. This similarity of data proves that the order of presentation is not an important variable.

At the Ceza Mission Hospital we tested also a group of eleven expectant mothers, only one of whom had ever left the reserve. Eight reported the illusion at twenty feet monocularly, two did not, and one was uncertain. None of the eleven, however, reported it at ten feet binocularly. These cases confirm the trend in all our tables that "primitives" are less able to perceive the sway in the trapezoidal window illusion under marginal-conditions (at ten feet binocularly) than are city dwellers.

Something should be said concerning the qualitative differences reported by subjects who first reported the illusion at twenty feet monocularly and then again at ten feet binocularly. Not infrequently their reports at ten feet binocularly were "mixed," that is to say, sometimes they saw the oscillation and sometimes not. In every case, the subject was asked to tell the "difference" if any existed between the movement seen at twenty feet monocularly and that at ten feet binocularly. Most subjects claimed that there was a difference: sometimes the window at the closer distance seemed to move faster, sometimes

Table 7.8

Percentage of cases reporting illusion among subjects preferring two circles. Combined African groups (Ceza and Lamontville); N = 44

Condition	Preferring Two Circles N = 15	Preferring Less than Two N = 29
20 ft. monocular	92	97
10 ft. binocular	27	38

in a bigger arc, sometimes even in the reverse direction. And often, as we have said, the reports at ten feet binocularly were mixed—the subjects reporting sometimes a full rotation and sometimes a sway. We record "yes" to the illusion at ten feet binocularly if at any point in the experiment the subject reports a clear oscillation. Since the same criteria were applied at both Ceza and Lamontville, no source of error is introduced.

If the reader is acquainted with the illusion he will no doubt recognize this ambiguity in the perception at ten feet when binocular cues are powerful evidence for true rotation, and yet the tendency to see illusory sway likewise exists. Because of this dual tendency we consider ten feet binocularly as a *marginal* condition for the illusion. What is important for our purposes is the finding that under such marginal conditions urban children, who are familiar with Western architecture, report the illusion much more frequently than do herd boys on the Zulu reserves.

As in the major experiment our subjects expressed their preference, in three paired comparisons, for a circle, trapezoid, or square. Since only seven of the forty-five cases failed to choose the circle at least once, we changed our criterion slightly from that used in Table 7.6. We determined the occurrence of the illusion among those who chose the circle *twice* as compared with those who chose it only once or not at all. Table 7.8 shows that in this population likewise, subjects who show a preference for circles tend—particularly in the binocular condition—to report the illusion somewhat less frequently than those who do not. The differences are not statistically significant but are in the same direction as those reported in Table 7.6. The implication of this finding, we repeat, seems to be that subjects whose aesthetic preference lies with the circularity of their tribal culture are the more resistant to the illusion.

At the conclusion of the experiment the investigator showed each subject the rectangular window and asked, "What is this?" (In order to make certain that the children would have an opportunity to say "window" if they perceived the resemblance, the question was asked in three different ways in the Zulu language.) To one or more of these three questionings sixty-seven percent of the urban children said "window," but only twenty-six percent of the Ceza children gave the same reply. If we combine all cases who said "window" at both Ceza and Lamontville we find an appreciable, though not statistically significant, tendency for them to report the illusion more often than do children who did not recognize the windowness of the stimulus object (corrected 2×2 $X^2 = 2.81$; $p < 0.10$ when both conditions are combined). So far as it goes, this finding (Table 7.9) lends support to the object-connotation theory of the perception of movement, especially under the ten-feet binocular condition.

Discussion

Our most striking finding is that under optimal conditions (monocularly at twenty feet) virtually as many primitive Zulus report the trapezoidal illusion as do urban Zulus or Europeans. Taking this one partial result by itself we

Table 7.9

**Percentage of subjects recognizing stimulus
as a "window" who report the illusion**

Condition	Recognizing "Window" N = 20	Not Recognizing "Window" N = 24
20 ft. monocular	100	88
10 ft. binocular	55	29

can say that the experiment supports either the nativistic or the cumulative-habit theory. It does not by itself give us grounds for choosing between them.

Nativists might argue, for example, that whenever a longer and a shorter projection on the retina occur simultaneously the longer will assume a figure character and therewith a frontal position in the perception (other conditions being equal). Thus, some form of isomorphism obtains between retinal-cortical processes and the perception itself.

An empiricist with a "cumulative habit" preference might say that myriad ocular-motor adjustments from infancy have built up a dependable expectancy that longer projections on the retina will betoken nearer objects. One learns through repeated experience that longer retinal images of trees, cattle, people, stand for *nearer* objects (provided, of course, that one assumes such objects to be of equal size whether far or near from the eyes). It is not necessary for the subject to have acquaintance with specific objects (in this case a window) in order to make a similar inference. The transfer effect is wide. Even the shadows painted on the rotating window are reminiscent of the subject's experience with shadows in nature. Old experiences automatically condition novel experiences even though the latter are only analogous.

One assumption that may play a decisive part in this case is the assumption of "right angularity." From earliest life the child is conditioned to the fact that perpendicular objects best withstand the force of gravity. Circular though his culture is, his basic frame of reference is still one of verticals and horizontals. Seeing an entirely new object (the trapezoidal window) he assumes unconsciously (no less than do people who are familiar with windows) that its shape is rectangular. Just like people in Western culture he may make this assumption even if he "knows" that the object is not in reality rectangular. This assumption, together with the assumption that longer objects on the retina are usually nearer objects, would predispose him to perceive that the longer edge of the window is always nearer (thus inducing the perceived oscillation). No less than people in Western culture he would fail to "correct" his assumptions of right-angularity and of long-edges-being-near-edges by his "knowledge" of the trapezoidal shape of the stimulus.

Our major result is clearly not compatible with a narrowly conceived object-connotation theory. It is not necessary for the subject consciously to assume that the object is a window in order to experience the illusion. True, as Table 7.9 suggests, the specific object connotation seems somewhat to favor the illusion, but it is clearly not the decisive determinant. Thus, for example, 88 percent of those who did not consciously recognize the frame as a "window" nevertheless experienced the illusion at twenty feet monocularly.

Yet, at the same time, our results show that object connotation cannot be disregarded. It also plays a part. Let us review the evidence:

1. Under all *suboptimal* conditions, as we see in Tables 7.4 and 7.7 (ten feet monocularly, and binocularly at ten or twenty feet) there is a tendency for unacculturated subjects to report the illusion less frequently than do the acculturated.

2. The subjects who recognize the "windowness" of the stimulus object tend to report the illusion somewhat more frequently especially at ten feet binocularly (Table 7.9).

3. African subjects expressing a preference for circles (assumed here to indicate a subjective closeness to the rotund Zulu culture) tend to report the illusion less often than those expressing preference for angular figures (Tables 7.6 and 7.8).

We conclude that experience with, and identification with, Western culture make it more likely that the illusion will be perceived under marginal (suboptimal) conditions.

One fact reported by Ames, and mentioned above, supports our interpretation. He finds that a plane trapezoidal frame yields appreciable oscillation, but that the addition of mullions, panes, and shadows enhances the illusion. In other words, specific "thingness" contributes to the experience though it does not account for it wholly. And we may again allude to von Schiller's contention that expectancy is effective in determining perceived movement under marginal (*alternative*) conditions.

May Brenner (1956) likewise makes the point that when marginal conditions obtain, the subject is forced to depend on stimulus *meaning*. On the other hand, when optimal stimulus conditions obtain, even brain-damaged cases report apparent movement to much the same degree as do normal cases.

Several other experiments have dealt with the effects of meaning on apparent movement. Thus, Jones and Bruner (1954) report that in a stroboscopic experiment the line drawing of a man is seen to be in motion more actively than is a nonsense figure. De Silva (1926) had previously established this same fact. Jones and Bruner conclude that "the more probable and practiced the movement, the more adequately will the movement experience maintain itself under suboptimal conditions." This conclusion is in agreement with our own.

Toch and Ittelson (1956) report an experiment in which drawings of a bomb stroboscopically presented are seen in a downward (falling) motion, whereas drawings of an airplane presented in an identical fashion are seen in an upward (rising) motion. Though this experiment taken by itself favors an object-connotation theory, the authors argue in general for the cumulative-habit theory. They contend, rightly no doubt, that the nativist position cannot be adequately tested short of a longitudinal study of infants from birth. They believe that generalized past experience accounts for our major dispositions to perceive stroboscopic or other illusory movement, but allow that under conditions of ambiguity or equivocation specific meaning connotations will enter to determine the direction and nature of the movement. Here, too, our findings are concordant.

If we leave the field of experimental testing for a moment, we can find many familiar instances of the role of object connotation in resolving perceptual ambiguities. A streak of light in the night sky may be seen as a shooting star, as distant fireworks, or as a jet plane, depending largely on one's expectations. Bartlett tells of the Swazi chieftain who perceived all traffic policemen in London as friendly beings, because in Swazi culture the upraised arm is an amiable greeting. A child in a dentist's chair, more familiar with space-ships than with nitrous oxide, perceives the inhalator as a spaceship toy. Every projective test assumes that ambiguous (multivalent) stimuli will receive subjective structuring on the basis of need, set, expectancy, or habit.

Our experiment does not introduce factors of need or of set, but deals only with the relevance of past experience (meaning) as a determinant of perceived movement. It may, however, be pointed out that among sophisticated observers of the trapezoidal illusion under marginal conditions (e.g., at ten feet binocularly) a voluntary effort to see or not to see the window as oscillating (or as rotating) can also be effective, especially if the observer picks out some detail of the window to watch during the rotation, thus inhibiting the impression as a whole. Meaning is not the only determinant entering into the resolution of perceptual ambiguity, but it is one of them.

Returning to James's statement that, "Perception is of definite and probable things," we may say that under optimal conditions of stimulation definite structure is conferred by physiological conditions or by deeply ingrained functional habits of spatial adjustment, or by both. But when marginal conditions prevail, an association with the most "probable" object is often called upon to provide the definiteness that is otherwise lacking.

What we have called "marginal" conditions should receive a further word of explanation. We use the term in our experiments to indicate that perceptual conflict is present. Under binocular conditions (especially at ten feet) there are many cues that "give away" the true rotation; at the same time there are operating also the assumptions that the window is rectangular and that longer objects are nearer. Under such a condition of conflict our finding is that urban children resolve the conflict with the aid of the supplementary assumption of "windowness." Not being able to draw on this supplementary assumption, the rural children as a rule resolve the conflict in favor of the binocular (or true) evidence. In this particular case, therefore, one might say that the primitive children see things "as they are" more often than do the children of civilization.

Conclusion

The perception of motion as represented in the rotating trapezoidal window is governed, under *optimal* conditions, by nativistic determinants or by the unconscious utilization of residual (but not immediately relevant) experience or by both. (Our experiment does not enable us to decide this issue.) At the same time, object connotation (meaning) based on closely relevant cultural experience helps to determine the nature of the perceived movement under *marginal* conditions.

An adequate theory of perceived movement must therefore allow a place for the subjects' specific assumptions of meaning even though it cannot be based solely on this foundation.

Editor's Note: Further Research on Rotating Figures

The rotating trapezoidal window has found utilization beyond a simple demonstration of the interaction of previous experience and perceptual tendency in a new situation. The experimental analysis of the cues which inform the observer about the figure's movement would extend our general knowledge of visual perception. In the case of the rotating window, the subject obviously is not misled by the cues, because he is unable to ascertain the true motion. On the other hand, a rotating square is usually perceived as rotating rather than oscillating.

Allport and Pettigrew applied and developed a hypothesis in the tradition of the empiricistic theories; the variable of importance was previous experience, and the experiment attempted to establish the effect of little experience in one sphere (windows and square forms) upon perceived motion. More recent research with rotating figures has been oriented toward nativistic theories in an attempt to establish the relationship between the retinal and figural cues (provided by the stimulus) and the perceived motion.

One of the first findings was that the oscillating motion described by the observer while viewing the trapezoidal window was not confined to the trapezoidal window alone. Circular, elliptical, and several varieties of irregular shapes were often reported as oscillating while, in fact, they were rotating. This oscillating motion usually was not reported in figures which subtended a visual angle greater than 10°. The expression, "subtends a visual angle," refers to the size of the angle at the retina formed by one line connecting the lowest portion of the distal stimulus and another to the highest portion of the distal stimulus. Small visual angles result when small or distant figures are viewed.

If such a wide variety of forms can be seen as oscillating or reversing, and others, such as squares and rectangles, seldom are reported as oscillating, certain cues of the true motion of the figure must be missing in the case of the former figures. R. P. Power of the University of Sydney in Australia has attempted to ascertain what these cues of movement are (*Journal of Experimental Psychology*, 1967).

Stimulus Properties which
Reduce Apparent Reversal
of Rotating Rectangular Shapes

R. P. Power

Plane shapes rotating in depth relative to a subject are frequently reported as reversing their direction of motion (AR) so that they appear to oscillate about their axes. Although this phenomenon is most commonly associated with rotating trapezoidal shapes (Ames, 1951) it is now established that a wide variety of shapes exhibit the effect (Canestrari, 1956; Day and Power, 1963, 1965; Mulholland, 1956, 1958; Pastore, 1952). These include circular, elliptical, and irregular shapes. Rectangular shapes which subtend small visual angles are reported as reversing their direction of motion (Mulholland, 1956, 1958; Pastore, 1952) but those whose subtense is greater (about 10° or more) are rarely reported as reversing (Ames, 1951; Day and Power, 1963, 1965; Zegers and Murray, 1962). It may be assumed that when visual angle is small the resolving power of the eye is insufficient for use of the information provided by the properties of the stimulus object.

The experiment described here was designed to isolate those properties of the stimulus object which determine reduction in AR frequency with rectangular shapes.

When a rectangular shape rotates in depth about a vertical axis relative to the subject those transformations which occur in the image projected at the retina can be classified as changes either in the vertical or in the horizontal dimensions. (a) As one vertical edge approaches the subject, its vertical projection lengthens while the projection of the other edge becomes shorter as it recedes. Thus there is continuous change in the relative lengths of the vertical edges of the image. (b) Associated with changes in the vertical dimensions of the image there occur changes in the orientation of its horizontal dimensions. As one vertical edge recedes from the subject the projections of the two horizontal edges converge on that side, and diverge on the opposite side. Thus there is a "see-saw" motion of the horizontal edges about the axis during rotation (Figure 7.4).

In order to isolate the relative effectiveness of these two types of change in the image as information for the direction of rotary motion, Shapes 1, 2, 3, and 4 were constructed (Figure 7.5). Shape 1 provided both types of information, Shape 2 provided the "see-saw" type of information, Shape 3 the information of changing vertical edges, and Shape 4 gave neither type of information. Shape 2 was equivalent to Shape 3 rotated through 90°, while Shape 4 was equivalent to the most extreme contours of Shape 2 mounted on Shape 3.

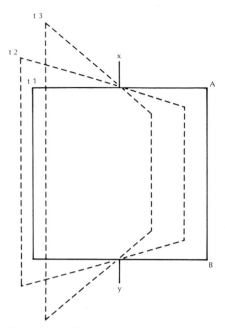

Figure 7.4: Three projections of a square object: t_1, in the frontal plane; t_2, after rotation through 30° about the axis xy with the edge AB receding; and t_3, after rotation through a further 30°.

However, it is possible that the information for true rotation direction is provided not by the absolute orientation of the edges, but by their relationship to the axis of rotation. That is, the information for rotation could be (c) the relative change in length of the edges parallel to the axis independently of their verticality, or (d) it could be the "see-saw" motion of the edges perpendicular to the axis independently of their horizontality. To test these further possibilities Shapes 5 and 6 were constructed (Figure 7.5). They were Shapes 2 and 3 rotated on a horizontal axis.

Comparisons between mean frequency of AR obtained with the shapes would allow a decision about the effectiveness of the four sources of information: (a) the changing relationship between vertical edges; (b) the changing relationship between horizontal edges; (c) the changing relationship between the edges parallel with the axis of rotation; and (d) the changing relationship between the edges perpendicular to the axis of rotation.

Method

Apparatus.   The apparatus consisted of a masonite box three feet wide, 3 feet high, and 6 feet long. Two brass viewing tubes, 1.5 inches in diameter

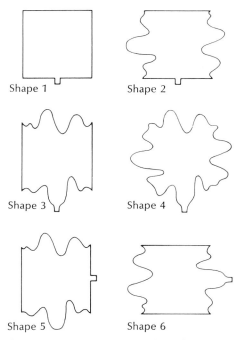

Figure 7.5: Six shapes used in the experiment (all straight sides six inches long).

and allowing a 15° field of vision, were set into one end of the box, as was an adjustable chin rest. A forty-watt circular fluorescent tube fifteen inches in diameter was mounted symmetrically about the inner ends of the viewing tubes. Each viewing tube could be blocked by means of a lens cap, and an occluding shutter could be raised or lowered by the experimenter from outside the box. The shapes were suspended from a socket on the driving shaft of a synchronous motor, which was geared to 4.75 rpm. The motor was mounted on a swinging arm, and could be placed so that the axis of rotation was either vertical or horizontal (motor on the ceiling or right-hand side of the box). Once on each revolution a cam on the driving shaft closed a microswitch, and this deflected one pen of a paper recorder. The other pen was activated by a press switch held by the subject. The axis of rotation was fifty-two inches from the subject's end of the viewing tubes, and the shapes occupied the center of the subject's field of vision.

The shapes (Figure 7.5) were made of 0.06-inch Plexiglas and mounted on Plexiglas rod, 0.375 inch in diameter. They were sprayed matte white, and a band of black tape 0.75 inch in width was placed so as to cover the slit cut in the rod when the shapes were mounted. When in the frontoparallel plane the shapes had a luminance of 2.53 ftl. Shape 1 was a six-inch square, Shape 2 had the sides parallel to the axis cut so that the edges were uneven, Shape 3 was equivalent to Shape 2, except that it was mounted on one of the uneven sides, Shape 4 was equivalent to the most extreme contours of Shapes 2 and 3, Shape 5 was Shape 2 when rotated horizontally, and Shape 6 was Shape 3 when rotated horizontally. Shapes 5 and 6 have been designated in this fashion to simplify discussion.

Subjects.   The subjects were 144 students in an introductory course in psychology, and they were randomly allocated to the six experimental groups. There were seventy-one men and seventy-three women, none of whom had served before in an experiment on AR.

Procedure.   The subject was told that he would be observing monocularly, and asked which eye he preferred to use. A lens cap was then placed over the other tube, and the chin rest adjusted. The subject was given the instructions, and the driving motor was switched on when he said he understood them. The occluding shutter was opened when the shape was in the sagittal plane. After twenty revolutions the shutter was closed, and the subject's score (number of reversals during twenty revolutions) was read from the paper record.

Instructions.   As it has been shown that they affect reports of AR (Power, 1965), the instructions are given in full.

In this experiment you are going to observe an object which is rotating, like this (the experimenter demonstrates rotation with a disc mounted on a rod). When people look at some objects they sometimes see them changing direction, like this (experimenter changes the direction of the disc after about three revolutions) or even like this (experimenter demonstrates oscillation through 180°). That is, they experience an illusion that the direction of motion changes. I want to find out how often you see this particular object change direction. I want you to press this button if the object appears to change direction. Remember, I want you to press the button when it seems to change. I am not concerned with what you know or think is really happening. Look at the centre of the object rather than any other part.

The subjects were told that the changes were illusory because subjects often stop responding if they realize that the changes are not objective (Spitz, 1964).

Experimental Design.   Preliminary experimental work indicated that the number of reversals produced by the shapes was independent of the axis of rotation, and that Shapes 1 and 2 had similar frequency of reversal.

Five predictions were then made: Prediction I—that Shapes 1 and 2 would produce a similar number of reversals; Prediction II—that Shapes 3 and 4 would produce a similar number of reversals; Prediction III—that Shapes 2 and 5 would produce a similar number of reversals; Prediction IV—that Shapes

3 and 6 would produce a similar number of reversals; and Prediction V—that Shapes 1 and 2 would produce fewer reversals than Shapes 3 and 4.

If these predictions were confirmed it would be concluded that the cue to rotation of a rectangular shape is the "see-saw" motion of the edges perpendicular to the axis of rotation, and that changes in the relative lengths of the edges parallel to the axis of rotation do not reduce AR of a rectangular shape.

Since it was proposed to interpret the nonrejection of four of the null hypotheses specified above, it was desirable to set a Type II error-rate (β) for the false acceptance of each of these. The values $\alpha = \beta = 0.05$ and $N = 24$ were chosen, and these values (Guenther, 1965) allow the detection of a "true" difference between population means as large or larger than σ (where σ is the unknown population standard deviation). For the fifth null hypothesis ($\mu_1 + \mu_2 = \mu_3 + \mu_4$) the values $\alpha = \beta = 0.05$ and $N = 24$ give a detectable "true" difference of $0.75\ \sigma$. (After the data were obtained σ was estimated at $\sqrt{MS_{Error}} = 9.69$ reversals, and $0.75\ \sigma$ at 7.27 reversals.)

Results

The means and standard deviations are reported in Table 7.10, and a summary of the analysis in Table 7.11. The hypotheses were tested by the method of planned contrasts. This method was used because it gives a higher probability of detecting a "true" difference than the usual method of protected t tests (Hays, 1964; Rodger, 1965). For Contrasts I to IV $p > 0.05$ so these null hypotheses were not rejected, and thus Predictions I to IV were confirmed. For Contrast V $p < 0.05$ so this null hypothesis was rejected and Prediction V was confirmed.

The means and standard deviations are significantly correlated, $r\ (4) = 0.85$, $p < 0.05$, so the scores were transformed (using the formula $Y = \log_{10} \dfrac{X}{(6.726 + 1)}$ where Y is the transformed score and X the original score) so that the means and standard deviations were uncorrelated, $r\ (4) = 0.02$, $p > 0.05$. The transformed scores did not depart significantly from a normal distribution when tested with the Kolmogorov-Smirnov one sample test, $D\ (144) = 0.07$, $p > 0.2$ (Siegel, 1956). The above analysis was repeated on the transformed data with analogous results.

Table 7.10

Means and standard deviations (SD) of frequency of reversal for each of the six stimulus conditions

Shape	1	2	3	4	5	6
$\overline{X}$	4.75	8.08	18.75	18.04	6.42	17.46
SD	7.08	8.82	12.72	9.08	6.51	11.33

Table 7.11

**Analysis of the data using the method
of planned comparisons**

Source	df	MS	F
Contrast			
I ($\mu_1 = \mu_2$)	1	133.067	1.42
II ($\mu_3 = \mu_4$)	1	6.049	0.06
III ($\mu_2 = \mu_5$)	1	43.777	0.47
IV ($\mu_3 = \mu_6$)	1	19.997	0.21
V ($\mu_1 + \mu_2 = \mu_3 + \mu_4$)	1	3,444.490	36.71*
Error	138	93.834	

* $p < 0.05$.

Discussion

Since all the hypotheses were confirmed it was concluded: (a) that all three shapes with straight edges perpendicular to the axis of rotation produce a similar number of reversals; (b) that the three shapes without straight edges perpendicular to the axis of rotation produce a similar number of reversals; and (c) that the second class of shapes produces more reversals than the first. As the first class of shapes gives the information produced by the "see-saw" motion of the edges but not the information from the relative size change of the edges the final conclusion was that the cue to true rotation direction of a rectangular shape is the "see-saw" motion of the edges parallel to the axis, and that the relative size change of the edges parallel to the axis is ineffective as a cue to direction of rotation.

Summary

The subjects give fewer reports of apparent reversal (AR) with rectangular shapes than other shapes. Four cues could be used by the subject as information for true rotation direction. They are: (a) the changing relationship between the vertical ends of the object; (b) the changing relationship between the horizontal edges; (c) the changing relationship between the edges parallel to the axis of rotation; and (d) the changing relationship between the edges perpendicular to the axis of rotation. An experiment was carried out in which these cues were systematically pitted against one another and it was shown that in the case of a rectangular shape, the straight edges perpendicular to the axis of rotation constituted the cue to rotation direction and that straight edges parallel to the axis of rotation do not reduce frequency of AR.

CHAPTER 8
Set and Perception

In Chapter 7, emphasis was placed on previous experience as a source of influence on perceptual-response tendencies. Such previous experiences of an organism produce response sets; that is, they cause a preparedness on the part of the individual to perceive a stimulus in a certain way. A perceptual set is manifested when an individual responds by paying more attention to certain aspects while disregarding other aspects of the stimuli. If, for example, one has established a set for recognizing a particular friend, whom he has agreed to meet on a busy street corner, he might well fail to recognize a second friend, who was not expected on that corner at that time. The set concentrated his attention on the first friend, causing him to disregard the second friend.

The Experimental Study of Set

In the typical experimental study of set, the subject is instructed to respond to certain aspects of the stimuli. Because the instructions cause the subject to respond to particular aspects of stimuli and not to other aspects, the conclusion can be made that the set directed or modified his behavior relative to the stimuli.

An experiment by Siipola (1935) may serve to clarify the concept of set. The following list of nonsense words were flashed on a screen for brief periods and the subject was required to identify the words: Chack, Sael, Wharl, Pasrot, and Dack. Although the stimuli were in fact nonsense words, the subjects were set to perceive real words. One group of subjects was informed that they would be viewing words related to travel, whereas a second group was instructed that they would be identifying animal words. The effects of the set were determined by recording the responses most frequently given for each word (the most frequent responses are given below).

Stimulus	Travel Group	Animal Group
Chack	Check	Chick
Sael	Sail	Seal
Wharl	Wharf	Whale
Pasrot	Passport	Parrot
Dack	Deck or Dock	Duck

A famous experiment by Gottschaldt (1929) demonstrates the establishment of set without specific instructions. Subjects were presented with simple geometric figures, called the a-figure, several times in rapid succession. On a critical trial, the new and more complex figure (b-figure) was introduced with the original figure (a-figure) embedded in it (Figure 8.1).

The subjects reported perceiving the a-figure in the b-figure, presumably because the set had been established through repeated, rapid presentation of the a-figure prior to the introduction of the b-figure. Under conditions not allowing the establishment of a set for the a-figure, subjects seldom reported perceiving the a-figure in the b-figure.

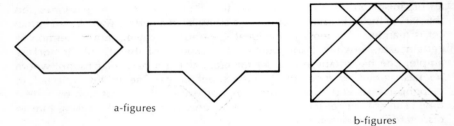

a-figures

b-figures

Figure 8.1: Example of the Gottschaldt Hidden Figures. One of the a-figures is hidden within the complex b-figure.

Establishing the mechanism of set is controversial. One mechanism, developed and proposed by Leo Postman, Jerome S and Elliott McGinnies (*Journal of Abnormal and Social Psycholog* was explained as *perceptual selectivity*, the modification of perceptual response tendencies on the basis of personal values and needs of the subject. In other words, the subject's values and needs constitute a set which enables him to respond more readily to certain kinds of stimuli or aspects of stimuli. As we shall see, the results of the study have been confirmed in several replications and not confirmed in others. Furthermore, the greatest source of controversy surrounding the study by Postman, Bruner, and McGinnies relates to the interpretation of their results.

Personal Values as Selective Factors in Perception

Leo Postman, Jerome S. Bruner, and Elliott McGinnies

What one sees, what one observes, is inevitably what one selects from a near infinitude of potential percepts. Perceptual selection depends not only upon the "primary determinants of attention" but is also a servant of one's interests, needs, and values.

Can one lean on the slender reed of "the limited span of attention" and its primary determinants to explain the selectivity of perception? That there is a limited span can hardly be denied. But to invoke it in explanation of itself leaves unexplained the differences in the perceptions of individuals faced with the same stimuli and all hampered by a "limited span of attention" and governed by common primary determinants.

The properties of the stimulus field as they affect the range and fluctuation of attention have been amply investigated: "intensity, quality, repetition, suddenness, movement, novelty, congruity with the present contents of consciousness are one and all (primary) determinants of attention" (Titchner, 1910, p. 270). Yet, however far one pushes such research, half of the question remains unanswered: What does the individual contribute to perceptual selection over and above a healthy pair of eyes and the appropriate response mechanisms? The concepts of secondary and derived primary attention are merely restatements of the problem, affirming that the organism can and does attend to things in spite of the absence of primary determinants. To say that there are "individual differences" in perceptual behavior is merely another way to restate the problem and to dismiss one of the most fruitful sources of psychological research.

Psychologists have in recent years been increasingly concerned with what may be called organismic or adjustive determinants in perception. Professor E. G. Boring (1946) has, for example, pointed out that "the purpose of perception is economy of thinking. It picks out and establishes what is permanent and therefore important to the organism for its survival and welfare." In general, however, "survival and welfare" have been treated as synonymous with the "primary biological needs" of the organism. The supposed utility of perceptual constancies described in terms of "regression to the real object" illustrates well this generalized organismic approach to the problem.

But survival and welfare obviously encompass more than purely biological needs. There remains the evanescent residual category of "personality," at once too broad to be operationally useful to the student of perception and too ubiquitous to be neglected. What is required are dimensions of variation in personality which are both measurable and intrinsically important, and which can be related to individual differences in perception.

One such dimension of variation in personality is personal interest or value. It is with this dimension of personality in its relation to perceptual selectivity that the present study is concerned. Our hypothesis, briefly, is that personal values are demonstrable determinants of what the individual selects perceptually from his environment.

The Experiment

Perceptual selectivity may be investigated in different ways. A subject may be faced with a complex field from which he selects this or that item or configuration. This type of selection may be called *spatial selection*. Or, a subject may be presented with a series of items one at a time, each well within his span of attention, and the *speed* with which the various items are correctly recognized may be compared. This type of selection may be called *temporal selection*. These two forms of selectivity are alike in that they both reflect differential tuning of the individual to stimulus objects in the environment. In the experiment here reported temporal selection was studied.

Twenty-five subjects, students at Harvard and Radcliffe, were shown thirty-six words, one at a time, in a modified Dodge tachistoscope. The words, typed in capital letters, were chosen to represent the six values measured by the Allport-Vernon Study of Values—theoretical, economic, aesthetic, social, political, and religious. These words were unanimously chosen by three independent judges familiar with the Spranger value classification from a preliminary list of ninety-six words equally distributed among the six values. The final list, comprising six words for each value, was balanced for length of words by using an equal number of six- and seven-letter words for each value. Insofar as possible, an attempt was made to choose words of equal familiarity. The stimulus words are listed by value category in Table 8.1.

The thirty-six words were shown to the subject in random order. Each word was exposed three times for 0.01 second. If the subject failed to recognize the word, three exposures were then given at 0.02, 0.03 second, etc., at exposure times increasing in even steps of 0.01 second until recognition occurred. A full record was kept of all the subject's pre-recognition responses. Subjects were instructed simply to report everything that they saw or thought they saw.

To obtain an independent measure of personal value orientation, the Allport-Vernon Study of Values (1931) was administered individually to each

Table 8.1

**Stimulus words representing the six
Spranger value categories**

Theoretical	Economic	Aesthetic	Social	Political	Religious
theory	income	beauty	loving	govern	prayer
verify	useful	artist	kindly	famous	sacred
science	wealthy	poetry	devoted	compete	worship
logical	finance	elegant	helpful	citizen	blessed
research	economic	literary	friendly	politics	religion
analysis	commerce	graceful	sociable	dominate	reverent

subject. The test was given either some weeks in advance of the perceptual experiment or after the experiment.

In summary, then, the following records were obtained for each subject:

1. Time of recognition for thirty-six words representing the six Spranger values.
2. Attempted solutions preceding recognition of the actual words.
3. Score profiles on the Allport-Vernon test, which could be evaluated against population norms.

Results of the Experiment

Analysis of Recognition Thresholds. Is time of recognition significantly influenced by the value which a given stimulus word represents? Each subject's value profile was compared with his "time-of-recognition profile." The value profile is a type of psychograph on which the subject's scores in the six Spranger values as measured by the Allport-Vernon Study are plotted. The average times of recognition for the sets of six words representing each of the value areas constitute the time-of-recognition profile. The two profiles for each of the twenty-five subjects are presented in Figure 8.2. Along the baseline the value-areas are indicated. Allport-Vernon scores are plotted against the left-hand ordinate and average times of recognition against the right-hand ordinate. Inspection of these profiles at once reveals considerable variability but also a marked tendency for high-value words to be recognized at shorter time exposures than low-value ones. In a few cases there is virtually one-to-one correspondence between the two profiles (e.g., the profiles of RB and IV). Such striking relationships are not, of course, the rule. One isolated case (JC) shows what appears to be a reversal, high-value words requiring, on the whole, a longer exposure time than less-valued words. Certainly visual inspection indicates that, for the sample as a whole, time of recognition varies as a function of value.

Statistical analysis confirms this impression. The value scores of each subject were classified as falling above or below the population mean (30) for the Allport-Vernon test. His time-of-recognition scores were similarly divided

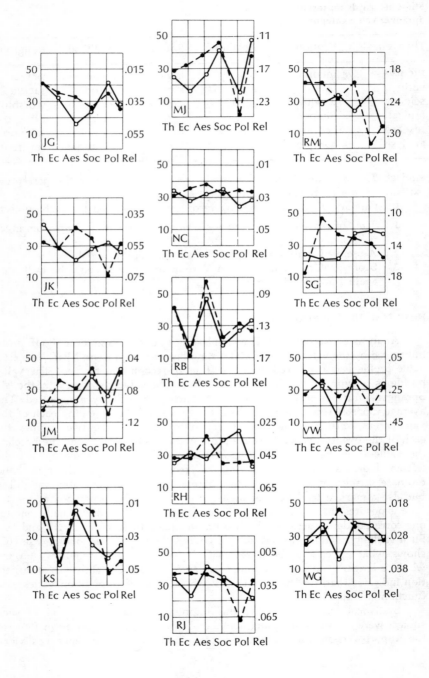

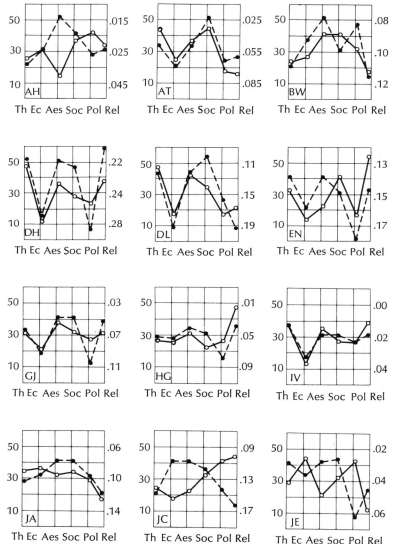

Figure 8.2: Value profiles and time-of-recognition of the individual subjects. The values tested by the Allport-Vernon Study are indicated along the abscissa. Value scores are plotted against the left-hand ordinate. Average recognition times for the words representing these values are plotted against the right-hand ordinate. Solid lines represent value scores, dotted lines represent times of recognition.

Table 8.2

**Chi-square test of significance of association
between value preference and time of recognition
(theoretical frequencies are in italics)**

		Value Scores		
		Above Mean	*Below Mean*	
Time of recognition	Above mean	156 *181.40*	216 *190.55*	372
	Below mean	283 *257.56*	245 *270.45*	528
		439	461	

$$X^2 = 11.87 \quad P = <0.01$$

into those falling below or above *his own* mean time of recognition. Combining the results for all subjects into a two-by-two contingency table (Table 8.2), a chi-square test of independence was performed. The obtained chi-square value of 11.87 indicates, at a high level of confidence, that the association between value orientation and time of recognition is not random.

An analysis in terms of a two-by-two table, though useful, can do little more than indicate that a general relationship does exist. For purposes of more detailed analysis, each subject's value scores were, therefore, ranked from highest (Rank 1) to lowest (Rank 6). For the group as a whole, the average time of recognition was computed for each of the six ranks. Note that the analysis here is in terms of *rank of value* rather than in terms of *specific* value areas. That is to say, Rank 1 could be any one of the six values for a given subject, and so on down for the remaining ranks. The mean times of recognition for the six value ranks are presented numerically in Table 8.3 and graphically in Figure 8.3. The significance of the difference between the mean times of recognition of stimulus words was tested for all possible combinations of value ranks. As Table 8.4 shows, the words symbolizing the subjects' highest ranking value are recognized at exposure times significantly shorter than those required for words symbolizing their lowest ranking value. A comparison of the highest ranking and second lowest value (Ranks 1 and 5) yields a similar result. All other differences fail to reach statistical significance although they are predominantly in the expected direction.

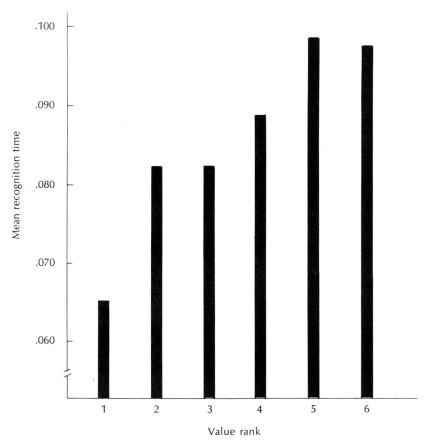

Figure 8.3: Average times of recognition for the words representing the six values of the Allport-Vernon Study arranged in rank order.

The great majority of subjects, then, conform to a general pattern. *The higher the value represented by a word, the more rapidly is it likely to be recognized.*

Analysis of Attempted Solutions. Statistical analysis shows that value acts as a *sensitizer*, lowers the perceptual threshold. But value orientation does more than that. It is an active, selective disposition which in many subtle ways affects the hypotheses and attempts at solution which precede the actual recognition of a stimulus word. Much can be learned about the role of value as an organizing factor in perception from an analysis of pre-solution behavior.

Each subject's perceptual behavior forms an individualized pattern and our preceding analysis of group data inevitably sacrifices a great deal of highly

Table 8.3

Mean times of recognition as a function of individual value ranks represented by the stimulus words

Value Rank	Mean Time of Recognition in Seconds
1	0.075
2	0.082
3	0.082
4	0.089
5	0.098
6	0.097

suggestive information about individual "styles" of perceiving. As a first approximation to a more intensive investigation of perceptual behavior, we have examined carefully and sought to classify individual pre-solution responses. Our effort has been to find categories of classification which might throw into relief the directive influence of value orientation of perception.

Table 8.4

Significance of differences between mean recognition times for all combinations of value ranks. Entries in the table represent values of *t*, and *P* (in italics)

	1	2	3	4	5
2	0.83 *0.40*				
3	0.80 *> 0.40*	0.07 *> 0.90*			
4	1.64 *0.10*	0.76 *> 0.40*	0.87 *0.40*		
5	2.32 *0.02*	1.52 *> 0.10*	1.62 *0.10*	0.84 *0.40*	
6	2.42 *< 0.02*	1.54 *> 0.10*	1.67 *0.10*	0.80 *> 0.40*	0.09 *> 0.90*

The following categories for the analysis of pre-solution responses or hypotheses have emerged:

1. *Covaluant Responses.* This category comprises responses which can be unambiguously classified as representing the same value area as the stimulus word. The subject who saw the word *Easter* when the stimulus word was *sacred* illustrates the covaluant category.

2. *Contravaluant Responses.* In some cases, the words reported in the pre-solution period were opposite in meaning to the stimulus word or served to derogate it. An instance is provided by a subject who saw *scornful* upon presentation of the stimulus word *helpful.* Or *revenge* instead of *blessed.*

3. *Structural Responses.* Under this heading fall the very frequent incorrect hypotheses based on the structural characteristics of the stimulus word. An illustrative sequence of hypotheses given by one subject in response to the word *loving* was: *movies, mowing, moving, lowing,* and finally *loving.* A frequent stimulus-bound, structural hypothesis was the response *turkey* for *theory.*

4. *Nonsense Responses.* Two types of responses are included here: (a) nonsense words, such as *linone* for *income,* or *weelby* for *wealthy;* and (b) partial responses in which the subject's hypothesis consisted of an enumeration of parts of a word or individual letters.

5. *Unrelated Responses.* This is our residual category. All responses which could not be related to the stimulus word in terms of any of the above categories were provisionally classified as unrelated. Responses such as *upper* and *carol* to a word like *useful* may serve as an illustration. We do not for a moment believe that they are haphazard responses. The fact that this category turned out to be the most numerous is a commentary on the inadequacy of existing analytic categories in the study of pre-solution behavior in perception.

Table 8.5 represents the mean frequency with which each of these kinds of pre-solution hypotheses occurred per stimulus word in the subjects' high-value (Ranks 1, 2, and 3) and low-value (Ranks 4, 5, and 6) areas. Table 8.5 also shows the significance of the differences in the mean frequency of the various response categories when high- and low-value areas are compared.

We are ready to grant at the outset that the categories of classification used in the analysis of pre-solution hypotheses are tentative. Their reliability has not as yet been demonstrated. The categories, moreover, are not always mutually exclusive. Without claiming any high degree of precision in our measurements, we nonetheless present the results of our classification as the simplest and most convenient description of general trends.

That several of our categories did discriminate between pre-solution responses to high- and low-value words may be taken as a presumptive demonstration of their validity. Covaluant hypotheses occur with significantly higher frequency in response to high-value words than they do in response to low-

Table 8.5

Mean frequency per word of different pre-solution hypotheses for high-value and low-value words

Type of Hypothesis	All Words	High-Value Words	Low-Value Words	Significance of Differences*
Covaluant	0.13	0.16	0.10	2.04 ($<$ 0.05)
Contravaluant	0.03	0.02	0.05	2.0 ($<$ 0.05)
Structural	0.44	0.49	0.40	1.35 ($>$ 0.10)
Nonsense	0.13	0.09	0.16	2.05 ($<$ 0.05)
Unrelated	0.56	0.56	0.57	0.10 (0.92)

* Entries represent values of t, entries in parentheses are values of P.

value words. A complementary finding is that both contravaluant and non-sense hypotheses appear more prominently among responses to low-value words. There is a similar tendency for structural hypotheses to be associated more frequently with high-value words, though the difference falls short of statistical significance. Our residual category, unrelated hypotheses, favors neither high- nor low-value stimulus words, nor is there any particular reason why it should.

The Role of Value Orientation in Perceptual Selection

Selection is one of the three basic adaptive processes that operate in perception. Inextricably linked with selection are accentuation and fixation. Once selected, a percept may be accentuated, i.e., certain of its features may be emphasized. Fixation denotes the persistence and preferential retention of certain selected percepts. Any perceptual behavior exhibits the three processes. The experiments reported here focus upon one aspect of this tripartite process which as a whole constitutes perception: the mechanisms through which value orientation becomes a determinant of selection.

Our results lead us to propose three complementary selective mechanisms. Value orientation acts as a sensitizer, lowering thresholds for acceptable stimulus objects. Let us call this mechanism *selective sensitization*. Value orientation may, on the other hand, raise thresholds for unacceptable stimulus objects. We shall refer to this mechanism as *perceptual defense*. Finally, the perceiver, whatever the nature of the stimulus, favors the pre-solution hypotheses which reflect his value orientation. He will, therefore, perceive more readily stimulus objects which lie within the same value area as his preferred pre-solution hypotheses. This third mechanism we shall term *value resonance*.

Selective Sensitization. The primary evidence supporting this concept is provided, as we have indicated, by the significantly lower thresholds of recognition for high-value words. Selective sensitization may well be a specific case of a more general phenomenon. Lashley (1938) has proposed, for example, that one of the mechanisms through which "instinctive" or "drive" behavior operates is perceptual sensitization. The organism's threshold is lowered for objects which may serve to reduce drive. We should like to emphasize here that such a process of perceptual sensitization is not limited to the types of behavior commonly regarded as instinctive. Value orientation too, the result of a long process of socialization, may serve as a sensitizer in much the same way.

That value orientation significantly affects the threshold time for the recognition of words leads to a reconsideration of the parameters which must be taken into account in the measurement of any threshold. It is not always sufficient to state the stimulus conditions and instructions to the subject under which threshold measurements are made. The words representing the six value areas were all equated as far as possible in terms of such physical properties as length, size, degree of illumination, and all responses were given under the same general instruction. Yet widely different thresholds are obtained when the subjects' "set" or orientation toward the stimulus materials is taken into account. Had we failed to consider the subjects' *predisposition* to respond to some values more readily than to others, we should probably have ascribed these individual differences merely to "chance fluctuations in the measurement of the span of attention"! If the concepts of threshold and sensitivity are to be extended to types of perceptual phenomena more complex than sheer sensory acuity, the crucial role played by such attitudinal factors as value and need must be recognized.

Perceptual Defense. Value orientation not only contributes to the selection and accentuation of certain percepts in preference to others, it also erects barriers against percepts and hypotheses incongruent with or threatening to the individual's values. We suggest that a defense mechanism similar to repression operates in perceptual behavior. The high thresholds for low-value words may result in part from such perceptual barriers. Not only do low-value words fail to benefit from selective sensitization, their recognition is also blocked by perceptual defense mechanisms. The clearest evidence for the operation of such perceptual defenses comes from the analysis of pre-solution responses.

Pre-solution responses to low-value words appear to take the form of avoidance of meaning. As indicated in Table 8.5, subjects have a pronounced tendency to see nonsense words when low-value stimulus words are presented for recognition. Such nonsense hypotheses take either the form of meaningless words or incomplete segments of words. Avoidance of meaning manifests itself even more accurately in the greater incidence of contravaluant hypotheses preceding the recognition of low-value words. Consider some examples. A subject, with little interest in religious values, when confronted with the word *sacred* gives the following sequence of hypotheses: *sucked, sacked, shocked, sacred.* Another, lacking in aesthetic values, sees *hypocrisy* for *elegant.*

Still another manifestation of perceptual defense is a frequent failure to use such available cues as word structure in forming hypotheses. Fewer pre-solution responses based on letter structure were given to low-value words than to high-value. Reluctance to use structural hypotheses fits well into perceptual defense behavior. Formation of an hypothesis based on structure too easily leads to recognition of the word being avoided. One may inquire at this point, "How does the subject 'know' that a word should be avoided? In order to 'repress' he must first recognize it for what it is." We have no answer to propose. What mediates the phenomena of hysterical or hypnotically induced blindness? Of only one thing we can be fairly sure: reactions do occur without conscious awareness of what one is reacting to. Psychological defense in perception is but one instance of such "unconscious" reaction.

Value Resonance.   The nature of pre-solution hypotheses, no less than recognition itself, reflects value orientation. "Guesses" are not haphazard. As frequently as possible and as long as possible perceptual guesses are made in congruence with prevailing value orientation. This congruence between "guesses" and dominant values accounts, we believe, for the significantly greater number of covaluant responses to high-value words.

When stimulus words reflecting the same values as the subject's preferred hypotheses are presented to him, they are recognized more rapidly since they conform to, or are resonant with, his general set to respond in terms of his major values. That a generalized set lowers the recognition threshold for specific stimuli within its compass, has, of course, been known since the early work of the Würzburg School. Thus, covaluant responses and sensitization work, as it were, hand in glove. Covaluant responses, reflecting the person's major values, help to prepare him for recognition of stimuli symbolizing these same major values. Consider, for example, the responses of a religious subject to a religious stimulus word, *reverence,* at the low exposure time of 0.01 second; *divinity, sentiment, reverence.* The first two responses, structurally unrelated to the stimulus, are clearly covaluant responses. That the subject recognized the correct word on the third exposure at 0.01 second illustrates the sensitizing action of a generalized set.

If the subject's typically preferred hypotheses reflect a value different from that symbolized by the stimulus word before him, his generalized set may serve to slow down recognition. His hypotheses, in such cases, may appear to the investigator as candidates for our "unrelated" category. An instance is provided by a subject of strongly theoretical bent who also scores high in aesthetic and social values but who is low in economic interest. Confronted with the word *income,* he gave these responses prior to recognition at 0.11 second: *learning, tomorrow, learning, knowledge, literature, learning, loving, income.* The exposure of 0.11 second required for recognition of this low-value word compares poorly indeed with his overall mean recognition time of 0.03 second.

Our aim in these pages has been to point to the relation of value orientation and perceptual selectivity. The experimental evidence leads us to the formulation of three mechanisms to account for the interrelationship of these phenomena in perceptual behavior. Value orientation makes for *perceptual sensitization* to valued stimuli, leads to *perceptual defense* against inimical stimuli, and gives rise to a process of *value resonance* which keeps the person responding in terms of objects valuable to him even when such objects are absent from his immediate environment. These processes of selectivity must be considered in any perceptual theory which lays claim to comprehensiveness.

Editor's Note: Further Research on Set

Many studies have concerned identification of the manner in which set influences behavior. Postman, Bruner, and McGinnies, in the preceding presentation, interpreted their results to mean that the perceptual process itself was modified by the set. The perceptual system was conceived as becoming tuned to respond to certain aspects of stimuli and to filter out other aspects.

A classic study by Chapman (1932) indicates an alternative explanation. Subjects were shown a series of cards at threshold duration in a tachistoscope. Each card contained letters of the alphabet. The array of letters on each card could vary along the following three dimensions:

1. Number of letters (four to eight)
2. Identity of the letters
3. Spatial arrangement of the letters

Two groups of subjects participated in the experiment. One group was informed of the attribute to attend to on that trial (number, identity, or spatial arrangement of letters). This information was given four seconds prior to the tachistoscopic presentation of the card. The subjects in group two were also informed of the attribute of the cards to which they were to attend. However, this information was given two seconds after the presentation of the card.

Perceptual tuning could occur only if the attribute was mentioned prior to the stimulus presentation, and the results showed that the before group's performance was better than the after group's. However, the after group did better than a group not receiving information at all. In a group not receiving any information, perceptual tuning could not have occurred. Facilitation in the after condition, therefore, must be due to memory. The set allows unimportant memory traces on the irrelevant dimensions to be discarded and attention placed on the relevant dimensions.

Memory-trace may also be accountable for the improved performance in identifying the correct attribute prior to presentation of the card. The unimportant traces are forgotten or allowed to decay immediately after presentation and the subject recalls only the important or relevant traces. With reduction of the number of items which he must remember, performance is improved.

Most of the empirical research can be interpreted in terms of the perceptual-tuning hypothesis or in terms of the memory hypothesis. The next task, design of an experiment to differentiate between memory and perceptual tuning in the before condition, was recently attempted by Howard Egeth and Edward Smith (*Journal of Experimental Psychology*, 1967).

Perceptual Selectivity in a Visual Recognition Task

Howard Egeth and Edward Smith

Since at least the time of Külpe's (1904) experiment on abstraction, psychologists have been concerned with the mechanism or mechanisms of selectivity through which accuracy of recognition is influenced by instructional sets. The existence of several thorough reviews of this general topic (e.g., Egeth, 1967; Pierce, 1963) permits us to single out for careful examination one of the most important and compelling arguments concerning the locus of such a mechanism.

Lawrence and Coles (1954) attempted to assess the relative importance of three possible selectivity mechanisms that might be operative in a perceptual recognition experiment: perceptual selectivity, selective remembering, and modification of response availability. Previously, investigators interested in examining selective processes in recognition had relied on a before versus after technique, one in which a to-be-reported aspect of the display was specified either before or shortly after the tachistoscopic presentation of a test stimulus. Accuracy of report was usually found to be higher with instructions preceding the stimulus display (e.g., Boring, 1924; Chapman, 1932), and several investigators had concluded that this result was an indication that the subject's perception of the stimulus could be selectively directed to critical aspects of the stimulus that had been specified by the instructions. However, Lawrence and Coles realized that this apparent selectivity might be reflecting a memory process rather than a perceptual one. Specifically, they reasoned that the before instructions might simply have been able to modify the memory trace more quickly than the after instructions since there was no delay in receiving the former kind of instructions although there was for the latter. In order to circumvent this difficulty, Lawrence and Coles resorted to a more elaborate experimental design. They reasoned that a percept must be richer and more full of detail than a memory trace. Granting this, consider the possible effect of giving alternatives (four verbal labels, one of which was appropriate to a briefly presented test picture) either before or after the presentation of the test picture. If the objects connoted by the four verbal labels are quite disparate, then even the relatively crude memory trace ought to carry enough information to enable the subjects to discriminate fairly adequately among them and thus choose the correct alternative. Hence, there should not be much decrement if the alternatives which connote disparate objects are presented after rather than before the test picture. However, if the objects connoted by the alternatives are similar to one another, then the crude memory trace may well be inadequate for discrimination when the alternatives are presented after the picture; but if the alternatives are presented before the picture then the subjects may be able to selectively direct their attention to those aspects of the picture that can best distinguish among the four alternatives. Therefore, in their experiment the existence of perceptual selectivity would be evidenced by an interaction between kind of alternatives, similar (the objects connoted by the verbal alternatives were similar to one another) or dissimilar (the objects connoted were different from one another) and time of presentation of the alternatives, before versus after the test picture. In particular, perceptual selectivity ought to result in less difference in recognition accuracy between similar and dissimilar alternatives when the sets of alternatives are presented before rather than after the test picture. Since the predicted interaction was not statistically significant those authors concluded that the presentation of alternatives influenced either memory or response availability rather than perception. Their conclusion was greatly strengthened by the further finding that time of presentation of alternatives failed to produce even a significant main effect.

Although the logic underlying the design of their experiment still seems sound, we propose that the experiment itself does not provide an opportunity for a mechanism of perceptual selectivity to operate. Consider a hypothetical case where the four similar alternatives "church," "school," "house," and "barn" are presented before a test picture. In order for perceptual selectivity to be manifested the subject would first have to consider the alternatives and determine a set of critical features which could distinguish among the alternatives. He would then have to direct his attention to those parts of the test picture that contain these critical features. However, it is not clear just how subjects could extract a set of critical visual features from a set of four verbal labels since it is not at all obvious just what set of features would distinguish reliably among the four *classes* of objects named above. In short, it does not seem reasonable to expect a perceptual process to be modified by this kind of conceptual information. Consideration of this point leads to a revision of the Lawrence and Coles experiment which does seem to provide a fair test of the perceptual-selectivity hypothesis. This revision involves the use of pictorial alternatives as well as pictorial test stimuli. In this situation the subject would have an opportunity to examine a set of alternatives in order to find features which distinguish among them, and he could then selectively direct his attention to the informative areas of the test picture.

Method

Subjects.   Forty-eight male and forty-eight female students at the University of Michigan served as paid volunteers and were tested individually.

Apparatus. The test pictures were displayed for 20 msec in a Gerbrands two-field mirror tachistoscope. In order to reduce the persistence of after-images, the adaptation field consisted of a jumble of small bits and pieces of pictures. A small black fixation cross was clearly visible in the adaptation field at the viewing distance of twenty-three inches. At that viewing distance a typical test picture subtended about 7° of visual angle. However, since the pictures did not have regular outlines, such a determination of an average size is only an approximation.

Procedure. In an attempt to remain fairly close to the methodology of the Lawrence and Coles (1954) study, the present experiment was originally designed as a 2 × 2 factorial design with alternatives presented either before or after the test picture, and with the alternatives within a set being either similar to or dissimilar from one another. However, the results from a group of pilot subjects indicated that the before conditions imposed much greater memory loads on subjects than did the after conditions. This point is treated further in the Results and Discussion sections; for now it is only important to note that as a result of the pilot data the experimental procedure was modified. Another level was added to the time-of-presentation-of-alternatives factor, viz., before *and* after (before-after). With this design, the chief comparison is between the after conditions and the new before-after conditions. (For a precedent in the use of this design see Long, Reid, and Henneman, 1960.) Although the logic of the original Lawrence and Coles study is still intact, in the present experiment it is in the before-after conditions that the effects of perceptual selectivity might be expected to occur unobscured by the confounding effects of a difficult memory task.

A different set of eight randomly chosen men and eight randomly chosen women served in each of the six experimental conditions. The subjects were briefly familiarized with the nature of tachistoscopically presented stimuli by requiring them to describe a picture shown for 20 msec. They were given five such trials with the same picture, after which the picture was exposed for several seconds. Then, subjects were given instructions appropriate to the conditions to which they had been assigned and these instructions were followed by five practice trials which were also appropriate to their assigned conditions.

In the before-after conditions, on each trial subjects were shown a plaque containing four pictures which they were allowed to examine for thirty seconds. At the end of thirty seconds the experimenter said, "Time," which was the cue for subjects to look into the tachistoscope and fixate the black cross. As soon as they had done so they were to say, "Ready," at which signal the experimenter flashed the picture for 20 msec in the center of the field. The subjects then looked back at the plaque containing the alternatives and pointed to the one that they thought had been flashed. They were permitted up to thirty seconds to reach a decision, and they were instructed to respond even if they were not certain of their answer. At the end of the thirty-second decision period another set of four alternatives was presented and the procedure was repeated. There were twenty trials not including the five given for practice. The subjects were paid one dollar for participating, and, in addition, received five cents for every correct choice.

The before conditions were essentially the same as the above with the single difference that the alternatives were removed while subjects were peering into the tachistoscope. Therefore they were available before the presentation but not after. The subjects indicated their choice by pointing to the appropriate position on a blank plaque that was divided into four positions by two perpendicular lines. This plaque was kept in place for thirty seconds so that the interstimulus intervals would be identical across conditions.

In the after conditions, subjects were told to wait until they were informed that it was time for them to look into the tachistoscope; this waiting period was thirty seconds. While subjects were looking into the apparatus a plaque containing four alternatives was slipped into place. Immediately after the presentation of the stimulus picture the subjects looked down at the plaque and then made their choice.

Stimuli. The sets of pictures used in the similar conditions were constructed by searching through magazines and merchandise catalogs for instances in which there were four similar pictures of essentially the same object. (For example, pictures of four different styles of men's shoes were used.) Care was taken to select pictures of roughly the same size for a given set of alternatives. The alternatives within these sets of similar alternatives were at least as similar to one another as the objects connoted by the similar alternatives in the Lawrence and Coles study, since in the present experiment all four visual alternatives would be given the same label (e.g., shoe), while in the Lawrence and Coles study the similar alternatives were disparate enough to be associated with different labels.

The selected pictures were cut out and several monochromatic reproductions of each were made on a Thermofax copier. The twenty-five clearest four-picture sets were used; twenty in the experimental series and five in the practice series. From each set one of the alternatives was chosen to be used as a test picture and a copy of each of these pictures was reserved for this purpose. Then, copies of the four alternative stimuli in each set were attached to cardboard plaques so that they could be displayed as sets. The pictures were arranged on the plaque as if at the corners of a square. Consistent use of this arrangement allowed for identification of the critical member (the set member identical to the test picture) by a simple pointing response. This was particularly useful in the after conditions since the alternatives themselves were not present when the subject was making his decision. Each of the four possible positions contained a critical member equally often in the experimental series.

The sets of pictures for the dissimilar conditions were constructed by recombining the pictures used in the similar conditions. From a particular set of four similar alternatives only one was included in any given set of dissimilar alternatives. Again, the sets of alternatives were mounted on plaques at the corners of an imaginary square. The twenty test stimuli of the similar series were also the test stimuli in the dissimilar series. The critical members corresponding to these test pictures were kept in the same relative positions on their plaques in the two series. For example, if a particular shoe served as a test picture in the similar series and the critical set member corresponding to it was displayed in the upper left of its plaque, then this same shoe would be a test picture in the dissimilar series and would again correspond to a set member in the upper left of its plaque. To carry this illustration further, it should be made clear that this shoe would be presented as an alternative along with three other shoes in the similar series, but in the dissimilar series it would be displayed along with pictures of three quite disparate objects, e.g., a motorcycle, a radio, and a vacuum cleaner.

Six different orders of presentation of the stimuli were used in each condition during the course of the experiment.

Results

Each subject received a score from 0 to 20 based on the number of trials on which his choice was correct; these data were used in the analysis below.

Pilot subjects had indicated that the before conditions were qualitatively different from the other conditions because of the burden placed upon them of having to remember the positions in which the various alternatives had appeared on their plaques. Although this may not be an extremely difficult task in itself, it should be recalled that the thirty-second examination period was supposed to be spent in a search for critical features, not in paired-associate learning. Thus the before conditions not only imposed greater memory loads on subjects but may have also reduced the time period during which the first stage of selectivity (determination of a critical set of discriminating features) operates. This preliminary finding led to the inclusion of the before-after conditions in the experimental design. Now, the logical test of the perceptual selectivity hypothesis consists in a comparison of the after conditions with the before-after conditions. Although the before conditions were retained in the design and their results reported below, they did not enter into the statistical analysis.

Two steps were taken to reduce the error variance of the data. First, sex was used as an additional factor in the analysis of variance. Second, subjects were eliminated from consideration if their scores deviated by more than two standard deviations in either direction from the means of their respective cells. The subjects eliminated in this way (only two) were replaced with new subjects. The means and standard deviations for all conditions are presented in Table 8.6.

An analysis of variance performed on the data of the after and before-after groups indicated the following significant effects: Time of presentation of alternative, $F(1, 56) = 5.91$, $p < 0.05$; similarity of alternatives, $F(1, 56) = 75.16$, $p < 0.01$; sex of S, $F(1, 56) = 7.59$, $p < 0.01$. The only significant interaction was the one of major interest—that between time of presentation of alternatives and similarity of alternatives, $F(1, 56) = 5.15$, $p < 0.05$. Examination of the data in Table 8.6 indicates that the nature of this interaction is

Table 8.6

Means and standard deviations of number of correct responses on twenty trials as a function of time of presentation of alternatives, similarity of alternatives, and sex of subject

| | Time of Presentation of Alternatives | | | | | |
| | Before | | After | | Before and After | |
	M	SD	M	SD	M	SD
Males						
Similar	7.75	1.71	8.00	3.71	11.00	3.68
Dissimilar	13.75	3.34	16.25	1.64	15.12	2.87
			(15.12)*	(2.31)*		
Females						
Similar	7.50	2.69	4.75	1.98	9.00	3.12
Dissimilar	12.88	3.39	13.37	2.94	14.75	2.49
			(12.62)*	(4.23)*		

* These values are based on the data obtained before deviant subjects were replaced.

exactly as expected on the perceptual-selectivity hypothesis, viz., there is less difference in recognition accuracy due to the similarity of alternatives under the before-after conditions than under the after conditions.

Examination of Table 8.6 also indicates that recognition accuracy is lower in the before conditions than in the before-after conditions in all four possible comparisons. This supports the assumption that subjects in the before conditions had greater memory loads and/or less time to search for critical features.

Discussion

The major findings of the present experiment are: (a) Presentation of pictorial alternatives both before and after a test picture results in greater recognition accuracy than the presentation of alternatives only after the test picture, and (b) time of presentation of the alternatives interacts with the similarity of the alternatives in just the way that is predicted on the assumption of a mechanism of perceptual selectivity. Both of these results lend support to the notion that perception can be selectively directed by instructional information, and both stand in direct contradiction to the results of the Lawrence and Coles study. The major reason for this discrepancy in results was advanced in the introduction, viz., the conceptual information used to specify the alternatives in the Lawrence and Coles study (the verbal labels) was not sufficient to modify the perceptual recognition process. The results from the present before condi-

tions also suggest that any perceptual selectivity that might have been operative in the before conditions of the Lawrence and Coles study might have been
obscured by the increased memory requirements of this kind of condition.

Although an interpretation of the results of the present experiment in
terms of perceptual selectivity seemed quite justified, it was pointed out to
the authors that it is possible to account for these results solely in terms of
some well-established principles of short-term memory. Assume that perception of a test picture is uninfluenced by the presentation of alternatives. In
order to respond correctly, subjects must compare a memory trace of the test
picture with some or all of the four alternatives. It seems reasonable to think
that subjects would "like" to make these comparisons in an intelligent order;
specifically, it seems plausible to think that they would like to compare it with
the most likely alternative first. Note, however, that subjects in the after conditions cannot know which alternative is most likely because they do not get to
see the alternatives until after the test picture is flashed. But subjects in the
before-after conditions could make use of this strategy since they have at least
some knowledge of the alternatives and their positions, and thus could first
compare their memory trace of the test picture with the alternative that they
consider most likely to yield a match. If subjects in the before-after conditions
used this strategy successfully on some of the trials then on the average they
could reach a decision on the basis of fewer comparisons than their counter-
parts in the after conditions. Since each comparison involves the inspection
of an alternative, and since every inspected alternative is a potential source of
interference with the memory trace, fewer comparisons result in less interference. Therefore the before-after conditions should result in greater recognition
accuracy than the after conditions. Furthermore, the magnitude of interference
effects in short-term memory varies directly with the degree of similarity between the interfering events, so the similar conditions ought to result in lower
overall recognition accuracy than the dissimilar conditions. It is also possible
to predict the obtained interaction between similarity and time of presentation
of alternatives since similarity of alternatives has less opportunity to affect
accuracy differentially in the before-after conditions than in the after conditions, because the former require fewer comparisons with the potentially interfering alternatives. (Note that this argument assumes that paired-associate
learning of pictorial alternatives and their relative positions occurs during the
first, "before," segment of a trial in the before-after conditions, just as was
the case in the before conditions.)

As a test of the validity of the preceding argument an additional eight
males and eight females were run in a before-after condition with similar
alternatives that was modified in such a way that the alternatives were presented in different locations on their plaques before and after the test picture.
This change made it impossible for subjects to utilize knowledge of the positions of the alternatives and thus seek out first the alternative they felt was
most likely. In all other respects it was identical to the corresponding condition in the main experiment. The results: male mean, 11.35 correct; female
mean, 9.12 correct. A comparison of these figures with the corresponding ones
from Table 8.6 indicates that these subjects performed no worse in the modi-

fied situation than the original subjects performed in the unmodified task, and therefore that the proposed memory effect in the before-after conditions was probably unimportant. Furthermore, since this result indicates that subjects in the before-after conditions did *not* memorize and utilize the positions of the alternatives and since previously presented results indicate that subjects in the before condition *did* (and in fact had to) memorize these positions, the assumption that the before-after conditions are more sensitive to perceptual selectivity than the before conditions is further strengthened.

Further justification for omitting the before conditions from consideration because of the large memory component in that task is given by the results of a recent study by Steffy and Eriksen (1965). Either before or after the brief presentation of a test stimulus (a single nonsense form) a set of three alternative nonsense forms was presented, also very briefly. There was a variable delay of from 10 to 700 msec between the two presentations (the duration of the delay is the interval between the offset of one display and the onset of the other). Thus, except for the great difference in durations, this study bears an obvious formal similarity to the present one. Steffy and Eriksen found that presentation of the alternatives after the test stimulus resulted in higher recognition accuracy than presentation of the alternatives before the test stimulus. Equally important, as the interval between the two presentations increased from 10 to 700 msec, accuracy decreased in the conditions in which the set of alternatives was presented before the single test stimulus, but in the conditions in which the test stimulus appeared first, accuracy remained at a constant level. It was concluded that the set of three alternatives was harder to remember over the delay interval than the single test stimulus because of the greater interference engendered by the larger number of items (see, e.g., Melton, 1963). It seems reasonable to invoke the same principles to account for the superiority of the before-after conditions to the before conditions in the present study.

In light of the overall pattern of results presented above it was concluded that selective visual perception could indeed be demonstrated in the laboratory. These results seem to be consistent with those of Harris and Haber (1963) on the effects of various coding strategies on recognition accuracy for tachistoscopically presented stimuli. They found that subjects were capable of encoding the various aspects of a multidimensional stimulus roughly in the order of importance of those dimensions. Such behavior is clearly adaptive since the visual image resulting from a complex tachistoscopic presentation fades rapidly. Therefore, if the valuable dimensions are encoded (prepared for storage in memory) early, there is a greater probability that subsequent responses to them will be correct. The application of this general rationale to the present study is straightforward; subjects in the before-after conditions had an opportunity to determine which dimensions were likely to be effective for discriminating within a set of alternatives, and they also had the opportunity to use this knowledge in extracting information from the test picture. The subjects in the after conditions could not know what kind of information to extract first; they got what they could from the flash, but there was an excellent probability that, in the similar conditions, it would not be adequate for discrimination. Hence the interaction between similarity and time of presentation.

Summary

The present experiment is an attempt to localize the mechanism or mechanisms of selectivity through which recognition accuracy may be influenced by instructional sets. Sets of four stimuli (pictures) each were displayed before, after, or before and after the tachistoscopic presentation of a single critical picture. The subjects had to report which one of the four alternatives was used as the critical picture. The stimuli within each set of four alternatives were either highly similar to one another or distinctively different from one another. The results indicated that perceptual processes were capable of being selectively tuned. This result stands in contrast to previous research which indicated that recognition accuracy was influenced solely by memorial processes.

Editor's Note: Set and Stimulus Attributes

Knowledge about a particular object constitutes a set, which exerts influence on perception of that object. Under conditions of very low illumination, in which visual sensations are relayed via the rods, color sensations are not possible. Yet a front lawn, even at night, appears green. We are not responding to the color; rather, we assign the color on the basis of past experience. Green is one attribute of lawns. Although no sensory foundation exists for the sensation of green under conditions of low illumination, the set, which has assigned green as a characteristic of the lawn, allows us to perceive green.

The specific characteristic of an object or the attributes of the object dictate perception of the object. A blue lawn, for example, might not be recognized as a lawn. On the other hand, despite the actual blue color, we might perceive the lawn as green. Such modifications of perception have received experimental analysis in a variety of situations. Perhaps the best known of such studies was that conducted by Karl Duncker (1939), who presented to subjects the silhouette of a donkey and a leaf. Both objects were cut from the same green material, but were illuminated with a reddish color—the complementary color for green—so that the objects appeared as an achromatic gray. After viewing one of the two test objects, the subjects were shown a color mixer and asked to match the mixed color to the previously presented stimulus. The disc on the color mixer contained red and green, which, if mixed in the proper proportions, could produce the achromatic gray of the preceding stimuli. Upon instructions from the subject, the experimenter then made adjustments in the color mixer. After each adjustment, the experimenter recorded the proportion of red to green utilized in obtaining a mixture which the subject felt best matched the preceding stimulus. The major result was the tendency for subjects to use more green when matching the leaf than when matching the donkey; hence the interpretation that set—green as an attribute of leaves—influenced the subjects' perceptions of the leaf silhouette.

Several subsequent studies have confirmed the basic observation made by Duncker. A problem arose, however, in the interpretation of the results: Were the subjects actually matching their perception of the previous color or their memory of the color modified by their perceptual set? Did the set affect the perception of the leaf silhouette itself, or did the set modify the subject's memory of the previously viewed leaf? Robert Harper of Knox College designed an experiment which attempted to answer this question (*American Journal of Psychology*, 1953).

The Perceptual Modification of Colored Figures

Robert S. Harper

The past decade has seen a renewed interest in the study of perception, and some of the problems considered at the turn of the century are being attacked again. One of the problems of yesterday—formulated in the language of the time—was whether the elements that theoretically make up a percept are discernible in it. Today, in spite of attempts to avoid it, the same problem is posed by the results of experiments on the effects of motivation and past experience on perception. In a recent examination of some of these experiments, Pratt (1950) has concluded that there is no evidence for the direct influence of motivational and experiential variables on perception—that the reported relationships can be explained, in effect, in terms of response-generalization. Here is a significant question concerning the characteristics of the "mechanism" which intervenes between stimulus and response: although it may be avoided by an operational or behavioral logic, it is capable of experimental analysis.

In an experiment by Bruner, Postman, and Rodrigues (1951), each of a number of selected figures (physically equal in color) was matched with a differential color-mixer. Some of the figures (such as a lobster-claw or a lemon) had a characteristic red or yellow color, while others (such as geometric forms) had no characteristic color. The results indicated that more red was added to the mixture for characteristically red figures than for neutral figures, and that more yellow was added to the mixture for characteristically yellow figures than for neutral figures. Unfortunately, however, these results are ambiguous; they can be interpreted either in terms of perceptual modification or in terms of response-generalization. From Pratt's point of view it might be maintained that the observer responded to a particular red color on the mixer *as if* it were the same color as that of characteristically red figures and *as if* it were redder than a neutral figure.

In the present experiment, a more adequate method was employed. A figure was superimposed on a background the color of which was varied until the figure was no longer detectable. The criterion of "undetectability" makes it possible to distinguish between variation in perception and variation in response. If the observer is unable to detect a colored figure superimposed on a colored background, then the figure and ground are not merely being *responded* to as the same but are being *perceived* as the same. As in the experiment by Bruner, two classes of figures were used to study the effect of organizational factors in perception.

Procedure

Three pairs of stimulus-figures were made. One member of each pair was a "meaningful" figure (one with a characteristic color). The other member of each pair was a "nonmeaningful" figure (one with no characteristic color) which had the same area and the same general contour characteristics as did its meaningful correlate. The three meaningful figures, all of them characteristically red, were an apple, a heart, and a lobster. Their respective "nonmeaningful" correlates were an oval, an isosceles triangle, and the letter "Y." All six figures, cut from the same sheet of orange paper (a scrap of which was, for the experimenter, indistinguishable from a background composed of 45° red and 315° orange), were mounted on cardboard grounds attached to small wire hangers.

A reflecting differential color-mixer was used to vary the background color. The observer sat three feet in front of a 3 × 4 feet screen, in the center of which was a two-inch aperture completely filled with the reflected background color. A small semi-cylindrical holder was so fitted into this aperture that the cut-out figures could be suspended in the middle of the patch of variable colored background. A black-cardboard shield was attached to the front of the holder, and the two-inch opening in the shield was covered with a thin sheet of frosted plastic which blurred the sharp contours of the stimulus-figures. The apparatus was set up in a darkened room, with the figures being illuminated by an incandescent light placed above the holder, and with the variable colored background being illuminated by lights symmetrically placed to the left and right of the aperture. The two color-disks of the mixer were light orange and dark red, respectively.

Five observers, of varying degrees of psychological sophistication, were asked to tell the experimenter, as the experimenter continuously varied the background color, when the figure was no longer distinguishable from the background on which it was superposed. When the observers entered the experimental room, they were given the following instructions.

Instructions

"I am going to place some small figures in this opening, and then I will gradually change the color of the background. I want you to tell me when the figure can no longer be distinguished from the background—when it merges with the background."

The experimenter then placed, successively, each figure in the holder and, starting either from a background with 0° of red or from a background with 180° of red, made two determinations for each figure. Three observers were shown the three nonmeaningful figures first and then the meaningful ones. The other two observers were shown the meaningful figures first. The figures were concealed from the observer until they were in the holder. As the experimenter stepped back from inserting the figure, he said, if it was a meaningful figure, "There is a reddish apple" ("heart" or "lobster"); if it was a nonmeaningful figure, "There is a yellowish-orange oval" ("triangle" or "Y").

Varying the amount of red in the background not only changed the hue of the background, but, since the red was darker than the orange, it also changed the brightness of the ground. The presence of the shield in front of the holder for the stimulus-figures prevented absolutely uniform illumination on the figures, since the light source could not be placed perpendicular to them. The observers experienced some difficulty in getting a setting of the background which would make the whole figure, with its differential brightness at top and bottom, completely merge with the ground. When the observers reported this difficulty, the experimenter suggested that they attend to the upper central portion of the figure, since this was the area in which existed the defining characteristics of the figures.

Results

The observers reported the merging of the figure with the ground with a very confident "Gone," sometimes preceded by a tentative "Going, going. . . ." Two sophisticated observers were used to evaluate the criterion-effect. While they were fixated on a particular part of the figure, and without stopping to record their settings in order not to influence their fixation, the experimenter changed the amount of red in the background fairly rapidly. In as many as seven "passes" through the color-range, these two observers consistently reported the figure as "Gone" within a range of only 3°. These incidental observations simply serve as evidence that, perceptually, the figures truly disappeared, and that the results obtained were not due to some unknown artifact of the situation.

The results are given in Tables 8.7 and 8.8. Table 8.7 shows the two settings of each observer for each figure. Table 8.8 shows the average number of degrees of red that each observer added to the background to make the nonmeaningful figures and the meaningful figures merge with the background. The mean difference in the number of degrees of red required for the two sets of figures to become undetectable (63.56°), evaluated by t for paired scores, was highly significant ($t = 13.27$, $P < 0.001$). Since, in this situation, when the figure merges with the background, a reasonable assumption is that the observer experiences both the figure and the ground as the same color, the conclusion can be drawn that the two classes of figure were *perceived* as being of different colors.

Table 8.7

**Background color required for indistinguishability.
Degrees of red in the background-color required
by the observer to cause the figure to merge
with the background.**

Observer	Triangle	Heart	Oval	Apple	Letter "Y"	Lobster
M	31	121	6	153	124	158
	51	105	63	136	136	171
L	111	90	58	157	111	165
	66	105	81	161	117	156
C	84	123	30	129	117	170
	85	130	42	121	66	132
S	63	105	36	156	117	156
	45	110	15	137	91	153
H	57	75	33	144	117	157
	15	92	46	125	126	154

Table 8.8

**Background color required for indistinguishability
of each class of figures**

Observer	Nonmeaningful	Meaningful
M	68.50	140.67
L	90.67	139.00
C	70.67	134.17
S	61.17	136.17
H	65.67	124.50
Mean	71.34	134.90

$M_{diff.}$ 63.56; SE_D 4.79; t 13.27; $P < 0.001$.

Summary

In this experiment the effect of past experience on the perception of color was studied. The method employed was based on the assumption that if a colored figure is indistinguishable from a colored background, the two colored surfaces are perceived as identical and not merely "responded to" as identical. Significant perceptual changes were found.

CHAPTER 9

Temporal
Factors
of Perception

Another major concern in contemporary research of perception is temporal aspects. Starting in 1964, the Center for Visual Science at the University of Rochester in New York has conducted, for example, an international Symposium on Temporal Factors in Vision and Visual Perception, presenting research on the relationship between time and perceptual tendencies.

Time Dependencies

The perceptual process is, in fact, a true process. Perception is not a static event, but rather a continuing interaction of organism and environment over the dimension of time. The variable time is inevitably present in perceptual response patterns. A stimulus which does not vary in itself always varies in time. The physical aspects of a stimulus may not change over a period of five minutes; however, the perception of the stimulus may be quite different after five minutes, as opposed to ten seconds, of observation.

Another time variable relates the interval between successive stimulus presentations. If the interval between incoming sensory units is rather long, we perceive two distinct stimuli which are independent of each other. For example, if we were shown an equilateral triangle for five seconds, then a blank (no stimulus) for one minute, followed by an inverted equilateral triangle, the two figures would be seen independently of one another. If, on the other hand, the time interval separating the triangles was only 5 msec, we would probably report perceiving a single six-sided figure. In this case the two stimuli would be perceived as one. Somewhere between 5 msec and one minute there must be a threshold after which successive figures are perceived independently.

In the discussion on the phenomena of metacontrast (Chapter 3), Eriksen and Collins found that a second stimulus following or preceding a critical stimulus impaired the subject's recognition of the critical stimulus if the interval between the two stimuli was under 100 msec. Professor Eriksen has conducted a variety of experiments aimed at establishing the exact effect of the time interval between successive stimulations. The basic question is: How do we perceive successive stimulations separated by short durations?

In an earlier presentation, Eriksen and Hoffman (1963) attempted to ascertain the effects of an unrecognized stimulus upon the recognition of a subsequent stimulus as a function of the interval between stimulations. If the first stimulus is too weak to be perceived or to be recognized by the subject, will this stimulus have any effect upon a second stimulus presentation? If such an effect is observed, what is the effect of the time interval between stimuli? The experiment also adds a physiological variable to the design: the condition of light or dark adaptation of the eye at the time of stimulus presentation. Adaptation has proved to be relevant in many aspects of perception and has shown its importance in the present context.

As Eriksen and Hoffman point out in the following introduction (*Journal of Experimental Psychology*, 1963), this question relates to another area of research, namely, subliminal perception. If the subject is not aware of the presentation of the first stimulus, yet his perceptual response is affected by it, we would have a demonstration of subliminal perception—a stimulus-induced modification of perception which the subject does not consciously perceive.

Form Recognition at Brief Durations as a Function of Adapting Field and Interval between Stimulations

Charles W. Eriksen and Melvin Hoffman

The research reported below is concerned with two distinct but nevertheless interrelated problems in visual perception. The first pertains to whether or not a low-intensity undetected stimulation leaves any residual effects upon the organism as assessed by changes in subsequent behavior or more specifically changes in the probability of recognition of the signal on reoccurrences. The possibility of such an effect is analogous to the concept of incremental strengthening of responses in learning. The second problem concerns the duration of the time interval (lag) between successive presentations of a weak signal in order for the recognitions of the signal to be independent of one another.

Clinical and personality psychologists have been concerned with the first of these problems in attempting to substantiate their concepts of the unconscious. Experiments such as those of Shevrin and Luborsky (1958), Hilgard (1962), Klein, Spence, Holt, and Gourevitch (1958), and Goldstein and Barthol (1960), have attempted to show that stimulation that is unreported by the human subject is nonetheless capable of changing or influencing subsequent behavior. As has been pointed out elsewhere (Eriksen, 1960, 1962; Johnson and Eriksen, 1961) these experiments in general have been too poorly controlled to shed much light on the basic question. They have, however, been valuable in pointing up gaps in our knowledge concerning basic perceptual functioning.

The threshold or detection function for various signals typically shows a range of signal intensity where the subject's detection or recognition is above chance accuracy but below 100 percent. At this signal-intensity level does an unrecognized signal leave the perceptual system in the same state as though the signal had not occurred; or are there residual effects in the system that would be revealed in terms of changed probabilities for recognition of a second signal occurring within defined lag times? One possible effect might be that of summation.

A possible mechanism for such summation to occur is suggested by the recent work of Sperling (1960), and Averbach and Coriell (1961). These investigators have found evidence of a perceptual storage in the visual system that seems to have a duration in the neighborhood of 250 msec. If the lag time between successive stimulations is within this value, it is possible that this raw memory process could be reinforced or strengthened.

The signal detection theory of perceptual judgments (Egan, Greenberg, and Shulman, 1961) is relevant to the second problem of this investigation.

This model dispenses with the concept of the threshold and considers detection essentially as a situation where the subject must discriminate the signal from the general noise background that exists within the sensory perceptual system itself. Thus a subject's failure to detect a signal is assumed to be due to the masking of the signal at that moment in time by noise within the perceptual system. If such noise exists in the perceptual system, it is assumed to be variable in intensity and must have a distribution in time. By systematically varying the lag interval between two presentations of a signal it should be possible to obtain a rough mapping of the distribution of this noise envelope. There should be some lag interval beyond which the noise magnitude present on the occurrence of the first signal is uncorrelated with the noise level present at the time of the second signal.

The problem of the independence of successive perceptual judgments is not a new one in psychology. Numerous investigators, e.g., Senders and Sowards (1952), Verplanck, Collier, and Cotton (1952), McGill (1957), and Day (1956), have shown that successive or serial perceptual judgments have a high degree of interdependence. However, these studies have not been successful in showing to what degree these interdependencies of successive responses are due to characteristics of the perceptual process itself as opposed to response effects.

Method

Experiment I

Subjects. Five practiced subjects, one female, were used in Experiment I. Each gave an equal number of judgments under all combinations of experimental treatments and conditions.

Procedure. The forms used were the capital letters A, T, and U. Preliminary work had shown that these letters had approximately equal recognizability at brief exposure durations and were approximately equal in confusability, one with another. The experimental procedure made use of a three-field tachistoscope, an adapting field, and two stimulus-exposure fields. The adapting field was used to vary the pre- and postadaptation brightness and the forms were presented in Fields I and II, the exposure fields. In addition to permitting precise control of the duration of exposures in Fields I and II, the apparatus also allowed precise control of the interval between termination of stimulation in Field I and onset of stimulation in Field II.

Three kinds of stimulus presentation were used: (a) a form presented in Field I followed by light alone in Field II; (b) a form presented in Field II preceded by light alone in Field I; (c) same form presented in Fields I and II. Intervals or lag times between termination of Field I and onset of Field II of 0, 5, 250, and 450 msec were studied.

In addition, two other variables were manipulated. Recognition for single and double presentations at each of the lag times was studied using a dark pre- and postadaptation field with only a faintly glowing fixation point as well as with a relatively bright pre- and postadaptation field. Also the effect of leaving the adapting field on during the stimulus presentations in Fields I and II and during the lag period was compared with the condition where the adapting field went off with the onset of the first field and remained off until the termination of Field II.

Thus, in summary, the three methods of form presentation (Field I, Field II, and double stimulation) at each of the four lag times were studied under four conditions. The conditions were: Condition A, adaptation field dark with dimly luminous fixation point that terminated with onset of Field I and returned with termination of Field II; Condition B, adaptation field dark but luminous fixation point remained on during presentation of Fields I and II and during the lag interval between them; Condition C, adaptation field bright but terminated with onset of Field I and returned with termination of Field II; Condition D, bright adaptation field that remained on during presentation of Fields I and II and during the lag time between fields. Table 9.1 diagrams the events and their time relations for a single trial under each of these four conditions.

In Experiment I each subject sat for twenty forty-minute sessions. With the exception of the first, sixth, eleventh, and sixteenth sessions each of the three forms was presented six times under each of the three methods of stimulus presentation and at each of the four lag times. Four successive sessions were devoted to judgments under each of the four conditions and within each session the three methods of presentation and four lag times were counterbalanced. The order in which the different conditions were judged was counterbalanced on the first four subjects. The fifth subject followed a different condition order than obtained for the first four subjects.

The first, sixth, eleventh, and sixteenth sessions initiated a new condition for each subject and these sessions were devoted to obtaining a function showing the subject's recognition accuracy as a function of duration of exposure under the conditions of pre- and postadaptation field obtaining for that particular condition. The stimulation sequence was adaptation field (light or dark depending upon the condition), exposure of one of the three forms, and then return to the adapting field. The three forms were presented randomly and the duration of exposure was varied systematically to obtain a range of recognition varying from chance (33⅓ percent) to approximately 90 percent. The subject was required to make a judgment of A, T, or U following each stimulation sequence. To insure comparability of the two exposure fields in the T-scope, half of the presentations occurred in Field I and half in Field II in a counterbalanced order. On the basis of the data obtained from these base rate determinations a level of duration was selected for stimulus exposure in Fields I and II for that condition and for the individual subject that yielded recognition of approximately 50 percent. The duration levels remained constant for this particular subject for all judgments made under that particular condition. Due to the differences in pre- and postadapting fields, the duration

Table 9.1

Events occurring in the adapting and the two stimulus exposure fields and their relative chronological relationships during a single trial under each of the four conditions

Condition	Fields	
		Fixation Point ← Off →
	Adapting	Dark
A	I	Off on ⎍
	II	Off on ⎍
	Adapting	Dark Fixation Point Remains On
B	I	Off on ⎍
	II	Off on ⎍
	Adapting	Light Dark
C	I	Off on ⎍
	II	Off on ⎍
	Adapting	Light
D	I	Off on ⎍
	II	Off on ⎍
		Lag (Variable) Time →

of exposure in the stimulus fields necessary to obtain 50 percent recognition accuracy in each of the four conditions varied markedly. The respective durations in milliseconds for Conditions A, B, C, and D averaged through the subjects were: 14, 14.4, 46, and 61.4.

Following the base-rate determination, the four experimental sessions for the condition were preceded by a seven-minute period of visual adaptation to the experimental situation during which time the subject made practice judgments before undertaking the experimental judgments.

The subject was instructed that he was participating in a study of form perception or recognition. He was told that on each trial one of three letters A, T, or U would be presented and that the letter would occur sometimes in the flash of the first field, sometimes in the flash of the second field, and that on some trials the same letter would occur in both fields. He was further informed that these methods of presentation would vary randomly and also that the interval between flashes would vary. It was stressed that on those trials where a letter appeared in both fields it would always be the same letter in both of the fields.

Judgments were obtained in the following manner. After the experimenter had arranged for the particular method of stimulus presentation to be used on that trial and set the lag time, he presented a ready signal to the subject. The subject then fixated the fixation point and when the cross was clear and sharp, indicating his eyes were accommodated to the proper plane, he pressed a thumb switch which presented the sequence of stimulation. The subject was required always to make a forced-choice response as to which of the three letters had been presented. He also was required to make a judgment as to whether the form had been presented in only one or in both of the exposure fields. The interjudgmental interval was approximately fifteen seconds, determined by the time required for the experimenter to change lag times and methods of stimulus presentation.

The exposure fields always had a brightness level of 0.201 apparent foot-candle as determined by a MacBeth illuminometer. Under the bright adaptation conditions (C and D) the adaptation field had a brightness of 0.582 apparent footcandle. For the two conditions involving a dark adaptation field the brightness level was too low to be measured. The fixation point for these conditions was obtained by painting a sheet of cardboard flat black and then carefully cutting a cross through the cardboard. This in turn was then back-lighted by a ten-watt incandescent bulb. The cross used as a fixation point for all conditions subtended twelve minutes of visual angle. The letters A, T, and U were obtained from printed sheets of paper and also subtended twelve minutes of angle. To prevent possible retinal summation or metacontrast masking effects (Averbach and Coriell, 1961) care was taken to insure that the forms did not fall on retinal areas immediately adjacent to the fixation stimulus. This was arranged by presenting the form on the points of an imaginary square of 1.25° of angle centered on the fixation point. Thus a form stimulus could occur in any one of these four possible positions determined on a random basis with the restriction that for double stimulation the same position would not occur for both presentations.

Apparatus. The three-field tachistoscope was built to special order by Merle Ridgely and Company. Two four-watt fluorescent tubes were used in each of the exposure fields which provided square onset of illumination although a somewhat tapered decay. During experimentation the timing section of the T-scope was periodically checked for calibration by means of photocells and a Hunter Klockounter.® Duration settings throughout the range employed in this experiment were found to be exceedingly stable and to have less than a 5 percent maximum error. Due to limitations in the timing equipment the return to the adapting field illumination following termination of the flash in Field II was delayed in the order of 250–300 msec. The three forms were each mounted on plastic cards off-white in color. The size of the exposure fields and the adaptation field was a square subtending 7.6° of angle on each dimension.

Experiment II

Subjects. Twelve undergraduate students at the University of Illinois, five females, were used in this study. All were experimentally naive with respect to perceptual experiments but before undertaking the present experiment they were given two practice sessions during which they made judgments of tachistoscopically exposed stimuli.

Procedure. The procedure and method in this experiment were identical to that of Experiment I except for the statistical design. Here three different subjects were assigned to each of the four conditions. Within a condition each of the three subjects had twenty-four presentations of each of the three forms under each of the three methods of presentation for each of the four lag times. The durations of exposures in milliseconds in the stimulus fields necessary to obtain fifty percent recognition under Conditions A, B, C, and D were, respectively: 18.8, 18.3, 40, and 76.

Results

In both Experiments I and II the number of correct recognitions was summed through the three forms and through sessions. In Experiment I these recognition scores were analyzed by a four-way classification analysis of variance (method of presentation, lag time, condition, and subjects). The summary of this analysis is given in Table 9.2. For Experiment II, where a different statistical design was employed, the recognition scores were analyzed by a modified four-way classification analysis of variance. The summary of this analysis is contained in Table 9.3.

In both experiments the main effects of lag times and method of form presentation (fields) are significant ($p < 0.05$). Further, conditions is a significant effect in Experiment I although failing to achieve significance in Experiment II. This discrepancy was anticipated due to the difference in statistical design between the two experiments. In Experiment I the same five subjects

Table 9.2

**Summary of analysis of variance
of recognition: Experiment I**

Source	MS	F
Lag times (L)	117.2	20.21*
Fields (F)	130.2	22.44*
Conditions (C)	48.7	8.40*
Individuals (I)	63.1	10.88*
L × F	8.1	1.40
L × C	21.4	3.69*
L × I	9.5	1.64
F × C	59.3	10.22*
F × I	6.3	1.09
C × I	18.1	3.12*
L × F × C	9.1	1.57
L × F × I	4.2	< 1.00
L × C × I	9.2	1.59
F × C × I	6.6	1.14
Error	5.8	

* $p < 0.05$.

Table 9.3

**Summary of analysis of variance
of recognitions: Experiment II**

Source	MS	F
Lag times (L)	113.4	9.56*
Fields (F)	100.5	7.89*
Conditions (C)	64.9	1.79
Individuals (I)	36.2	7.67*
L × F	9.6	2.03
L × C	15.9	1.34
F × C	30.6	2.40
L × F × C	7.3	1.55
Error 1	11.86	
Error 2	12.74	
Error 3	4.72	

* $p < 0.05$.

gave data under all four conditions whereas three different subjects were employed for each of the four conditions in Experiment II, thus making this second experiment less sensitive for testing condition effects.

In the first experiment the second-order interactions of Lags × Condition and Method of Stimulation (fields) × Condition are significant. In Experiment II neither of these interactions reaches significance although, as will be seen in Figure 9.1, the relationships between these variables are nearly identical in both experiments. There is a suggestion ($p < 0.10$) in both experiments of an interaction of Lags × Method of Stimulation × Conditions.

The nature of the results can be seen more clearly in Figure 9.1. Here, number of correct recognitions has been plotted as a function of method of stimulation and lag time by condition for each of the two experiments. Percent correct recognitions obtained at the base-rate level are plotted for purposes of comparison. The suggestion of a triple interaction in statistical analyses taken in conjunction with the very marked similarity of the functions from the two experiments indicates that interpretation of the effects of method of stimulation and of lag time is best made separately for the four conditions.

The effect of lag times and method of stimulation appears quite similar for both Conditions A and B. Under both conditions and in both experiments there is a definite tendency for recognition to improve irrespective of the method of stimulation as lag time increases from 0 to 450 msec. There is also a slight tendency for the double method of presentation to be slightly superior to that obtained for a single presentation in either field. However this superiority is not marked. In Condition C there is again a marked tendency for increasing lag times to result in increased recognition of forms presented twice (double stimulation) and with forms presented in Field II, but here there is a discrepancy for Field I. Increasing lag time does not improve recognition of forms appearing in Field I.

Condition D is the most discrepant of the four conditions. Here none of the three methods of stimulation show increasing recognition as a function of increasing lag time. However for both Conditions C and D there is again a slight tendency for the double stimulation to be slightly superior.

In addition to requiring a forced choice as to which of the three forms had been presented on each trial subjects were required to make a judgment as to whether the presentation had been a single form stimulation or a double presentation of the form, i.e., once in each of the two exposure fields. To determine whether subjects were capable of making reliable discriminations as to single and double stimulation the number of single judgments to each of the three methods of presentation was averaged through forms and sessions and analyzed by a four-way classification analysis of variance (lags, methods of stimulation, conditions, and subjects) for Experiment I and a modified four-way classification for Experiment II.

In Experiment I all four main effects are significant ($p < 0.01$). In Experiment II similar results are obtained except the main effect due to conditions is not significant as might be anticipated due to the lack of sensitivity of this particular design for testing condition effects. The individual difference is appreciably larger on these judgments as also might be anticipated since no

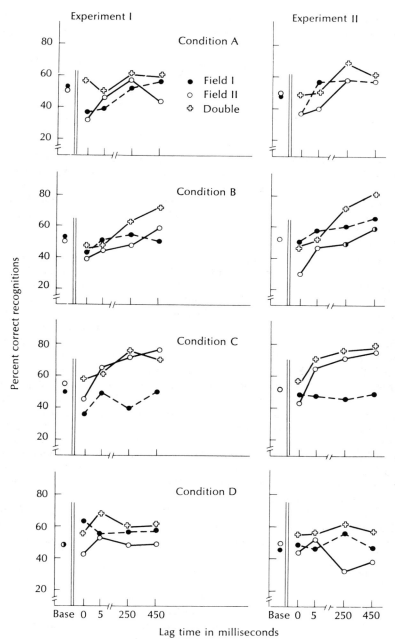

Figure 9.1: Percentage of correct form recognitions as a function of method of presentation, time lag between fields, and adapting brightness condition.

attempt was made to equate subjects on this variable by adjusting exposure levels beforehand as was done for recognition accuracy. The subjects would be expected to vary in terms of the subjective criteria they adopt for making a judgment of double. This is reflected not only in a significant subject main effect but in the Subject × Experimental Variable interactions. In addition to the subject interactions in Experiment I the second-order interactions among the three experimental variables are all significant. In the second experiment only the Lag × Condition interaction obtains statistical reliability.

In Figure 9.2 the data are again presented by condition for each of the two experiments showing number of single judgments as a function of the three methods of stimulation and the four lag times. Inspection of Figure 9.2 reveals that in both experiments under all four conditions subjects were capable of making discriminations between a single and a double stimulation as shown by the fact that the number of single judgments to the double stimulation decreases with increasing lag times whereas the number of single judgments to a single stimulation in either Field I or Field II remains relatively constant and at an appreciably higher level.

Again the data for Conditions A and B are quite similar. In both conditions as well as in both experiments discrimination between a single and a double stimulation is quite poor at 0- and 5-msec lag times. Considering the results across both experiments it would also appear that even at the 0 lag between stimulations subjects under Conditions C and D were able to discriminate on some trials between single and double presentations but were unable to do so under the A and B conditions. This finding is perhaps related to the superiority of the light-adapted eye to detecting flicker and to Weyer's (1899) finding that the light-adapted eye can discriminate single from double light flashes with less time separation between flashes than the dark-adapted eye.

Further data analyses were performed to determine the degree of dependence between the two judgments required of subject and to determine whether there was a correlation between accuracy of single and double judgments and identification of the form. For the first of these analyses fourfold chi squares were computed for single-double judgments versus correct-incorrect identification of the form. These chi squares were computed for individual subjects under each lag and condition. The resulting chi squares were then summed through subjects by lag and condition using the Fisher-Pearson test (Gordon, Loveland, and Cureton, 1952) and taking direction of relationship into account. The results of this analysis showed no significant nor appreciable tendency for subject's same-difference judgments to be correlated with accuracy of form identification.

A similar chi-square analysis was undertaken to determine whether *accuracy* in same-difference judgment was correlated with accuracy in form identification. Here two of the sixteen chi-square values were significant beyond the 0.05 level for Experiment I and three for Experiment II. Considering that the significant chi squares did not cluster in particular lags and conditions within and across experiments and also considering the number of repeated comparisons that were made, these five significant relationships would appear to be within chance expectancy. Accordingly we can conclude there is no evidence

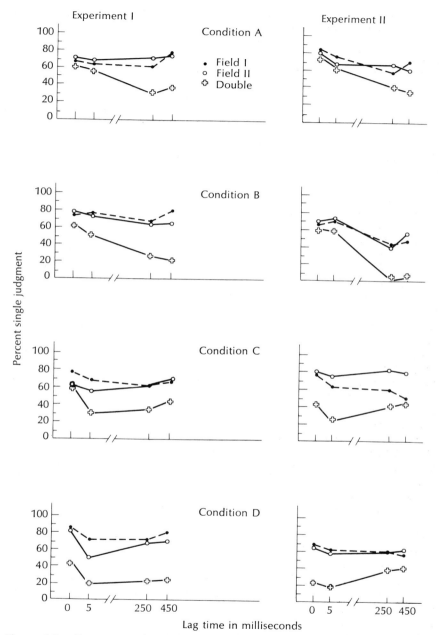

Figure 9.2: Percentage of judgments of "single" as a function of method of stimulation, time lag between fields, and adapting brightness condition.

Table 9.4

Recognition errors in Experiment I to the three forms under single and double presentations

| Responses | Single Presentation | | Double Presentation | | Total |
	Errors	Percent	Errors	Percent	Errors
Form A					
T	482	53.7	123	49.8	605
U	416	46.3	124	50.2	540
Total	898		247		1145
Form T					
A	422	51.8	119	49.0	541
U	392	48.2	124	51.0	516
Total	814		243		1057
Form U					
A	484	50.8	161	56.5	645
T	468	49.2	124	43.5	592
Total	952		285		1237

that the accuracy of a single-double judgment to a presentation is related to the subject's recognition accuracy on that presentation.

The question can be raised as to whether the subjects judged the double stimulus presentation with the same subjective criteria for A, T, or U responses as they used for single stimulus presentations. At least a partial answer to this question can be provided by examining the distribution of errors to the A, T, and U stimuli presented under both methods of presentation. If the subjects were responding to the two methods of presentation as similar or identical judgmental tasks and were employing the same criteria for A, T, or U responses, then the distribution of errors should be proportional for the two methods.

The errors made in judging each of the three forms, summed through fields, lags, and conditions for Experiment I subjects, are shown in Table 9.4. Inspection of these data shows that incorrect recognitions or errors are distributed virtually the same for single and double stimulations.

Discussion

Before considering the effects of double stimulation, the differences in form recognition for stimuli presented only in Field I or Field II as a function of lag time and adapting field should be considered. An explanation for these differences may be found in figure-ground contrast and brightness summation. Contrast between form and ground is an important variable in recognizability. Its importance in the present experiment can be seen in the duration of exposures required for 50 percent recognition under Conditions A and B as opposed to Condition D. Under the former conditions approximately 14 msec were required while under the D condition approximately 60–70 msec were necessary for the same recognizability level. In Conditions A and B the adaptation field was dark and the form was presented in the flash of either Field I or Field II. However in Condition D the adaptation field was bright and exposures of the form in Field I or II were superimposed upon the illumination of the adapting field. Thus the illumination of the adapting field added equal increments to the light and dark sections of the stimulus which reduced figure-ground contrast. The differences in exposure required for a given level of recognizability between these conditions cannot be explained in terms of light adaptation since Condition C employed the same adapting field as the D condition but here the stimulus exposures were not superimposed upon the illumination of the adapting field. Nonetheless Condition C required appreciably shorter durations for 50 percent recognizability (40 msec).

The differences in form recognizability can be explained in terms of contrast differences if we consider the phenomenon of brightness summation. Clark and Blackwell (1959) have shown that two pulses of light show at least partial summation in terms of a detection criterion if one pulse follows the other within an interval of approximately 65 msec or less for a light-adapted eye and 85 msec or less for a dark-adapted eye, the amount of summation being inversely proportional to the lag time. From their findings we would expect at least partial brightness summation to occur in the present study whenever two light fields are separated by lag intervals of less than 80 msec. Specifically these cases would be: (a) in Conditions A and B when Fields I and II are separated by lags of 0 and 5 msec; (b) in Condition C for Field I under all lag conditions and for Field II at lag times of 0 and 5 msec; and (c) in Condition D for both fields under all lag times (see Table 9.1).

The effectiveness of a contrast brightness–summation explanation can be seen if the data in Figure 9.1 are examined. Consider first Conditions A and B. Here the base-rate recognition levels for each field were determined separately by presenting the dark adaptation field followed by a flash containing the form and then a return to the dark adaptation field. Using these base-rate values as a point of comparison it is noted that in both experiments recognizability in Field I and in Field II tends to be depressed below the base value at lag times of 0 and 5 msec. This is what would be expected since experimental stimulus presentations at these two lag times should result in brightness summation between Field I and Field II with a reduction in figure-ground contrast due to the fact that whichever of the two fields contains the stimulus, the flash of the other field, through this brightness summation, adds equal increments to both the light and dark areas of the following or preceding stimulus-containing field. However at lag times of 250 and 450 msec recognizability in the two fields has improved at least to the point of the base-rate levels. This is again consistent with the explanation assuming that summation does not occur at these longer lag times. It is to be noted that a bidirectional brightness summation is assumed so that the contrast would be reduced in Field II if it was immediately preceded by a flash in Field I and similarly, contrast in Field I would be reduced if followed by a flash in Field II at the shorter lag times.

In Condition C the base-rate values were obtained by the use of a bright adaptation field followed at 0 lag by exposure of the stimulus in either Field I or II and approximately 250 msec later a return to the bright adapting field. Thus the base-rate values contain the circumstances necessary for brightness summation, namely between the adapting field and the exposure field. Recognizability of forms presented in Field I at 0- and 5-msec lag should under this condition be expected to be close to the base rate or perhaps slightly depressed due to the flash in the second field which would provide an opportunity for brightness summation to occur at both ends of Field I presentation. Field II would also be expected to give essentially base-rate level at 0- and 5-msec lag since again the summation would be occurring from the flash in Field I that preceded a presentation of a form in Field II. However, at the longer lag intervals recognizability for Field II presentations should improve relative to the base-rate level whereas for Field I they should tend to remain constant since Field I is always immediately preceded by the bright adapting field.

In Condition D the results again are quite consistent with our explanation. Here the base-rate level was obtained by superimposing a stimulus exposure upon the bright illumination of the adapting field. Irrespective of lag times in the experimental judgments, conditions existed for brightness summation in whichever field the form was presented. Even at 450-msec lag, presentation of a form in Field II is equivalent to the presentation of a form in Field I under Condition C and the base-rate situation for Condition D. As a consequence, no improvement over the base-rate levels in recognizability would be expected as a function of lag time.

The results in Figure 9.1 fit quite well with the contrast brightness–summation explanation. Minor discrepancies such as a tendency for recognizability to rise somewhat above the base-rate level at longer lag times in Conditions A and B and not to show appreciable reduction below base levels at the 0- and 5-msec lag times would seem to be attributable to practice effects. The experimental judgments were always made following the base-rate session so that the subjects had opportunity to become more proficient at perceptual recognition under the particular viewing conditions. Also it is to be remembered that due to limitations in the timing equipment the return of the adapting field in Condition C following the flash in Field II was delayed in the order of 250–300 msec. This time delay is consistent with the findings that there would be no brightness summation effects due to the return of the adapting field for stimulation presented in Field II at the longer lag times.

Another possible explanation for the above-discussed effects might be found in terms of dark adaptation which would be expected to yield better recognition. However, a dark adaptation explanation is contradicted by several findings in the data. Dark adaptation would have to work in reverse in order to explain the gain in form recognizability in Field I stimulations under

Conditions A and B. Also in the A, B, and C conditions 5 msec of lag or dark time gives an appreciable increase to recognizability of forms in Field II and it seems questionable whether enough dark adaptation could occur in 5 msec to account for this large increase in recognizability.

Another possible explanation might be advanced in terms of subjects blinking to the flashing light in Field I. If the flash of light in Field I caused occasional blinks in subjects, this would be expected to effect the recognizability of forms presented in Field II when the lag time corresponded with the latency of the blink. However, an explanation along these lines would be unable to explain why there is a gain in recognizability of forms presented in Field I under the A and B conditions and also the latency for the blink would have to be in the order of approximately 14 msec in these conditions and approximately 50 msec in Condition C to appreciably effect the results.

Another finding of interest in the Figure 9.1 data is the apparent ability of an event to act backward in time and effect the recognizability for forms that preceded. In Conditions A and B the flash of light from Field II following within 5 msec of a form presented in Field I impairs recognition of the form. Since this form had been presented for approximately 14 msec in Field I with full contrast before any brightness summation could be present, this would imply that the 14-msec period was insufficient for consolidation of perception to occur. It further implies that the recognition level achieved during the base-rate level assessments under these conditions was achieved not in the approximately 14 msec exposure of the form but actually occupied part of the dark period following the exposure. (Concern with this problem dates back to Wundt's laboratory, and Sperling, 1960, has provided a recent review of this older literature.) This effect is quite similar to the metacontrast phenomena that have been reported by various investigators (Alpern, 1952; Toch, 1956; Werner, 1935) and some of the metacontrast phenomena might well reduce to the effects of figure-ground contrast and brightness summation that seem to be involved in our results.

The recognizability of forms presented with the double stimulation as opposed to a single stimulation in either field was found to be slightly but consistently superior at most lag times. This can be seen most readily in Figure 9.3 where we have presented separately for the two experiments the percent correct recognitions for forms presented in Field I, in Field II, and for double presentation as a function of lag time. The data points have been summed through forms, subjects, and conditions in order to obtain the most stable values. The interpretation of these gains in recognizability with double presentation must consider that the subject had two opportunities to correctly perceive the form. If we wish to raise the question whether an incorrectly recognized stimulus has some residual effects in the nervous system as manifested in the recognition behavior for a subsequent presentation of the stimulus, in other words a summative or perhaps inhibitory effect, then we need to know the level of recognition that would be expected if the two opportunities were independent perceptual events. Similarly the question of how long a time duration is necessary between two stimulations in order for error in the perceptual system to be uncorrelated requires an estimate of what the recognizability level should be for a double stimulus presentation if the two events are indeed independent. The lag time at which the empirical level reaches the level for independence would then indicate the lag time necessary for non-correlated error.

A computation of the recognition level to be expected under the case of independent perceptual events poses a number of difficulties. Clark and Blackwell (1959) employed a standard formula for statistical independence which applied to the present situation would yield:

$$P_D = P_{F1} + P_{F2} - (P_{F1} \cdot P_{F2})$$

where P_D is the proportion of correct recognitions for the double presentations and P_{F1} and P_{F2} are the observed proportion of correct recognitions for stimulation in Fields I and II, respectively. To use this formula for the present data would require making three important assumptions concerning the perceptual recognition process. First it would be necessary to assume that there are no guess trials; second that the subject uses the same criteria for double as opposed to single stimulus presentations; and third that when the subject has an incorrect and a correct perception as a result of the double stimulation and is allowed only one response he always decides in favor of the correct perception.

The first two assumptions are not too implausible. The concepts from the theory of signal detection as applied to psychophysics by Egan, Greenberg, and Shulman (1961) and Swets, Tanner, and Birdsall (1961) are consistent with the assumption that there are no pure guess trials. Similarly the data presented in Table 9.4 support the assumption that the subjects employed the same criteria for responses or judgments under the double and the single presentations. The third assumption that the subject can always correctly discriminate between the choice of a correct and an incorrect perception on the double presentation however seems much less tenable.

In Figure 9.3 the upper curve represents the level of recognizability that would be predicted for double presentations employing the formula for statistical independence. While the use of this formula for predicting the case of independence is greatly restricted by the third assumption discussed above, the curve nonetheless provides an anchor point for evaluating the empirically determined level of performance.

The curves in Figure 9.3 do show that double stimulation results in proportionately greater recognizability relative to single stimulation in either field as lag time increases. There is a suggestion that an asymptote is reached or approached at the 250–450 msec level but further experimentation with longer lag times would be needed to substantiate this. The relatively smaller gain in recognizability for the double stimulations at the 0- and 5-msec lag may be due either to the correlation of perceptual system noise on the two presentations or may be due to some interfering effect of one stimulation upon the recognizability of the other. Research on the concept of a psychological refractory period has led some experimenters to speculate that a finite time

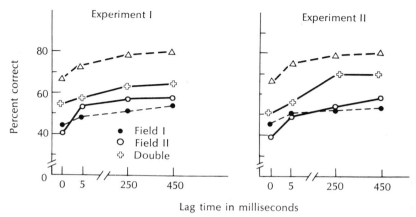

Figure 9.3: Percentage of correct form recognitions for single and for double stimulations.

is required by the perceptual system to code or process a stimulation or signal. If a second signal should arrive during this processing time it is either degraded or ineffective. If such an effect does exist, it could explain the results of the present experiment but Clark and Blackwell's (1959) data on the detection function for double presentations of flashes of light would suggest that the concept was limited to the recognition as opposed to the detection situation.

Summary

Two experiments explored the questions as to whether an unrecognized stimulation has an effect upon the recognition of a subsequent stimulation and the duration of the time interval between successive presentations of a weak stimulus in order for the recognitions of the stimulus to be independent of one another. By means of a three-field tachistoscope the recognition for a form presented twice where the interval between presentations was 0, 5, 250, or 450 msec was compared with recognition for a single exposure of the form at the same duration. Four conditions involving variation of the brightness of adapting field and of the interval between form presentations were investigated. In Experiment I, five practiced subjects made judgments under all conditions. In Experiment II, twelve subjects were assigned, three to each condition. Recognizability was found to be a complex function of whether a form was followed or preceded by a flash of light, the lag time between stimulations and the brightness of the adapting field. The results were explained in terms of brightness summation that resulted in reduced figure-ground contrast for the form. Double presentation was slightly superior to single presentations, the amount of gain being a negatively accelerated function of lag time between the two presentations.

Editor's Note: Perceptual Memory

When we consider memory, we think primarily of some form of verbal memory. We remember names, places, and general information in terms of verbal units or cues. We also have and utilize a perceptual memory, which records information about perceptual events. In reality it is most difficult to separate perceptual and verbal memory; usually both are storing information for future reference.

Let us consider first, the memory for physical shapes and objects. We find it much easier to remember the shape of a hexagon, for example, than the shape of an irregular six-sided figure such as this:

One reason for this is that we remember the perfect hexagon through utilizing both perceptual and verbal memory systems. The irregular figure has no verbal cue and must be recalled from perceptual memory alone. A second factor is the frequency of presentation, or experience, with the figures involved. Obviously we encounter hexagons more frequently than irregular six-sided figures.

In order to study verbal or perceptual memory independently of each other and of previous experiences specific stimulus materials must be devised. In 1885 Ebbinghaus attempted to introduce such a unit, the nonsense syllable. One procedure is to show a list of nonsense syllables to a group of subjects, who, in turn, are divided into subgroups and each group is tested for retention of the nonsense syllables after a given period of time (thirty seconds, sixty seconds, ten minutes, twenty-four hours). In the method of retention testing known as *recognition*, subjects are asked to select the originally viewed syllables from a larger list containing, in addition to the original syllables, a great number of syllables not appearing in the original list. Typically such studies have revealed that the subject can recognize about 70 percent of the syllables after a period of forty-eight hours (Luh, 1922). Obviously, the recognition method involves both verbal, as well as perceptual, memory. If the subjects are asked, for example, to recall the nonsense syllables of the original list rather than to recognize them, they are able to recall only about 20 percent after forty-eight hours.

A variety of similar procedures have been devised to study perceptual memory. Early studies often confused verbal and perceptual memory mechanisms by presenting the subject with visual items which had verbal names. For example, the subject viewed a complex picture and was asked to recall the items depicted after different periods of time. In other studies the subjects were asked to reproduce (to draw) nonsense forms and the degree of accuracy with which they reproduced the original form was taken as an indicator of perceptual memory. Individual drawing abilities detracted from the objectivity of the obtained retention curves.

More recent research has utilized a recognition method in which subjects are shown nonsense forms for brief periods, then, after varying periods of delay, are asked to select them from a group of alternatives.

Some of the problems involved in such research appear to be the same for verbal and for perceptual memory. One major problem involves the degree of similarity of the alternative nonsense figures or syllables. It would be more difficult to recall which of the syllables (QIX, QAX, QYX) was on the original list, than to recognize the critical syllable from less similar alternatives such as (LIN, QAX, PYZ). In the case of nonsense forms, degree of similarity of the alternatives is a critical factor in the number of forms that will be recognized after a given delay interval.

In an additional study by Professor C. W. Eriksen at the University of Illinois (*Journal of Experimental Psychology*, 1967), the delay intervals were much shorter than the forty-eight hours utilized in the verbal memory study. Perceptual memory, under the conditions of Eriksen's experiment, is observed after intervals less than 1,000 msec.

Selective Attention and Very Short-Term Recognition Memory for Nonsense Forms

Charles W. Eriksen and Joseph S. Lappin

The concept of attention arises primarily from the need to account for the selective capacity of humans and lower animals as well to respond to certain stimuli and effectively ignore others that appear equally potent on physical and time dimensions. The present study is addressed to three questions about the operation of visual attention. (a) To what extent do the effects of attention depend upon foveal fixation, can selective attentional effects be found when both attended and nonattended stimuli are on equally sensitive foveal areas? (b) Is the differential memory for attended and nonattended stimuli attributable to events or processes occurring at or shortly after the stimulation event or to differential rehearsal or processing following the stimulation? (c) A somewhat related question has to do with how long it takes for the selective attentional process to act upon stimulations.

Results from a previous experiment (Steffy and Eriksen, 1965) suggested a procedure for an initial attack upon these questions. In that study, recognition memory over short durations of 700 msec or less was impaired when the form to be recognized was presented briefly together with two other nonsense forms as opposed to the condition where the form was presented alone. The result was interpreted in terms of an interference process among the three forms similar to interference effects over longer memory periods. The question arises as to whether the selective capacity of attention can be used to eliminate or reduce the interfering effect of the extraneous forms. For example, can the interference be eliminated or reduced if an indicator is present in the display directing the subject's attention to a subset of the forms?

In the present studies subjects were shown displays containing two or four nonsense forms presented for 125 msec and followed by the occurrence of a single test form at delays of 0–1,000 msec. The subject was required to judge whether the test form was or was not included among the forms in the display. The displays of four forms were presented under two conditions, one where the display contained directional bar markers directing subjects to the top or the bottom pair of the forms and another condition where no indicators were present. In this latter condition an indicator occurred at the time of the test form directing the subject to make his decision on the basis of the top or the bottom pair of forms that had been presented in the preceding display.

In addition to providing information on the selective attentional process these experiments also provided further information on interference effects in recognition memory over very short time intervals.

Experiment I

Method

Subjects.   Twenty-four students at the University of Illinois served as paid volunteers. They were assigned randomly to two groups of twelve each, each group containing eight females.

Apparatus and Stimuli.   A three-field Scientific Prototype Model GB tachistoscope was used for stimulus presentation. The stimuli were 9–16-sided nonsense forms constructed according to the method of Attneave (1957). The forms were drawn on black paper, cut out, and placed on a white field where they were photographed. The photographs were then mounted on cards to be inserted in the fields of the tachistoscope. A total of twenty-four nonsense forms were used to construct four different sets of twenty-four stimulus cards. Three of the sets were displays, one set consisting of two-form displays, another set of four-form displays with indicators, and the third set, four-form displays without indicators. The two sets of four-form displays contained four different nonsense forms on the corners of an imaginary square around the fixation point. Both sets of four-form displays were identical except that one set had small horizontal lines (indicators) at each side of either the top or bottom row of two forms. The set of two-form displays consisted of the two forms designated by the indicator lines in the four-form display set. To maintain control for perceptual complexity, these displays also had the indicator lines. The set of test forms had a small vertical line above or below the nonsense form.

In constructing the sets each of the twenty-four nonsense forms appeared once in each corner of the four-form display and the form in the display matched by the test stimulus appeared equally often in each position. When viewed through the tachistoscope the nonsense forms subtended approximately twenty minutes of visual angle and were positioned fifty minutes of angle from the fixation point, a small cross of two fine black lines subtending seven minutes of angle. The test form always contained a black indicator line either above or below the form which when it appeared was centered on the fixation point. The indicator on the test form was used for the condition of the four-form display without indicators. The position of the indicator on the test form directed the subject to make his choice either from the top or the bottom pair of the four stimuli previously presented in the display. The same indicator line occurred on the trials when the display with indicator had also appeared and in this case was congruent with the position of the display indicators. To control for stimulus complexity the same test-form displays, although here, as with the four-form displays with indicator, the indicator appearing with the test form had no meaning for the subject.

The luminance in the adapting and two stimulus fields was five ftl. The adapting field was on continuously except during presentation of the display and test forms. The adapting field luminance also filled the delay intervals.

Procedure.   Prior to undertaking the experimental sessions each subject engaged in two practice sessions during which he made same-different judgments of two nonsense forms (not identical to any used in the experimental sessions) simultaneously presented at brief duration. For the experimental sessions the subjects were assigned randomly to either one of two conditions. In the indicator with display (ID) condition the subjects were given two kinds of trials during each experimental session. In random ordering they were presented with either the two-form display or the four-form display *with indicators* which upon termination was then followed by the test form at one of four delay times, 0, 50, 200, and 600 msec between offset of the display and onset of the test form. The subject was required to make a judgment as to whether the test form was the same or different from the forms that had appeared in the two-form display or the indicated two forms in the four-form display. The subjects assigned to the indicator with test-form group (IT) were treated identically to the ID group except that no indicators occurred with their four-form displays. Instead they were instructed to use the indicator occurring with the test form to narrow down their decision as to whether the test form was the same or different from the designated two forms in the four-form display. Thus the subjects in the ID group possibly were able to direct their attention to the two relevant forms in the four-form display simultaneously with the display occurrence whereas the subjects in the IT group were unable to selectively attend to a subset of the two forms until the indicator appeared simultaneously with the test form.

Each subject was run for four sessions. During a session there were four blocks of twenty-four trials, one for each of the delay intervals. Within a session the delay interval was constant within trial blocks but the order of the delay interval within sessions was counterbalanced across sessions and across the subjects. Each trial block contained twelve trials of the two-form displays and twelve with four-form displays in random ordering. Half of the trials for both the two- and the four-form displays had the test form the same as one of the designated two forms and in the other half the test form was different from all of the display forms. For all subjects the display and test forms were each presented for 125 msec.

Results

The number of correct same-different discriminations were analyzed by a modified four-way analysis of variance (ID and IT groups, subjects, test-form delay, and two- and four-form displays). Significant beyond the 0.01 level were the effects due to subjects, $F (22, 66) = 4.25$, the difference between two- and four-form displays, $F (1, 22) = 157.23$, and the effects of delay of the test form, $F (3, 66) = 9.54$. Also the interaction of groups, two- and four-form displays, and delays was significant beyond the 0.05 level, $F (3, 66) = 3.74$.

Figure 9.4 shows recognition accuracy as a function of delay of the test form for the two groups and for the two- and four-form displays. There is a clear and consistent superiority in recognition memory when the display contained two as opposed to four forms. There is close agreement between the performance of the ID and IT groups on the two-form displays except when the test form occurred 50 msec following termination of the display. Since the stimulation conditions were identical for the two-form displays in both groups, this difference would appear attributable to sampling fluctuation.

Of major interest is the effect of the indicator on the four-form displays. The ID group which received the indicator simultaneously with the display is superior in performance to the IT group except at the delay interval of 50 msec. The overall trend of the data is for performance to continue to improve for the ID group with increasing delay of the test form with a suggestion of an asymptote in common with the two-form display data. Performance for the IT group is maximum at 50-msec delay of the test form and remains essentially constant throughout the 600-msec delay interval.

The effect of delay of the test form is somewhat surprising. There is no indication of a forgetting function over the 600-msec interval for either the two- or four-form displays. Instead recognition performance is improved when the test form is delayed 200 msec rather than presented immediately upon display termination or even 50 msec later. This result suggests a visual masking effect which could be a masking of the test form by the preceding display (forward masking), a masking of the display by the test form (backward masking), or a mutual masking.

Experiment II

Since the difference between the ID and IT groups on the four-form displays was of borderline significance in the preceding experiment, Experiment II was carried out to see if the obtained recognition memory differences would hold up on a new sample. Also the failure to obtain forgetting effects as a function of the delay of the test form raises the question as to what would happen if the delay interval range was extended to 1,000 msec.

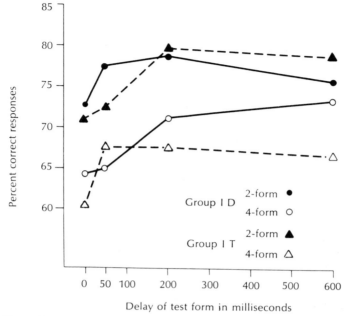

Figure 9.4: Percentage of correct same-different recognitions as a function of the number of alternative forms in the display, and delay of the test form for the ID and IT groups.

Method

Subjects. Eight students at the University of Illinois, three female, served as paid volunteers in this experiment.

Procedure. Apparatus, stimuli, and procedure were identical to those employed in Experiment I with the following exceptions. Only one experimental group was constituted and only four-form displays were used. On alternate experimental sessions the indicators occurred with the displays (ID condition) and on the other sessions the indicator occurred with the test form (IT condition). The order in which ID and IT condition sessions were given was counterbalanced across the subjects. In addition to the delay intervals for the test form that were employed in the preceding experiment a 1,000-msec delay interval was added to the present study. Thus subjects were given five blocks of twenty-four trials each for the five delay intervals during a given experimental session. The subjects had a total of forty-eight trials at each of the five delay intervals and under each of the two display conditions.

Results

Number of correct same-different recognitions were analyzed in a three-way classification analysis of variance (ID and IT conditions, subjects, and delay intervals). The main effects for conditions, $F(1, 7) = 33.4$, and for subjects, $F(7, 28) = 5.9$, were significant beyond the 0.01 level. The effect of delay intervals was not significant, $F(94, 28) = 1.5$, and none of the interactions approached significance ($F < 1$).

Figure 9.5 shows recognition accuracy as a function of indicator conditions and delay interval of the test form. While overall accuracy is slightly higher, the shape of the functions for the ID and IT conditions is essentially the same as was obtained in Experiment I. The only discrepancy occurs at 50-msec delay. In the previous experiment this was the only delay where performance was poorer when the indicators occurred simultaneously with the display. In the present study performance under this condition is consistently superior to the IT condition where the indicator occurs with the test form. This suggests that the previous discrepancy was a chance fluctuation.

Although the effect of delay intervals was not significant in the A-V, this second experiment replicates quite closely the impairment in performance previously found when the test form occurred immediately following termination of the display.

Extending the range of delay intervals to 1,000 msec has not produced unequivocal evidence of a forgetting function. There is a decrease in performance for the ID condition at 1,000 msec suggesting a forgetting effect but this interpretation is clouded by a slight increase for the IT condition at this delay.

Discussion

The results of these two experiments taken together are quite convincing that a selective attentional process in visual perception is operative within a time interval of 125 msec. If subjects are given an indication of which pair of nonsense forms is relevant at the time the two pairs are presented, they are more accurate in their judgments of whether a subsequent nonsense form was or was not a member of the pair. Delaying the designation of the relevant pair until the time the test form occurs results in poorer performance. This superiority in recognition accuracy with simultaneous indicators is apparent even when compared with the case where the indicator occurs immediately following termination of the display and in fact may become slightly greater as the indicator is delayed out to an interval of 600 msec.

This finding would suggest that whatever is involved in the selective attentional process is occurring within the first 125 msec. The subjects in both the simultaneous and delayed indicator groups have only two forms to compare with the test form. If both groups had perceived and/or stored the total input of the four forms in the display in the same manner, then selection of the relevant pair of forms at the time of the test form's occurrence should reveal no difference in performance for the two groups. There are also several indications that selectivity is not occurring after the input since the difference between simultaneous and delayed indicators is present even when the delayed indicator occurs immediately upon termination of the display. For the delay

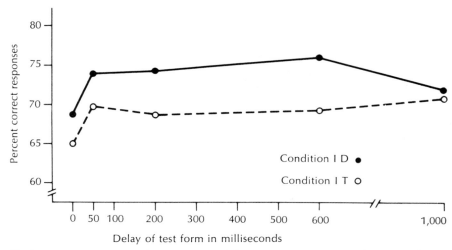

Figure 9.5: Percentage of correct same-different recognitions as a function of the delay of the test form and whether the indicators appeared with the display (ID) or the test form (IT).

group there is no advantage in having the indicator delayed only by 50 msec as opposed to 1,000 msec. Performance for both the 50- and 1,000-msec delays is almost identical, a result that would argue against the generality of a short-term perceptual storage process as has been advanced by Averbach and Coriell (1961) and Sperling (1963). In the present experiments, at least, the occurrence of the indicators must be simultaneous with the display for an advantage to occur in subsequent recognition memory.

It is of interest to look at the present results from the point of view of serial versus parallel processing of information. Sperling (1963) and Averbach and Coriell (1961) have presented models of visual perception in which it is assumed that items are processed serially. If we assume that the subject serially processed each of the items in the four-form display, then the advantage of the simultaneous indicators would have been to tell him which two forms to process first. If the total duration of the stimulation and resultant perceptual event were too short to process all four items before the perception decayed, then the advantage of the simultaneous indicators can be understood. With the delayed indicator subjects would have to guess whether to begin processing the top or the bottom two forms with only a 50 percent chance of guessing correctly.

If we apply these assumptions to the data from the IT group in Experiment I where we have appropriate observations, it turns out that the data for the four-form displays in this group are approximately what would be expected from these assumptions. Average recognition accuracy for the two-form data for this group at the 200- and 600-msec delay was 78.7 percent. Chance is 50 percent and if the assumption is made that subjects guessed correctly the same number of times they guessed incorrectly, we are left with an estimate of 57.4 percent as the time that the subjects were responding correctly to a real memory of the stimulus. If 57.4 percent is then taken as an indication of the times the subject can process or partially process two items, we can extrapolate to the data for the four forms with delayed indicator. Half of the time the subject chooses the correct two forms to process with a recognition accuracy of 57.4 percent. Thus on 28.7 percent of the trials he will be correct on the basis of having processed or encoded the relevant forms. On the remaining 71.3 percent of the trials, he either processed the irrelevant forms or failed to complete the processing of the relevant pair and is thus forced to guess. By chance he would be expected to be correct half of this 71.3 percent of the trials for an overall accuracy of 64.3 percent. As will be observed from the data in Figure 9.4 this is quite close to the percentage accuracy (66 percent) obtained for the four-form displays by the IT group at 200- and 600-msec delay.

It is quite tempting to adopt this model of the underlying processes in the present experiments but a major difficulty arises when one considers that four-form displays with simultaneous indicators are appreciably less effective than if only two forms are presented in the display. A model such as is described above would seem to require little or no difference between two-form displays and four-form displays with simultaneous indicators. In both cases the subject should be able to process the correct two forms.

Whatever the basis of a selective process, it is not completely effective in eliminating the effects of extraneous stimuli. Even when the indicator occurs simultaneously with the two pairs of nonsense forms, the subject is not as accurate in his decisions as when only a single pair of nonsense forms is presented. In other words, extraneous input is not completely ignored since it apparently provides interfering effects even for such short memory intervals as are involved in the present experimental arrangements. In this respect the present results confirm the previous findings of Steffy and Eriksen (1965).

The results do indicate that whatever is involved in selective visual attention does not depend primarily upon fineness of foveal fixation. In the present experimental arrangement all forms were presented equidistant from the center of foveal fixation and the duration of stimulus presentation was too short for eye movements to have occurred even under the condition where the cue occurred concurrently with the displays.

The apparent masking effect when the test form follows immediately the termination of the display appears to be a real phenomenon. Experiment I shows the effect quite clearly for both the two- and four-form displays under both indicator conditions. Although the main effect of delay intervals was not significant in Experiment II when the 1,000-msec delay was included in the analysis, the consistency of the finding for 0 delay is certainly confirmatory. This impairment is also verified by introspective reports of subjects who quite uniformly reported that when the test form followed the display at 0 delay they tended not to see the test form (forward masking). Typical comments were to the effect that the test form occurred while they were still busy "looking" at the display.

This masking effect is quite similar to previously found effects resulting from luminance summation–contrast reduction (Eriksen, 1966; Eriksen and Hoffman, 1963; Thompson, 1966). However in the present experiment other processes must be involved since the experimental procedure was designed in terms of adapting and delay field luminances to control luminance summation–contrast reduction effects.

It is possible that this "masking effect" is attributable to saccadic eye movement. The problem of "blanking out" of vision during eye movements has a long history in experimental psychology (Dodge, 1900; Holt, 1903; Woodworth, 1906). Recently Volkmann (1962) has presented convincing evidence that thresholds are markedly raised during saccadic eye movements and Latour (1962) has further indicated that suppression occurs approximately 40 msec before the eye begins to move. When these observations are combined with the findings that latency of eye movement varies from 125 to approximately 230 msec, depending upon individual subjects (Diefendorf and Dodge, 1908), an explanation for the "masking effect" is obtained.

The impairment in performance found when the test form occurred immediately following termination of the display could be due to an eye movement that is just beginning or occurs shortly after the test form occurs. Since the display form was on for 125 msec followed by 125 msec of the test form, an eye movement would occur during the time the test form was being presented to the subject. If we consider the approximately 40 msec of visual suppression occurring before an eye movement, as reported by Latour (1962), and add another 20 msec for the time for the eye to travel approximately 1° from the fixation point to one of the forms presented in the display, we end up with an interval of about 70 msec of visual impairment that occurs during the time the test form is being presented. This could well account for the subjects' phenomenal reports that at 0 delay they did not seem to see the test form.

Summary

In two experiments the subjects received displays containing two or four nonsense forms presented for 125 msec and followed by a single test form at delays of 0–1,000 msec. The subject judged whether the test form was or was not included among the forms in the display. Four form displays were presented under two conditions, one where directional bar markers directed the subjects to the top or bottom pair of forms and another condition where no indicators were present. In the latter condition an indicator occurring at the time of the test form directed the subject to make his decision on the basis of the top or bottom pair of preceding display forms. Recognition was superior at all delay intervals for two-form displays, and four-form displays with the simultaneous indicator were superior to four-form displays where the indicator was delayed until the test form. The results were interpreted in terms of a selective process in visual attention and a masking effect apparent in the data was interpreted in terms of saccadic eye movement.

Editor's Note: Subliminal Perception

The area of perceptual research known as subliminal perception was mentioned in conjunction with the experiment conducted by Eriksen and Hoffman, presented at the beginning of this chapter. Subliminal *sensation* refers to the entrance of a novel sensory stimulus into a sensory system without the subject being aware of the presence of the stimulus. Subliminal *perception* refers to some modification of behavior as a result of the subliminal stimulus. The word novel indicates that the subject has had no prior experience with the stimulus. Many if not most of the perceptual cues, such as monocular depth cues (Chapter 5), we respond to unknowingly. For example, we judge the distance of objects through a wide variety of external and internal stimuli, which would be rather difficult for us to identify. Such effects are caused, however, by our excess experience with these cues rather than their subliminal nature.

The study of subliminal perception, although dating back to the 1850s, attained fame when several advertising agencies claimed to increase, through subliminal advertising, the sales of various products. One such famous report claimed increases in the sales of Coca-Cola and popcorn after the subliminal presentation of the messages "BUY POPCORN" and "BUY COCA-COLA" during a movie. Subsequent research, conducted under adequately controlled conditions, has failed to lend credulance to such claims.

The studies of subliminal advertising and those studies conducted in hopes of demonstrating empirically the existence of the unconscious have been characterized by poorly controlled experiments and subjective measures of evaluating the effects of the stimuli. No studies have provided well-founded evidence for the effects of subliminal stimuli upon cognitive behavior or mental processes. Verbal information does not appear to be transferable via a subliminal massage. Rather, the observations made with subliminal stimuli seem to indicate that some change has occurred in the physiological response tendencies of the visual system. The effects observed are similar to the effects of masking stimuli in the metacontrast experiments. Brief or weak sensory stimuli seem to initiate changes in the response tendencies of the receptors involved. The observed behavior, then, is a result of this physiological change rather than the result of some influence upon mental process.

An experiment conducted by the present writer attempted to ascertain the duration of the change in receptor responsiveness after stimulation by a subliminal stimulus (*The Psychological Record*, 1967). The research was conducted at the experimental laboratories of the University of Göettingen in West Germany.

Temporal Gradients of Responses to Subliminal Stimuli

Gerald M. Murch

Although subliminal perception has received a great deal of theoretical, experimental, and even political attention, little is known about the conditions under which responses to subliminal stimuli are to be measured. Most previous research has been aimed at providing support for or against the hypothesis that subliminal perception exists (Bevan, 1964). Despite numerous studies the answer to this question remains equivocal and is lost in the wide variety of experimental designs attempting to answer it.

By subliminal perception we understand a process by which a stimulus which has been presented below the verbal threshold, that is, the threshold at which a subject is capable of adequately describing the stimulus, is discriminated from alternative stimuli which were previously not given subliminally.

To observe this process a stimulus is presented below the verbal threshold; the same stimulus is then presented again, this time, however, supraliminally together with several alternatives as response categories. The subject chooses one of these categories, allowing the experimenter to observe the frequency with which the stimulus previously presented subliminally is chosen.

We are assuming, based on previous research, that subliminal perception involves a response to the figural elements of the stimulus material and is noncognitive in nature (Murch, 1966). This may not be the only design with which consistent results are to be found; however, it has proved successful enough that we are able to accept the existence of subliminal perception, defining it within the borders of this approach to the problem.

The present study poses the question of the duration of the effects of subliminal stimulation. That is to say, how long after the presentation of a subliminal stimulus can a response to that stimulus be measured. Outside of previous research by the present author, we know of no further work on this question, although many previous claims, especially from the areas of motivation research, have assumed that the effects of the stimulation remain for indefinite periods.

Experiment I

Method

Twenty-six students taking part in a first semester course in psychology served as subjects for the present design. Each subject was run individually. The first part of the experiment concerned itself with the establishment of the verbal threshold for each subject. The subject entered a darkened room and was seated in front of the tachistoscope (Scientific Prototype, three-field Model GB). After a five minute adaptation period the subject was instructed to look into the viewer of the tachistoscope, where a 6 × 6 cm square was to be seen. The square was divided centrally by a vertical and horizontal line, making four fields. At the junction of these lines was a fixation point. The subject was then told that a series of letters, one after another, would be presented for very short durations. The length of presentation was to be increased in each case until the subject was able to correctly identify the letter in question. This was accomplished by beginning with a presentation period of 1 msec and increasing the duration by 0.1 msec after each ten-stimulus presentation. The inter-stimulus interval was 250 msec. The luminance for both fields, and in the main experiment for all three fields, was held constant at 3.6 ftc. This process was continued until the subject had correctly identified the letter. A total of six letters (O, M, H, V, S, K) was used, each 2 cm high, three of which were drawn in red and three in black. Previous results had indicated that the threshold values for a black letter were lower than for a red letter (Hurvich and Jameson, 1963; Murch, 1965); however, these threshold values served as an adequate stimulation duration for a red subliminal stimulus. That is, the red subliminal stimulus remained below the verbal threshold. The mean threshold values found for the three black letters was taken as the projection value for the subliminal stimulus in the main experiment which was begun immediately after completing the threshold measurements.

An example of the stimulus materials used in the main experiment is to be found in Figure 9.6. The complete set of stimulus items has been published elsewhere (Murch, 1967a). The letters were stenciled with a red Guteberg "Signierstift" 3 mm felt through a Standardgraph Stencil 202/20.

The supraliminal stimulus (position 1 of Figure 9.6) consisted in each case of parts of two letters with a fixation point between them. The subliminal stimuli consisted of a completed pair of letters which were superimposed around the supraliminal parts (bottom of Figure 9.6). The response categories consisted of three equally likely pairs, all of which were possible extensions of the supraliminal parts. One of the response categories corresponded exactly to the subliminally presented pair. Fixation points were also given on the response categories.

The supraliminal stimuli (parts of letters) were presented in each case for a period of ten seconds which was interrupted forty times by the presentation of the subliminal stimulus. The interstimulus interval for the subliminal presentations was held at 250 msec. The interval between each problem was twenty seconds during which a blank field of the same intensity as the stimulus fields was shown. At the end of the ten seconds the three response categories were presented in the third channel of the tachistoscope. The response categories appeared simultaneously and appeared either after the last subliminal stimulation (0 msec), or after delay periods of 100, 250, 500, 1000, and 2000 msec. Each subject received a total of ten problems per delay period. The order of the delay periods was permuted across all subjects.

The instructions to the subjects for the design emphasized that they should

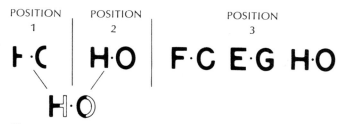

Figure 9.6:   An example of the stimulus material, see text.

not attempt to analyze the problems. Rather they should fixate upon the fixation point during the ten-second presentation of the supraliminal stimulus, then, upon the presentation of the response categories, rapidly fixate the left, center, and right response category in that order, responding by hitting a key corresponding to that pair which made the first best impression. Heavy emphasis was put upon rapid responding, fixating in the order left, center and right, and not attempting to analyze the problems, but rather to attempt to respond intuitively. The subjects responded to each problem by pushing one of three Morse-keys, located around the subject's right hand in such a manner that the subject could orient himself on the spatial relationships between keys, as the subjects were not allowed to look away from the viewer during the entire experiment. The keys were connected to an Esterline Angus Event Recorder which was put in operation at the time of presentation of the response categories, allowing the response latency to be measured (chart speed twelve seconds per minute). A small light located immediately below the viewer came on if the subject responded correctly by selecting the category being previously subliminally presented, giving him some performance feedback.

The program for the presentation of stimuli, length of delay, performance feedback was run by a Massey-Dickenson Programming device through which all aggregates were automatically activated. The experimenter, who remained out of sight and without contact with the subject after having read the instructions, needed only to change the stimulus materials at the end of each problem.

At the end of the experiment each subject was asked to explain how he had gone about responding to the problems. Three questions were asked of each subject:

1. How did you go about choosing a response category?
2. Did you see anything outside of the parts of letters and the three choices in the apparatus?
3. During the presentation of the parts of letters one of the response possibilities was blended in for very short durations. Did you notice this at any time?

In cases in which an indication was found that the subject had perceived the subliminal stimuli at a level allowing verbalization, he was left out of the evaluation. This was the case for two subjects. The subliminality of the stimulus is then defined as the inability of subject to verbally identify the stimulus as the basis of his discrimination behavior.

The subjects were divided randomly into two equal groups after completing the threshold measurements representing a control and an experimental condition. The control group was treated in the same manner as described with the exception that a blank stimulus slide was presented instead of one of the response categories.

Results

The number of responses corresponding to the subliminally presented letters for all subjects was counted for each of the six delay intervals. This total was then divided by the total number of responses giving an indication of the response probabilities. Figure 9.7 shows these results.

The response probabilities for the control group vary around the expected value of $p = 0.33$. None of the probabilities deviate significantly from chance expectations. The experimental group, however, shows a significant tendency to respond to the subliminal stimulation for the delay periods of 0 msec ($z = 5.05$, $p < 0.001$), 100 msec ($z = 4.65$, $p < 0.001$) and 250 msec ($z = 5.23$, $p < 0.001$). No other values deviate significantly from $p = 0.33$.

The fact that the three possibilities were presented together made it necessary to examine the response probabilities for the correct discrimination of the subliminal stimulus when it appeared in the left position, center position and right position. For delay periods of 0, 100, and 250 msec the experimental group showed the highest probability of selecting the subliminal stimulus when it appeared in the left or first position. The presentation of the correct response in the right or third position, in the order of fixation, led to a response probability not deviating from chance expectations. On trials in which the correct response was shown in the center or second position the obtained response probability deviated from chance on the three delay intervals. These were, however, consistently lower than those obtained when the category of the subliminal stimulus was presented in the first position.

Secondly we wished to see if the response latency was indicative of a response to the subliminal stimulus as had been found in a previous study. We therefore computed the mean latency periods for responses corresponding to the subliminal stimulation on one hand and for the responses deviating from the subliminal stimulation for each delay period. The results of this calculation are to be found in Figure 9.8.

As can be seen the latencies of responses in which the category representing the subliminal stimulus was selected were shorter for the delay periods of 0, 100, and 250 msec. Differences between the response latencies were tested with a t-test after the data had been normalized by means of a logarithmic transformation. The latencies were compared for correct versus incorrect responses made by the subjects of the experimental group, and for correct versus correct responses made by the experimental and control group for each of the six delay intervals. The results indicate, as was to be expected from Figure 9.8, that the response latencies for the periods of 0, 100, and 250 msec for correct

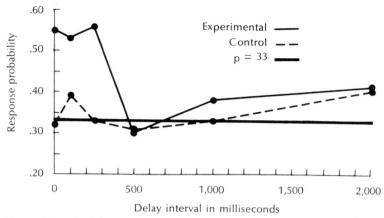

Figure 9.7: Probability of selecting the subliminally presented stimulus (ordinate) as a function of the response delay interval.

responses of the experimental group were significantly shorter ($p < 0.01$) than those for incorrect responses or for correct responses made by subjects of the control group.

Experiments II and III

In Experiment I the subjects were not given a specified period within which a response was to be made, although the results indicated that more rapid re-sponding was indicative of responses to the subliminally presented stimuli. Un-der the conditions of Experiment I significant responding to the subliminal stimulation was found up to delay periods of 250 msec. The purpose of Experi-ments II and III was to reduce the period of time in which the subjects were allowed to contemplate the response in order to observe the effects on the temporal response gradients.

Method
The method of Experiments II and III was essentially the same as in Ex-periment I. In the first design the response categories were presented after each delay period and remained until the subject responded by depressing one of the three response keys. The correct response was acknowledged by means of a light. In the present design the response categories were presented for a period of two seconds. The subjects were required to depress one of the keys within this time limit. In the case of Experiment II (Experiment Group 2SP and Control Group 2SP) failure to respond within the two-second time limit was punished by means of an electric shock administered to the left hand of the subject by means of a tube held by the subject. A Lafayette Shocker Model 5226 was used with a plug-in resistor of 100,000 ohms, which con-verted the shocker from constant voltage to constant current. A constant value

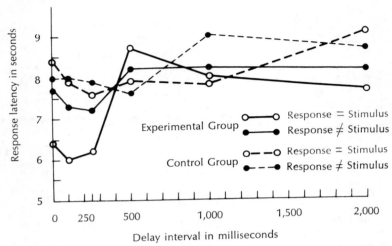

Figure 9.8: Response latencies (in seconds) for correct responses (Stimulus = Response) and incorrect responses (Stimulus ≠ Response).

of 1.9 ma was used as the shock intensity for all subjects. The shock was administered automatically at the end of the two-second presentation of the three response categories unless any one of the keys had been activated during the two-second period. The duration of the shock was 100 msec. Furthermore, failure to respond during the two-second period also meant the deletion of the feedback (light) as to whether or not the response was correct.

In Experiment III (Experiment Group 2S and Control Group 2S) the response categories were also presented for only two seconds; however, failure to respond within this limit was not punished with a shock. No feedback for responses occurring after the two seconds was given. All four groups consisted of twelve subjects drawn from a first semester psychology class.

All other elements of these two experiments, such as threshold determination, stimulus materials, delay periods, were the same as in Experiment I.

Results
The results of Experiments II and III are to be found in Figure 9.9.

As was the case in Experiment I the response probabilities for selecting the subliminally presented category lie above the chance expectations at the delay periods of 0, 100, and 250 msec. However, in general the probabilities are lower than those obtained in Experiment I. That is to say, the subjects did not perform as well with a two-second response time limit. Furthermore, in the case of Experiment I Group 2SP the obtained deviation from chance expectation at 250 msec ($p = 0.41$) fails to reach significance ($z = 1.86$, $p > 0.01$). All other values for the Experimental Groups deviate significantly from $p = 0.33$ for the delay periods of 0, 100, and 250 msec (Experiment $2S_0$, $z = 4.89$; Experiment $2S_{100}$, $z = 2.22$; Experiment $2S_{250}$, $z = 2.44$) (Experiment $2SP_0$, $z = 2.79$; Experiment $2SP_{0.00}$, $z = 4.65$).

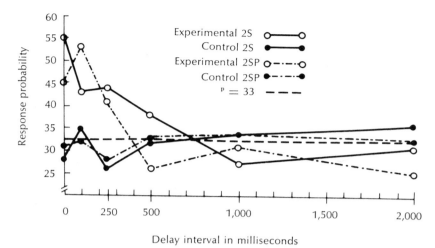

Figure 9.9: Probability of selecting the subliminally presented stimulus as a function of the response delay interval for groups 2SP (two-second punishment) and groups 2S (two-second).

Discussion

The results of the present experiments indicate that the stimulus elements leading to the correct discrimination of the subliminal stimulus are extinguished or inhibited in some manner unless the response categories, allowing the stimulus elements to be applied, are presented within a period of 0.25 sec.

At first glance, the results of these experiments are somewhat surprising in light of the claims made by some individuals concerning the effects of subliminal stimulation. If we compare, however, these results with those found in the area of short-term perceptual memory certain analogies are obvious. The fact that no effects of the subliminal stimulation upon the discrimination behavior of the subjects was to be found after delay intervals greater than 250 msec appears to coincide, at least numerically, with the results of several other authors. Evidence of perceptual storage in the visual system has been reported lasting for about 270 msec (Averbach and Coriell, 1961; Sperling, 1960).

In the way of a theoretical explanation of the results obtained, we assume a change in threshold level, perhaps at the level of the bipolar or ganglion cells, caused by the presentation of successive temporally separated stimuli (light). The subliminal stimulation is considered to activate a local graded potential change which does not reach the level necessary to cause a spike; that is, the stimulus remains below the threshold. (In the case of the spike the stimulus would no longer be subliminal but rather supraliminal.) The presentation of the same stimulus with complete foveal congruency, which was previously presented subliminally, this time at a supraliminal level as a response category, reactivates the receptors previously caused to change their threshold level by the subliminal stimulus. Due to the lower threshold the response category corresponding to the subliminal stimulus is selected, providing all other things are equal.

The greatest response probability would then be expected at a 0 delay period—that is immediately after the refractory period at the time of greatest threshold change—decaying as a function of the length of delay between subliminal and supraliminal stimulation. Although no differences in the response probabilities were found between 0, 100, and 250 msec in Experiment I, this may be due to the rather small number of observations. In Experiments II and III the response probabilities after a delay of 250 msec were found less than after shorter delays. In fact, in the case of the Experimental Group 2SP, the response probability failed to deviate from chance expectations.

This interpretation presumes that a summation takes place between two stimulus presentations, varying in intensity (one subliminal and one supraliminal), over short temporal gaps. Some previous work is relevant to this hypothesis. It has been found that the double presentation of a stimulus (letters) was "slightly superior to single presentations, the amount of gain being a negatively accelerated function of time lag between stimulations" (Eriksen and Hoffman, 1963). The results suggest that an asymptote was reached at the interval between 250–450 msec, although due to the failure to use longer intervals, as the authors themselves point out, no final conclusions can be made.

Summary

This paper presents three experiments aimed at determining the duration of the effects of subliminal stimulation in a discrimination situation. Parts of two letters were shown supraliminally in a three-field tachistoscope. Subliminal completions of these letters were presented which were to be discriminated from two other equally likely alternatives not previously presented subliminally. The presentation of the response categories was delayed for 0, 100, 250, 500, 1000, or 2000 msec. The major results of each experiment indicated increased response probabilities after delays of 0, 100, and 250 msec. A tendency for more rapid responding to correspond to the selection of the subliminal stimulus was observed, however. Lengthening the time in which a response could be made did not increase response accuracy. A general model based on threshold changes of stimulated receptors is presented.

References

Abney, W. 1913. *Research in colour vision and the trichromatic theory.* London: Longmans, Green, and Co.

————, and Watson, W. 1916. *Trans. Roy. Soc.* (London) 216A:91.

Allport, F. H. 1955. *Theories of perception and the concept of structure.* New York: Wiley.

Allport, G. W., and Pettigrew, T. F. 1957. Cultural influences of the perception of movement: The trapezoidal illusion among Zulus. *J. Abnorm. Soc. Psychol.* 65:104–13.

————, and Vernon, P. E. 1931. *A study of values.* Boston: Houghton Mifflin.

Alpern, M. 1952. Metacontrast: Historical introduction. *Amer. J. Optom.* 29:634.

Ames, A., Jr. 1951. Visual perception and the rotating trapezoidal window. *Psychol. Mono.* 65: whole no. 324.

Asch, S. E., and Witkin, H. A. 1948. Studies in space orientation I. Perception of the upright with displaced visual fields, *J. Exp. Psychol.* 38:325–37.

Attneave, F. 1954. Some informational aspects of visual perception. *Psychol. Rev.* 61:183–93.

————. 1957. Physical determinants of the judged complexity of shapes. *J. Exp. Psychol.* 53:221–27.

————, and McReynolds, P. W. 1950. A visual beat phenomenon. *Amer. J. Psychol.* 63:107–10.

Auerbach, E., and Wald, G. 1954. Identification of a violet receptor in human color vision. *Science* 120:401–4.

————, and ————. 1955. The participation of different types of cones in human light and light adaptation. *Amer. J. Ophthal.* 39, no. 2, pt. 2, p. 24.

Averbach, E., and Coriell, A. S. 1961. Short-term memory in vision. *Bell Sys. Tech. J.* 40:309–28.

Bales, J. F., and Follansbee, G. L. 1935. The after effect of the perception of curved lines. *J. Exp. Psychol.* 18:499–503.

Behar, I., and Bevan, W. 1961. The perceived duration of auditory and visual intervals: Cross modal comparison and interaction. *Amer. J. Psychol.* 74:17–26.

• Bevan, W. 1963. The pooling mechanism and the phenomena of reinforcement. In *Motivation and social interaction,* ed. O. J. Harvey. New York: Ronald Press.

————. 1964. Subliminal stimulation. *Psychol. Bull.* 61:61–69.

————, and Adamson, R. 1960. Reinforcers and reinforcement: Their relation to maze performance. *J. Exp. Psychol.* 59:226–32.

————; Barker, H.; and Pritchard, J. F. 1963. The Newhall scaling method, psychophysical bowing, and adaption level. *J. Gen. Psychol.* 69:95–111.

————, and Pritchard, J. F. 1963. Effect of "subliminal" tones upon the judgment of loudness. *J. Exp. Psychol.* 66:23–29.

Bitterman, M. E., and Elam, C. B. 1954. Discrimination following varying amounts of nondifferentiated reinforcement. *Amer. J. Psychol.* 67:133–37.

Black, R. W.; Adamson, R.; and Bevan, W. 1961. Runaway behavior as a function of apparent intensity of shock. *J. Comp. Physiol. Psychol.* 54:270–74.

————, and Bevan, W. 1960. The effect of subliminal shock upon the judged intensity of weak shock. *Amer. J. Psychol.* 73:262–67.

Blackwell, H. R. 1953. Threshold psychophysical measurements. *Univ. Mich. Eng. Research Inst. Bull.* no. 36.

Block, W. 1964. A conceptual framework for the clinical test situation. *Psychol. Bull.* 61:168–75.

Boardman, W. K., and Goldstone, S. 1962. Effects of subliminal anchors upon judgment of size. *Perc. Motor Skills* 14:475–82.

• Boettner, E. A., and Wolter, J. R. 1962. Transmission of the ocular media. *Invest. Ophthal.* 1:776–83.

Bolles, R. C., and Bailey, D. E. 1956. Importance of object recognition in size constancy. *J. Exp. Psychol.* 51:222–25.

Boring, E. G. 1924. Attributes and sensation. *Amer. J. Psychol.* 35:301–4.

————. 1933. *The physical dimensions of consciousness.* New York: Century.

————. 1936. Koffka's principles of Gestalt psychology. *Psychol. Bull.* 33:59–69.

————. 1946. The perception of objects. *Amer. J. Physics* 14:99–107.

————. 1952. Visual perception as invariance. *Psychol. Rev.* 59:141–48.

Bouman, M. A. 1950. Quanta explanations of vision. *Doc. Ophthal.* 4:23–115.

Brenner, M. W. 1956. The effects of brain damage on the perception of apparent movement. *J. Pers.* 25:202–12.

Broadbent, D. E. 1956. Successive responses to simultaneous stimuli. *Quart. J. Exp. Psychol.* 8:145–52.

————. 1957. A mechanical model for human attention and immediate memory. *Psychol. Rev.* 64:205–15.

Brown, P. K., and Wald, G. 1963. Visual pigments in human and monkey retinas. *Nature* (London) 200:37–43.

Bruner, J. S., Postman, L., and Rodrigues, J. 1951. Expectation and the perception of color. *Amer. J. Psychol.* 64:216–27.

Brunswik, E. 1933. Die Zugänglichkeit von Gegenständen für die Wahrnehmung und deren quantitative Bestimmung. *Arch. für die gesamte Psychol.* 88:377–418.

————. 1947. *Systematic and representative design of psychological experiments: With results in physical and social perception.* Berkeley: U. of California Press.

————. 1952. *The conceptual framework of psychology.* Chicago: University of Chicago Press.

————, and Kamiya, J. 1953. Ecological cue-validity of "proximity" and of other gestalt factors. *Amer. J. Psychol.* 66:20–32.

Bryden, M. P. 1960. Tachistoscopic recognition of non-alphabetical material. *Canad. J. Psychol.* 14:74–82.

Callaway, E., III, and Alexander, J. D., Jr. 1960. The temporal coding of sensory data: An investigation of two theories. *J. Gen. Psychol.* 62:293–309.

Campbell, D. T.; Hunt, W.; and Lewis, N. A. 1957. The effects of assimilation and contrast in judgments of clinical materials. *Amer. J. Psychol.* 70:347–60.

————; Lewis, N. A.; and Hunt, W. A. 1958. Context effects with judgmental language that is absolute, extensive, and extra-experimentally anchored. *J. Exp. Psychol.* 55:220–28.

Canestrari, R. 1956. Ossenazioni sul fenomeno del tropezio ruotante. *Riv. Psicol. Soc.* 50:1–20.

Carlson, V. R. 1960. Overestimation in size constancy judgments. *Amer. J. Psychol.* 73:199–213.

————. 1962. Size constancy judgments and perceptual compromise. *J. Exp. Psychol.* 63:68–73.

Chaplin, I. P. 1968. *Dictionary of Psychology.* New York: Dell.

Chapman, D. W. 1932. Relative effects of determinate and indeterminate Aufgaben. *Amer. J. Psychol.* 44:163–74.

Clark, W. C., and Blackwell, H. R. 1959. Visual detection thresholds for single and double light pulses in the temporal element contribution hypothesis. *U. Mich. En. Res. Inst. Proj. Mich. Rep.* (Ann Arbor) no. 2144–343–T.

Clowes, M. B. 1959. Eye movements and the discrimination of brightness and colour. Ph.D. dissertation, University of Reading.

Cohen, W. 1957. Spatial and textural characteristics of the Ganzfeld. *Amer. J. Psychol.* 70:403–10.

Cornsweet, T. N. 1956. Determination of the stimuli for involuntary drifts and saccadic eye movements. *J. Opt. Soc. Amer.* 46:987–93.

Corso, J. F. 1956. The neural quantum theory of sensory discrimination. *Psychol. Bull.* 53:371–93.

Crozier, W. J. 1950. On visibility of radiation at the human fovea. *J. Gen. Physiol.* 34:87–136.

Dartnell, H. J. A. 1948. Visual purple and photopic luminosity curve. *Brit. J. Opthal.* 32:793–811.

Day, W. F. 1956. Serial non-randomness in auditory differential thresholds as a function of interstimulus interval. *Amer. J. Psychol.* 69:387–94.

Day, R. H., and Power, R. P. 1963. Frequency of apparent reversal rotary motion in depth as a function of shape and pattern. *Aust. J. Psychol.* 15:162–74.

————, and ————. 1965. Apparent reversal (oscillation) of rotary motion in depth: An investigation and a general theory. *Psychol. Rev.* 72:117–27.

De Silva, H. R. 1926. An experimental investigation of the determinants of apparent visual movement. *Amer. J. Psychol.* 37:469–501.

Diefendorf, A. R., and Dodge, R. 1908. An experimental study of the ocular reactions of the insane from photographic records. *Brain* 31:451–89.

Ditchburn, R. W., and Fender, D. H. 1955. The stabilized retinal image. *Opt. Acta.* 2:128–33.

————; ————; and Mayne, S. 1959. Vision with controlled movements of the retinal image. *J. Physiol.* 145:98–107.

————, and Ginsborg, B. L. 1952. Vision with a stabilized retinal image. *Nature* (London) 170:36–37.

————, and Pritchard, R. W. 1956. Stabilized interference fringes on the retina. *Nature* (London) 177:434.

Dodge, R. 1900. Visual perception during eye movement. *Psychol. Rev.* 7:454.

Dollin, A., and Sakoda, J. M. 1962. The effect of order of presentation on perception of TAT pictures. *J. Consult. Psychol.* 26:340–44.

Doob, L. 1957. An introduction to the psychology of acculturation. *J. Soc. Psychol.* 45:143–60.

Duncker, K. 1939. The influence of past experience upon perceptual properties. *Amer. J. Psychol.* 52:255–65.

Ebbinghaus, H. 1885. *Über das Gedächtnis.* Leipzig: Duncker.

Egan, J. P.; Greenberg, G. Z.; and Schulman, A. I. 1961. Operating characteristics, sign detectability, and the method of free response. *J. Acous. Soc. Amer.* 33:933–1007.

————; Schulman, A. I.; and Greenberg, G. Z. 1959. Operating characteristics determined by binary decisions and by rating. *J. Acous. Soc. Amer.* 31:768–73.

Egeth, H. 1967. Selective attention. *Psychol. Bull.* 67:41–57.

————, and Smith, E. E. 1967. Perceptual selectivity in a visual recognition task. *J. Exp. Psychol.* 74:543–49.

Ellis, W. D. 1939. *A source book of gestalt psychology.* New York: Harcourt, Brace & Co.

Eriksen, C. W. 1960. Discrimination and learning without awareness: A methodological survey and evaluation. *Psychol. Rev.* 67:279–300.

————. 1962. Figments, fantasies, and follies: A search for the subconscious mind. In *Behavior and awareness,* ed. C. W. Eriksen, pp. 3–26. Durham, N.C.: Duke University Press.

————. 1966. Temporal luminance summation effects in backward and forward masking. *Perc. Psychophysics* 1:87–92.

————, and Collins, J. F. 1964. Backward masking in vision. *Psychon. Sci.* 1:101–102.

————, and ————. 1965. Reinterpretation of one form of backward and forward masking in visual perception. *J. Exp. Psychol.* 70:343–51.

————, and ————. 1967. Some temporal characteristics of visual pattern perception. *J. Exp. Psychol.* 74:476–84.

————, and Hoffman, M. 1963. Form recognition at brief durations as a function of adapting field and interval between stimulations. *J. Exp. Psychol.* 66:485–99.

————, and Johnson, H. J. 1964. Storage and decay characteristics of nonattended auditory stimuli. *J. Exp. Psychol.* 68:28–36.

————, and Lappin, J. S. 1967. Selective attention and very short-term recognition for nonsense forms. *J. Exp. Psychol.* 73:358–64.

————, and Steffy, R. A. 1964. Short-term memory and retroactive interference in visual perception. *J. Exp. Psychol.* 68:423–34.

Erulkar, S. D., and Fillenz, M. 1960. Single-unit activity in the lateral geniculate body of the cat. *J. Physiol.* 154:206–218.

Fechner, G. T. 1860. *Elemente der Psychophysik.* Leipzig: Breitkopf & Hartel.

Fender, D. H. 1956. The function of eye movements in the visual process. Ph.D. dissertation, University of Reading.

Fick, A. 1879. Die Lehre von der Lichtempfindungen. In *Handbuch der Phsysiologie,* ed. L. Hermann, vol. 3. p. 139. Leipzig: Duncker.

Fuchs, W. 1920. Untersuchungen über das Sehen der Hemianopiker und Heiamblio-piker, II. In *Psychologische Analysen hirn-pathologischer Fälle*, ed. Gelb and Goldstein. Leipzig: Barth.

Ganz, L. 1966. Mechanism of figural after-effects. *Psychol. Bull.* 73:128–50.

Gellermann, L. 1933. Chance orders of alternating stimuli in visual discrimination experiments. *J. Genet. Psychol.* 42:206–7.

Gibson, E. J., and Walk, R. D. 1956. The effect of prolonged exposure to visually presented patterns on learning to discriminate them. *J. Comp. Physiol. Psychol.* 29:320–42.

Gibson, J. J. 1933. Adaption, after-effect, and contrast in the perception of curved lines. *J. Exp. Psychol.* 16:160–72.

————. 1934. Vertical and horizontal orientation in visual perception. *Psychol. Bull.* 31:739.

————. 1937. Adaption, after-effect, and contrast in the perception of tilted lines. II. Simultaneous contrast and the areal restriction of the after-effect. *J. Exp. Psychol.* 20:553–69.

————. 1950. *The perception of the visual world.* Boston: Houghton Mifflin.

————, and Dibble, F. N. 1952. Exploratory experiments on the stimulus conditions for the perception of a visual surface. *J. Exp. Psychol.* 43:414–19.

————, and Mowrer, O. H. 1938. Determinants of the perceived vertical and horizontal. *Psychol. Rev.* 45:300–323.

————, and Radner, M. 1937. Adaption, after-effect, and contrast in the perception of tilted lines. *J. Exp. Psychol.* 20:453–67.

————, and Waddell, D. 1952. Homogeneous retinal stimulation and visual perception. *Amer. J. Psychol.* 65:263–70.

Gibson, K. S., and Tyndall, E. P. T. 1923. *Nat. Bur. Standards* 19:131.

Gilinsky, A. S. 1955. The effect of attitude upon the perception of size. *Amer. J. Psychol.* 68:173–92.

Goldstein, K. 1926. Über induzierte Veränderungen des Tonus. *Arch. f. Neur. u. Psychiat.* 17:210–25.

Goldstein, J. J., and Barthol, R. P. 1960. Fantasy responses to subliminal stimuli. *J. Abnorm. Soc. Psychol.* 60:22–26.

Goldstone, S., and Goldfarb, J. L. 1964. Adaption level, personality theory, and psychopathology. *Psychol. Bull.* 61:176–87.

————; ————; Strong, J.; and Russell, J. 1962. Replication: The effect of subliminal shock upon the judged intensity of weak shock. *Perc. Motor Skills* 14:222.

Gordon, M. H.; Loveland, E. H.; and Cureton, E. E. 1952. An extended table of chi square for two degrees of freedom for use in combining probabilities from independent samples. *Psychometrika* 17:311–16.

Gottschaldt, K. 1929. II. Über den Einfluss der Erfahrung auf die Wahrnehmung von Figuren. *Psychol. Forsch.* 12:1–87.

Graham, C. H., ed. 1965. *Vision and visual perception.* New York: Wiley.

Granit, R. 1947. *Sensory mechanisms of the retina.* London: Oxford University Press.

Grant, D. A., and Schipper, L. M. 1952. The acquisition and extinction of conditioned eyelid responses as a function of the percentage of fixed ratio random reinforcement. *J. Exp. Psychol.* 43:313–20.

Green, D. M. 1960. Psychoacoustics and detection theory. *J. Acous. Soc. Amer.* 32:1189–1203.

Grice, G. R. 1948. The acquisition of a visual discrimination habit following response to a single stimulus. *J. Exp. Psychol.* 38:633–42.

Guenther, W. C. 1965. *Concepts of statistical inference*. New York: McGraw-Hill.

Haber, R. N., and Hershenson, M. 1965. Effects of repeated brief exposures on the growth of a percept. *J. Exp. Psychol.* 69:40–46.

Hake, H. W. 1957. Contributions of psychology to the study of pattern vision. *USAF WADC Tech. Rep.* 2:277–94.

Hall, J. F. 1961. *Psychology of motivation*. Philadelphia: Lippincott.

Harper, R. S. 1953. The perceptual modification of colored figures. *Amer. J. Psychol.* 66:86–89.

Harris, C. S., and Haber, R. N. 1963. Selective attention and coding in visual perception. *J. Exp. Psychol.* 65:328–33.

Hays, W. L. 1964. *Statistics for psychologists*. New York: Holt, Rinehart & Winston.

Hebb, D. O. 1937. The innate organization of visual activity. I. Perception of figures by rats reared in total darkness. *J. Genet. Psychol.* 51:101–26.

————. 1949. *Organization of behavior*. New York: Wiley.

Helmholtz, H. L. F. von. 1852. On the theory of compound colours. *Phil. Mag.* 5:519–34.

Helson, H. 1938. Fundamental problems in color vision. I. The principle governing changes in hue, saturation, and lightness of non-selective samples in chromatic illumination. *J. Exp. Psychol.* 23:439–76.

————. 1947. Adaption-level as a frame of reference for prediction of psychological data. *Amer. J. Psychol.* 60:1–29.

————. 1963. Studies of anomalous contrast and assimilation. *J. Opt. Soc. Amer.* 53:179–84.

————. 1964. Current trends and issues in adaptation level theory. *Amer. Psychol.* 19:26–28.

————; Blake, R. R.; and Mouton, J. S. 1958. Petition signing as adjustment to situational and personal factors. *J. Soc. Psychol.* 48:3–10.

————; ————; ————; and Olmstead, J. A. 1956. Attitudes as adjustments to stimulus, background, and residual factors, *J. Abnorm. Soc. Psychol.* 52:314–22.

————, and Joy, V. 1962. Domains of lightness assimilation and contrast effects in vision. *Psychol. Beitr.* 6:405–15.

————; Judd, D. B.; and Warren, M. H. 1952. Object-color changes from daylight to incandescent filament illumination. *Illum. Engr.* 47:221–33.

————; ————; and Wilson, M. 1956. Color rendition with fluorescent sources of illumination. *Illum. Engr.* 51:329–46.

————, and Michels, W. C. 1948. The effect of adaption on achromaticity. *J. Opt. Soc. Amer.* 38:1025–32.

————, and Rohles, R. H., Jr. 1959. A quantitative study of reversal of classical lightness-contrast. *Amer. J. Psychol.* 72:530–38.

————, and Steger, J. A. 1962. On the inhibitory effects of a second stimulus to react. *J. Exp. Psychol.* 63:201–5.

Hering, E. 1895. Über das sogennante Purkinjesche Phänomen. *Arch. für ges. Physiol.* 60:519–42.

Heron, W. 1957. Perception as a function of retinal locus and attention. *Amer. J. Psychol.* 70:38–48.

————; Doane, B. K.; and Scott, T. H. 1956. Visual disturbances after prolonged perceptual isolation. *Canad. J. Psychol.* 10:13–18.

Hess, W. 1924. Reactions to light in the earthworm: Lumbricus terrestris. *J. Morphol. Physiol.* 39:515–42.

Hilgard, E. R. 1962. What becomes of the input from the stimulus? In *Behavior and awareness*, ed. C. W. Eriksen, pp. 46–72.

Hillebrand, F. 1889. *Akad. Wiss. Wien. Math. Naturwiss. Klass. Abt. III* 98:70. Durham, N.C.: Duke University Press.

Hochberg, J. E., and Silverstein, A. 1956. A quantitative index of stimulus similarity proximity vs. difference in brightness. *Amer. J. Psychol.* 69:456–58.

———; Triebel, W.; and Seaman, G. 1951. Color adaption under conditions of homogeneous stimulation (Ganzfeld). *J. Exp. Psychol.* 41:153–59.

Holt, E. B. 1903. Eye-movement and central anesthesia. *Harvard Psychol. Stud.* 1:3–45.

Holway, A. H., and Boring, E. G. 1941. Determinants of apparent visual size with distance variant. *Amer. J. Psychol.* 54:21–37.

Hovland, C. I., and Sherif, M. 1952. Judgmental phenomena and scales of attitude measurement: Item displacement in Thurstone scales. *J. Abnorm. Soc. Psychol.* 47:822–32.

Hsia, Y., and Graham, C. H. 1952. Spectral sensitivity of the cones in the dark adapted human eye. *Proc. Nat. Acad. Sci.* 38:80–85.

———, and ———. 1957. Spectral luminosity curves for protonopic, deuteranopic and normal subjects. *Proc. Nat. Acad. Sci.* 43:1101–19.

Hubel, D. H., and Wiesel, T. N. 1962. Receptive fields, binocular interaction and functional architecture in the cat's visual cortex. *J. Physiol.* 160:106–54.

———, and ———. 1965. Receptive fields and functional architecture in two non-striate visual areas (18 and 19) of the cat. *J. Neurophysiol.* 28:229–89.

Hurvich, L. M., and Jameson, D. 1951. The binocular fusion of yellow in relation to color theories. *Science.* 114:199–202.

———. 1963. Spectral sensitivity of the fovea. I. Neutral adaptation. *J. Optical Soc. Amer.* 43:485–94.

Hymovitch, B. 1952. The effects of experimental variation on problem solving in rats. *J. Comp. Physiol. Psychol.* 45:313–21.

Ittelson, W. H., and Kilpatrick, F. P. 1951. Experiments in perception. *Sci. Amer.* 185:50–55.

James, W. 1890. *Principles of psychology.* New York: Henry Holt & Co.

Jameson, D., and Hurvich, L. M. 1951. Use of spectral hue-invariant loci for the specification of white stimuli. *J. Exp. Psychol.* 41:455–63.

Jenkin, N., and Hyman, R. 1959. Attitude and distance-estimation as variables in size matching. *Amer. J. Psychol.* 72:68–76.

Johnson, J., and Eriksen, C. W. 1961. Preconscious perception: A re-examination of the Poetzl phenomenon. *J. Abnorm. Soc. Psychol.* 62:497–503.

Jones, E. E., and Bruner, J. S. 1954. Expectancy in apparent visual movement. *Brit. J. Psychol.* 45:157–65.

Judd, D. B. 1943. Facts of color-blindness. *J. Opt. Soc. Amer.* 33:294.

———. 1951. Basic correlates of the visual stimulus. In *Handbook of experimental psychology,* ed. S. S. Stevens, pp. 811–67. New York: Wiley.

———. 1960. Appraisal of Land's work on two-primary color projections. *J. Opt. Soc. Amer.* 50:254–68.

Kader, F. J. 1960. Target complexity and visibility in stabilized images. B.A. thesis, McGill University.

Kahneman, D. 1964. Temporal summation in an acuity task at different energy levels —a study of the determinants of summation. *Vis. Res.* 4:557–66.

———. 1966. Time intensity reciprocity in acuity as a function of luminence and figure ground contrast. *Vis. Res.* 6:207–15.

———, and Norman, J. 1964. The time-intensity relations in visual perception as a function of observer's task. *J. Exp. Psychol.* 68:215–20.

————, ————, and Kubovy, M. 1967. The critical duration for the resolution of form: centrally or peripherally determined? *J. Exp. Psychol.* 73:323–27.

Katz, D. 1935. *The world of colour.* London: Kegan, Paul, Trobner, & Co.

Kilpatrick, F. P., and Ittelson, W. H. 1953. The size-distance invariance hypothesis. *Psychol. Rev.* 60:223–31.

Kimura, D. 1959. The effect of letter position on recognition. *Canad. J. Psychol.* 13:1–10.

Klein, G. S., Spence, D. P., Holt, R. R., and Gourevitch, S. 1958. Cognition without awareness: Subliminal influences upon conscious thought. *J. Abnorm. Soc. Psychol.* 57:255–66.

Koffka, K. 1935. *Principles of gestalt psychology.* New York: Harcourt, Brace & Co.

Koffka, D., and Harrower, M. R. 1931. Colour and organization. *Psychol. Forsch.* 15:145–75.

Köhler, W. 1929. *Gestalt psychology.* New York: Liveright.

————. 1940. *Dynamics in psychology.* New York: Liveright.

————, and Wallach, H. 1944. Figural aftereffects. *Proc. Amer. Phil. Soc.* 88:269–357.

Kolers, P. A. 1962. Intensity and contour effects in visual masking. *Vis. Res.* 2:277–94.

————, and Rosner, V. S. 1960. On visual masking (metacontrast): Dichoptic observation. *Amer. J. Psychol.* 73:2–21.

Krauskopf, J. 1957. Effect of retinal image motion on contrast thresholds for maintained vision. *J. Opt. Soc. Amer.* 47:740–44.

Kreis, J. V. 1905. Die Gesichtsempfindungen. In *Handbuch der Physiologie des Menschen,* ed. W. Nagel, vol. 3, p. 109. Braunschweig: Vieweg.

Külpe, O. 1904. Versuch über Abstraktion. *Versuch über den Internationaler Kongress für experimentelle Psychologie:* 56–58.

Land, E. H. 1959. Color vision and the natural image. Parts I and II. *Proc. Nat. Acad. Sci.* 45:115–29 and 636–44.

Lashley, K. S. 1938. Experimental analysis of instinctive behavior. *Psychol. Rev.* 45:445–71.

————. 1941. Patterns of cerebral organization indicated by the scotomas of migraine. *Arch. Neurol. Psychiat.* 46:331–39.

————. 1958. Cerebral organization and behavior. *Res. Publ. Ass. Nerv. Ment. Dis.* 35:1–18.

————, and Russell, J. T. 1934. The mechanism of vision. XI. A preliminary test of innate organization. *J. Genet. Psychol.* 45:136–44.

Latour, P. L. 1962. Visual threshold during eye movements. *Vis. Res.* 2:261–62.

Lawrence, D. H., and Coles, G. R. 1954. Accuracy of recognition with alternatives before and after the stimulus. *J. Exp. Psychol.* 47:208–14.

Leibowitz, H. W., and Harvey, L. O., Jr. 1967. Size matching as a function of instructions in a naturalistic environment. *J. Exp. Psychol.* 74:378–82.

————, and ————. 1969. The effect of instructions, environment, and type of test object on matched size. *J. Exp. Psychol.* 81:36–43.

Lewin, K. 1951. *Field theory in social science.* New York: Harper & Row.

Lichten, W., and Laurie, S. 1950. A new technique for the study of perceived size. *Amer. J. Psychol.* 63:280–82.

Licklider, J. C. R. 1959. Three auditory theories. In *Psychology: A study of science,* ed. S. Kock, vol. I, pp. 41–144. New York: McGraw-Hill.

Lindquist, E. F. 1953. *Design and analysis of experiments in psychology and education.* Boston: Houghton Mifflin.

Lindsley, D. B., and Emmons, W. H. 1958. Perception time and evoked potentials. *Science* 127:1061.

Logan, F. H. 1960. *Incentive.* New Haven: Yale University Press.

Long, E. R.; Reid, L. S.; and Henneman, R. H. 1960. An experimental analysis of set: variables influencing the identification of ambiguous, visual stimulus-objects. *J. Exp. Psychol.* 73:553–62.

Luce, R. D. 1960. Detection thresholds: a problem reconsidered. *Science* 132:1495.

Ludvigh, E., and McCarthy, E. F. Absorption of visible light by refractive media of human eye. *Arch. Ophthamol.* 20:37–51.

Luh, C. W. 1922. The conditions of retention. *Psychol. Mono.* no. 142.

McGill, W. J. 1957. Serial effects in auditory threshold judgments. *J. Exp. Psychol.* 53:297–303.

MacKay, D. M. 1957. Some further visual phenomena associated with regular patterned stimulation. *Nature* (London) 180:1145–46.

McKennell, A. C. 1960. Visual size and familiar size: individual differences. *Brit. J. Psychol.* 51:27–35.

Marks, W. B., Dobelle, W. H., and MacNichol, E. F., Jr. 1964. Visual pigments of single primate cones. *Science* 143:1181–83.

Maxwell, J. C. 1855. On the theory of colours in relation to colour blindness. In *Researches on Colour-Blindness,* p. 153. Edinburgh: Sutherland and Knox.

———. 1871. *Proc. Roy. Inst. Gr. Brit.* 6:260.

———. 1890. On the unequal sensibility of the foramen centrale to the light of different colours. In *Scientific Papers,* ed. W. D. Niven, vol. 1. London: Cambridge University Press.

Melton, A. W. 1963. Implications of short-term memory for a general theory of memory. *J. Verb. Learn. and Verb. Behav.* 2:1–21.

Metzger, W. 1930. Optische untersuchungen am Ganzfeld. II. Zur phänomenologie des homogenen Ganzfelds. *Psychol. Forsch.* 13:6–29.

Michels, W. C., and Helson, H. 1949. A reformulation of the Fechner law in terms of adaption-level applied to rating-scale data. *Amer. J. Psychol.* 62:355–68.

Miller, N. E. 1959. Liberalization of basic S.-R. concepts: Extensions to conflict behavior, motivation, and social learning. In *Psychology: A study of science,* ed. S. Koch, vol. 2. New York: McGraw-Hill.

Milner, P. M. 1957. The cell assembly: Mark II: *Psychol. Rev.* 64:242–52.

Mishkin, M., and Forgays, D. G. 1952. Word recognition as a function of retinal locus. *J. Exp. Psychol.* 43:43–48.

Muenzinger, K. F. 1946. Reward and punishment. *U. Colo. Stud., Gen. Sec.* 27:1–16.

Mulholland, T. 1956. Motion perceived while viewing rotating stimulus objects. *Amer. J. Psychol.* 69:96–99.

———. 1958. The "swinging disc" illusion. *Amer. J. Psychol.* 71:375–82.

Münsterberg, H. 1889. *Beiträge zur experimentellen Psychologie* 2:204–5.

Murch, G. M. 1965. A simple laboratory demonstration of subception. *Brit. J. Psychol.* 56:467–70,

———. 1966. *Über subliminale Reizwirkungen bei der Wahrnemung optischer Figurationen.* Göettingen: Psychologisches Institut.

———. 1967a. Die Nachwirkung unterschwelliger Reizung als eine Funktion der Zeit zwischen Reizdarbietung und Reaktion. *Z. f. Exp. und Ang. Psychol.* 14:463–73.

———. 1967b. Temporal gradients of responses to subliminal stimuli. *Psychol. Rec.* 17:483–91.

———. 1969. Growth of a percept as a function of interstimulus interval. *J. Exp. Psychol.* 82:121–28.

————, and Wesley, F. 1966. German psychology and its journals. *Psychol. Bull.* 66:410–15.

Musatti, A. 1938. In *Experimental psychology*, ed. R. S. Woodworth. New York: Holt.

Ogle, K. N. 1963. Stereoscopic depth perception and exposure delay between images to the two eyes. *J. Opt. Soc. Amer.* 53:1296–1304.

Orbach, J. 1952. Retinal locus as a factor in the recognition of visually perceived words. *Amer. J. Psychol.* 65:555–62.

Osgood, C. E., and Heyer, A. W. 1951. A new interpretation of figural after-effects. *Psychol. Rev.* 59:98–118.

Parducci, A. 1964. Sequential effects in judgment. *Psychol. Bull.* 61:163–67.

————; Calfee, R. C.; Marshall, L. M.; and Davidson, L. P. 1960. Context effects in judgment: adaption level as a function of the mean, midpoint and median of the stimuli. *J. Exp. Psychol.* 60:65–77.

Pastore, N. 1952. Some remarks on the Ames oscillatory effect. *Psychol. Rev.* 59:319–23.

Pavlov, I. P. 1927. *Conditioned reflexes.* Ed. and trans. C. V. Anrep. London: Oxford University Press.

Pierce, J. 1963. Determinants of threshold for form. *Psychol. Bull.* 60:391–407.

Pitt, F. H. G. 1935. Characteristics of dichromatic vision. *Med. Res. Council Spec. Rept,* no. 200. London: H. M. Stat. Office.

Podell, J. E. 1961. A comparison of generalization and adaption level as theories of connotation. *J. Abnorm. Soc. Psychol.* 62:593–97.

Polyak, S. 1941. *The retina.* Chicago: University of Chicago Press.

Postman, L.; Bruner, J. S.; and McGinnies, E. M. 1948. Personal values as selective factors in perception. *J. Abnorm. Soc. Psychol.* 43:142–54.

Power, R. P. 1965. The effect of instructions on the apparent reversal of rotary motion in depth. *Quart. J. Exp. Psychol.* 17:346–50.

————. 1967. Stimulus properties which reduce apparent reversal of rotating rectangular shapes. *J. Exp. Psychol.* 73:595–99.

Pratt, C. C. 1950. The role of past experience in visual perception. *J. Psychol.* 30:85–107.

Pritchard, R. M. 1958. Visual illusions viewed as stabilized retinal images. *Quart. J. Exp. Psychol.* 10:77–81.

————. 1961. A collimator stabilizing system. *Quart. J. Exp. Psychol.* 13:181–83.

————, and Vowles, D. 1960a. The effects of auditory stimulation on the perception of the stabilized retinal image. Unpublished report, McGill University.

————; Heron, W.; and Hebb, D. O. 1960b. Visual perception approached by the method of stabilized images. *Canad. J. Psychol.* 14:67–77.

Raab, D. H. 1963. Backward masking. *Psychol. Bull.* 60:118–29.

Rambo, W. W., and Johnson, E. L. 1964. Practice effects and the estimation of adaption level. *Amer. J. Psychol.* 77:106–10.

Ratliff, F., and Riggs, L. A. 1950. Involuntary motions of the eye monocular fixation. *J. Exp. Psychol.* 40:687–701.

Riesen, A. 1950. Arrested vision. *Sci. Amer.* 183:11–16.

Riggs, L. A.; Ratliff, F., Cornsweet, J. C.; and Cornsweet, T. N. 1953. The disappearance of steadily fixated test-objects. *J. Opt. Soc. Amer.* 43:495–501.

————; Armington, J. C.; and Ratliff, F. 1954. Motions of the retinal image during fixation. *J. Opt. Soc. Amer.* 44:315–21.

Rivers, W. H. R. 1901. Introduction and Vision. In *Reports of the Cambridge anthropological expedition to Torres Straits.* Reports, vol. 2, ed. A. C. Haddon. Cambridge: Cambridge University Press.

Rodgers, R. S. 1965. *Intermediate statistics*. Sidney: University Co-operative Book-shop.

Rosenbaum, M. 1956. The effect of stimulus and background factors in the volunteering response. *J. Abnorm. Soc. Psychol.* 53:118–21.

Rubin, E. 1921. *Visuell wahrgenommene Figuren*. Copenhagen: Glydendalska.

Rushton, W. A. H. 1959. Visual pigments in man and animals and their relation to seeing. *Prog. in Biophys. and Biochem.* 9:239.

———. 1964. Interpretation of retinal densitometry. *J. Opt. Soc. Amer.* 54:273.

———, and Cohen, R. D. 1954. Visual purple level and the course of dark adaption. *Nature* 173:301–2.

Russell, B. 1948. *Human knowledge*. New York: Simon & Schuster.

Schultze, M. 1866. *Arch. Mikr. Anat.* 2:175.

Schurman, D. L., Eriksen, C. W., and Rohrbaugh, J. 1968. Masking phenomena and time-intensity reciprocity for form. *J. Exp. Psychol.* 78:310–17.

Senders, V. L., and Sowards, A. 1952. Analysis of response sequences in the setting of a psychological experiment. *Amer. J. Psychol.* 65:358–74.

Shannon, C. E. 1951. Prediction and entropy of printed English. *Bell Syst. Tech. J.* 30:50–64.

Sherif, M., and Hovland, C. I. 1961. *Social judgment*. New Haven: Yale University Press.

———; Taub, D.; and Hovland, C. I. 1958. Assimilation and contrast effects of anchoring stimuli on judgments. *J. Exp. Psychol.* 55:150–55.

Shevrin, H., and Luborsky, L. 1958. The measurement of preconscious perception in dreams and images: An investigation of the Poetzl phenomenon. *J. Abnorm. Soc. Psychol.* 56:285–95.

Siegel, A. I. 1953. Deprivation of visual form definition in the ring dove. I. Discriminatory learning. *J. Comp. Physiol. Psychol.* 46:115–19.

Siegel, S. 1956. *Nonparametric statistics for the behavioral sciences*. New York: McGraw-Hill.

Siipola, E. M. 1935. A group study of some effects of preparatory set. *Psychol. Mono.* 46: whole no. 210.

Sloan, L. L. 1928. *Psychol. Mono.* 38: whole no. 1.

Snedecor, G. W. 1946. *Statistical methods*. Ames, Iowa: Iowa State College Press.

Spence, K. W. 1936. The nature of discrimination learning in animals. *Psychol. Rev.* 43:427–49.

Sperling, G. A. 1960. The information available in brief visual presentations. *Psychol. Mono.* 74: whole no. 498.

———. 1963. A model for visual memory tasks. *Hum. Factors* 5:19–31.

Spitz, H. H. 1964. A comparison of mental retardates and normals on the rotating trapezoidal window illusion. *J. Abnorm. Soc. Psychol.* 68:574–78.

Steffy, R. A., and Eriksen, C. W. 1965. Short-term, perceptual recognition memory for tachistoscopically presented nonsense forms. *J. Exp. Psychol.* 70:277–83.

Stevens, S. S. 1957. On the psychophysical law. *Psychol. Rev.* 64:153–81.

———. 1958. Adaption level vs. the relativity of judgment. *Amer. J. Psychol.* 71:633–46.

———. 1961. The psychophysics of sensory function. In *Sensory communications*, ed. W. A. Rosenblith, pp. 1–33. New York: Wiley.

Stiles, W. S. 1949. *Ned. Tijdschr. Natuurk.* 15:125.

———. 1959. Color vision: the approach through increment threshold sensitivity. *Proc. Nat. Acad. Sci.* 45:100.

———. 1964. Foveal threshold sensitivity on fields of different colors. *Sci.* 145:1016–17.

———, and Crawford, B. H. 1933. Luminous efficiency of rays entering the eye pupil at different points. *Proc. Roy. Soc.* (London) 112:428–50.

Stroud, J. M. 1956. The fine structure of psychological time. In *Information theory in psychology*, ed. H. Quastler, pp. 174–207. Glencoe, Ill.: Free Press.

Swets, J. A. 1959. Indices of signal detectability obtained with various psychophysical procedures. *J. Acoust. Soc. Am.* 31:511–13.

———. 1961. Is there a sensory threshold? *Science* 134:168–77.

———; Tanner, W. P.; and Birdsall, T. G. 1961. Decision processes in perception. *Psychol. Rev.* 68:301–40.

Tanner, W. P., Jr. 1956. A theory of recognition. *J. Acous. Soc. Amer.* 28:883–88.

———, and Birdsall, T. G. 1958. Definitions of d' and n as psychophysical measures. *J. Acous. Soc. Amer.* 30:922–28.

———, and Swets, J. A. 1954. A decision-making theory of visual detection. *Psychol. Rev.* 61:401–9.

———; ———; and Green, D. M. 1956. Some general properties of the hearing mechanism. *Electronic Defense Group, Univ. Michigan, Tech. Rep.* no. 30.

Thompson, J. H. 1966. What happens to the stimulus in backward masking? *J. Exp. Psychol.* 71:580–86.

Thompson, S. P. 1879. The pseudophone. *Phil. Mag.* 8:385–90.

Thomson, L. C. 1951. The spectral sensitivity of the central fovea. *J. Physiol.* 112:114–32.

Thorndike, E. L., and Lorge, I. 1944. *The teacher's word book of 30,000 words*. New York: Teacher's College, Columbia University.

Titchener, E. B. 1910. *A textbook of psychology*. New York: Macmillan Co.

Toch, H. H. 1956. The perceptual elaborations of stroboscopic presentations. *Amer. J. Psychol.* 69:345–58.

———, and Ittelson, W. H. 1956. The role of past experience in apparent movement: A revaluation. *Brit. J. Psychol.* 47:195–207.

Troland, L. T. 1922. *Nela Park Abstract Bull.* no. 799:388.

Vernon, M. D. 1934. The perception of inclined lines. *Brit. J. Psychol.* 25:186–89.

Verplanck, W. S.; Collier, G. H.; and Cotton, J. W. 1952. Nonindependence of successive responses in measurements of the visual threshold. *J. Exp. Psychol.* 44:273–82.

Volkmann, F. C. 1962. Vision during voluntary saccadic eye movements. *J. Opt. Soc. Amer.* 52:571–78.

Von Senden, M. V. 1932. *Raum-und Gestaltauffassung bei operierten Blindgebornen vor und nach der Operation*. Leipzig: Barth.

Wald, G. 1945. Human vision and the spectrum. *Science* 101:653–58.

———. 1949. The photochemistry of vision. *Doc. Ophthal.* 3:94–137.

———. 1954. On the mechanism of the visual threshold and visual adaptation. *Science* 119:887–92.

———. 1958. Retinal chemistry and the physiology of vision. In "Visual Problems of Colour." *Natl. Phys. Lab., Gt. Brit. Proc. Symp.* 8, vol. 1, p. 7.

———. 1964. The receptors of human color vision. *Science* 145:1007–15.

———. 1965. Receptor mechanisms in human vision. *Proc. 13th Int. Physiol. Congr.* (Tokyo) 69–79.

———. 1966a. Defective color vision and its inheritance. *Proc. Nat. Acad. Sci.* 55:1347–68.

————. 1966b. The retinal basis of human vision. *Proc. 4th ISCERG Symp.* (Tokyo) *vol. 10 suppl.*, pp. 1–11.

————, and Brown, P. K. 1958. Human rhodopsin. *Science* 127:222–26.

Wallach, H. 1948. Brightness constancy and the nature of achromatic colours. *J. Exp. Psychol.* 38:310–24.

Walters, H. V., and Wright, W. D. 1943. Spectral sensitivity of the fovea and extra-fovea in the Purkinje range. *Proc. Roy. Soc.* (London) 131:340–61.

Weale, R. A. 1951. Foveal and para-central spectral sensitivities in man. *J. Physiol.* (London) 114:435–46.

————. 1953. Spectral sensitivity and wavelength discrimination of the peripheral retina. *J. Physiol.* (London) 119:170–90.

————. 1959. *Opt. Acta.* 6:158.

Werner, H. 1929. Untersuchungen über Empfindungen und Empfinden. *Z. Psychol.* 114:152–66.

————. 1935. Studies on contour: I. Qualitative analysis. *Amer. J. Psychol.* 47:40–64.

Wertheimer, M. 1912. Experimentelle Studien über das Sehen von Bewegungen. *Z. Psychol.* 61:161–65.

————. 1922. Untersunchungen zur Lehre von der Gestalt. I. *Psychol. Forsch.* 1:47–58.

————. 1923. Untersuchungen zur Lehre von der Gestalt. II. *Psychol. Forsch.* 5:301–50.

Weyer, E. M. 1899. Die Zeitschwellen gleichartiger und disparater Sinneseindrucke. *Phil. Stud.* 15:68–138.

White, C. T. 1963. Temporal numerosity and the psychological unit of duration. *Psychol. Mono.* 77: whole no. 575.

————, and Cheatham, P. G. 1959. Temporal numerosity: IV A comparison of the major senses. *J. Exp. Psychol.* 58:441–44.

Willmer, E. N. 1953. Physiological basis for human colour vision in the central fovea. *Doc. Ophthal.* 56:235–313.

Wohlwill, J. 1963. The development of "overconstancy" in space perception. In *Advances in Child Development*, vol. 1, ed. L. P. Lipsitt and C. C. Spiker. New York: Academic Press.

Woodworth, R. S. 1906. Vision and localization during eye movements. *Psychol. Bull.* 3:68.

————. 1938. *Experimental psychology.* New York: Holt.

————, and Schlosberg, H. 1954. *Experimental psychology.* New York: Holt.

Wright, W. D. 1952. The characteristics of tritanopia. *J. Opt. Soc. Amer.* 42:509–21.

Yarbus, A. L. 1957. The perception of an image fixed with respect to the retina. *Biofizika* 2:683–90.

Young, H. H.; Holtzman, W. H.; and Bryant, W. D. 1954. Effects of item context and order on personality ratings. *Educ. Psychol. Msmt.* 14:499–517.

Young, P. T. 1928. Auditory localization with acoustical transposition of the ears. *J. Exp. Psychol.* 11:399–429.

Young, T. 1802. On the mechanism of the eye. *Phil. Trans. Roy. Soc.* (London) 12.

————. 1807. On the theory of light and colours. In *Lectures in natural philosophy*, vol. 2, pp. 613–32. London: Printed by William Savage for Joseph Johnson, St. Paul's Church Yard.

Zegers, R. T., and Murray, P. A. 1962. Perception of distortion I. An experimental approach to illusion. *Technical Report No. 506–1*. Port Washington, New York: U.S. Naval Training Device Center.

Index